12-97

The New
PSYCHIATRY

Also by Jack M. Gorman, M.D.

The Essential Guide to Psychiatric Drugs

The
NEW PSYCHIATRY
THE ESSENTIAL Guide *to State-of-the-Art Therapy,*
Medication, and Emotional Health

Jack M. Gorman, M.D.,
Columbia University College of Physicians and Surgeons

ST. MARTIN'S PRESS ❧ New York

Design by Bonni Leon-Berman

Library of Congress Cataloging-in-Publication Data

Gorman, Jack M.
  The new psychiatry : the essential guide to state-of-the-art therapy, medication, and emotional health / by Jack M. Gorman.—1st ed.
      p.   cm.
  Includes bibliographical references and index.
  ISBN 0-312-14690-6
  1. Psychiatry—Popular works.   I. Title.
RC460.G57   1996
616.89—dc20   96-2878
                                                                              CIP

First Edition: September 1996

10   9   8   7   6   5   4   3   2   1

MEDICAL CAUTION

The information in this book is intended to guide potential patients and their families, but not to substitute for the advice and directions of your personal physician or therapist. Do not take any medications or make changes in the way you take current medications or any other type of treatment without first consulting your physician and/or therapist. Also, report all side effects or reactions to any medications or other treatment to your doctor.

Contents

Acknowledgments

SOMETIMES I THINK the major reason I write books is for the pleasure of thanking people who are important to me and whom I admire. Then I worry about all the people I will inevitably forget. Still, this is a rare opportunity to put in writing my gratitude and affection for people who do so much.

I have wonderful colleagues at Columbia University and the New York State Psychiatric Institute who are of immeasurable help to me and from whom I learn a lot of psychiatry. I thanked many of them in my last book, *The Essential Guide to Psychiatric Drugs.* Now, I would like to thank Dr. John Oldham, Director of the New York State Psychiatric Institute; Drs. Laszlo Papp and Jeremy Coplan and all of my coworkers in the Biological Studies Unit; Dr. Dolores Malaspina and Dr. David Strauss and coworkers in the Schizophrenia Research Unit; and Dr. Charles Nemeroff of Emory University. These are dedicated mental health professionals and friends. I would also like to thank Dr. Robert Spitzer, Dr. Michelle Friedman, Dr. Lawrence Welkowitz, and Mr. Orville M. Simon for help in preparing parts of the book.

Special thanks to Barbara Barnett, who assists me in many editorial and administrative ways; to my agent, Vicki Bijur; and very specially to my editor and now friend at St. Martin's Press, Robert Weil. If this book is to be praised, Bob deserves much of it.

But, as last time, it all boils down for me to three people who are really the only reason I do anything. Both of my daughters, Sara and Rachel, are now old enough to read some of the things that I write. Perhaps they will notice here and there how much they influence me; it is because of them that I am convinced the world can be a wonderful place and that our efforts to help people feel happy and satisfied are worthwhile. My wife, Dr. Lauren Kantor Gorman, really wrote this book. She will deny this merely because it is I who sat for hours at the word processor getting the text down. But she is the best psychiatrist I know and at every turn of writing this book I asked myself, "Is that what Lauren would do or say or recommend?" Many busy people who write books thank their families for their patience during the long hours the author needed to be tied up with his or her work; I do thank my family for that as well. But they are also busy people and I have much more to thank them for. To Sara, Rachel, and Lauren, I thank you simply for being wonderful people.

Introduction

THERE ARE TWO bad images of psychiatrists. One is of the middle-aged man with a beard and cigar who talks patients into lying on the couch in his office and then proceeds to see them several times a week for years. Little progress seems to be made from this. The other is of a slightly younger doctor with a white coat and prescription pad who thinks that every problem in the world can be solved with a pill. You get ten minutes once every few months to talk to this kind of psychiatrist.

And then there is the image of psychiatry that I hope to promote in this book. It is called the "New Psychiatry" and reflects what every psychiatrist should aspire to and what every patient has a right to insist upon.

The New Psychiatry has several basic principles that I will emphasize over and over again throughout this book. They are:

THE PRINCIPLES OF THE NEW PSYCHIATRY

1. The goal of treatment is to help the patient get better.
2. Only treatments that have been proven to work should be employed.
3. Psychiatrists should recommend to patients the treatments that will work best for them, not the treatments the psychiatrist happens to like the best.
4. Patients with psychiatric problems have the right to know what their diagnoses are, what all possible treatment options might be, and the adverse risks associated with those treatments.
5. Psychiatric treatment is highly effective for many conditions.
6. Psychiatric treatment is ineffective for many problems that people face.
7. People with psychiatric problems should be treated by doctors and society in general with care and compassion.
8. Psychiatrists are experts on the diagnosis and treatment of mental and behavioral illnesses; they are not qualified to make moral, political, or economic decisions for anyone besides themselves.

Increasingly, the public thinks psychiatrists are limited to making diagnoses and prescribing medication. This is seen as a cold, emotionally sterile enterprise. Nobody expects that psychiatrists will be interested in their daily problems, their families and backgrounds, their hopes and desires, yet the revolution that began in the late 1950s and brought effective medication to the fight against mental illness is now seen as having reduced psychiatrists to a bunch of unfeeling pill pushers.

Sweeping generalizations like this are, of course, never true. But it is best to lay out on the table right away what the criticisms of psychiatry have been and to carefully detail what the New Psychiatry tries to do. Potential consumers of psychiatric care and their families must understand what psychiatric illnesses are, including all the different categories and symptoms, and what treatment approaches are available.

In the last decade, scientific progress in understanding how the brain works has been remarkable. At the same time, however, psychiatry is endowed with a long tradition of respect and insight into the vagaries of human emotion and behavior. Brilliant pioneers like Sigmund Freud and B. F. Skinner stand side by side with modern neurobiologists in shaping a medical specialty that has at its disposal an array of powerful and effective tools for treating illness. *The New Psychiatry integrates all of this into a compassionate and humane, yet always scientifically, rigorous approach that is aimed at helping individuals overcome the ravages of emotional suffering.*

If there is a "New Psychiatry," what was the "Old Psychiatry"? Let me be clear that the New Psychiatry does not represent a sudden break with previous schools of thought or the emergence of a rivalrous band of psychiatrists. Rather, what has occurred is a gradual process of maturation of the field which, when employed correctly, benefits the patient. In other medical areas, like internal medicine and surgery, there has been a gradual recognition in recent decades that no one doctor can possibly master all the necessary knowledge and skills to treat every possible illness. Hence, the advent of subspecialties like cardiology, gastroenterology, and head and neck surgery. Medical and surgical subspecialists do not think they have all the answers for all possible diseases. Psychiatry also had its subspecialists, including psychoanalysts, psychopharmacologists, hypnotherapists, and behaviorists. Unfortunately, these subspecialists often did believe they had all the answers for all conditions. Today, psychiatrists are much more willing to admit that some psychiatric illnesses respond to some methods better than others. There are still subspecialists, but psychoanalysts are more likely to refer patients who need medication to a psychiatrist with special skill in that area, while psychopharmacologists are increasingly sending their patients to psychotherapists when it is clear that medication alone won't help. In the Old Psychiatry, each clinician learned a set of techniques from one school of thought and insisted on applying them to all comers. In the New Psychiatry clinicians may still feel most comfortable with the tools of one school, but they readily admit when they don't have the right skill for a particular patient.

It is time that people who might need psychiatric treatment have a resource where they can obtain sufficient information to be able to make informed decisions about their treatment. *The New Psychiatry* is not a drug book or a psychotherapy book or a self-help book. It does not single out one illness, such as depression or bulimia, for special attention. After all, how does one know if he is suffering from depression or anxiety in the first place? Why look in a book about medication if you really would do better with psychotherapy? When you pick up this book, all you need to know is that you, or perhaps a friend or member of your family, are not happy with the way your life is going and you wonder if a psychiatrist might help. By reading through these chapters, either from beginning to end or by jumping from one topic to the next that seems relevant to you (either way will work), you should come to an understanding of what your problem might be, whether a psychiatrist could help, and what is involved in getting treatment.

There are a few practical details you will need to know. Modern authors struggle with handling pronouns, which can be masculine or feminine. I take this seriously because language is a powerful tool for shaping our view of the world and if we persist in always using the pronouns "he" and "him" we will certainly bias ourselves to believe this is a male-dominated society. On the other hand, our ears are trained to revolt somewhat when we encounter the phrase "he or she" over and over again or the neologism "s/he." Here is what I have done. When I am discussing an illness that is clearly more common among one sex or the other, I use the corresponding gender's pronoun. So, for example, because anorexia nervosa is an illness that overwhelmingly afflicts women, I always use feminine pronouns when discussing it. Alcoholism is more common among men, so here I use masculine pronouns. At other times, I have tried to use masculine or feminine pronouns at random intervals. This is but one possible solution to the language problem, but perhaps an acceptable one.

Another struggle in a consumer-oriented book is whether to use brand or generic names for drugs.* When a drug is first released to the market it is usually patented and only available under a single brand name. After the patent runs out, other companies can make the drug and sell it under a generic name. Valium is that brand name for diazepam and Prozac is the brand name for fluoxetine. Generic drugs are much cheaper than brand-name drugs and it is considered best to encourage doctors to prescribe generic forms whenever possible. Furthermore, using brand names might lead readers to think I am promoting one drug company or another. On the other hand, many drugs are so widely known by their brand names that it inevitably confuses readers if one uses only generic names, some of which can be real tongue twisters. My solution is to give both whenever possible. Brand names always have the first letter capitalized. I will usually give a brand name and then its generic in parentheses or the generic and then brand name in parentheses. I want to be clear, however, that in no instance am I attempting to endorse the use of brand name over generic drugs or am I trying to promote any particular company. No drug companies were involved in writing this book in any way.

Finally, I want to be straightforward about the many clinical examples and case stories you will find in *The New Psychiatry*. None of them are actual cases. They are not even disguised versions of real people's stories; I have made them all up. The reason should be clear. Maintaining confidenti-

---

*Most medications have both a brand name and a generic name. When a drug name is capitalized it is a brand name; when all lowercase letters are used it is the generic name. I have tried to use whichever name for a drug I think people will recognize best.

ality is critical for patients with any medical problem, including psychiatric. Even if I disguised a story, the person whom it is based upon would surely recognize himself. The cases in this book are all plausible and based on conditions and events I have seen, but none of them concerns a real person I've treated or known.

So much for these practical details. Let me return now to the eight principles of the New Psychiatry given at the beginning. At first glance, these may seem obvious. But further examination reveals that in many ways each one of the eight principles is controversial.

AN EXPANDED DEFINITION OF THE EIGHT PRINCIPLES OF THE NEW PSYCHIATRY

1. The goal of treatment is to get better: in the past, some have argued that psychiatric treatment is working merely if the patient understands himself in more depth. The New Psychiatry insists that the patient feels better, does better, and is better. If treatment does not provide this, it should be changed or abandoned.

2. Only proven treatments should be employed: Examples include cognitive behavioral psychotherapy for mild to moderate forms of depression and antipsychotic medication for schizophrenia. There is a method of establishing whether a medical treatment works. Psychiatric treatment has not always been held to that standard. In some legitimate cases, it is very difficult to apply the usual standards of proof to some forms of psychiatric therapy. Nevertheless, only treatments for which there is some scientific evidence of benefit should be recommended.

3. Recommend only what will work for a patient, not what the doctor knows best: Psychiatry is often divided into various schools of thought. Practitioners include psychoanalysts, behaviorists, and biologists, among others. Each is most comfortable with a particular type of treatment, but that may not be the best treatment for an individual. *A psychiatrist has a duty to transcend her own theoretical orientation when making recommendations to a patient.* If the right treatment isn't one the psychiatrist likes to administer, she should refer the patient to someone else.

4. Patients have a right to know what they have, what treatments are available, and what the risks are: Diagnosis has not always been treated as a central feature in psychiatry, so many patients have entered treatment without knowing exactly what they are being treated for. Without this information, it is impossible to be part of the decision-making process to determine which treatments are going to be the most helpful and carry the fewest risks.

5. Treatment is effective: Many people still labor under the misconception that people with psychiatric problems never get better and that treatments don't work. In fact, the rate of response to psychiatric therapy rivals that

of any medical problem. Psychiatric patients routinely respond positively to treatment.

6. Treatment is not effective for every problem in life: Psychiatric treatment works for many specific psychiatric illnesses, but it doesn't make people taller, stronger, smarter, or sexier. Unreasonable expectations on the part of either patient or doctor dooms a psychiatric therapy to failure.
7. Patients with psychiatric illnesses deserve care and compassion: It is bad enough to have a depression or panic attacks or alcoholism without having to face doctors who are curt or rude and a society that acts as if mental illness is a moral failing. Psychiatric illnesses should receive the same attention as high blood pressure, cancer, or diabetes.
8. Psychiatrists are not qualified to make moral, social, or economic decisions: Psychiatrists are trained to make diagnoses and to treat psychiatric illnesses; they should keep their personal opinions out of the treatment. They are not substitutes for ministers, rabbis, accountants, or political scientists. They should never make a patient feel judged.

While you are reading this book and when you are receiving psychiatric treatment, you might refer back to these eight principles from time to time. They are the basis for establishing psychiatry as a medical specialty with a scientific grounding that nevertheless maintains its comprehensive interest in the individual experiences of its consumers.

This book is divided into four main sections, all of which reflect the synthesis of the New Psychiatry. In the first I discuss ways to decide if you need psychiatric help and how to pick a good psychiatrist for yourself. The second section gives details about the three major types of psychiatric treatments: psychodynamic psychotherapy, cognitive/behavioral therapy, and medication. There is also information about combining treatments and about marital, family, and group therapy. The third section provides information on the main kinds of psychiatric illnesses, including how the different diagnoses are made and which treatments work best. The final section is composed of special topics, such as the cost of psychiatric treatment, the issue of confidentiality, psychiatry and the courtroom, and sex with psychotherapists.

Obviously, it would be impossible to ''prescribe'' in a book the exact treatment for every particular individual's psychiatric problem. This guide is not a substitute for seeing a doctor. But if it helps you become an informed consumer, well versed in the ideas of the New Psychiatry, and makes you less afraid to seek psychiatric help, then it will be successful.

PART I Considering TREATMENT

1. The Fundamental Principles of the
   New Psychiatry

1.
The Fundamental Principles of the New Psychiatry

WHENEVER I SEE a new patient in my office, after shaking her hand and asking her to have a seat, I begin with a simple question: "How can I help you?" Sometimes the patient replies, "I don't know, that is why I am here." But I ask that question for a reason: I believe it goes to the heart of the fundamental principle of all of medicine, including psychiatry. Our only mission as psychiatrists is to help people. That may seem sickeningly obvious, but it will provoke a lot of disagreement from the practitioners in the field.

For many years, young psychiatrists were taught not to focus too much on a patient's "real life" and not to become too involved in whether a patient actually felt or did better during treatment. The main goal of psychiatric treatment was supposed to be insight. If a person learned more about himself, the treatment was considered a success. It was even assumed that many patients would actually feel worse during this adventure in self-discovery. Learning about one's repressed and darkest secrets might reasonably cause embarrassment and shame, it was reasoned. Depression and self-loathing might even result. But these were considered temporary necessities on the road to more insight. The thinking went that psychotherapy was not unlike treating an abscess: in order to do the job right you first have to probe the infection and often lance it. That might hurt the patient, but ultimately the relief would be great.

The problem with this kind of thinking is that in the case of the abscess there is objective proof that the pain and suffering has been worth it—the abscess is drained and never comes back. In the case of psychiatric treatment, however, no such evidence was ever required. We were taught that as long as there was an increase in self-understanding, then the treatment was a success. Whether the patient felt any better or performed better in life was not a major concern of the treatment. Naturally, it would be nice if a person felt better after years of treatment, but the therapist would never consider himself to have failed if such a "real-life" benefit was not realized.

Today, there is no place for such thinking in psychiatry. Every patient has a right to demand that she gets a good result from treatment. If the result is not satisfactory, the treatment should be terminated and something else tried. As I will explain, there are many complexities when dealing with human emotions that sometimes make an assessment of treatment success difficult. Therefore, I am not recommending that a patient walk out of treatment on a whim or badger the doctor to prove that the treatment is working every five minutes. Rather, I am asserting that both patient and doctor should agree at the beginning of any psychiatric treatment that the goal is to get the patient better and that treatment need not necessarily go on forever.

Throughout this book I will emphasize the necessity of setting specific goals at the beginning of every treatment, offer some practical aspects about setting those goals, and suggest ways of evaluating whether progress toward meeting those goals is being made.

How Do I Know If I Need Help?

In making the decision about whether to see a psychiatrist, a potential patient—or family member of a patient—should also turn the question around and ask two related questions: What will happen if I don't see a psychiatrist? and (2) What harm could occur to me if I do see one?

Fighting Stigma

There are many reasons why people shun psychiatrists. Perhaps the most unfortunate is the fear of the stigma of getting (or needing) psychiatric treatment. During the era when psychoanalysis reigned supreme in psychiatry, it was almost a mark of intelligence and success in some parts of the country to be seeing an analyst. Patients would compare notes about their analysts and loudly announce they were off for the analytic hour several times a week. Today, however, it is much more likely that people who think they need to see a psychiatrist will fear ridicule from others if they do seek treatment. And to be sure, there are elements of discrimination against patients who see psychiatrists. Health insurance companies, for example, generally limit the amount they will reimburse for psychiatric care to a fraction of the amount they will allow for other medical care. It is as if the insurance companies are saying it is okay to get your acne treated but not to get help for your panic attacks. People who admit they have seen a psychiatrist or have been to a clinic or hospital for substance abuse or illness may also find it difficult to get life and disability insurance. A vice presidential candidate, Thomas Eagleton, withdrew from the race in 1972 when it was learned he had received electroconvulsant therapy (ECT) for depression.

The ridiculing of psychiatric patients continues unabated in the movies and on television. The term *schizophrenic* is often used casually to describe someone who can't make up his mind about things, and people are called "crazy" when they act a little bit odd. On a recent episode of the popular television show *Doogie Howser,* which features a precocious young doctor, time was running out to get gifts on Christmas Eve to patients in the hospital.

A senior physician came up with what he thought was a brilliant idea: "We'll start with the pediatric ward and then get to the cardiology ward. If we don't make it to the psychiatric ward until tomorrow it will be okay because they don't know what day of the week it is anyway." It would be hard to think of anything more offensive to the millions of Americans who, while suffering from depression and other serious mental illnesses, know all too well what day of the week it is.

We cannot dismiss the fact that ignorance does still breed stigma for psychiatric patients. We can take some satisfaction, however, from the courageous public figures who acknowledge they have had treatment for psychiatric illness, thus decreasing the stigma attached to seeking help. Psychiatrists and their patients are always grateful to people such as former football star Earl Campbell, actor Philip Bosco, and the governor of Florida, Lawton Chiles, for acknowledging unashamedly the help they received from psychiatrists.

The Fear of Personal Failure

Deeper than the fear of public stigma is the belief that seeing a psychiatrist represents a personal failure. In our culture we are constantly taught that we must take care of ourselves and not succumb to our emotions. A person who feels he needs to talk to a psychiatrist often believes he has failed in some major way. Hopefully, after reading this book, such people will recognize that psychiatric problems are not that much different than those associated with pneumonia, diabetes, high blood pressure, and heart disease. Getting help at the appropriate time from the appropriate caregiver and working hard to ensure the success of the treatment is still part of a vigorous self-help program, whether the problem is depression or arthritis.

Feeling Persistently Unhappy

If we can help a person overcome the fear of stigma and self-criticism, we can turn to the question of whether she should see a psychiatrist or not. In the boldest terms, it is fair to say that someone should consider seeing a psychiatrist if she is persistently unhappy or senses that other people are persistently unhappy with her. By persistently I mean more than just a few days here or there.

There are many reasons people may find themselves persistently unhappy. Depression is, of course, one of the leading reasons. Anyone who feels consistently depressed for more than a few weeks should consider seeing a psychiatrist, especially if the cause of the depression is not obvious and if the depressed mood begins to interfere with the ability to function in one's work and social roles. Because depression is one of the easiest to treat of all the psychiatric illnesses, it is always a tragedy when someone waits to get help until he is attempting to improve his mood by abusing alcohol or until he feels suicidal.

Besides depression, however, there are many other problems that can lead to persistent unhappiness. Anxiety disorders are among the most common psychiatric illnesses in the United States. A person who has recurrent, severe panic attacks or is phobic and cannot leave home or worries about unimportant things all the time and cannot sleep at night is likely to be unhappy about life even if his mood is not depressed. These problems are, once again, relatively easy to treat and should not be ignored.

"Neurotic" Problems

The so-called neurotic problems are more complex. What if a man recognizes he is persistently unable to remain in a romantic relationship, even though he wants to get married and have a family? What if a woman notices that she always says the wrong thing at work and never gets promoted, even though she is one of the best workers? Once again, these problems may produce unhappiness without actual depression, but they are more difficult to treat because they often represent long-standing personality problems. Nevertheless, people with these problems often get help from psychiatrists and it is best for them to have at least one or two consultations in order to make an informed decision.

People Are Always Mad at Me

What about the situation in which a person senses that others are persistently unhappy with him? There are many psychiatric illnesses that annoy people associated with the patient more than they annoy the patient. Some would argue that this is society's problem, but that is just a convenient political cop-out in my opinion. Left unchecked, such illnesses will ultimately drive people away and leave the patient isolated and unfulfilled. An example is chronic hypomania, a condition in which a patient has a persistently elevated mood and believes he is better than other people. Such people are typically overconfident, irritable, and argumentative, talk fast, spend too much money, and engage in promiscuous sex. They may have a good time but they are very irritating to be around and ultimately wind up wondering indignantly why they have no friends and no money. Another example is attention deficit disorder, usually seen in elementary-school-aged boys. These children cannot concentrate for sustained periods of time and are often temperamental and excessively emotional. Some become hyperactive and disruptive in class. Although the child may not at first be bothered by this, teachers usually become exasperated and other children become frightened. If not treated, such children usually do poorly in school—even if they are smart—and have few friends. Here again, treatment can be very successful.

If the thought crosses your mind, then, that you might want to see a psychiatrist because you are unhappy or people are unhappy with you, you might next ask what could happen if you don't get help. Some problems may actually go away by themselves if given some time. If your problems are not seriously affecting your ability to work or function with friends and family and if they are not life-threatening, it is not unreasonable to try to work things out by yourself for a bit. You might give yourself some timetable to be sure you don't let your problems go unchecked forever. Tell yourself, for instance, "If I don't feel better in two weeks, I am going to see someone."

Unfortunately, however, the majority of problems leading to persistent unhappiness either don't improve over time or get worse. The risk someone takes in not getting help is that he will have to live his entire life feeling sad or dissatisfied. Against that scenario, the idea of seeing a psychiatrist at least to judge whether treatment could be helpful seems a far more preferable path.

The Risks of Seeing a Psychiatrist

What harm can come from seeing a psychiatrist? The biggest harm that can occur, in my opinion, is getting talked into a treatment that won't help and only drains time and money. Contrary to popular belief, neither psychotherapy nor psychiatric medications are powerful enough to really control minds or turn thinking, feeling people into robots under the command of the doctor. The biggest risk a person takes in getting involved in psychiatric treatment is wasting time and money while not getting better. Once again, a major reason I have written this book is to try to indicate how treatment that works can be obtained without getting involved in futile and prolonged adventures.

How to Pick a Psychiatrist

Perhaps reluctantly, perhaps at the urging of family or friends, you have decided to see a psychiatrist. Still, you have heard horror stories about what psychiatrists do, and things you have seen in the movies confirm your fears. How do you pick a good psychiatrist?

People seem to be much more troubled by this question than they are when seeking help from a lawyer, accountant, or pediatrician. That is probably because most people, however correctly, think they know how to evaluate a lawyer's, accountant's, or pediatrician's performance. Your lawyer is good if you win your case, your accountant is competent if you get a refund on your tax return, and your pediatrician is good if your children grow properly. On the other hand, it is still a mystery to most people what psychiatrists do and how psychiatrists work and so it appears that it will be difficult to tell if the psychiatrist is any good.

Ask a Friend or Relative

It may sound so simple but picking a good psychiatrist should not be that much different from picking a good accountant. The first thing to consider is whether you know anyone who has had a good result from a psychiatrist

TABLE 1

REASONS TO CONSIDER SEEING A PSYCHIATRIST

1. You have been feeling sad and tearful for no obvious reason.
2. You have lost your appetite and cannot sleep, but your medical doctor says nothing is wrong.
3. You have been feeling helpless and hopeless and feel that you have nothing to look forward to.
4. You have been thinking that life is not worth living.
5. You have been drinking or taking medicine not prescribed for you to help you sleep or cheer you up.
6. You have had more than two anxiety attacks in which you feel as if you are about to die but nothing physically wrong is found.
7. You are afraid to do things most people do, like drive in your car or go to a restaurant or go shopping in a mall.
8. You spend much more time than most people doing simple things like washing your hands or taking a shower.
9. You have been feeling nervous and tense constantly for weeks.
10. Your mind has been playing tricks on you and you hear things or see things other people do not hear or see.
11. You have eating disorders.
12. Other people have been complaining that you talk too loud and too fast; you think everything is fine but no one else thinks your ideas are reasonable.
13. You are in an abusive relationship (emotionally and/or physically) and can't get out.

and is happy with her treatment. Unfortunately, many people keep the fact that they have seen a psychiatrist a secret, so it may be hard to find a relative or friend you trust who can recommend one. Nonetheless, more and more people are willing to acknowledge they have consulted a psychiatrist, and a good recommendation from a satisfied customer you trust is probably the best guide.

Ask Your Family Doctor

Another way is to ask your family doctor. This is, of course, standard practice when one needs to consult any type of medical specialist. Often, people who need to see a cardiologist, surgeon, or gynecologist will see whomever their family doctor recommends without question. This can work when seeking a psychiatrist, but is not always as reliable. The biggest problem here, in my experience, is that family physicians, general practitioners, and internists are usually reluctant to bring up the idea of seeing a psychiatrist with a patient, fearing the patient will be insulted. Thus, a general practitioner may see a patient complaining of chest pain, shortness of breath, and dizzy spells several times, each time finding nothing medically wrong and reassuring the patient that everything is fine. After two or three such visits the doctor may suspect that the patient is really suffering from a psychiatric condition, perhaps depression or panic disorder. Unfortunately, the doctor may avoid mentioning his suspicion or recommending a psychiatric consultation because he is concerned his patient will simply go and see another medical doctor.

Even if the medical doctor does refer the patient to a psychiatrist, he may not ever find out how the patient does. This is because of a misguided idea among medical doctors and psychiatrists about what "patient confidentiality" means. A cardiologist will always send a note to a referring physician thanking her for the referral and explaining the findings. The patient is also encouraged to return to the referring doctor for follow-up treatment. In that way, the referring doctor has a chance to determine whether patients like the cardiologist and whether the cardiologist seems to do a good job. This is how doctors develop their lists of specialists to whom they will refer their patients. However, in the case of psychiatrists, doctors mistakenly think that it is a violation of the patient's confidentiality for the psychiatrist to report back to the referring doctor or for the referring doctor to ask how things went with the psychiatrist.

Because of this, many medical doctors do not actually know the name of a good psychiatrist. It is still worthwhile to ask your family doctor for the name of a psychiatrist, but you should also ask the doctor how much he really knows about the psychiatrist.

Seek a Patient Advocacy Group

A third way to select a psychiatrist is to contact a patient advocacy group. In recent years, organizations have sprung up that represent the needs of patients with psychiatric illnesses and their families. One of the major principles of the New Psychiatry is to welcome these groups and to seek their advice. Many keep lists of psychiatrists and take the trouble to evaluate how these doctors actually perform by questioning members about their experiences. Examples of such groups are the National Alliance for the Mentally Ill (NAMI), the National Depressive and Manic Depressive Association (NDMDA), the Anxiety Disorders Association of America (ADAA), and the Mental Health Association (MHA). These organizations have national offices (see Table 2) and many also have local chapters. It is wise to call these organizations and request the name of a psychiatrist.

TABLE 2
PATIENT ADVOCACY GROUPS

Name	Address	Phone Number
National Alliance for the Mentally Ill	2101 Wilson Boulevard Suite 302 Arlington, VA 22201	703/524-7600 800/950-NAMI
National Depressive and Manic Depressive Association	730 N. Franklin Suite 302 Chicago, IL 60610	312/642-0049
Anxiety Disorders Association of America	6000 Executive Boulevard Suite 200 Rockville, MD 20852-3801	301/231-9350
The National Mental Health Association	1021 Prince Street Alexandria, VA 22314-2971	800/969-6977

Call a Local Medical School

Another way to obtain information about good psychiatrists is to call a medical school in your area and ask for the department of psychiatry. They will usually, of course, give you the name of a doctor who is on staff in their department. Nevertheless, it is often possible to give the administrator of the department a brief description of your problem and get the name of a good doctor. It is also possible to call local branches of organizations like the American Psychiatric Association, but they will generally give out randomly selected names of psychiatrists who are members, rather than names of particularly talented doctors.

What Qualifications the Psychiatrist Should Have

Many people are confused about what goes into becoming a psychiatrist and most people do not know the difference between psychologists and psychiatrists. In some states there are no regulations or qualifications concerning psychotherapists: anyone who thinks he gives good advice and has an understanding ear is often permitted to call himself a psychotherapist.

How Do Psychiatrists Train?

Psychiatrists are medical doctors who must go to medical school and obtain an M.D. degree. It is important to note that in most medical schools the first three years are the same for all students regardless of what specialty they will ultimately pick. Medical students are taught the basic sciences, like biochemistry and physiology and anatomy, and must also do clinical work in medicine, neurology, surgery, pediatrics, psychiatry, and all the other medical specialties. In the last year of medical school students have more leeway to pick electives, and someone planning on becoming a psychiatrist will usually select special courses and clinical electives in psychiatry.

After medical school, future psychiatrists must do a year-long internship. This may be in medicine, surgery, or pediatrics, or may be a "rotating" internship in which some months are spent in psychiatry and others in medicine and neurology. The idea is that psychiatrists should know general medicine well enough so that they will not someday miss a brain tumor or other serious medical condition in a patient who complains of hallucinations or is feeling depressed. In addition, the more a psychiatrist knows about general medicine the better equipped he will be to prescribe the sometimes complicated medications psychiatrists administer these days.

After the internship, a psychiatrist must do at least a three-year psychiatric residency. These three years are entirely devoted to caring for psychiatric patients and usually include work with hospitalized patients, outpatients, children with psychiatric illnesses, and medically ill patients with psychiatric problems. The resident should learn how to administer most of the standard psychiatric treatments, including psychotherapy, group and family therapy, and medications.

There are definite differences among psychiatric residencies. Some residencies emphasize psychotherapy more than others, while some are quite negative about psychotherapy. Some residencies are geared toward encouraging psychiatrists to enter research or academic careers, others emphasize public psychiatry and work in state-operated psychiatric hospitals that care mainly for patients with schizophrenia, and some encourage residents to enter private practice after training is complete.

Some of these differences vary to some extent by region of the country. For example, many of the Midwestern psychiatric residency programs, such as those at the University of Iowa and Washington University in St. Louis, are known for emphasizing training in psychiatric diagnosis and medication treatment. Long-term psychotherapy is generally not encouraged. Programs in the Northeast, on the other hand, are often more influenced by the psychoanalytic tradition and offer more training in long-term psychotherapies.

At the end of residency some psychiatrists choose to do further training in a subspecialty of psychiatry. These are very diverse and include child psychiatry, forensic psychiatry (dealing with psychiatric problems in the legal system), consultation psychiatry (dealing with medically ill patients with psychiatric problems), geriatric psychiatry, and psychopharmacology (using medications to treat psychiatric problems). These ''fellowships'' typically last one to two years and are mainly done by psychiatrists interested in research careers.

Some psychiatrists enter psychoanalytic training after residency. This is a very specialized form of psychotherapy which will be described in more detail in a later chapter. Briefly, psychoanalysts believe that psychiatric problems arise from conflicts in the patient's unconscious mind. The patient is not aware of these unconscious conflicts, but the struggle caused by them produces psychiatric symptoms. Psychoanalysis is a technique aimed at making these unconscious conflicts conscious, so that the patient is aware of them and can control them. Psychoanalysis as a treatment usually involves having the patient lie on a couch for four or five sessions per week and typically takes five or more years to complete. To become a psychoanalyst a ''candidate'' must have her own psychoanalysis, called a training analysis, take courses, and treat several patients in psychoanalysis under careful supervision.

Many people assume that psychiatrists have themselves been in psychiatric therapy, but that is not necessarily the case. Only psychoanalysts are generally required to undergo psychoanalysis by the institutes that train and certify them. There is no legal requirement that a psychiatrist undergo psychotherapy and residencies do not require psychotherapy in order for someone to complete the residency. While many psychiatrists do have psychotherapy at some point, often for personal rather than training reasons, this is not required.

Most psychiatrists who complete a psychiatric residency in the United States are eligible to take the examinations of the American Board of Psychiatry and Neurology and thus become ''board certified.'' There is, again, no legal requirement that a doctor in any specialty become board certified. Many doctors never take the boards; others do and fail. The boards in psychiatry have two parts, one written and the other oral. The written part is a comprehensive examination involving all aspects of psychiatry and also tests knowledge in neurology. The oral part involves interviewing a patient in front of several examiners and then answering questions about the patient's diagnosis and possible treatment. Theoretically, a psychiatrist who passes the boards and becomes certified has a broad knowledge of all aspects of psychiatry and is therefore best qualified to treat psychiatric patients.

Psychiatrists differ from other mental health practitioners because they go to medical school. Psychologists usually have a doctorate in psychology obtained from a university and then can become licensed in many states after passing an examination. Psychiatric social workers receive a master's degree in social work from a school of social work, which usually takes two years to obtain. There is no requirement that they have special training in psychiatric problems, although many do obtain such training and have excellent backgrounds. Nurses, occupational therapists, and recreational therapists often provide psychotherapy, and many are extremely talented.

Psychiatrists and Psychologists

Many people are under the impression that psychiatrists are at the "top of the heap" among mental health caregivers and that if you can afford it you should see a psychiatrist rather than a psychologist or a social worker. It is true that psychiatrists train longer than other mental health professionals, are the only ones who are legally permitted to prescribe medication (with a few exceptions mentioned later on), and generally charge the most money. But are they always best?

There is no simple answer to that question. A very good psychologist is always preferable to a very bad psychiatrist. Psychiatrists are trained to do some things that psychologists cannot, like prescribe medication and evaluate the possibility that there are other medical problems causing or complicating a psychiatric problem. But psychologists and social workers are often very good psychotherapists. I generally recommend that a person who suspects she has a psychiatric problem begin by having a consultation with a psychiatrist. The consultation should focus on the diagnosis and treatment options. If the treatment recommended is exclusively psychotherapy and no medical problems are involved, the patient can consider seeing a nonpsychiatrist therapist. The therapy will probably be less expensive and may be just as good. On the other hand, even when the treatment is going to be psychotherapy only, it is certainly reasonable to continue to see the consulting psychiatrist if a good connection has been made. There is an emerging public perception that psychiatrists are only interested in prescribing medication for psychiatric illness. Although psychiatric drugs have become an important part of treatment in the last thirty years, most psychiatrists actually prefer treating patients with psychotherapy and feel quite qualified to do this. It is not true that psychologists and social workers automatically make better therapists. In the chapters on psychotherapy I will discuss ways to know what constitutes a good psychotherapist for an individual patient.

The important point here is that the New Psychiatry dictates patients get the treatment they need, not the treatment with which an individual practitioner feels most comfortable. The New Psychiatry says, "There are no schools of thought when it comes to treating a patient, there are, instead, many useful approaches that must be tailored to the needs of each individual patient."

What Should Happen in the First Meeting

The first meeting with a psychiatrist is critical and has a dual purpose. Obviously, the doctor should take steps to make a diagnosis and a treatment recommendation. Just as important, the patient should evaluate the psychiatrist and decide whether he or she is the right doctor for her.

What should the doctor do? First, she should be courteous and professional. A new patient should not generally be kept waiting more than a few minutes past the appointment time. Some psychiatrists schedule so many patients in an hour's time, and take phone calls as they go along, that they inevitably get behind schedule. This is a bad practice. While modern psychiatry need not be practiced in a secret hideout with ten-foot-thick walls, the doctor must still try not to answer the phone during an appointment and to have a reasonable schedule. The doctor should also welcome the new patient into her office, invite the patient to sit down, and ask questions. Strange as it may seem to some people, there are still psychiatrists who believe that talking to patients is a bad practice. I will address this more fully in later chapters, but it is important to note here that a psychiatrist is allowed to be a real person. I always introduce myself to a new patient and shake his hand. To me, that is simple courtesy.

Establish the Problem

The business of the first meeting is to try to establish what the problem is. This means that the psychiatrist must be clearly interested in each individual's particular situation. Make sure you get a good sense that the doctor is listening to what you say, treating you with respect, and not putting words in your mouth. There are psychiatrists who "specialize" in specific treatments—medications, psychoanalysis, behavior therapy—or in specific problems and illnesses—depression, schizophrenia, marital difficulties. There is nothing wrong with this, but it is important that such doctors not attempt to apply their specific treatment or diagnosis preferences to every patient they see. Once again, this may seem obvious but it is a common problem. A patient with depression may be told that her real problem is a bad marriage. Perhaps so, but it could also be that the patient has stumbled on a doctor who is expert at marital problems and tends to see everything in those terms. Most of the time, in my experience, patients realize this but deny it. A depressed person is easily persuaded that he is wrong and may therefore fail to speak up and say, "Doctor, there may be things about my marriage I need to work on, but the idea that marital problems are the main cause of my depression just doesn't seem correct."

Hence, a new patient should feel that she is getting enough time to speak about and describe what is going on with her. By the same token, the doctor should never leave a new patient adrift but must instead ask questions and guide the patient. In essence, the patient and doctor should work together in the first visit to come to an understanding of the problem that seems on target to both.

The Need for a Diagnosis

Throughout this book I will stress the need for diagnosis. This is not a universally accepted concept among psychiatrists. Some psychiatrists and psychologists prefer to think of a patient in terms of their ''conflicts'' or ''dynamics.'' These are useful concepts, but a diagnosis is always necessary first. I do not mean to imply that patients are to be pushed into convenient pigeonholes; once again, let me stress that it is critical to understand each patient's individual problems and life situations. Nevertheless, treatment will always be misguided if there is no diagnosis first. We are fortunate today to have a fairly accurate and comprehensive system of diagnoses for psychiatry. This is called the *Diagnostic and Statistical Manual*, or *DSM*, and was created by experts commissioned by the American Psychiatric Association. Every few years committees revise and update the diagnostic system, so at the time of this writing we have *DSM-IV*. The *DSM* is a list of all psychiatric diagnoses with criteria for making each diagnosis. It is not a legal document and no one is required to use it, although insurance companies often require a *DSM* diagnosis for reimbursement purposes and a *DSM* diagnosis usually carries considerable weight in court proceedings. In order to arrive at a *DSM* diagnosis, the psychiatrist must ask specific questions about possible symptoms. For example, if a new patient says in response to the question ''How can I help you?'' that he has been feeling depressed for several months, the psychiatrist will ask the following kinds of questions:

- How long have you felt this way?
- Do you have an idea about what started you feeling depressed?
- Has your ability to sleep been affected?
- Has your appetite changed and have you lost weight?
- Do you find it hard to concentrate and are you often tired?
- Do you feel the worst in the morning or evening?
- Do you ever feel things are so bad that you would be better off dead?
- Have you considered suicide?

This is only a partial list of potential questions, but each one moves the doctor closer or farther away from making a diagnosis of depression, depending on the patient's responses. A person who says he feels depressed but who has no trouble sleeping through the night, has no change in appetite, never has problems concentrating, enjoys work and hobbies, and has a good sex drive is probably not suffering from a true, clinical depression. In this case, the psychiatrist will try to find out what the patient means by ''I feel depressed.'' It may be closer to anxiety, or it may be a feeling of dissatisfaction with some aspect of life.

All of this information-gathering usually takes at least an hour in the first visit, and 90 minutes is a reasonable amount of time for an initial consultation. Be wary of a psychiatrist who schedules much less time than this for a first visit. It usually represents a doctor with rigid ideas about the range of psychiatric problems or one who doesn't like to listen very much.

More Critical Questions

In addition to asking questions to arrive at a diagnosis, there are standard things that the doctor should find out about. Sometimes, these will seem insulting but they are necessary. Every first consultation should include an inquiry about suicidal thoughts and about drug and alcohol abuse. It is amazing how many doctors, fearing they will insult their new patient, do not ask how much they drink. There is no way to know by looking at a person if they have an alcohol problem. Some of the most upright, respectable, and successful people drink to excess or become addicted to alcohol and there is virtually no psychiatric problem that alcohol is incapable of causing. The doctor should also ask if the patient has any medical problems. This includes asking specific medical questions, such as the history of different illnesses, findings at the last physical examination, and current medication use. Finally the doctor should ask if there is a family history of psychiatric illness, as some conditions are now believed to be genetic.

In addition to all of these diagnostic questions, the doctor should try to get to know the person a little bit. Where was the patient born, what was his childhood like, are his parents still living? Is the patient married, are there children and if so how are they doing, what kinds of work has the patient done, and how much money does she earn? What are the patient's hobbies and interests?

At the end of this, the doctor should be in a position to venture a diagnosis. Sometimes, more information will be required and the psychiatrist may ask to speak to family members, spouses, or previous doctors. In the case of a patient who has been hospitalized in the past, it is always useful for the psychiatrist to review the hospital record. Occasionally, medical tests are necessary, especially if an underlying medical problem is suspected to be causing or contributing to the psychiatric symptoms.

The Results of the First Meeting

For the most part, the doctor should be able to say at the end of the first visit, ''This is what I think you have, based on the information you have given me so far.'' In this regard, a patient seeing a psychiatrist should expect the same performance he would from an internist or neurologist. An internist might say to a patient, ''I am not sure about the correct diagnosis, but I can tell you what I think are the possibilities and I will be more sure after some tests.'' An internist would not be expected to say to a new patient, ''After several more visits I will tell you what treatment you need,'' or ''You are obviously suffering from deep-rooted problems that we will discuss more at subsequent meetings.'' Similarly, a psychiatrist might say, ''I think you are either suffering from panic disorder or social phobia, and I would like to ask more questions next time I see you to arrive at a final diagnosis,'' but should never say, ''You are obviously having great difficulties and need treatment for them.''

With the diagnosis established, the doctor should then make treatment recommendations. As I will describe in later chapters, there are many possible ways to treat each psychiatric illness. It is the art of psychiatry to be able to design a treatment protocol for a given patient that will produce the best result with the fewest side effects in the shortest period of time. The goal of treatment is always the same: to make the patient better.

The Treatment Approaches

Basically, there are three main kinds of psychiatric treatment—psycho-dynamic psychotherapy (sometimes called long-term or psychoanalytic psychotherapy), cognitive/behavioral psychotherapy, and medication. More and more psychiatrists believe each of these has value and can work. The worst psychiatrists become married to only one form of treatment and attempt to influence patients to accept only that one form. This does not mean that specialization is a bad thing. Some psychiatrists spend years specifically learning psychoanalysis, some are particularly skilled and interested in behavior therapy, and others are specialists in medication (called psychopharmacologists). The problem arises only when the specialist has blinders and refuses to acknowledge that the treatment he knows best may not be best for all patients.

In this regard, it is my belief that psychiatry still lags behind other medical specialties. Specialists in internal medicine, for example, often take sub-specialty training in fields like cardiology, gastroenterology, and infectious diseases. If a cardiologist's patient complains one day of a stomachache, the cardiologist does not order a cardiogram and prescribe digitalis just because those are the tools of his specialty. Instead, the cardiologist determines that the problem is not related to the patient's heart and seeks the consultation of a gastroenterologist. What happens, however, to a psycho-pharmacologist's patient who one day complains that despite the success of antidepressant medication in relieving symptoms of depression, he still feels bored at his job and keeps missing every possible promotion. A rigid psycho-pharmacologist might think these are lingering signs of depression and increase the dose of medication. In fact, these complaints might have nothing to do with depression and often do not respond to medication. Rather, the patient's complaints are very likely the result of conflicts about competition and success, areas that respond better to psychotherapy. Yet it is relatively uncommon for a psychopharmacologist to refer her patient to a psychotherapist.

What the Doctor Should Explain

Because of these factions in psychiatry, a patient must be prepared to listen carefully to the doctor's treatment recommendation. Ideally, the psychiatrist who knows the New Psychiatry should explain how he arrived at the recommendation and what are the alternatives he rejected. If the doctor recommends behavioral psychotherapy, he should explain what evidence there is that this is effective for the patient's particular problem and why that choice is better than drugs or psychoanalysis. A doctor who says, "I do not believe in medication" or "Psychotherapy is a waste" is not equipped to design a good treatment program.

Equally important, the doctor should be prepared to explain the risks and adverse side effects of the treatment he recommends. All psychiatric medications have side effects, but it is less often recognized that psychotherapies also have side effects. Psychotherapies are time-consuming and costly and patients sometimes become dependent on the therapist and have difficulty terminating the treatment because of this. No psychiatric treatment is completely risk-free and a new patient has an absolute right to know what these risks might be.

What the Doctor Should Answer

At the end of the initial consultation the psychiatrist should leave time for questions. These can be about the reasons behind the diagnosis and treatment recommendation. They can also be about the psychiatrist's qualifications. Many patients want to know where their doctors went to college and medical school and at which hospitals they did their internships and residencies. Doctors should answer these questions, but it is unlikely that most people will know which medical schools and residencies are particularly good for psychiatric training. More important are the following questions:

- Does the psychiatrist have any specialty training after residency?
- Is the psychiatrist board certified?
- Does the psychiatrist have special areas of interest and special areas of expertise?
- How long has the psychiatrist been in practice?

It is important for patients to know that these are perfectly legitimate questions. If the psychiatrist appears defensive about such questions or if he attempts to offer "interpretations" rather than answers, it is probably wise to go somewhere else. For example, if you ask a psychiatrist, "Are you comfortable with psychotherapy and with psychopharmacology?" and the doctor answers, "I wonder why you are asking that question," you should reply, "I am asking because it is important to me in deciding whether I want to have you be my doctor." If the psychiatrist does not answer the question, I would not want that psychiatrist to treat me.

Finally, the psychiatrist should explain the practical aspects of the treatment she recommends. How long will it take and how much will it cost? How available is the doctor in between visits? If there is an emergency, can the psychiatrist be reached promptly?

T A B L E 3
WHAT SHOULD BE COVERED IN THE FIRST VISIT

1. The psychiatrist should establish himself as a courteous and caring physician.
2. The doctor should ask enough directed questions to establish a psychiatric diagnosis.
3. The patient should have ample opportunity to explain what is bothering him and to list all of his complaints.
4. Information should be obtained about potential medical problems, family history of psychiatric illness, drug and alcohol abuse, life stresses, and marital and work situation.
5. A treatment recommendation should be made and defended by the doctor.
6. The patient should be given time to ask questions about the basis for the diagnosis and treatment recommendation and about the psychiatrist's qualifications.
7. Practical aspects of the proposed treatment, including length and cost, should be explained.

In Table 3, I have summarized the things that should be covered in the first meeting with a new psychiatrist.

For some people suffering from psychiatric illness, the task of evaluating the psychiatrist's performance and providing all the necessary information may seem daunting. People with severe depression, for example, may have difficulty concentrating on questions and may feel so badly about themselves that they are unable to question the psychiatrist's recommendations. For that reason, a patient should always be made to feel free to bring along a spouse, relative, adult child, partner, or close or intimate friend to the initial visit. These people can help in three ways. First, such "significant others" may be able to provide information that the patient has forgotten. Second, they may be better able to remember the doctor's comments and recommendations later on. Third, they may feel more comfortable answering questions and even challenging the psychiatrist's recommendations. At some point in the evaluation, the psychiatrist may want to speak to the patient alone, but otherwise there is absolutely nothing wrong with bringing someone with you to the first visit.

What You Should Do in the First Visit

So far, I have stressed the things you should demand from a psychiatrist during the initial consultation. These include promptness, polite and courteous demeanor, a carefully developed diagnosis, and well-justified treatment recommendations. I also want to stress the things that patients should try to do.

Keep the Appointment

First, show up. If you make an appointment to see a psychiatrist you will be taking up at least an hour and possibly more of her time. Psychiatrists have nothing to sell except their time—unlike other physicians they do not have procedures to perform that generate income. If you don't show up, the doctor loses a substantial part of that week's income. At very least, you should cancel an appointment you don't intend to keep several days in advance.

Don't Abuse the Phone

Also, do not attempt to get the consultation over the telephone. It is perfectly okay to give the psychiatrist a few details about your situation when you call for an appointment to make sure she deals with cases like yours. You might let the doctor know that you are suffering from depression or panic attacks, for example, or that you are calling about a son who has schizophrenia. You might also ask if the psychiatrist has an exclusive interest in one particular type of treatment, like psychoanalysis or psychopharmacology. And you can certainly ask what the fee will be and how long the consultation will last. Do not, however, try to give the doctor your entire history over the phone or get the doctor to call in a prescription or give you advice without seeing you in person first. It is dangerous and unethical for physicians to provide medical care to patients they have never met, and without a formal consultation the doctor cannot reasonably be expected to help.

Be Prepared

Next, try to gather information the doctor will likely need to know before the visit. Write these things down if they are complicated. Such important information includes all previous episodes of serious psychiatric illness, types of treatment you have received and whether or not they were successful, names and doses of medication you have used, and any instances of psychiatric hospitalization. You should also try to gather medical records including a recent report from your family doctor and copies of laboratory reports if you have had blood tests, X rays, or other diagnostic procedures. I have had the experience many times of thinking a patient complaining of depression might actually have thyroid disease, only to have the patient tell me at the end of the first visit that she recently saw a doctor and had blood tests. Until I know whether thyroid tests were done and what the results were, it may be hard to determine the diagnosis and develop a treatment plan.

Have Reasonable Expectations

I have emphasized the need to ask questions freely. I have also stated emphatically that psychiatrists have a responsibility to answer questions about how they arrived at a particular diagnosis, why they chose a specific treatment, and what kind of experience and credentials they have. On the other hand, it is not necessary to make the psychiatrist submit to a job interview. It is generally ill-advised to ask the doctor personal questions.

There is some legitimate debate about how important personal characteristics of a therapist are to the success of treatment. A patient who has difficulty dealing with her children may feel that a psychiatrist who has children will be the most understanding. An elderly patient may think a young doctor will be unable to grasp all the issues surrounding aging. A gay patient may want a gay psychiatrist. Although I believe these aspects of the therapist's life are much less important than skill and warmth, in keeping with the New Psychiatry they are not to be dismissed without careful consideration. Inquiries about such things should not be met by such comments from the psychiatrist as, "I wonder why you ask that question?"

Do not be unreasonable in your demands or expectations. I have had patients tell me at the end of an initial consultation, "Doctor, I have seen five other shrinks and none of them made me better. If you don't help me in two weeks I am going to kill myself." To such patients I advise immediate hospitalization, because I do not think that within two weeks I can do better than five other psychiatrists. You have the right to ask the doctor how long he thinks it will take for treatment to help, but not for magic. Do not expect to get medications that have no side effects or the appointment time that ensures you will not miss your weekly tennis lesson. Many patients want to see a psychiatrist before or after work and many psychiatrists do have early-morning and evening hours. There are only so many hours in a day, however, and it is not reasonable to expect the doctor to have the perfect hour for your schedule.

Finally, do not ask the psychiatrist to doctor insurance forms. It is a sad fact that most health, life, and disability insurance companies—including Medicare and Medicaid—actively and deliberately discriminate against patients with psychiatric illness. Exactly why they are permitted to get away with this is a mystery to me, but it certainly is not a system devised by psychiatrists. Contrary to popular belief, psychiatrists are actually among the lowest paid medical specialists. Many patients will ask the psychiatrist to put a "medical sounding" diagnosis on an insurance form or to indicate visits that the patient did not actually have in order to improve the reimbursement rate. Don't even ask. Psychiatrists are trained to understand human behavior and are supposed to be especially tolerant of individual needs and fears. We don't like to see people labor under a financial burden in order to obtain medical care and are deeply concerned that reimbursement for psychiatric treatment is so poor. Nonetheless, psychiatrists are understandably adverse to lying on insurance forms, both because it is a bad message to convey to patients and because it is a dangerous practice. If you think the psychiatrist you want to see charges more than you can afford, ask if the fee can be adjusted. If not, consider a lower-cost alternative.

I have attempted to set down the basics of getting psychiatric treatment. In the next section I will describe in more detail the major types of treatment and then, in section four, the major psychiatric illnesses. Section five contains information on special topics. The most important advice I can give is, don't neglect your mental health. Nobody—not you, your family, your boss, or society—benefits if you suffer from treatable psychiatric illness. Forget about the stigma you think you may suffer if you see a psychiatrist and consider instead the prospect of living your whole life without relief from emotional suffering. Use the same threshold for calling a psychiatrist that you would use to call your pediatrician or general practitioner. The worst that will happen is that the psychiatrist will say that you do not need psychiatric treatment and you will have wasted a little time and money. When you have decided to see a psychiatrist, be an informed and aggressive consumer. Pick the psychiatrist you will see carefully and do not be afraid to see more than one to get several opinions. Read everything you can about psychiatry and psychiatric problems and ask questions. Most important, insist that you get results that matter to you. Once again, let me assert that the object of psychiatric treatment is to get better. Set goals with the psychiatrist and make periodic evaluations of whether you are meeting them. Following these guidelines, psychiatry can work.

PART II **The**
TREATMENTS

THERE ARE THREE main kinds of psychiatric treatment: psychodynamic psychotherapy, cognitive/behavioral psychotherapy, and medication. In this section, descriptions are provided of each of these, including some information on how each was developed, what the theory and science behind each method is, and which conditions each type of treatment may help. Also explained are modalities that use each of the three main treatment types, like family therapy, group therapy, and hospitalization. It is important to remember that most patients will need aspects of more than one main type of treatment to get the most benefit from psychiatric care. It is very important, however, to understand what the different techniques are so that an individual patient and his or her family can determine if they are necessary and if they are being applied correctly. In the next section, on the illnesses themselves, detailed information about combining different kinds of treatment for specific problems is given.

2.
Psychodynamic Psychotherapy

WHEN MOST PEOPLE think about being treated by a psychiatrist they think about what we call *psychodynamic psychotherapy.* In old movies, psychiatrists usually sat behind a desk, stroked their beards and puffed their cigars, and said things like "Tell me about that" and "How did that make you feel?" The patient talked and talked and ultimately the doctor said with almost no tone in his voice, "Our time is up for today. See you tomorrow."

The implication is that at this rate, the therapy will go on for a very long time. But that is really not what we mean when we group a number of psychotherapeutic approaches under the somewhat misleading but traditional rubric "psychodynamic." These psychotherapies have in common an adherence to the principles of psychoanalysis as first laid down by Sigmund Freud in the early part of the twentieth century. Psychodynamic psychotherapy includes psychoanalysis itself and something called psychoanalytic psychotherapy. Terms like *non-directed* and *insight-oriented* are also used to describe psychodynamic psychotherapy, as we will see later in this chapter.

Psychodynamic psychotherapies are in trouble these days for at least two important reasons. First, they are expensive, and fewer and fewer people can afford to see a therapist one or more times per week for years. Second, and probably most important, they are accused of violating principle No. 2 of the New Psychiatry: There is renewed concern that they do not work. Despite the fact that psychoanalysis has been around for almost one hundred years, there is very little scientific documentation proving that it works.

A History of Psychoanalysis

Like many things in psychiatry, the fate of psychoanalysis and the psychodynamic psychotherapies has gone from one extreme to the other. In the 1940s and 1950s psychoanalysis ruled the day among psychiatrists. It was widely believed that long-term, psychodynamically oriented therapy was the correct treatment for all psychiatric problems, from neuroses to depression to sexual fetishes to schizophrenia. Using principles laid down by Freud, some psychiatrists reported remarkable success in rapidly rehabilitating American soldiers suffering from "battle fatigue" and "shell shock" during World War II. This lead in part to a glorification of the psychodynamic method. It was asserted that long-term psychotherapy could "get to the bottom" of psychiatric illness, affording the only true "cure."

But the limelight for psychoanalysis did not last long. As I noted in the Introduction, psychoanalysis came under heavy attack during the 1960s by people who felt they had better ways of improving the world's quality of life. Suddenly, psychoanalysis, which itself had once been seen as a radical way of looking at human behavior, stood accused of being reactionary. Freud's idea that the goals of life were to love and work seemed to young intellectuals of the 1960s a conservative manifesto. Psychoanalysis was seen as dominated by white males, and feminists especially took umbrage at concepts like "penis envy."

By the beginning of the 1970s, psychiatry's "scientific revolution," described in Chapter 4 (Medication), became firmly entrenched. Psychopharmacology gradually replaced psychoanalysis as the fad of the moment. Then, in the 1980s, the crisis over paying for health care began, and insurance companies started refusing to pay for long-term psychiatric treatment.

At this point there is an extremist position that psychoanalytic psychotherapies are worthless. Insurance companies love this kind of talk and so do radical psychopharmacologists and behavioral therapists who hope to replace psychoanalysts and corner the mental health care market.

It is important to stress that it would be a serious mistake to jump on this kind of bandwagon and casually dismiss psychoanalytic therapies. Although very few patients really need five years of four-times-a-week psychoanalysis, many people do, in fact, benefit from different versions of psychodynamic psychotherapy. It is important to understand something about the principles of psychodynamic therapy, how it works and, perhaps most important, for what specific problems it may be helpful.

Psychodynamic Psychotherapy: What Is It?

There are really two main principles behind psychoanalysis and other forms of psychodynamic psychotherapy. They are:

1. All human beings have unconscious thoughts. These are thoughts that we are not aware of but that have a great deal of influence over our behavior. When there are conflicts among these thoughts or when we have unconscious thoughts that are in conflict with our conscious ideas of right and wrong, emotional problems can result.
2. Early childhood experiences are critically important in shaping our personalities, our unconscious thoughts, our emotions, and our behaviors.

How do we know if these things are true? The answer is, we really don't. It is obvious that some things go on in the brain out of immediate consciousness. Some part of your brain has stored the information about what you had for breakfast this morning even though, until I brought it up, you weren't actually thinking about it. We store thousands of memories in various parts of our brains that are "unconscious" in the sense that we don't have to be thinking about them all the time to make them stay there. They can be summoned up whenever we need them. These memories, however, are not exactly what psychoanalysts have in mind. They believe that there is a whole life of thoughts and feelings in our minds that we are not aware of but that can control us. These thoughts are often not exactly the kind of things most people are pleased to know they have. They tend, according to psychoanalysts, to mainly involve sex and violence. Freud believed that humans have a part of the unconscious mind called the Id that basically wants us to have sex with whomever we feel like having it with and to murder anyone who displeases us. Another part of the unconscious mind, called the Superego, is our conscience and tells us not to do such bad things. The Superego can get so stern, however, that sometimes it overdoes it and makes us feel guilty for every sexy or angry thought we have. A third part of the unconscious mind, called the Ego, is supposed to mediate between the Id and the Superego and figure out how to live an ordinary life in the real world. It is the Ego that Freud believed makes it possible for us to reach the pinnacle of human life and be able to "work and love."

It is easy to make fun of these ideas, and many people have done just that. Sophisticated X rays of the human brain do not show us where the Id, Ego, and Superego are, nor can we prove that complex unconscious thoughts actually exist. Nonetheless, let us look at an example of behavior that just might involve unconscious thoughts.

The Power of the Unconscious Thought: An Example

A 45-year-old man is having a discussion with his wife about her day at work. She tells him about a deal she worked out with another lawyer, about where she went for lunch, about an expensive dress she bought during her lunchtime, and about a difficult client she will meet with tomorrow. During the conversation the husband, who is also an attorney and who has a long history of hypochondriacal complaints, begins to feel a slight pain in his chest. While his wife is talking he starts thinking about what life will be like for his family after he dies of a heart attack and whether he has enough life insurance. He begins to obsess about his life insurance policy: How much does he have? Is there enough to cover the mortgage? Did he remember to pay the last premium? Soon, he feels he must rush home and call his insurance agent.

Our hypochondriac husband is conscious of three thoughts: his chest hurts, he might die, and, most important to him at the moment, his life insurance might not be enough. But one might ask, why at this moment did he start having these pains and thoughts? Only minutes earlier he felt physically fine and he has not thought about his life insurance policy for months. Why now?

The answer, it turns out, is that he is angry at his wife for spending money on the dress. Although the couple earns a good salary, the husband believes his wife spends more than they can afford. Yet at no time did the husband actually think to himself, "I am upset because my wife spent too much money." Instead, all of his thoughts focused on life insurance. We might say that his angry thoughts toward his wife in this case were unconscious, yet they had a profound influence on his behavior. The end result was a rush home to check on an insurance policy.

Now this example is admittedly simple, but I picked it because it is one many people will relate to. We all have had the experience of entertaining worried thoughts and only later realizing that something else was really bothering us. In the example above, the husband did not consciously entertain the angry thoughts about his wife for several reasons. First, a part of him actually enjoyed seeing his wife dressed in expensive clothing. Second, he was afraid of his anger—his unconscious anger was really out of proportion to the situation. Third, he was afraid of his wife's reaction; in reality, she had done absolutely nothing wrong. So the actual angry thought about his wife was repressed and an alternate thought emerged instead into consciousness. In this case the alternate thought was completely off base—the man has a healthy heart and plenty of life insurance. But it was easier for him to worry about dying than be angry at his wife. One might say that he would rather think about dying himself than almost murdering his wife.

Now I have already said that this particular man had a long history of hypochondriacal complaints. Almost every week he convinced himself he was either having a heart attack or had developed cancer. Doctors were constantly telling him he was healthy, but soon after such reassurance he would develop another medical complaint. A psychiatrist listening to the story of his conversation with his wife might come to the following tentative conclusion: the man has a tendency to translate unconscious anger into conscious physical complaints. The psychiatrist might then take the position that in order to cure the man of his hypochondriasis it will be necessary to make him aware of his unconscious anger. In the above example, the patient needs to recognize that in fact he is angry at his wife for buying a dress. With this knowledge made conscious he can then recognize that his anger is inappropriate, that his wife is really not a spendthrift, and that he needs to loosen up about his ideas about money.

Next, the psychiatrist might ask, "How did this patient get the way he is? Why does he have this tendency to bury anger in the first place?" Here, the second principle of psychoanalytic thinking comes into play. This is the idea that early childhood experiences shape our innermost thoughts and behavior. An exploration of the patient's life history reveals that as a boy he witnessed his parents having many angry and occasionally violent arguments.

Whenever his parents fought, the young boy would become terrified, fearing that his parents would kill each other. He also felt neglected and abandoned; his warring parents were in no position to pay him any attention during their battles. When he was only seven, his parents separated and his father spent less and less time with him over the years.

As a young child, then, this patient got the idea that anger is a terrible and destructive thing, especially between a husband and a wife. Day in and day out he witnessed a married couple fight and come to hate each other. To the impressionable young boy, anger between husband and wife became associated with terror and neglect. There was no happy ending to this anger. A fighting couple meant divorce and a little boy with no father.

If you asked the little boy grown up whether it is okay for married couples to fight he would probably answer, "Of course, couples always fight." So the man's conscious mind can give the right answer. But unconsciously, this man has come to believe the opposite. Anger toward his wife is dangerous and must be avoided at all costs. Symbolically, anger between a husband and wife is deadly and so every time he feels anger at her he gets a pain and fears for his life.

With this information, the psychiatrist is able to make what is called a "formulation," a more comprehensive description of the way the patient's unconscious mind developed and how it operates in the present. The formulation is then presented to the patient as the framework for developing a treatment plan. The patient must come to recognize how his unconscious developed and how it works in order to get over his physical complaints.

The Object of Psychoanalysis

I do not think this example will seem terribly farfetched to most readers, but some psychoanalysts and their critics will object. Many psychoanalysts will insist that I have vastly oversimplified their field. For example, they will say I have overlooked one important tenet of their field: the Oedipus conflict. Going back to our example, the psychoanalysts will say that the real problem with our patient is that during his childhood, while witnessing his parents' fights, he became confused about where he fit in. Little boys, according to psychoanalytic theory, have erotic feelings toward their mothers and feel jealous of their fathers. A part of them wants to get the father out of the picture so that they can marry Mother themselves, but another part fears that these murderous thoughts will wind up motivating Father to kill them, or at least to cut off the little boy's penis. All of this is unconscious, according to psychoanalysts. The conflict is resolved as the boy comes to identify more and more with his father and ultimately to find a woman of his own. But in our example, the little boy unconsciously believes he has a real chance to get rid of his father; after all, his mother seems to hate her husband herself. The possibility of success is actually terrifying to the little boy, who is even more afraid of the father's retaliation. So, to protect himself the boy develops mythical feelings that he is sick and about to die. These "dynamics" persist into adult life, but always out of consciousness.

The psychoanalysts will say, therefore, that simply making angry thoughts conscious is not enough. In order for our patient to get better, he will have to recognize the details of his Oedipal conflict. Unless that is resolved, he will never get better.

Criticism of Psychoanalysis

Critics of psychoanalysis will similarly object to my example. A nice story, they will say, but one without any proof. How do we know that angry thoughts make a person believe he is going to die? It could be purely coincidence. They will note that our patient is a generally anxious man who worries about everything. He worries that he does not have enough money and he worries that his heart is weak. He worries that his wife is angry at him and he worries that the stock market is going to crash. The critics will say that the patient is suffering from an anxiety disorder. Psychopharmacologists might then say he has this anxiety disorder because of defects in the biochemistry of his brain. Behaviorists will say he has this problem because his parents were anxious and he learned to be anxious from them. In any event, the critics will say that trying to convince the man that he worries about his health because he is unconsciously angry at his wife is a waste of time and probably not even true.

A confused patient who has to listen to these different opinions might say, "Well, the most sensible solution would be to start with the quickest treatment and if that doesn't work, then I'll go on and try something that is more expensive and time-consuming." Following such a plan would make the choice of treatment easy: medications for psychiatric problems, including anxiety in this example, take about one month to work; behavioral psychotherapies take three to six months; and psychodynamic psychotherapies involving psychoanalytic principles take more than one year. But the patient is likely to get some scary cautionary advice before taking this route. Both behavioral and psychodynamic psychotherapists will insist that medications only cover up symptoms and produce adverse side effects. The psychoanalytic psychotherapists will further assert that all other treatments only produce symptomatic improvement: the only way to root out the deepest causes of psychiatric problems, they will say, is to undergo a psychodynamic psychotherapy.

Before giving my advice on how to proceed it will be necessary to describe a little more about how long-term therapies work and about some of the variations among them.

Psychodynamic Psychotherapy: How Does It Work?

Basic Principles

The basic principle behind psychodynamic psychotherapy is to make conscious what is unconscious. Because unconscious material is deeply buried, often since early childhood, the process is slow. Furthermore, it is not a simple matter of telling the patient that she does this or that because specific thoughts are in her unconscious. Merely telling the patient what is buried is not sufficient; the patient in long-term therapy must come gradually to discover what is there.

In order to accomplish this process of self-discovery, Freud recommended that patients be asked to "free-associate" during therapy sessions. That is, the patient in classical psychoanalysis is told to say out loud whatever pops into her mind. The therapist tries not to interfere too much with this process; after all, the critical thing is not what the therapist thinks but what turns out to be buried in the unconscious. Dreams are believed to be particularly helpful. Freud called dreams the "royal road to the unconscious" and in his most famous book, *The Interpretation of Dreams,* explained that while asleep the dreamer allows unconscious material to come out and reveal itself, although usually behind a complicated disguise. By disentangling the dream's story, analysts believe they can gain insight into the unconscious.

Throughout this the analyst intervenes only at select moments when he thinks the patient is ready to recognize elements coming from the unconscious. Because the unconscious is held to contain a lot of disagreeable information, it must be revealed slowly. Otherwise the patient will either object, get upset, or think the whole thing is stupid. One cannot abruptly tell an analytic patient, "You act this way because you always wanted to murder your father and have sex with your mother." This repugnant idea would either sound disgusting or moronic to most people. In time, however, patients come to accept such interpretations.

What Is Transference?

One other crucial part of psychodynamic treatments is the development of something called *transference.* The exact definition of transference is not universally agreed upon, but the one I think that is most understandable is as follows: A patient gradually comes to act toward and think about the therapist in the same way she came to think about her parents. In essence, the patient "transfers" onto the analyst attitudes that she developed toward her mother and father early in childhood. By identifying these transference attitudes, the patient and therapist can get an understanding of what went on during the patient's childhood.

Let me try to give an example of transference. A patient is stuck in a traffic jam on the way to her appointment with her therapist. In the car, she first becomes worried she will be late and then fearful that the analyst will be angry with her. As it gets later and later she begins to shake and tremble, picturing the analyst unleashing on her an angry reprimand for being late. She becomes so fearful that she turns the car around and goes home, unable to face the imagined wrath of her doctor.

In fact, the therapist can very well understand that a traffic jam might from time to time make a patient late to a session. While recognizing that being late to a session is unfortunate, the woman's particular therapist had never reprimanded any patient in his entire career for anything, let alone being late because of unavoidable circumstances. The woman's fear of the analyst's reaction to lateness was really entirely a product of her own personality and had nothing to do with the way the therapist really ever acted. It turned out after examination at later sessions that her father had been stern about most things and never tolerated sloppiness, lateness, or almost any ordinary human foible. The patient reacted to the analyst as she would have to her father, but she was entirely unaware of this. In fact, she believed that most people would be angry if she were late to a meeting because of traffic. This is an example of a "transference" reaction, one which was useful in ultimately helping the patient learn an important fact about herself.

In classical psychoanalysis, the patient lies on a couch and free-associates for an hour from three to five times a week. The therapist rarely talks for fear of disrupting the process. The patient is generally not permitted to know much about the therapist—real information about the therapist might interfere with the development of transference. Thus, the analyst is a silent and somewhat mysterious figure to the patient. In fact, a patient in analysis once commented that when his analyst spoke he would jump up off the couch in a startled reaction, having come to forget sometimes that anyone else was actually in the room.

There are variants of this version and these are what I will discuss next.

Psychodynamic Psychotherapy: What Are the Different Versions?

What I have described above is the most classical form of psychoanalysis, deriving directly from the works of Sigmund Freud. Psychoanalysts who train in one of the institutes approved by the American Psychoanalytic Association learn this fairly rigorous and traditional method.

But over the years, for both practical and theoretical reasons, many modifications have been made in classical psychoanalytic technique. I won't try to explain all of them; some are fairly simple alterations like having the patient come three times a week instead of four, or allowing the analyst somewhat more freedom in reacting to what the patient says.

Over the years since Freud's original works, many analysts realized that there are lots of patients who cannot withstand the demands of psychoanalysis. For some patients this is because their illness will not permit it. A patient suffering from a severe depression, for example, may simply be incapable of free association and may not be able to wait years for improvement. Patients with severe neurotic disorders, discussed in later chapters, may not be able to stand the severe deprivation that comes from not getting much feedback and direction from the analyst. For others the problem with traditional psychoanalysis has a more practical basis: the patient cannot afford to see someone four times a week, for instance. For these reasons, a variant of psychoanalysis was developed in which patients sit up in a chair instead of lying on a couch, see the therapist once or twice a week (occasionally three times), and get much more direction and input from the therapist than is the case with psychoanalysis. This variant is usually called psychoanalytic psychotherapy or insight-oriented psychotherapy.

This kind of therapy still adheres to the fundamental principles of all psychodynamic therapy that I mentioned above: unconscious factors are important in influencing behavior and early childhood experiences shape personality. The psychoanalytic psychotherapist still attempts to make unconscious material conscious and to draw upon childhood experiences to help the patient understand what is at the root of his problems. The main difference between psychoanalysis and psychoanalytic psychotherapy really has to do with the degree to which the therapist interacts with the patient. In the latter the therapist is much more apt to make comments, give advice, and ask questions. Long silences lasting an entire session are rare in psychoanalytic psychotherapy and complicated transference feelings are not permitted to build up. In psychoanalysis the therapist may permit the patient to harbor all kinds of neurotic feelings toward him for long periods of time. Patients in analysis develop strong romantic attachments to the analyst, for example, that are often permitted to brew for months without comment or dissection. In psychoanalytic psychotherapy such deep feelings are more likely to be identified and interpreted as soon as they occur.

For classical analysts, psychoanalytic psychotherapy is a relatively superficial treatment that is necessary for many patients but rarely sufficient to produce a "cure." They argue that if a patient can possibly be in analysis she should be. Sometimes, they see psychoanalytic psychotherapy as a preparatory phase to psychoanalysis.

In reality, the number of patients who currently go through a classical psychoanalysis is becoming smaller and smaller. Top analysts can now charge up to $200 per session and a monthly bill for psychoanalysis can easily reach $3,000 to $4,000. Insurance companies rarely reimburse for this any longer, and it is a rare individual, with a lot of time on his hands, who can afford $30,000 or more a year for many years in order to get analyzed. Hence, most patients who have long-term psychotherapy now have psychoanalytic psychotherapy. This is still quite expensive and time-consuming and is only partially paid for by most health insurance policies.

Before I answer the critical question of ''What does psychodynamic psychotherapy work for?'' I want to reassert my belief that it does indeed work. I say this because as a scientist and clinician I have to be honest and admit that there are really no scientific studies that prove that long-term psychotherapy works in the same way that we can prove a medication works.

There are a few conditions for which I can say psychodynamic psychotherapy is not a good treatment. Most psychoanalysts would agree, although even here some traditionalists will still insist that long-term psychotherapy is good for everything. The conditions for which I never recommend psychoanalysis or psychoanalytic psychotherapy as the only treatment are: schizophrenia, bipolar affective disorder (formerly called manic depressive illness), psychotic depression, obsessive compulsive disorder, panic disorder, simple phobia, bulimia, anorexia nervosa, and drug and alcohol abuse. These conditions either do not respond to long-term therapy, or even if they do, the treatment would take too long to be worth it. A patient suffering from a psychotic depression (described in more detail in Chapter 10) would probably be dead long before psychoanalysis could possibly make a difference.

There are conditions that may or may not respond to long-term psychotherapy, depending on a great number of factors. These conditions include social phobia, generalized anxiety disorder, sexual problems, family and marital problems, and dysthymia (a form of chronic depression). These are conditions for which there is scientific evidence that drugs and/or behavioral psychotherapy are effective, but it is my own experience that many patients with these problems get only partial help from drugs and behavioral psychotherapy and can benefit from psychodynamic psychotherapy. I usually recommend that patients with these problems first try the much shorter and less expensive medication and behavioral therapies before committing themselves to long-term psychotherapy.

Finally, there are conditions that, if they are going to respond to anything, will only respond to psychodynamic psychotherapy. These are mainly the neuroses (also called personality or character disorders) and include such things as compulsive, histrionic, borderline, and narcissistic neuroses. Drugs and behavioral therapy don't work for these deeply ingrained difficulties. An important caution, however, comes from the fact that not everybody with these problems will get better even if they undergo years of long-term psychotherapy. The question then becomes, how to decide if it is worth having psychodynamic psychotherapy in the first place.

Psychodynamic Psychotherapy: How Do I Decide If I Should Do It?

What should you do if, after listening to your story, a psychiatrist recommends psychoanalytic psychotherapy or psychoanalysis? First, ask the psychiatrist if there is any other treatment that might possibly help you and be on the lookout for such answers as ''I don't believe in medication'' or ''Only psychodynamic psychotherapy will get to the root of your problem.'' These are ''party line'' responses and mean the psychiatrist is locked into psychodynamic therapy. If you get answers like this, get another opinion.

Second, ask the doctor if it is possible to try another treatment that is shorter and less expensive first to see if it will work. If you have a phobia, for example, you should probably try behavioral psychotherapy, described in the next chapter, first, and only if it is ineffective should longer-term therapy be considered. If you have depression, an antidepressant medication will surely work before psychodynamic therapy. You can wait until you feel less depressed to make a commitment to psychodynamic psychotherapy.

Finally, ask yourself if you are dealing with a relatively specific problem or with a whole set of problems that have been affecting your life for years. Are you looking for help getting over depression or handwashing compulsions or panic attacks? Or are you looking for help improving your relationships with other people, your ability to compete for job promotions, and your feelings of inferiority. The first set of specific problems usually respond to focused behavioral or psychopharmacological treatments. Often, when people undergo these shorter therapies and respond, they feel better about life and no longer consider years of psychoanalytic therapy. On the other hand, focused behavioral and medication treatments are not likely to correct deep-rooted and long-standing difficulties in the way a person relates to others or basic self-image.

If you are suffering from more generalized difficulties in life, the next question you should ask is, Will the treatment be worth it? Remember that psychodynamic treatments—be they therapy or psychoanalysis—will last a long time and there is no guarantee they will work. On the other hand, when they do work they can make a big difference and it would be a tragedy to casually pass up this kind of help. Let me give an example of one person's decision to enter psychoanalytic psychotherapy.

An Example of Useful Psychotherapy

Mrs. B. came to see me because she thought she might need antidepressant medication. She had read in a magazine article that depressed people often have difficulty relating to others because it is hard for them to be outgoing and talkative. Furthermore, Mrs. B. read, depressed people often perform beneath their potential at work because the depression blunts their motivation and makes them feel unworthy. Indeed, Mrs. B. complained of an unhappy marriage, few close friends, and substantial job dissatisfaction. And it is perfectly true that depression can make a person feel guilty, socially withdrawn, unmotivated, and unworthy. The important thing about Mrs. B. however, was that there was little evidence that she was really depressed. She came to my office dressed attractively in bright clothing with carefully applied makeup. She talked in an animated way, smiled occasionally, and laughed at a joke I told her. She told me that she never experienced insomnia and that her appetite was fine. She enjoyed going to the movies and read approximately one book every two weeks without any concentration difficulties. So what was the problem? First, Mrs. B. had married a man who was himself isolated and uncommunicative. She actually had misgivings about marrying him in the first place, but felt pressured by her parents, something she noted was characteristic of her life even into adulthood. She had many friends as a young girl, but somewhere beginning in adolescence she started thinking that her acquaintances were smarter and more attractive and began avoiding friendships.

This attitude also affected Mrs. B. at work: although she is a bright and talented economist, she never believed in herself enough to promote her work and call it to the attention of her superiors. Consequently, Mrs. B. was consistently passed over for promotions, making her feel even worse about herself. I could not make a diagnosis of depression in this case and certainly could not recommend any medication that would alleviate Mrs. B.'s problems. I explained that certain aspects of her difficulties might respond to behavioral psychotherapy. For example, a technique known as "assertiveness training" might help her take control in her relationship with her husband and be more aggressive at work. But my overriding feeling was that Mrs. B. was suffering from a whole series of conflicts about her place in the world and her self-image. I recommended psychoanalytic psychotherapy.

Mrs. B. was not suffering from a specific focused problem, nor were her problems trivial. She had made a series of wrong choices in her life and was denying herself many opportunities for self-fulfillment. Her constellation of problems does not usually respond to drugs or behavioral treatment and cannot be ignored. It would be ridiculous to tell Mrs. B. to "pull yourself up" or "learn to live with it." This was not a lazy person given to sitting back and making other people take care of her. Mrs. B. worked hard and deserved to have help overcoming stumbling blocks in her way.

What Makes Psychoanalytic Therapy Work

What are the chances that people like Mrs. B. can be helped with psychoanalytic psychotherapy? Unfortunately, this is hard to predict. In general, the things that indicate a person will get better in psychodynamic treatment are the following:

1. A high degree of motivation to change
2. A relatively stable life without much chaos
3. A better than average intelligence
4. A good relationship with the therapist

Let me expand on these four points. The first one may seem obvious, but it is surprising how many people begin psychotherapy who really don't want to change. People get used to their personalities and lifestyles over time and it may feel unacceptably disruptive to make significant changes. For example, for all Mrs. B complaints about her husband's lack of warmth, she must be willing to address this problem with her therapist and then with her husband if treatment is going to work. If she feels that, despite her complaints, it is too much trouble to try to alter her relationship with her husband, then it is worthless to make this a goal of treatment. A patient in psychoanalytic treatment must be ready to face many aspects of her life and work hard to change them.

The second point, that the patient have a relatively stable life, is important. Psychoanalytic psychotherapy can be applied to people with very chaotic lives who live on an emotional roller coaster and frequently change jobs, addresses, and "significant others." But the more extraneous chaos there is in a person's life, the more unpredictable becomes the likelihood of success with psychoanalytic psychotherapy. A person with a job and a stable relationship is more likely to improve. By "better than average intelligence," the third point, I do not mean that a person has to be a rocket scientist to get better in psychotherapy. Nevertheless, the process does seem to have a better chance of succeeding with people of relatively high intelligence levels.

The Doctor-Patient Relationship Is Key

Finally, and perhaps most important, is the relationship between doctor and patient. While this is important for all treatment situations, with doctors of all specialties, it seems of greatest significance for psychodynamic psychotherapy. Studies have shown that it is critical for the doctor and patient to actually like each other in order for the therapy to work. This is different than what is needed, for example, between patient and cardiologist. The patient does not have to think the cardiologist is a particularly interesting or nice person and the cardiologist does not necessarily have to like the patient. What is required in this situation is that the patient believe the cardiologist cares about him and treats him appropriately and that the cardiologist acts in a professional and kind manner. But the "fit" between psychotherapist and patient is more complex.

In the course of treatment, as I have discussed above, a patient may develop all kinds of feelings toward the therapist, some of which can be intensely negative. These are called transference and are part of the therapy. It is important not to drop out of treatment because of them. But transference does not enter into a patient's initial consideration of which therapist to pick. If you have intense negative feelings toward a therapist after the first or second meeting, regardless of the reason, don't get involved in a long-term therapy with that person. Even if you think your reasons may be silly or irrational, remember, there are plenty of psychotherapists in the world and you should try to find one with whom you feel comfortable at the outset.

When the Therapist Doesn't Like the Patient

By the same token, if a therapist does not like a potential patient, he should not accept that patient into long-term therapy. Let me give an example:

A 52-year-old man, Mr. K., came to see me. He complained of feeling bored at work and that his wife did not excite him. He was a very successful businessman, but was annoyed by all the people who asked for his help, including his children. He wanted work to go more smoothly, with less aggravation from his staff. I thought Mr. K. had legitimate problems, but I found myself feeling very critical of him. For example, his solution to his difficulties with his wife was to have multiple affairs. He seemed punitive with his children, ''nickel and diming'' them even though he was wealthy. He seemed to want the people who worked for him to be his slaves and had little empathy for them. He annoyed me by trying to get me to reduce my fee and put a misleading diagnosis on his insurance form, even though he was a millionaire several times over. Mr. K. is entirely deserving of psychiatric treatment, but I realized that I could never empathize with him and that the last thing a patient needs is a therapist who feels critical of him. Rather than struggle against these odds, I gave Mr. K. the names of several other psychiatrists who I thought might not be so bothered by what seemed to me his arrogance.

When the Patient Should Reject the Therapist

In the above case, I decided I did not like the patient and referred him elsewhere. Here is an example of a patient I saw who should have rejected his therapist:

Mr. L. was a 27-year-old man when he came to me for a consultation. He had been in psychotherapy with another psychiatrist for five years, since graduating from college. Now, five years later, he felt he had made very little progress. He told me that he found his therapist to be aloof and cold. Even at their first meeting, he felt the therapist was judging him; over the years he actually dreaded going to sessions. Nevertheless, he had dutifully gone to every session and felt disloyal to his therapist for seeing me.

My impression was that Mr. L. was actually suffering from an excessive case of obedience. He always did what everyone told him and never did what he wanted. Although this made his boss very happy, Mr. L. was chronically morose and angry. It would have been better for him to have had a more flexible therapist, someone who could help Mr. L. loosen up and take more risks. Instead, he picked, for his particular difficulties, about the worst therapist possible. The therapist told Mr. L. he needed psychoanalysis, when to come for the next appointment, and what the fee would be, and Mr. L. did what he was told. Some will argue that Mr. L. did these things out of deep, unconscious motivations and that he was only having a transference reaction to the analyst. Maybe so, but I still insist that if you find a psychiatrist disagreeable on the first meeting, for whatever reason, go see someone else.

Beyond the four points I have laid down, it is really impossible to know beforehand whether psychodynamic psychotherapy is going to work. So the next question is, What is it supposed to do and how do you judge if it is working before years have elapsed?

Psychodynamic Psychotherapy: How Do You Know If It Is Helping?

As with all treatments offered by the New Psychiatry, in order to know if any treatment is working you first have to figure out what it is you want it to do. That means setting goals at the beginning. This is often overlooked in psychodynamic psychotherapies. Some psychoanalysts, on theoretical grounds, will even refuse to set goals with the patient. These doctrinaire therapists will insist that the only goal is to explore the unconscious. I am happy for them to do that on their time.

Setting Goals

If you decide to start a psychoanalysis or psychoanalytic psychotherapy, you should absolutely make a list of goals, with your therapist, that you want to meet. These can be fairly general, like improving your relationship with your husband, having more self-confidence, or becoming able to compete better at work. Make sure that you and your therapist are clear about what you want to achieve.

Don't try to evaluate each goal at every session. By design, psychodynamic psychotherapy is a relatively slow process. Often, one or two sessions will go by that do not seem obviously related to the goals. An occasional session may even be a waste of time: the patient may have absolutely nothing to say or the therapist may be tired that day. These are the unavoidable bumps in the road of a long-term therapy. But these misfirings should be the exception, not the rule. For the most part, a patient must feel that each session accomplishes something toward the goals. By the end of the first month of treatment, the patient should feel comfortable telling the therapist almost anything and the therapist should have a very good idea of what needs to be done to move things along. By the end of the third month the patient should detect some real progress: an ability to identify mistakes he is making in relating to people more rapidly; a renewed feeling of hopefulness that things can get better. By six months some evidence of real improvement should be obvious to both patient and doctor. A patient who seeks to learn how his personality interferes with romantic relationships should now be doing somewhat better in choosing appropriate people to ask for dates and in making the date successful.

Certainly after a year in therapy a patient should recognize tangible evidence that his goals are being met. This does not mean that everything in his life will be perfect or that he will be a completely new person. These things will never happen and anybody who expects this is destined for disappointment. But a patient who went into therapy because she is blocked in her ability to compete at work and get ahead because of personal conflicts should, after one year in therapy, find herself less blocked, more competitive, and doing better on her job.

What If the Goals Aren't Being Met

What if none of these milestones are met and even after a year there is no sense of progress? At that juncture you should seriously question both yourself and your therapist about whether the treatment will ever work. Do not make excuses either for yourself or the therapist. Do not buy an explanation for lack of progress such as "These things take a lot of time," or "The reason you are not getting better is because you are resisting," or, especially, "We are not interested in practical improvement, only in your understanding yourself better." If you ask your therapist why you are not improving and are given a question in return, such as "I wonder why you feel frustrated?" or "Do you feel angry at me for not making you better?," you should tell your therapist that such replies are not satisfactory.

Sometimes it is helpful to get a psychotherapy consultation. This means going to see another psychiatrist, usually one who is very senior and experienced, and explaining what is going on in the therapy. The consultant will also speak to your current therapist and then try to figure out whether the therapy is likely to ever be productive and whether there are things that can be done to speed progress. Sometimes it turns out that the patient really is making progress, but for a variety of reasons fails to recognize this. Let me give an example of how a psychotherapy consultation can help.

A patient, Ms. R., was seeing a psychotherapist for therapy twice a week for slightly over one year. She was 32 years old and unmarried and felt she was doing something wrong in meeting men and staying in relationships. She set as her goal learning what was preventing her from entering and maintaining a relationship. The therapist determined that the patient was unconsciously comparing all the men she met to her very successful father. Her father had always taken care of her every need as a little girl and was universally recognized by all of his acquaintances as "perfect." Ms. R. met and dated many men, but she always found things wrong with them: they were not doing well enough in their careers or weren't athletic enough or handsome enough. She really did not recognize how critical she was; what would usually happen was that she would meet someone, pick on them until they became angry at her, and then the man would reject her. After about one month of therapy the psychiatrist recognized this pattern and began pointing it out to her. After six months the therapist began linking this behavior to Ms. R.'s feelings about her father, who actually turned out to be not so perfect after all, and by one year Ms. R. was dating the same man for three months with signs that, if anything, the relationship was getting stronger. Still, Ms. R. felt therapy was not working and insisted on a consultation. The consultant quickly recognized that Ms. R. had a strong transference reaction to her therapist, who she felt was a "perfect" man. Because of this, she had been comparing her new boyfriend with her therapist and consequently did not allow herself to recognize how well her new relationship was developing and how different this was from her past behavior. The consultant pointed this out to both the patient and her therapist and enabled them to continue their already successful work.

The above example is obviously a success story, but in my experience a therapy that does nothing in the first year is probably never going to help. Often, patients recognize this after less than one year and only stay in treatment longer because they are afraid to insult the therapist by dropping out or because they think it is their failure that therapy isn't working better. Such people can get trapped into years of therapy that doesn't work. There is absolutely nothing wrong with quitting therapy if you don't feel it is helpful. Always evaluate how you are doing and whether your goals are being met and never be afraid to question what is going on.

Psychodynamic Psychotherapy: What Are the Practical Arrangements?

Let us say that you have selected a psychotherapist and set your goals for a psychoanalytic psychotherapy or psychoanalysis. The next step is to make a suitable arrangement with your doctor about the practical details. These include what the fee will be, what your session times will be, how often you will come, and what will happen if you miss a session or go on vacation.

Psychoanalytic therapies should generally involve, at the very least, weekly sessions. Most therapists believe that this is really a minimum. When seeing a patient only once a week there is a tendency for the patient to merely report the events that occurred in his life during the past week and never get to any other material. So twice a week is recommended whenever possible. Patients with more serious character disorders, like borderline personality disorder (see Chapter 15), will sometimes require more than two sessions per week. A psychoanalysis is usually conducted with three to five sessions per week.

Scheduling the Sessions

You and the therapist should agree on a regular time for your sessions. Many patients want session times in the early morning before work or in the evening after work. Some patients request sessions on weekends. Although psychotherapists often have such hours, they are at a premium. Furthermore, most psychotherapists do not want to work every night and all weekend. It is not infrequent that a patient and doctor may think they are a perfect match, but cannot find agreeable times to meet. Before abandoning that therapist, find out if he or she may have some better times open in the next few months when a current patient finishes. Also, consider going less often to start until better times become available. Finally, be realistic about your schedule. Many people, with a little effort, can get away from work at lunchtime or at the end of the day. You may have to work later another day, but don't be resentful about this. Your therapist is probably working from early in the morning until late at night himself.

Setting the Fee

The fee for therapy should be discussed openly and early. I remember when I was just starting out my own psychiatric practice commenting to a similarly beginning psychotherapist that I had no difficulty discussing intimate details of patient's lives with them, but felt uncomfortable discussing fees. My colleague replied, ''That is because you don't have sex with your patients but you do have money with them.'' Contrary to popular belief, psychiatrists are at the bottom of the pay scale among doctors. They usually earn about half to a third of what surgeons make and less than neurologists, dermatologists, and dentists. That is because psychiatric treatments generally involve large, regular blocks of time and no procedures are involved. On the other hand, the patient who comes two or more times a week will find the bill at the end of the month quite large. Furthermore, the era of third-party reimbursement for long-term psychotherapy is just about over. It is rare nowadays that a health insurance company will pay more than a token amount for psychoanalytic psychotherapy and many specifically exclude psychoanalysis from the contract. You must know beforehand, therefore, exactly what you will be expected to pay.

Fees for a psychotherapy session vary in different parts of the country and by the experience of the therapist. In New York City a very senior psychiatrist may charge $200 for a 45-minute session. That means the bill could be close to $2,000 a month, depending on the frequency of visits. At the lower end of the pay scale are non-M.D. psychotherapists, including psychologists and psychiatric social workers, who may charge as little as $75 for a session. There are also clinics at most medical schools and some foundations that operate on sliding scales depending on a person's finances. Generally, the therapy in these settings is done by trainees who are supervised by more senior clinicians. The critical thing in selecting a therapist is to identify one who seems to fit you best. Naturally, as I discuss above, a therapist should have experience and good credentials, but a good social worker who you like and makes sense to you will probably be a better choice for therapy than the most experienced psychiatrist if you find him to be distant, arrogant, or bored. Do not get fooled into thinking that the most expensive therapist is necessarily the best.

Make sure the doctor tells you how much the fee will be before you agree to therapy. Do not settle for any ''interpretations'' of your behavior when discussing payment. If you ask how much therapy will be and the doctor replies, ''I wonder why you are asking that question?'' you should tell him, ''Because I am the one who has to come up with the money.'' You are entitled to know when you will be billed—at the end of every session, every week, or monthly—and when you are expected to pay.

It is not wrong to ask a therapist if his or her fee could be adjusted. But remember, the therapist is not obligated to do so and the worst scenario is one in which a therapist feels badgered into lowering his fee and then resents it. If you think the therapist is charging too much or more than you can afford, try someone else. Do not ask therapists to lie on insurance forms and make up extra sessions or bogus diagnoses that are covered under your health insurance contract. Also, do not expect the therapist to bill or hold responsible for payment someone besides you. Often an adult patient will go to see a therapist at the urging of her parents. The patient may ask the therapist to bill the parents, who have agreed to pay the fee. There are several problems, however, with this. First, a therapist's relationship is with his patient and neither patient nor therapist should feel that someone else, by virtue of ''holding the purse strings,'' has an influence over the treatment. This does not mean that parents and other important figures in the patient's life should be barred from talking to the therapist and giving their ideas about what the problems are. Also, there are exceptions to this rule in the case of people who are incompetent to pay bills, but they will rarely be in psychodynamic therapy. Second, it is not uncommon for a third party to decide abruptly, often when the therapy is going quite well, that they do not want to pay anymore. This puts the therapist in the terrible position of having to decide between working for free or terminating the patient. Remember that we are not talking about an occasional visit. A single patient in psychotherapy may account for 5 to 10 percent of a psychiatrist's income, so having to treat someone for free can have more than a trivial impact.

To summarize, patients are entitled to know exactly how much they will be charged and to seek a different therapist if the bill seems too high. Therapists are entitled to charge the fee they think is appropriate and to be paid. All of this is to be agreed upon at the beginning of treatment.

The issue of missed sessions is more controversial. Usually, a patient in psychodynamic therapy has an agreed upon time or times each week for sessions. The therapist has reserved these times and agrees not to schedule anyone else. If the patient does not show up, the therapist loses that part of his weekly income. So most therapists charge patients who do not show up for a scheduled appointment.

On the other end of the spectrum, however, are therapists who charge for missed sessions even if the patient gives weeks of advance notice. Some psychoanalysts charge for sessions when the patient goes on vacation. They argue that the patient has ''rented'' that time and is responsible for payment. Some insist that charging for such missed sessions has some sort of therapeutic value. I personally disagree with this approach and feel it sends a very bad message to patients. It seems to punish patients for living normal lives, like having appointments or going on vacation. It also gives the doctor too much control; the patient is essentially told he must go on vacation only when the doctor goes on vacation or he will be penalized.

My own policy is to charge patients who cancel appointments with less than 48 hours' notice. I tell the patient honestly that I earn my living by seeing patients and that it is economically necessary that I keep a certain number of hours filled, both to pay my expenses (like the office rent, telephone bill, and malpractice insurance) and to make a profit. With 48 hours' notice I can usually fill the spot with another patient, and if I cannot, that is my problem; the patient has given me the courtesy of providing advanced notice. If I get less than 48 hours' notice, I charge the patient, with rare exceptions (I cannot bring myself to charge someone who misses an appointment because of a medical emergency, for example, but some therapists do so).

The critical thing here is that the patient understands the therapist's policies beforehand and has the opportunity to refuse to agree to them and see someone else. While I do not agree that patients should be charged for sessions they miss if advanced notice is given, I think it is unconscionable for a doctor to charge someone for a missed session if that policy has not been clearly explained in advance.

There are a few other practical details. Most patients in long-term therapy will have sufficient contact with the doctor so that telephone calls in between sessions are not necessary. But occasionally a patient may have an emergency and feel the need to call the doctor. I tell patients before they start that I will always return their phone calls and that I do not charge for this time unless the patient regularly expects lengthy consultations over the phone. Some doctors do charge for every phone call once a patient has started therapy. I think this is wrong, but again I stress that you should know the doctor's policies in the beginning.

Finally, you should ask the doctor how often he or she plans to be away from the office. Some very senior psychiatrists are also heavily involved in academic life, forcing them to travel often and cancel many sessions. This may not be a problem for some patients but bothers others a great deal. Ask the therapist if she travels often and how many vacations she will take. You want the best therapist, but not one who will be around so little that it will take years to get through the therapy.

Psychodynamic Psychotherapy: Concluding Remarks

As you will see in reading the chapters on medication and behavioral therapies that follow, psychodynamic therapy is the most difficult psychiatric treatment to describe and the most difficult to say precisely for which conditions it works. A good therapist can be enormously helpful: he may be the warm person whom you feel understands your problems and to whom you can open up. He may also be the person you trust enough to tell you things that are true about yourself but painful to hear. Many people derive enormous benefit from long-term therapy, but many others seem to get trapped into endless sessions that produce little obvious benefit. Such people get ''hooked'' on therapy and become convinced that something awful will happen to them if they quit. These patients often substitute therapy for real life and live only from session to session. They derive satisfaction from what they do only insofar as they think it will make an interesting topic for the next session. They put off forming new relationships because they are so caught up in the relationship with their therapist that other people don't seem important.

For that reason I again stress the following points:

- Choose a therapist you feel comfortable with and like from the very beginning.
- Make sure you settle and agree upon all the practical details before starting therapy.
- Set goals for what you want to accomplish at the very beginning and make sure your therapist knows what they are.
- Review your progress periodically and make sure you are getting close to and often meeting your goals.
- Don't hesitate to tell your therapist that you feel progress is too slow or nonexistent. Get a consultation from another therapist if you and your therapist disagree on how things are going.
- Never let therapy become a substitute for living your life. It should help you live your life more happily and successfully, not become a world unto itself.

Because it has been around for a century, psychodynamic therapy may seem like an institution to a potential patient, frightening her away or intimidating—keeping her from asking questions. The real action in psychodynamic psychotherapy, however, is not between you and Freud or you and your mysterious unconscious or you and the American Psychoanalytic Association. It is between you and a single therapist. If you choose carefully and ask questions, you have the best chance of getting a good result. Your goal is not to understand your Id better, it is to have a better life. Make sure the therapy is aimed toward that goal at all times.

3.
Cognitive and Behavioral Therapies

THE PREVIOUS CHAPTER delves into the only world of psychotherapy that most people think exists. Certainly, this is the world of movie psychiatrists who, at least lately, are usually handsome men like Richard Gere with beautiful female patients lying on the couch. This is a world of mystery and intrigue where the psychiatrist is generally seen as a shrewd detective, piecing together highly obscure parts of a complicated puzzle. Sex and violence abound—just the things that make for entertaining movies.

I doubt there will ever be a movie about a cognitive therapist. In the first place, there are no couches in cognitive psychotherapy. In the second place, the cognitive therapist generally couldn't care less about Oedipus, early masturbation fantasies, or what happens during toilet training. Finally, cognitive and behavioral therapy is mostly business. There is little romance, mystery, or intrigue. Even sex is treated matter-of-factly. This is not exactly the common, everyday idea of what seeing a psychotherapist is like.

But the important thing is that cognitive and behavioral therapies are effective and practical treatments for a variety of psychiatric illnesses. And that makes them central to the New Psychiatry. They work and they work fairly quickly. Some predict that someday, largely because of economic factors, they will replace long-term, psychoanalytic-type treatments. Therefore, it is very important for anyone contemplating help for a psychiatric problem to understand what cognitive and behavioral treatments are and how they work. At times, cognitive and behavioral treatments do seem simplistic and even superficial. That is a charge that the cognitive therapists will take great exception to, but in fairness it is accurate. Telling somebody that essentially they are depressed because they are thinking about things in a depressed way or that they are anxious because they worry too much may seem ridiculously obvious and hardly therapeutic. But give this a chance; seemingly simple concepts have been turned into powerful treatment techniques.

Cognitive and Behavioral Therapies: What Are They?

To begin with, cognitive and behavioral treatments are not exactly the same and there are purists who insist that a therapist should do one or the other.

Nevertheless, as will become clear, they share many fundamental principles and, perhaps of greatest importance to a potential consumer, they are frequently administered to good effect together.

A Brief History

Actually, behavioral therapy preceded cognitive therapy. Perhaps the most famous experiment ever done in the field of behavior theory was the Russian scientist Pavlov's study of salivating dogs. Pavlov, as many people know, observed that his dogs salivated whenever they saw food. In technical terms, the food is called an unconditioned stimulus in this situation because the dog doesn't have to learn anything in order to salivate when it sees the food. Next, Pavlov started ringing a bell every time he showed the dogs the food. After a while, he was able to show that merely ringing the bell, without showing any food, caused the dogs to salivate. That is, the dogs had learned to associate the ringing of bells with getting food and hence the bell ringing, called in this case the conditioned stimulus, became a sufficient cue to cause the response of salivation.

Humans Can Be Conditioned

Behaviorists correctly believe that humans are also susceptible to learning by conditioning, just as Pavlov's dogs. Here is a very simple example: Ms. Q. is a 42-year-old business executive who has developed a phobia about eating in restaurants. Every time she even thinks of going to one she feels her heart start to race, her hands become sweaty, and her throat clogs up as if she is going to choke. The situation became serious when she had a terrible fight with her husband. He had arranged to take her and their three children to a restaurant to celebrate Ms. Q.'s birthday. At first, she agreed to go, but an hour before Ms. Q. told her husband she simply could not do it. The couple wound up having a big fight, mostly because Mr. Q. had been urging his wife to get help for this problem for several months.

A behavioral therapist listened to Ms. Q.'s story and made an interesting discovery. Ms. Q. used to go to lunches in expensive restaurants almost every day for business. At first, as a junior executive, she found these business lunches fairly exciting, but over the previous month they became increasingly tense and stressful for several reasons. First, at a recent series of lunches she and her partners had dealt with a business deal they had made that was losing a lot of money. Then, she began noticing that one of her partners was drinking too much and she worried he was developing a serious problem with alcohol. Then, an important client whom she had to have lunch with almost ten times made inappropriate sexual advances. At one business lunch, in the middle of an extremely stressful discussion about a very large deal, she felt as if she was choking on her food and had to rush into the restroom. At another, she felt as if she were going to pass out and feared she was about to crash on the table and embarrass herself.

Having dinner with her husband and children shouldn't have frightened Ms. Q. so much, but what the behavioral therapist realized is that she had come to associate restaurants with tension and fear. Merely thinking about going into a restaurant cued Ms. Q. to associations of financial problems, drunken partners, and sexual harassment. If you said to Ms. Q., "What are you afraid of about restaurants?" she would initially probably plead ignorance. But the therapist was able to show her that she was reacting just as Pavlov's dogs had. Even without the stress of business partners and rotten clients—the unconditioned stimulus, like the dogs' food—Ms. Q. had become fearfully reactive to restaurants—the conditioned stimulus, like the bells in Pavlov's experiment. Many people are not exactly pleased to learn that they are like a dog in a laboratory, but to some extent this is exactly what we are like. Fortunately, a key principle of behavioral therapy is that what is learned can be unlearned. Hence, the therapist was able to unlink restaurants from business in Ms. Q.'s mind, helping her to realize that what frightened her was the stress of business deals and not of family gatherings in the local McDonald's.

Going a step further with behavioral theory, most people have heard of the great scientist B. F. Skinner. Skinner showed us even more ways in which human behavior is shaped like that of animals by explaining how reward and punishment operate. Skinner and his followers were the first to make it clear that all kinds of animals, including rats, pigeons, and even some insects can learn new behavior if the proper reinforcements are given. Although cockroaches have minuscule brains, if you reward them enough for doing a particular behavior they will eventually learn to do it automatically. Rewards, incidentally, seem to work better in getting animals to do things than punishments. A little food goes farther than a lot of electric shocks in getting a hamster to learn how to run through a maze without making mistakes. Ms. Q. was actually being rewarded for choking: it enabled her to avoid the stress of going to business meetings.

The key thing here is that the behaviorists insist that humans develop their behaviors in much the same way as animals, although with far more complexity. Throughout life, behaviorists contend, humans are subject to a myriad of rewards and punishments that shape how we ultimately behave. After a while, we do things without needing immediate reward and sometimes we do not even pair performing a behavior with a reward at all. Most of us go to work everyday and try to do a good job without thinking every minute about our paycheck. We don't have to have an obvious reward, or obvious punishment, thrust in our face every minute in order to perform. But for the behaviorists, if you look carefully enough you will usually find an original set of reinforcements that shaped a particular behavior.

The important thing is that a lot can go wrong in shaping behaviors. Reward the wrong things and punish the right things and you can wind up with someone who behaves maladaptively. These forces can obviously have tremendous impact on a child's development and here we see a major disagreement between psychoanalysts and behaviorists. The psychoanalysts insist that our personalities develop as the unconscious mind grows. To them our behavior is driven by urges and conflicts that are far beneath consciousness. Behaviorists do not believe there is any need for an unconscious. True, there are things we have forgotten or are not immediately aware of, but these are not important for their theory. For them, everything is learning. We are what we have learned and we learn by associations, conditioning, rewards, punishments, and following role models.

Even in the life of an adult we can often see how the application of rewards and punishment shapes behavior. As a simple example, I am reminded of a medical student who was having increasing difficulty studying. He would sit down early in the morning on a weekend day and find himself totally unable to get started. Hours would go by and nothing would happen. Then he would beat himself mentally and finally get a little something done. After sitting for hours he would finally go to bed late at night, only to repeat the process the next day. He did nothing but try to study.

The first thing that struck me about this young man's approach to getting his work done was how onerous he had made it. Even before he developed severe problems getting his work done, he still believed it was necessary to begin studying early in the morning and keep going for hours and hours. When he did well on a test he felt slight relief, but nothing more. When he did poorly on a test he felt crushed and indulged in self-hatred. Although I know well that you have to study a lot to get through medical school, this student had turned every aspect of studying into a punishment. There were no rewards, no breaks, no positive reinforcement.

So we worked together to draw up new rules about studying. No matter how much he did or did not get done, he was not permitted to study more than ten hours in a weekend. He was required to do at least one thing each weekend day he enjoyed, like play tennis, go to the movies, or have a good dinner. Before he started studying he must make a reasonable list of things he could get done in the allotted number of hours; if he got them all done he had to give himself an especially good reward.

In this way the student built into his schedule enough positive reinforcement so that there was always something to look forward to. His studying efficiency improved remarkably.

Now the above example is a simple one, but gives us an excellent opportunity to see differences between the psychoanalytic and behavioral approaches. A psychoanalytic therapist would undoubtedly find the treatment approach described above for the medical student as entirely superficial. He or she would want to know why this medical student treated himself in such a rigid and cruel way. What unconscious forces were at work that made this young man believe that fun and rewards were dangerous and unacceptable? The behavioral therapist asks none of these questions. He or she analyzes the behavior and attempts to figure out what factors keep that behavior going in the present. Then, an intervention is designed specifically aimed at changing the behavior.

Cognitive Therapy Is a New Addition

Cognitive psychology is a relatively recent addition to behavioral theory. Here, in addition to observing behavior the therapist is trained to observe the kinds of thoughts a patient typically entertains. Cognitive theorists believe that the way people think about and interpret events in the world determine the way they feel and behave. When pressed they will usually say that people learn particular ways of thinking but in general cognitive therapists are not especially interested in causes of psychiatric problems. They take a very straightforward and practical approach: bad thinking and interpreting habits lead to psychological difficulties. The logical extension of this is, if you can teach a patient better habits you can relieve them of their depression, anxiety, or eating disorder.

A Comparison with Psychoanalytic Therapy

As an example of how this works, let us recall the example from the last chapter in which a 45-year-old man is having a discussion with his wife. Remember that in the course of this discussion, which included many different topics, the man's wife mentions that she has just bought an expensive dress. A few minutes later the husband has an episode of chest pain, fears that he might be about to die from a heart attack, and begins to worry that his life insurance policy is not sufficient to take care of his family when he dies. Suddenly, he rushes home to call his insurance agent.

We used this example to reveal some of the principles of psychoanalytic thinking, but it is interesting to take the same example and see how a cognitive/behavioral therapist would approach this problem. The patient has, it turns out, a long history of hypochondriasis. He also worries about everything and is rarely relaxed. The cognitive therapist breaks down with the patient every element of the incident, looking for something that may have triggered the chest pain. The expensive dress appears to have upset him, but it is quickly established that the couple can afford it, so money is really not the issue. What, then, is the problem? The cognitive therapist asks more questions:

"If you can afford the dress, why did it bother you?"

"I think because she never discusses these things with me. Sure, we can afford the dress, but if she is going to buy expensive things without talking to me first about it, how do I know how far she will go? It could have been a fur coat for $20,000, which we really can't afford. Then there would be trouble."

"So, you are afraid your wife will spend money recklessly and get you into financial trouble?"

"It's mostly that I think a husband and wife should discuss things like that. Her attitude is that because she has a job and earns money she should be able to buy whatever she wants. She thinks I'm trying to make it so that she has to ask for permission before she buys something, but that's not it at all. I just want to discuss things."

At this point, the cognitive therapist does something cognitive therapists always do: he asks for evidence.

"Has your wife ever actually gone on a reckless spending spree?"

"Well, I'm trying to think . . . not yet but I suppose it could happen if we don't discuss things."

"Well, it is one thing to suppose it could happen, but you have been married for 18 years and you can't think of a single example when she actually bought something that put your family into a financial crisis."

"No, but how do I know it couldn't happen in the future?"

"It seems," answered the therapist, "that 18 years of experience with your wife hasn't made much difference to you. You are worrying about something that has never happened and, after 18 years, I think a reasonable person might say, is probably never going to happen. Your wife knows your finances just as well as you do and she obviously has in mind exactly how much can and can't be spent."

What the therapist has done is to analyze the patient's thinking. The patient had leapt to a conclusion from very meager evidence: My wife bought an expensive dress, therefore she is going to go on wild spending sprees and soon we will be bankrupt. This is an example of what cognitive therapists call catastrophic thinking. There is no basis in fact for this conclusion, but the patient is prone to make these errors in thought all of the time. He has the problem, not his wife. His problem is that he always expects the worst. If you truly believe you are about to lose all your money, then it is understandable that you might develop chest pain. The therapist will now work directly on the patient's maladaptive thinking process, attempting to train him to train himself not to entertain catastrophic thoughts so readily.

There is yet another aspect to the cognitive/behavioral therapist's approach to this patient. After identifying the catastrophic thinking pattern that seems to have triggered the patient's anxiety and hypochondriacal chest pain, the therapist next asks about the fact that he and his wife do not discuss purchases.

"You said before that your wife never discusses what she is going to buy with you."

"That's right, and she thinks I am trying to make her report to me and get permission from me. But I would never buy anything without asking her first. That's the way it should be in a marriage."

"Does she know you feel that way?"

"Of course she knows."

"How does she know?"

"Well, I told her."

"When did you tell her?"

After thinking for a while, obviously having trouble coming up with an example, the patient finally remembers, "Oh yes, about a year ago she bought my daughter this expensive calculator, I think it cost $100, and I told her I thought I should have been consulted, but she just got mad at me and told me she can't call me up at the office every time she has to get something for the kids. What kid needs a $100 calculator? I could have given her one of mine; they cost about $10."

To this, the therapist pointed out, "It doesn't seem that you had a discussion with your wife about what things you think the two of you should be checking out with each other before buying them. It sounds to me more like you yelled at her for buying something, she got mad, and you have been afraid ever since to bring up the topic. Why are you so afraid to have a discussion about this if it means so much to you?"

"I hate when she gets angry. She makes me feel like I'm some kind of male chauvinist pig, like I think I'm her father and she has to report everything to me."

"But that isn't the case at all. You are someone who is very worried about money, probably more than you should be, and you want to have some control over how much you spend. Otherwise you wind up getting chest pain and buying more life insurance. Is your wife someone who would have trouble discussing that kind of thing with you?"

The approach here is, again, to figure out how the patient thinks about things. In this case, he fears that his wife will get mad at him and accuse him of being an imperious, controlling husband if he raises his concerns about their finances. But once again, he has no evidence to support his view. He has never tried to discuss money in an appropriate way with his wife and has no idea how she will react to a frank discussion that includes his acknowledging that he is a very nervous person when it comes to money. In essence, he has painted a portrait of what such a conversation would be like that has nothing to do with his true experience. Further, he is much too afraid that his wife might get mad at him. Sometimes, especially when discussing money, husbands and wives do get angry at each other, but that is not a reason to avoid the discussion forever.

The therapist will now work with the patient to correct his automatic thought that his wife will not tolerate a discussion with him about their finances and to become more assertive and less frightened if she gets angry. Incidentally, the outcome of all of this was quite different than he expected. His wife had been avoiding discussing money with him for years because she felt he couldn't handle it and would have one of his many "heart attacks." She was actually very prudent in spending and had a much better handle than he did on the family's income and expenses. Because she was less frightened by catastrophic fears of bankruptcy, she had been making budgets and keeping to them for years. Her husband, on the other hand, was so scared of the whole money topic that he just avoided ever looking in the bank account to see what was there.

Critical to our discussion of this example is once again what it reveals about cognitive and behavioral approaches and how they differ from psychoanalytic ones. Notice that the cognitive therapist deals only in the present and only with what the patient can agree to. Nothing is said about unconscious material or about early childhood experiences. There are maladaptive thinking patterns which the therapist can explain to the patient; the patient must then agree that those patterns are there. Then, therapist and patient work to correct them. In the process, the patient learns how these thinking patterns make him anxious and how this anxiety gets translated into physical symptoms. All is done on a completely conscious level. Further, the therapist is directly interested in symptom reduction; he wants the patient to stop being anxious and stop getting chest pain. He is not going to ask the patient, as did the psychoanalytic therapist in the last chapter, about his parents' fights when he was a little boy. The cognitive therapist is not interested in uncovering the idea that the patient feels a fight with his wife will result in a divorce because his parents got divorced. Nor will there be any discussion of Oedipal conflicts leading to a fear of beating out his father and becoming more financially successful.

It is obvious why the psychoanalytic and cognitive/behavioral approaches clashed. Psychoanalysts often scoff at cognitive/behavioral therapy, mainly insisting that it is superficial. What good, they ask, is trying to correct symptoms when the cause is left untouched? For them, what cognitive therapists do is little more than palliative, like giving aspirin to someone with pneumonia. You may bring the fever down and relieve some of the pain, but the bacteria in the lungs will still be there, and unless definitive therapy is initiated to get at the underlying cause, the patient will never really get well.

Psychoanalysts also point out that much of the theory behind behavioral approaches comes from animal experiments. Animals, even the most intelligent ones like chimpanzees, are clearly susceptible to all kinds of learning by association, reward, and punishment, but they do not have the complicated emotional and intellectual capacities that humans have. Hence, the analysts say, there is an awful lot to the human psyche that differs from animals, which such experimentation will never be able to reveal.

But the behaviorists have two main comebacks. First, they point out that psychoanalysts only *believe* that they know what the cause of psychiatric disturbance is. Most of psychoanalytic theory comes from the writings of a single person, Sigmund Freud, and is based on the analysis of individual cases. Hence, the claim that psychoanalysis really gets to the underlying causes of things is based on a wish.

As far as research is concerned, the behaviorists say that although it is true that some of their theories are based on animal experiments, at least they have been able to do research in the way that science conventionally understands it. And there is plenty of research involving humans, much of which supports cognitive and behavioral theory.

Ultimately, the two camps never really convince each other, but that is not what they are interested in doing. The people they want to convince are the potential patients. Both psychoanalysts and cognitive therapists are competing for the psychotherapy market and the consumer is their main target. In reality, economic forces are tilting the struggle in favor of the cognitive therapists; affording long-term psychotherapy is becoming so difficult that more and more therapists are learning cognitive and behavioral techniques so they can provide shorter, less expensive treatments.

It is still my firm opinion that psychoanalytic therapy is useful for some people with certain problems. In the preceding chapter I detail some of these specific circumstances. But for practical purposes, cognitive and behavioral treatments will be increasingly utilized as the psychotherapy of choice. Despite the great intellectual appeal of psychoanalysis and the writings of Freud, what works and can be delivered to patients is still going to be the most attractive form of psychotherapy.

Cognitive/Behavioral Therapy: How Does It Work?

The principle of cognitive and behavioral therapy is that what has been learned can be unlearned. The first task, then, is to examine the behaviors and thoughts a patient has that may be causing the disturbance under treatment.

The cognitive/behavioral therapist will be very specific about identifying what the problems are. Vague things like "not getting enough out of life," "worrying too much," or "having difficulty with relationships" will need to be narrowed down considerably. A good cognitive therapist will review each and every complaint a new patient has in detail and make up a list of what can and needs to be changed. Here, for example, is one scenario:

Treating Behavioral Problems

A 22-year-old woman saw a therapist because of bulimia. When she explained her situation to the doctor she described it as "I binge-eat and then I vomit."

"How often do you binge?" asked the therapist.

"Oh, you know, sometimes once, sometimes twice."

"Once a day, twice a day, or twice a week?"

"No, I mean once or twice a week."

"How much do you eat during a binge?"

"A lot!"

"I need to know exactly what you consume during each binge, how long it takes you to eat all of it, and how long it is after finishing bingeing before you vomit."

As you can see, the therapist is not content with being told there is a problem with eating. She wants to know all of the details so that each facet can be attacked separately. In this way, the therapist has a detailed picture of the *behavior*. Notice that she does not ask the patient anything about why she overeats. At this point the therapist wants just the objective facts.

Next, the therapist will move on to an understanding of the patient's thoughts and conditions under which the patient binges.

"At what point do you get the urge to binge?"

"Usually about an hour before I actually do it. I usually try not to eat anything all day but then I start to feel hungry around 4 or 5 o'clock, right before I leave work. Then I obsess about whether I am going to binge or not for an hour."

"Tell me exactly what thoughts you have while you are considering whether to binge or not."

"Well, I try to talk myself out of it. I tell myself I am already fat and that even if I vomit afterward some of the calories will stick on and I'll get fatter and then I'll hate myself. Then I usually think about how horrible I look and how I will never have a relationship with anybody because I look like a pig. And I try to think about whether I could just eat some lettuce, you know salad and stuff. And sometimes I do that, but other times I start in with the peanut butter and the cookies and stuff and then I can't stop."

Of course, this is a very abbreviated version of what actually goes on in assessing the problem, but from this we can give some idea of how the cognitive/behavioral therapist will start to work on the problem.

First, there might be a behavioral intervention. The patient says she eats nothing all day, apparently believing that in this way she will limit the number of calories she takes in and lose weight. In fact, this only results in her feeling terribly hungry and out of control by the end of the day. So the therapist will insist that the patient eat breakfast and lunch and work out with the patient exactly what should be eaten at those times. She will also give the patient scientific information on calories, weight loss, and dieting so that she will understand that prolonged fasting never promotes weight loss.

Next, there will be cognitive interventions. One key thing about the patient's thoughts is the amount of self-loathing that goes on. The patient wants to avoid bingeing, but she tries to do this by telling herself that she is fat and ugly and will never have a boyfriend. The therapist will point out that running oneself down only makes a person feel demoralized and angry. Such a person is less likely to withstand an urge to binge. Also, the patient is guilty of what cognitive therapists call "all or nothing" thinking: she feels that if she eats anything it is just as bad as eating everything. So the patient spends hours trying to convince herself not to eat at all. After all, who could exist on one salad a day?

"What makes you think you are fat?" the therapist asks.

"Look at me, I've gained weight. I used to weigh 120 pounds, now I weigh 135. It's disgusting."

"You may have gained weight, but that is not the same as being fat. It is reasonable to want to lose weight to get back to where you were a year ago, but no one would reasonably call you a fat person. By calling yourself fat, you are actually giving yourself a reason to binge. It is as if you were saying, I'm fat and ugly so why not eat everything in sight. A better, and also a more accurate, way to look at the situation would be to say to yourself, I have gained some weight, which happens to a lot of people, and I would like to lose some weight. This has nothing to do with what kind of person I am or whether I will have a good social life. It just means that I have a goal for myself of trying to lose 15 pounds. I'll have to work out a program I can live with to lose the weight; starving myself won't help."

Again, it is important to stress that I am condensing several sessions' worth of material and intervention. Notice, however, some of the key points in cognitive/behavioral therapy. The therapist is dealing with the patient entirely in the present; there is no discussion of eating habits or body image during childhood, for example. And the therapist is telling the patient what to do. There will be a lot of give-and-take on this between patient and therapist because the therapist will want to be sure that she has the behaviors and cognitions absolutely correct and that the patient agrees to do everything assigned. There will also be homework; this is a critical part of cognitive and behavioral therapies. First, the patient is expected to keep logs and records of binges, thoughts, and attempts to stop bingeing. Each time the patient has an urge to binge she will be asked to rate the strength of that urge on a rating scale, say from one to ten, and also to record all of her thoughts. There are two reasons for all this paperwork. First, it enables the therapist to see if symptoms are getting better or worse. Second, and of perhaps greatest importance, it teaches the patient how to monitor her own behavior and thoughts.

Informing this process is the basic idea that it is a set of maladaptive behaviors and thoughts that keeps the patient bingeing. The therapist takes the stance that starving herself during the day, accusing herself of being fat and ugly, and believing that if she eats anything more caloric than lettuce she will gain weight all serve to keep the main symptom, bingeing, alive.

As will be seen in the chapters on specific psychiatric illnesses, each disorder treated with cognitive/behavioral therapy involves specific sets of maladaptive behaviors and thoughts. Depressed patients, for example, characteristically jump to the most negative possible conclusion about events without examining all of the evidence and always assume that they have done something wrong. Behaviorally, depressed patients listen to people who give bad advice and are critical rather than seeking out more reasonable and supportive types. Anxious patients indulge in catastrophic thoughts and overestimate the probability of bad outcomes actually occurring. Patients with schizophrenia typically make a series of behavioral errors, such as failing to make eye contact, making threatening gestures to others, and ignoring personal hygiene. All of these are susceptible to behavioral and cognitive interventions. Among other things, the therapist teaches the patient how to examine more critically her thoughts. What is the evidence for or against a thought or conclusion? Are there alternative ways of looking at things? Even if the worst possibility came true, would it really be so bad? Could it be handled? Each cognitive error is therefore corrected.

Ultimately, the goal of behavior therapy is that the patient should become her own therapist, able to use all of the techniques learned during treatment in an ongoing way. Without needing to remain in therapy, the patient should be able to apply behavioral and cognitive techniques on her own to quickly reverse impending relapse.

Cognitive and behavioral therapies are generally short term. Depending on the illness involved, between 10 and 20 sessions are usually enough. In some cases of depression or phobia, the first few sessions may occur on a twice-a-week basis, followed by several weekly sessions and then a few sessions every other week. After the last regular session many cognitive/behavioral therapists allow the patient to call if there is difficulty and will see the patient for an occasional booster session if relapse occurs. But a therapy that goes on for more than six months, and certainly for more than one year, is probably not cognitive/behavioral.

Does this actually work? There is still some controversy attached to cognitive and behavioral therapy because research in this area is difficult. The main problem is designing a placebo therapy. Although patients are not encouraged to develop a deep relationship—called transference in psychoanalytic terms—with the cognitive therapist, a good cognitive therapist will be seen by the patient as a warm, caring, and concerned professional. The kind of attention and positive regard the patient gets from the therapist may in itself be psychologically beneficial, so it becomes hard to know how much of the success cognitive therapists have is actually due to their specific techniques and how much is due to nonspecific factors such as caring and attention.

But cognitive scientists have made significant gains in recent years in developing experiments to test cognitive/behavioral therapy and for some conditions, explained in the next section, they are able to show that the treatments are successful.

Some Things That Don't Work

There are certain things that some therapists do that have not been proven to work. One is biofeedback. In order to relax anxious patients, some therapists use fancy gadgets that supposedly train patients to lower their blood pressure or heart rate, especially when confronted with stressful situations. The gadgets look nice and patients sometimes think the whirring dials and clicking machines makes therapy more "medical," but none of this seems to be particularly helpful. The jury is still out on hypnosis as a treatment for psychiatric illnesses such as anxiety and depression; some therapists still use it, but it is probably not necessary for most patients. Hypnosis appears to have a legitimate role in helping patients cope with chronic pain. Its usefulness in treating anxiety and phobias is doubtful. Some claim it has utility in controlling bad habits, like cigarette smoking and overeating, but this too is far from firmly established. At least pending further research, which I personally doubt will change my recommendation, cognitive/behavioral therapy should involve a patient, a therapist, and lots of homework.

It is important to say something about therapist credentials. As insurance companies increasingly refuse to pay for long-term therapy for psychiatric problems, more and more therapists are claiming to be cognitive or behavioral therapists in order to legitimize their use of shorter therapies. In fact, many of these therapists have had little training in the area and were originally trained in psychoanalytic techniques. Some legitimate cognitive therapists insist that it is actually more difficult to train someone who has a background in psychoanalytic therapy than someone who has no therapy training at all. The techniques are very different and specific training is needed to do cognitive/behavioral therapy properly.

Potential patients should therefore carefully inquire about the therapist's training. There are many fewer training programs for cognitive therapy than for psychoanalytic training, but a cognitive/behavioral therapist should be able to describe a specific training program that he or she completed before becoming a cognitive therapist. Patients who want cognitive therapy should also be suspicious if the therapist suggests treatment may take more than the usual 10 to 20 sessions or if his interest seems to stray from the set of specific problems targeted for the treatment. Also, a therapist who does not talk much or says "uh-huh" a lot is not a cognitive therapist.

Cognitive/Behavioral Therapy: What Does It Work For?

Although cognitive therapists might assert that cognitive/behavioral therapy works for everything, there is general agreement that it clearly works for a number of specific illnesses.

A recently published, multicenter research study demonstrated that for mild depression cognitive/behavioral therapy is highly effective. Another form of brief, nonpsychoanalytic therapy called interpersonal psychotherapy was also beneficial. Both types of therapy worked just as well as antidepressant medication in these patients and better than placebo. In the chapter on depression I describe these treatments in more detail. It is important to note that the study, as well as clinical experience, indicate that as depression gets more severe, antidepressant medication becomes superior to cognitive/behavioral therapy. When the depression is severe enough to cause suicidal thoughts, weight loss from loss of appetite, and a general inability to function, antidepressant medication should usually be prescribed. But for mild depression a course of cognitive therapy often relieves the symptoms without medication.

It should also be noted that cognitive therapy does not seem to prevent recurrence of depression the way medications do. Hence, if you have had more than two bouts with depression you should consider taking antidepressant medication on a regular basis to prevent further episodes.

Cognitive/behavioral therapy is also an important part of the treatment for most anxiety disorders. These are discussed in more detail in Chapter 11. Anxiety is, in a sense, a "behavioral" phenomenon; we learn to be anxious and fearful of dangerous, threatening things. In the anxiety disorders, patients start becoming anxious about things that shouldn't be so frightening. Somehow, they have learned to associate danger with nonthreatening events. Behavior therapy can be extremely effective in treating this.

A prime example is what we call *specific phobia*. This involves a fear of a specific thing, like the fear of heights or fear of small animals or fear of closed in spaces (claustrophobia). Ordinarily, it is not scary to look out of a fifth-floor window. Most people would not feel anxious even opening the window and looking out. Not until you actually dangled the average person out of the window would we expect there to be fear, increase in heart rate, or rapid breathing. But people with a fear of heights start getting scared the minute the elevator door opens and they know they are on floor number five. They won't even approach the window; merely thinking about it gives them palpitations and makes them perspire. Soon, the experience is recalled with such dread that the person with this specific phobia won't even go up to the fifth floor. At this point, the phobia begins to have functional significance. If you live in a big city and can't go above the second floor of a building, your life is going to be very limited. The specific phobic knows the fear is irrational, but staying away from the fifth floor is the only way to escape the anxiety.

The treatment of most specific phobias with behavior therapy is very straightforward. The patient needs to learn that nothing terrible will happen to him if he goes up to the fifth floor; what really bothers him is the anxiety he experiences. If he keeps avoiding going to the fifth floor, he will remain calm, so in effect having the phobia keeps him relaxed. What he needs to do is get up to the fifth floor and have the anxiety; after enough time, the anxiety will start to go away by itself. Of course, no one will be able to convince the phobic to just go up to the fifth floor, so the treatment has to gradually expose him to heights. This is called *exposure* therapy and is one of the hallmarks of behavior treatment.

In a typical exposure therapy, the phobic may first be asked to imagine being on the fifth floor while comfortably seated in a chair on the first floor. Thinking about it makes him anxious at first, but not as anxious as actually doing it. In time—maybe four or five times, to be exact—the patient is able to imagine himself on the fifth floor without anxiety. Then, up to the second floor. This is not too frightening. The heart pounds a little bit, there is some perspiration, but the patient (often accompanied by the therapist on these first trials) learns that the anxiety itself is merely uncomfortable, not life threatening. Gradually, the patient ascends to higher floors, each time staying at the next level until the anxiety becomes tolerable. Ultimately, the patient is able to go the roof of a skyscraper and look down with no more than mild fear. We call this kind of exposure *hierarchical, in vivo* exposure. "Hierarchical" because the patient starts with simple tasks and moves on to harder and harder ones, and "in vivo" because it is done in real life, not just in the imagination. This kind of treatment is the only effective therapy for specific phobias.

As discussed in Chapter 11, behavioral and cognitive treatments are used in most of the other anxiety disorders as well, including panic, generalized, and obsessive compulsive disorders and social phobia. In these more complex anxiety disorders, other behavioral and cognitive techniques are added to exposure, including breathing retraining to stop hyperventilation, cognitive therapy to decrease catastrophic thoughts, and response blocking to prevent compulsive rituals.

As with depression, the more severe anxiety disorders are often treated with medication. Much research is now being conducted to see if combining medication with behavior therapy might not offer patients with anxiety disorder the best chance at getting well. Behavior therapists claim that their treatments do prevent recurrence of anxiety disorder once the patient has been successfully treated; I am personally skeptical about this and await proof.

Eating disorders like bulimia and anorexia nervosa are increasingly treated with cognitive/behavior therapy. This seems particularly effective for bulimia; the jury is still out on how well behavior therapy works for anorexia. As the case example described earlier in this chapter indicates, bulimic patients often have a characteristic set of beliefs and habits that seem to perpetuate their binges. Hence, behavioral and cognitive techniques, as research studies increasingly indicate, are very effective. Anorexia, often a life-threatening illness in which patients starve themselves, is very hard to treat by any method. It is not yet entirely clear how much behavior therapy has to offer here, but there are interesting leads.

In the cases of mild depression, anxiety disorders, and bulimia there is evidence and clinical experience that cognitive/behavioral treatment resolves the problem. People with these problems can consider cognitive therapy as a viable treatment option. In a few other psychiatric conditions, behavior therapy is not enough on its own but can be added to other types of treatment to improve outcome. Schizophrenia is a good example of this.

Schizophrenia, described in Chapter 12, must almost always be treated with antipsychotic medications. Without them, there is no clinically effective way to control such acute and florid symptoms as hallucinations and delusions. Furthermore, there is abundant evidence that only antipsychotic medication has a chance of preventing acute psychotic relapse in patients with schizophrenia; although these drugs are very far from perfect, they are absolutely necessary in treating most patients with schizophrenia.

There are still a lot of things about schizophrenia, however, that antipsychotic drugs do not treat. Patients with schizophrenia often lack social skills, for example. They do not look people in the eye when talking to them, they may make frightening and threatening gestures, blurt out incoherent things, and neglect personal hygiene. Because of these habits, people become frightened of patients with schizophrenia even though the vast majority of them are entirely nonviolent. Thus shunned, patients with schizophrenia often lead sad, lonely, and isolated lives.

Behavior therapies have made gains in recent years in developing programs to help teach patients with schizophrenia how to interact better. One of my colleagues, Dr. Xavier Amador, for example, is starting with the very important problem of deciding whether patients with schizophrenia should be told they have schizophrenia. Denial of the illness often makes the patient unwilling to address any of his interpersonal problems; on the other hand, schizophrenia is usually such a severe illness that some denial may protect the patient from becoming completely hopeless and even suicidal. Behavioral treatments are now aimed at helping patients with schizophrenia understand their illness without demoralizing them and then teaching them ways to avoid frightening others away.

There are also problems that are not, strictly speaking, psychiatric illnesses for which behavior therapy may be effective. Many sexual problems are treated successfully with behavior therapy, including premature ejaculation, problems achieving orgasm, and impotence. Weight-control techniques for obesity and programs to help people stop cigarette smoking often heavily involve cognitive and behavioral techniques.

Finally, comprehensive treatment programs for substance-abuse problems are heavily laced with cognitive and behavioral treatments. Alcoholics Anonymous, probably the most successful method of treating alcohol abuse, uses a "Twelve Step" program that is basically cognitive and behavioral therapy in a group format. Treatment programs for drug abuse similarly involve mainly cognitive and behavioral techniques.

TABLE 4
WHAT COGNITIVE/BEHAVIORAL THERAPY IS USED FOR

- *Mild depression*
- *Anxiety disorders*
  phobias
  panic
  generalized anxiety
  obsessive compulsive
- *Eating disorders*
  bulimia
  anorexia nervosa
- *Substance abuse*
  alcoholism
  drug addiction
- *Schizophrenia*
  social skills training
- *Sexual problems*
- *Bad habits*
  overeating
  cigarette smoking

Cognitive/Behavioral Therapy: How Do I Know If I Should Do It?

There are several conditions for which cognitive/behavioral therapy is considered the treatment of choice. If you are suffering from a specific phobia, like fear of heights or small animals, the first stop is the office of a behavior therapist. Usually, this is all the treatment that will be required. Treatment of sexual problems, like premature ejaculation, is usually behavioral. In the area of substance abuse, as Chapter 14 describes in more detail, there are some promising leads in using medication to combat addiction. Methadone is already one way to help heroin addicts; a drug called naltrexone may be useful for alcoholism. Still, an appropriate and comprehensive treatment program for any form of drug addiction is almost always going to include cognitive and behavioral therapy aimed at managing craving, reducing temptation, and acquiring alternative ways of handling stress.

For other conditions, behavior therapy is almost always recommended in conjunction with medication. Patients with obsessive compulsive disorder, for example, usually require a medication like clomipramine (Anafranil), fluoxetine (Prozac), or sertraline (Zoloft) to stop their relentless ruminations and rituals. Still, medications are only partially effective and clinicians commonly recommend combining them with behavior therapy. The examples of specific phobia and obsessive compulsive disorder are straightforward because the prescription of cognitive/behavioral therapy lacks controversy. In many other areas, however, potential patients are faced with debate, often acrimonious, among experts as to whether cognitive/behavioral therapy is effective. These battles are currently fought over the treatment of depression, panic disorder, social phobia, generalized anxiety disorder, and eating disorders.

For patients with depression, the best guidelines are along levels of severity. If you have a very serious depression with weight loss, suicidal thoughts, and marked inability to function, you should take antidepressant medication. Even mild depressions respond well to medication, but at this level there is less urgency to get better quickly and solid evidence that cognitive and behavioral treatments work. Hence, for mild depression characterized by sadness, poor concentration, and low energy a patient really has to decide whether to take medication, which will work in about four weeks and usually cause some side effects, or try cognitive therapy, which takes about three months to be fully effective. In the chapter on depression I give more details on how to go about making this decision.

For the anxiety disorders, especially panic disorder, the controversies about which treatment is best might interest Hollywood. Here, medications have been shown to be highly effective in numerous well-designed scientific trials, so for many years American psychiatrists recommended to almost all patients with panic disorder that they take medicine. Then, a trickle and later a steady flow of studies indicated that 10 to 12 sessions of cognitive/behavioral therapy could stop panic attacks, greatly reduce generalized anxiety, and relieve social phobia.

The problem in this area is that the psychobiologists and behaviorists seem largely hostile to each other, with patients caught in the middle. In the chapter on anxiety disorders I make some clear suggestions about choosing between medication and behavior therapy for anxiety disorders. At present, I must admit, there is no simple answer. With panic disorder, for example, medications will work in four to six weeks and the patient does not have to spend the time or money in psychotherapy. But all medications have some side effects and in many cases patients relapse when they are stopped. The behavior therapies appear to work but take longer and, at least until we get health-care reform in the United States that includes psychiatry, usually mean considerable out-of-pocket expense. Furthermore, it is not clear (despite claims from behavior therapists to the contrary) how long a remission from panic or social phobia can actually be achieved from behavior therapy once the treatment is completed.

There are some conditions for which behavior therapy is not recommended as the primary treatment. Patients with bipolar mood disorder—formally called manic depression—need to take lithium or one of the other drugs that control this illness. Behavior therapy is not helpful. Patients with schizophrenia will benefit from behavior therapy, as I describe above, but only *after* their psychotic symptoms are controlled with antipsychotic drugs.

Cognitive/Behavioral Therapy: How Do I Know If It Is Helping?

One of the basic premises of cognitive/behavioral treatment is that response should be obvious. Unlike psychodynamic psychotherapies, cognitive therapy is entirely directed to symptoms. Whatever the patient complains about is the target of cognitive therapy, and therefore it is straightforward to decide if the treatment is successful.

Cognitive therapists often use rating scales to judge how treatment is progressing. Because psychiatrists do not have the advantage of blood tests and X rays to help with diagnosis, there has always been the problem of finding objective measures of symptoms and illnesses. What one clinician may regard as extremely severe depression, for example, another might think only moderately severe. To help with this problem, innumerable rating scales have been devised to measure just about every conceivable thought, symptom, and type of behavior. Most of these assign a numerical value to scale the severity of the symptom or abnormal behavior under question.

Using Rating Scales

Perhaps the most famous of these scales is the Hamilton Depression Rating Scale (HAMD) devised by the late and very renowned British scientist, Max Hamilton. There are different versions of this scale, some with 17 items, others with 21 or more items, but the basic idea is to come up with a number that rates how severe depression is in any individual. Aaron Beck made an important scale for depression, called the Beck Depression Inventory, and Hamilton himself also made one for anxiety disorders, the Hamilton Anxiety Rating Scale (HAMA). Other examples are the Acute Panic Inventory for panic attacks, the Young Mania Scale for mania, and the Yale Brown Obsessions and Compulsions Scale.

By assigning a score to a patient at the beginning of treatment, cognitive/behavioral therapists are then in a position to give that scale at several points during the treatment and thereby determine if the patient is getting better. Some scales are given to the patient by the doctor, others are self-rating instruments in which the patient fills out answers to questions herself and then a score is derived. Because a good scale, like the HAMD or Beck Depression Inventory, has been given to thousands of people, it is standardized and therefore an individual's score should give some idea about how severe her illness is compared to that of other people. This is as close to a laboratory test as psychiatry has been able to come up with so far.

Rating scales have their drawbacks. First of all, although they are said to be objective they are obviously filled out by patients and doctors and therefore are in fact subjective to some degree. If a patient says she has anemia, no matter how much she believes it, if her blood test comes back with a normal hemoglobin she is not anemic. But if the same patient believes she is depressed, even a rating scale is not going to be powerful enough to prove whether she is or is not.

A second problem with rating scales is that they may miss the nuances of human behavior. Each rating scale is composed of a series of questions like "In the last week, have you had trouble sleeping?" and "How much of the time in the last two weeks have you thought about death and dying?" Patients then answer the questions on a scale, from "no trouble at all" to "extreme trouble, couldn't sleep at all." But many clinicians, especially psychoanalysts, argue that symptom checklists like these rating scales do not capture the full flavor of a person's personality or troubles.

A final problem with rating scales is that there is a lot of overlap among them, so that sometimes a patient can get a very high score on a rating scale for depression and also on a rating scale for anxiety disorder. Many of the items on the HAMD, for example, are really signs of high anxiety, like worry and obsessions. So the rating scales are not always clear in what they are supposed to be rating. But all of these problems aside, the rating scales do exemplify important aspects of cognitive behavioral therapy and how its progress can be evaluated.

A Typical Cognitive/Behavioral Therapy

The cognitive/behavioral therapist isn't really all that interested in the "nuances" of personality; he wants the depressed patient to start eating and sleeping, stop crying, and go back to work. By that I do not mean that the therapist is oblivious to how the patient *feels;* he does want her to feel happier. But cognitive/behavioral therapy is interested in reportable, objective (as much as possible), and obvious clinical signs rather than underlying meaning.

Here is an example:

A 52-year-old farmer felt increasingly depressed for three months. He was never a frivolous man, but now his family noticed he appeared constantly grim. His silence at the dinner table was striking, even for this man who was never known for the gift of gab. He still awoke at 5:30 A.M. every day to work, but now seemed to move more slowly. Sometimes he was already awake for an hour before the alarm clock went off. His appetite was poor and he seemed not to enjoy anything. He saw a psychiatrist at the medical school clinic about one hour's drive from his home. The doctor diagnosed major depression and medication was considered, but the patient was afraid to take drugs and wanted to try another solution. He agreed to try a course of 12 psychotherapy sessions.

In the first session, the patient filled out a number of self-rating instruments; others were completed by the doctor. These indicated a moderately severe depression. Although he felt depressed, the patient was not suicidal and still able to work. Next, the patient and doctor agreed on goals. There were three: (1) improvement in mood—the patient wanted to feel less burdened by his life and more cheerful, (2) improvement in sleep—no more tossing and turning all night or waking up at 3:00 A.M., and (3) better appetite—the patient had already lost five pounds.

In the next session, the therapist inquired about the patient's thoughts as he tossed and turned in bed at night. He was worried, it turned out, about his farm. It had been in his family for several generations, but times were tough for family farms at this point and profits smaller. Lately, he had just been able to meet bank loan payments that previously he had paid without trouble. From this worry, the farmer went on to many more. He envisioned losing the farm and being disgraced. He had no idea what kind of work he could do; he still had one of his three children at home to support, the other two having grown up and gone off on their own. He also worried that his wife could not stand losing the farm and would get sick.

The therapist identified the worry over financial ruin as the prime motivator of the depression. The question to be answered was, How realistic was the fear and was anything being done to resolve the problem? It turned out that although the patient worried incessantly about losing the farm, he had not made any review of his finances, spoken to an accountant, or consulted his banker. The banker, for example, was an old family friend, sympathetic to farmers, who were both his friends and the main source of his business. In the third and fourth sessions the therapist tackled the problem of why the farmer had been so passive about getting information that might shed light on his financial situation in a more realistic way. In fact, he was so worried that he was afraid to face the banker and the accountant, fearing the worst. Without any real evidence other than some diminution of the funds in his checking account, he had catastrophized the situation. He acted like a man with a huge tumor who is afraid to consult a doctor to find out if it is malignant.

In the next few sessions the doctor and patient worked out a plan for the farmer to get the information necessary about his finances. Here, the cognitive approach of identifying maladaptive worries and fears shifted to a behavioral approach of getting the farmer to do something he was avoiding. The farmer needed considerable cajoling; he was afraid he would seem stupid to the accountant and annoying to the banker.

When he finally did get the facts, they were midway between his fears and a fairy-tale ending. Like many Midwestern farmers, he had indeed experienced some loss of profitability over the recent years, but he was far from bankruptcy. Although the farm was not doing quite as well as it had ten years ago, it was felt to be solid and in no danger of going under. The banker regarded this farm as one to continue to support. Several changes in loan structure and payment plan were devised to ease the burden. The farmer was assured that he was likely to be in business for many years to come.

In the remaining sessions, the therapist worked to be sure the farmer incorporated these facts into his thinking. He showed him how these worries had produced the depression, including his inability to sleep and eat. Not unexpectedly, the farmer began reporting sleeping through the night and eating his meals, although he still complained of not feeling cheerful. Next, the therapist worked a bit on the farmer's feeling that financial trouble would kill his wife. The wife was interviewed and she turned out to be a resilient woman who had recently taken a job in the town library, mostly out of interest but not minding the extra income. She was clearly not the type to fold up her tent in times of trouble. So once again, the farmer had blown things out of proportion in a "depressing" way.

By the tenth session the farmer was smiling more and, for the first time, acknowledged that things were not as bad as he feared. In fact, he was surprised to calculate that he would have enough money to take the usual family vacation in the winter and wondered whether he should try to go to someplace warm for a change if he could afford it. The therapist supported this idea wholeheartedly. At the time of the twelfth session the original rating instruments were again administered and the farmer's scores on the depression scales were all substantially lower, mostly falling in the "not depressed" range. In this session the doctor and patient reviewed everything they had covered. The patient was told that if any signs of depression returned he should call the doctor immediately. Two years later, the patient is still feeling well and working on his farm. Incidentally, he had a very nice vacation in Florida that winter.

In this case, patient and doctor know that the cognitive/behavioral therapy helped because the original goals were met. Clear-cut goals were set before treatment was started and rating-scale scores obtained. The therapist informed the patient exactly how many sessions would be required and had a plan for what was to be accomplished during each session. The patient was required to do things in between sessions to move the treatment along—in this case obtain necessary information about his finances.

What If Cognitive/Behavioral Therapy Doesn't Work?

What would have happened if the patient did not improve by the end of the twelfth session? A responsible therapist at that point would have taken a stronger stance about antidepressant medication. As explained in the chapter about depression, the kind of depression experienced by this particular patient is also responsive to medication. Rather than permit him to continue to feel glum—or to get worse and become unable to work—medication should be recommended if cognitive therapy fails. Some would say that medication should have been started anyway in this patient at the first meeting with the doctor because he would have gotten better quicker. Then the therapy could be used to teach him how to get out of depression on his own. In this case the patient was reluctant to try medication and his doctor appropriately ceded to his wishes.

What should be done if he gets depressed again? If mild signs reappear, it would be reasonable to have one or two more sessions with the therapist to review the work done in the initial twelve sessions. Sometimes, a booster like this can get a patient back on track. If that doesn't work, however, antidepressant medication should definitely be started. Evidence suggests that medication, but not psychotherapy, can prevent relapse in patients with recurrent depression.

Is there a role for psychoanalytic-type therapy in this patient? Here we would run into differences of opinion. At the conclusion of the cognitive therapy there is no question that the patient feels better. He is less depressed, sleeping and eating better, and enjoying things again. Many would say that this is enough treatment.

But notice that some issues of this man's personality are left unaddressed. Why didn't he take more initiative and work out his financial problems instead of sitting around and worrying so much? Why is he so concerned about disgracing his father? Why is he so insecure about his wife's feelings and so wrong about how she would handle things? In short, why does our farmer seem to blame himself for everything and believe that everyone will be mad at him?

These appear to be deep-rooted issues that may not respond to cognitive therapy. The question becomes, Are they worth going after? If the farmer feels better, is there any reason for him to find out what his personality structure is like? These are difficult questions to answer. If we knew for sure that exploring such issues would prevent future depression and make the farmer a happier man for life, then few would argue that a long-term psychoanalytic therapy would be worthwhile. And many psychoanalysts insist that is exactly what they could do for this man if he is willing to spend the time and effort (and money) to go through a long-term treatment. I will not, unfortunately, be able to resolve this issue. Without psychoanalytic therapy the patient may never find out why he thinks and acts the way he does. On the other hand, there is no guarantee that a long-term treatment will make him feel any differently than he does at the end of a successful cognitive therapy. It may well be that the decision to have psychoanalytic therapy is itself rooted in the vagaries of personality: some people will be so curious about their underlying personality structure that they will not be able to resist while others are happy to leave well enough alone.

The example I have provided is of a very commonplace type of depression, but the principles are the same for all kinds of disorders treated by cognitive/behavioral therapy. In the case of phobias, for example, the doctor and patient will know if the treatment is working once the patient is able to confront whatever he is afraid of and no longer avoids the phobic situation. For obsessive compulsive disorder (OCD) patients, the treatment works if they spend less or no time engaged in compulsive checking or washing rituals. For eating disorder patients, treatment success is measured by a decrease or elimination in binges. In every case the treatment is judged on its ability to make practical, observable, and simple changes in symptoms and behaviors.

Cognitive/Behavioral Therapy: What Are the Practical Arrangements?

Cognitive/behavioral therapy should always be time-limited. In other words, at the start the number of sessions should be specified. This is one of the most important practical aspects because it will immediately inform the patient how long it should take until there is improvement and how much the treatment will cost. Furthermore, if a therapist says he is a cognitive and/or behavioral therapist but is vague about how long treatment will last, the chances are he is really not a bona fide cognitive/behavioral therapist. At the end of the first, or at most the second, session the therapist should outline a tentative treatment plan that includes the number of sessions expected.

Scheduling the Sessions

Most cognitive and behavioral treatments last about three to six months and range from just a handful of sessions to about 20. Often, the therapist will recommend more frequent sessions in the beginning, maybe one every few days, with the interval between sessions lengthening as work progresses. This is fine, as long as the therapist sticks to the original plan of a set number of sessions.

It is reasonable in a cognitive/behavioral situation to ask the therapist to give a general outline of what will be done in each treatment session. More and more cognitive/behavioral therapies are guided by manuals developed in the course of research studies that have shown the effectiveness of these treatments. These manuals specify exactly what will be done at each session, including what homework assignments are given. Even though I have done it many times, for example, I still use the manual developed by Drs. David Barlow, Michelle Craske, and Ron Rapee every time I do a cognitive behavioral therapy for panic disorder. I can therefore tell a potential patient exactly how many sessions I plan (eleven), the frequency of the sessions (two in the first week, then weekly through session nine, then every other week for ten and eleven), and exactly what will be covered in each session.

Obviously, more experienced therapists need not sit with manuals on their lap while doing the treatment (although many do) and some flexibility is important in cognitive/behavioral therapy. If a depressed patient reveals for the first time in session six that he has an alcohol problem, some change in the treatment plan, including the addition of extra sessions, may be required. So it is not fair to hold the therapist to the plan too rigidly. Nevertheless, the structure of cognitive/behavioral therapy is very different from that of psychoanalysis and it is imperative to insist on knowing the details.

Setting the Fees

One similarity with psychoanalytic psychotherapy is the fee structure. The fee for a cognitive/behavioral session should be the same as for a psychoanalytic session. The fee should be established before treatment starts and the therapist's policy about charging for missed sessions should be understood. Given the fact that there are only a few sessions altogether, cognitive/behavioral therapists are understandably reluctant to make fee adjustments. Nevertheless, it is fair to ask the therapist—if you feel you cannot afford his full fee—if he has a policy of fee reduction. I always recommend against running up a bill in psychotherapy, however. Some therapists allow patients to do this, but it usually just creates anxiety in both patient and therapist. If you can't afford the therapist, ask for a referral to a lower-cost option. As far as paying for missed sessions, remember that the therapist has nothing to sell but her time. If you make an appointment and then don't show up or cancel with less than a day's notice, you will leave a therapist sitting alone in her office. Therapists are human and have to pay the rent and feed the family just like anybody else, so it is not improper for them to have a policy of charging for no-shows or last-minute cancellations. That should not be interpreted as callous on the therapist's part. On the other hand, therapists should not charge patients for missed sessions if enough notice is given; the patient's life and schedule are important and it is expected that emergencies may arise necessitating a cancellation. The most important reason to make every session, however, is therapeutic; cognitive/behavioral therapy operates on a kind of momentum that should not be broken. Regular sessions over a brief period of time work better than conducting the treatment on an occasional basis over many months.

Even though medication is not involved, the patient should be permitted to call the therapist in between sessions if there is an emergency. For example, if a panic patient has an especially severe attack during the treatment, she should be allowed to call the therapist for advice and reassurance. If a depressed patient develops suicidal thoughts in the middle of the treatment period, he is *required* to call the therapist, who should return the call promptly.

Phone calls should not, however, be frivolous and under no circumstances should the patient attempt to have a whole psychotherapy session conducted on the phone. Remember that the cognitive/behavioral therapist is not there to get involved in the patient's daily life. If you are being treated for depression and have a fight with your wife, don't expect the therapist to spend an hour on the phone listening to your side of the story. Phone calls should be for emergencies only.

Cognitive Behavioral Therapy: A Summary

The message I have tried to convey is that cognitive/behavioral therapy works. I have tried to warn potential patients that there are "true believers" who think it is the answer to everything and who see both psychoanalysts and psychopharmacologists (who prescribe medication) as the devil. Stay away from them. Therapy is not religion and opinions don't count. The important thing is that cognitive/behavioral therapy is a reasonable and effective treatment for a variety of psychiatric problems. When conducted by a properly trained therapist using the correct techniques and procedures, it can make a difference in mild depression, phobias, anxiety attacks, compulsions, bulimia, and the rehabilitation of patients with schizophrenia.

4.
Medication

MANY WILL THINK that the New Psychiatry means drugs, and only drugs. That is wrong. Drugs for psychiatric disorders may be a more recent phenomenon than psychotherapy, but the New Psychiatry insists that we use all of the treatment modalities available to get patients better. In this chapter, then, I will rigorously assert when drugs* are useful, when they are not, and when they need to be combined with other kinds of treatment.

For thousands of years people have used drugs to alter mental functions, and that is the problem. Mention medication for a psychiatric problem and many people think of "mind-altering drugs," "brain control," "addiction," and "bad trips." Even the most educated operate under the serious misconception that medications used to treat psychiatric illness are laden with serious side effects and, they think, offer only superficial and temporary solutions.

It is true, of course, that many recreational drugs affect the brain. We all know that alcohol, the most widely abused substance in the world, produces many effects that people like. Some people feel calmer after a drink, others find they can be free of inhibitions, and a few believe they are more creative. In fact, alcohol operates on brain receptors that some psychiatric drugs also bind to, so it is no surprise that alcohol shares some positive properties with these medications.

And the situation is not limited to alcohol. Illegal drugs such as heroin, cocaine, and LSD all have effects on brain chemistry that, in very limited ways, are the same as those of medications psychiatrists prescribe. It isn't all that surprising—or even unreasonable, therefore—that many people wonder if psychiatric drugs will cause the same kinds of devastating problems as alcohol, heroin, and cocaine.

The fact is that psychiatric drugs are not the same as street drugs or vodka. Like any medication, from aspirin to penicillin to antihistamines, psychiatric drugs have adverse side effects and, if used improperly, can cause considerable harm. But more than 30 years of experience with psychiatric drugs has resulted in a collection of medicines that are almost always safe and that work to resolve serious psychiatric illness. It is very easy for science writers to pick up a copy of a drug manufacturer's label (the prescribing information for a given drug) and reel off a list of impressive-sounding side effects.

---

*Most medications have both a brand name and a generic name. When a drug name is capitalized it is a brand name; when a lowercase letter is used it is the generic name. I have tried to use whichever name for a drug I think people will recognize best.

Doing that frightens people needlessly because, as we shall see later in this chapter, such prescribing information is far more a legal document than the presentation of medical information.

A second serious misconception is that medications offer superficial, temporary solutions. This idea stems from old psychoanalytic concepts—not shared any longer by most psychoanalysts—that to "cure" a psychiatric problem you have to "get to the bottom of it." This is discussed on pages 25–26 and elsewhere, but to briefly reiterate, it is important to understand that no school of thought about psychiatric illness can legitimately lay claim to know what the root causes of any disorder are. What works, works, but we do not know if psychoanalysis or behavior therapy or drugs or prayer are actually getting to the "bottom of things." Medications relieve psychiatric symptoms, which is all any treatment can claim at this time. The results are no more temporary or superficial than those obtained by any other treatment.

Medication: The Pros and Cons

Having dispelled some of the most egregious myths, it is now possible to give a balanced view about the use of psychiatric drugs. There are, in fact, serious problems with them. They do not work for all psychiatric problems. They do not work for all patients. They do have adverse side effects. In the sections that follow in this chapter, and in the chapters on individual psychiatric illnesses, I am going to be very explicit about all these risks. Readers may also want to consult my previous book, *The Essential Guide to Psychiatric Drugs* (St. Martin's Press, updated edition, 1995), which gives an even more detailed account.

To begin to understand psychiatric drugs it is useful to review something about their history and how they work. Many people refer to the 1960s as the era of a "drug revolution" in psychiatry. Until then, psychiatrists used mostly "talk therapy." There were some drugs. Barbiturates such as phenobarbital and secobarbital were sometimes prescribed for anxiety and insomnia; a drug called Miltown (generically called meprobamate) was also hailed before the sixties as an antianxiety drug (nowadays it is generally looked on with disfavor). Very depressed patients were given shock treatment. But, for the most part, psychiatrists were described as "doctors who hate the sight of blood" and very little in the way of medical therapy was available.

Then, from the end of the 1950s through the early 1970s, a bevy of medications was introduced in several categories. There were drugs to treat anxiety, called benzodiazepines; drugs for depression, called tricyclics; a drug for manic depression (now called bipolar mood disorder), lithium; and drugs for psychotic symptoms in patients with schizophrenia, called phenothiazines. These drugs were slow to catch on in many circles; at the time psychoanalysis held sway in the United States and few believed that medication could really make a difference in what then were believed to be disorders of unconscious mental function.

But as scientific evidence accumulated that the medications worked, and as it got increasingly expensive to pay for long-term psychoanalytic psychotherapies, more and more psychiatrists became willing to try the new medications. By the early 1970s the psychiatric drug revolution was firmly in place. Patients were prescribed antidepressants and antianxiety agents in record numbers. Scientifically, the field now entertained the idea that if drugs work, psychiatric disorders must be at least in part biological.

The medications that psychiatrists prescribe fall in several categories. In each category there are many subcategories and many different drugs. In

TABLE 5
MAJOR CATEGORIES OF PSYCHIATRIC DRUGS

ANTIDEPRESSANTS—Drugs used to treat depression, include:
Tricyclic antidepressants (examples: Tofranil, Elavil, Sinequan)
Monoamine oxidase (MAO) inhibitors (examples: Nardil, Parnate)
Serotonin reuptake blockers (examples: Prozac, Zoloft, Paxil)
Other agents (examples: Wellbutrin, Effexor, Serzone)
ANTIANXIETY AGENTS—Drugs used to treat generalized anxiety, include:
Benzodiazepines (examples: Valium, Librium, Xanax, Ativan)
Non-benzodiazepines (example: BuSpar)
ANTIMANIC AGENTS—Drugs used to treat bipolar mood disorder, include:
Lithium
Anticonvulsants (examples: Tegretol, Depakote)
ANTIPSYCHOTIC AGENTS—Drugs used to treat psychosis, mostly in patients
with schizophrenia, include:
Typical antipsychotics (examples: Thorazine, Mellaril, Haldol)
Atypical antipsychotics (examples: Clozaril, Risperdal)

Table 5 you will find some of the broader subdivisions; chapters on individual psychiatric conditions have tables with more detailed subdivisions.

Table 5 is important because it should make it very clear that any one drug is not going to work for every condition. There are complexities in picking the right medication. The more a potential patient and/or his family members know about the different medications, the more they can join in a partnership with the doctor to decide if one should be tried.

The controversies that have grown up around psychiatric drugs, mainly in the last ten to fifteen years, are partly based on reasonable arguments and partly on irrational complaints.

Some Objections Are Reasonable

The reasonable arguments need to be carefully addressed. For one thing, it is probably true that physicians prescribe too much medication in general. How many viral illness are treated with antibiotics that have no effect on viruses? How many cases of simple upset stomach are treated with histamine blockers, such as Tagamet and Zantac, when these drugs are really mainly useful for people with ulcers? How many cases of anger at a spouse or upset about a reversal at work are treated with antidepressants, which only work for specific syndromes?

The answers to the above questions are not know, but I am sure that the figures are high. Often, I see patients who insist they are depressed or anxious and want medication when it is entirely clear to me that they do not have a psychiatric illness but are rather reacting appropriately to bad news and adverse life circumstances. The charge that it is easy to prescribe medication instead of taking someone's problems seriously and helping them find meaningful solutions is a reasonable one. Many have argued since psychiatric drugs were introduced that they are prescribed without careful attention to diagnosis. Over and over in this book I stress that psychiatric treatment, like treatment of any other disorder, should be linked to diagnosis. Nowhere is this more critical than in the use of medication.

Another legitimate criticism of psychiatric medication use is that it is often improperly supervised. Patients and physicians do not always fully appreciate the power of these drugs or the nuances of prescribing them. Most psychiatric drugs take weeks to work, so the doctor cannot usually say, "Take a few and see how you are." A careful phase of monitoring the patient to be sure the drug is working must occur during the first four to six weeks. Then, the decision about when to stop the medication must be made. Stop the drug too quickly and risk immediate relapse of a serious condition. Continue the drug too long and the patient may become dependent on it and have difficulty stopping. The doctor cannot, therefore, tell the patient, "Here is a prescription for a six-month supply. Take the pills every day and call me when you have used them up."

I suspect that originally doctors, patients, and health-care planners all had the idea that psychiatric medication would be a cheap way to treat psychiatric illness. It is true, of course, that it is far cheaper to treat a case of depression with an antidepressant drug than with five or six years of psychoanalysis. On the other hand, it is going to be more expensive to treat depression than a cold. Follow-up visits and telephone calls will be necessary and some counseling is almost always advised. The temptation to prescribe medication and then never see the patient again is very strong, especially for health insurance companies who don't want to pay for doctor's visits. This practice, however, is dangerous and results in some of the more unfortunate medication outcomes I have seen.

Some Objections Have No Basis

Many other objections to psychiatric drugs, however, are entirely irrational. I touched upon two of them in the beginning of this section: they don't get to the bottom of things and they have too many side effects. My answers to these objections, to reiterate, are: nobody can claim that any psychiatric treatment gets to the bottom of anything and all effective treatments have side effects, most of which are manageable. To these irrational objections have come others. One of the most egregious in recent history is the assertion that some antidepressants make people become homicidal and suicidal maniacs. This has been especially leveled at the antidepressant Prozac. Study after study has shown that antidepressants reduce the chances that someone will develop suicidal ideation. Where the notion that antidepressants can make people become suicidal is hard to fathom. One possibility, and the one I think is probably correct, is that it represents the chance occurrence of suicidal behavior. Patients with depression may become suicidal at any time in their illness; antidepressant drugs take four to six weeks to work. As more and more depressed patients are prescribed antidepressant medication, the chance that some will become suicidal in the period of time before the drug has a chance to work increases. The drug has not made the patient want to die; rather, it is the natural evolution of the illness.

Anytime a person has a clinical depression she should be closely monitored for the emergence of suicidal thoughts and plans. If these are judged to be serious, the patient should be hospitalized. Antidepressant medication should be seen as one scientifically proven method for the prevention of suicide.

Another recent case that is more difficult to figure out is the campaign against the sleeping pill Halcion. Halcion is a powerful sleeping pill and it was originally released in a dose (0.5 mg) that was higher than necessary to accomplish the purpose of helping insomniacs get some sleep. At that dose, some people complained of memory lapses in the hours after taking the pill. Anecdotes abound about people taking Halcion to sleep on overnight airplane rides, then making the wrong connection in an airport because they forgot where they were going. The dose has since been lowered; the pill comes in 0.25 mg and 0.125 mg, and many doctors recommend only taking half of that.

But to the stories of amnesia were soon added gruesome tales of patients becoming suicidal and homicidal from Halcion. A woman in Utah was acquitted of murdering her mother—and given a settlement by the manufacturer of the drug—because she was on Halcion at the time of the killing. Two famous authors, William Styron and Philip Roth, decried Halcion, insisting it made their depressions worse. Some of these horror stories led authorities in Britain and a few other countries to ban Halcion; the U.S. Food and Drug Administration refused to do this after hearings.

It is important to remember that stories people tell do not make good science. Does Halcion cause brain damage, murder, or suicide? When large populations of people taking the drug are looked at by scientists, it is hard to find any evidence to support these claims. Should we then discount the stories of people who claim the drug has harmed them? Certainly not. Patients should always be listened to, and if a patient truly believes a medication has made him worse, the drug should be stopped as soon as possible. Idiosyncratic reactions can occur. We love penicillin but know that the rare individual is allergic. There may be individuals who do have unusual and adverse reactions to drugs, and for that reason it is important for doctors to share this information with one another, with the Food and Drug Administration, with pharmaceutical companies, and with patients. But decisions about whether to use medication to treat a psychiatric problem should never be based on anecdotes, newspaper stories, or television shows. Patients and their families should ask doctors to explain to them the scientific evidence that supports the use of a treatment.

Psychiatric Drugs: How Do They Work?

Psychiatric drugs work in the brain and therefore it is necessary to know something about how the brain is organized to understand them. Although the brain is by far the most complex part of the body—and probably the most complicated thing in all of nature—it is absolutely possible to understand something about how it works. In this case, a little knowledge will be helpful in understanding what psychiatric drugs do.

The brain is composed of cells called neurons. Unlike other cells in the body, when neurons die they cannot be replaced. That is why injuries to the brain and spinal cord are permanent. There are millions of neurons in a human brain, more in a single brain than there have been people who have ever lived on earth. Each neuron sends out tiny appendages called axons, which connect to other neurons. The axons of one neuron do not actually touch another neuron, but come very close. The space between one neuron and another is called a synapse. Figure 1 shows schematically what this looks like. There are billions of synapses in a human brain; it is said that if all the neurons with their axons from a single human brain were stretched out end to end it would go to the moon and back.

Neurons send and receive information along their axons. One simple example is the jerking of a hand away from a flame. The flame stimulates a nerve cell in the hand, which conducts up to the spinal cord. The information that something hot is near the hand is then passed to other neurons that send a message to the hand to "pull back." Other neurons are then sent the information that flames are hot, so the fact is remembered and you keep your hand farther away the next time. All of this happens in a mere flash,

FIGURE 1

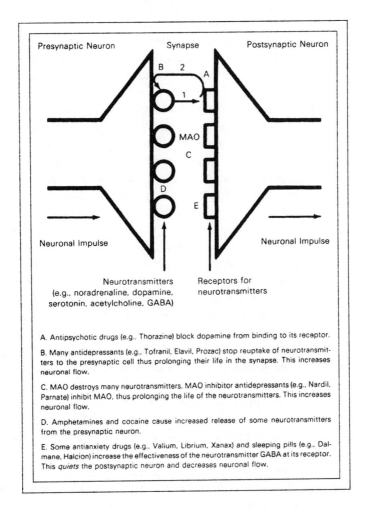

Presynaptic Neuron   Synapse   Postsynaptic Neuron

Neuronal Impulse   Neuronal Impulse

Neurotransmitters
(e.g., noradrenaline, dopamine,
serotonin, acetylcholine, GABA)

Receptors for
neurotransmitters

A. Antipsychotic drugs (e.g., Thorazine) block dopamine from binding to its receptor.

B. Many antidepressants (e.g., Tofranil, Elavil, Prozac) stop reuptake of neurotransmitters to the presynaptic cell thus prolonging their life in the synapse. This increases neuronal flow.

C. MAO destroys many neurotransmitters. MAO inhibitor antidepressants (e.g., Nardil, Parnate) inhibit MAO, thus prolonging the life of the neurotransmitters. This increases neuronal flow.

D. Amphetamines and cocaine cause increased release of some neurotransmitters from the presynaptic neuron.

E. Some antianxiety drugs (e.g., Valium, Librium, Xanax) and sleeping pills (e.g., Dalmane, Halcion) increase the effectiveness of the neurotransmitter GABA at its receptor. This *quiets* the postsynaptic neuron and decreases neuronal flow.

although not as fast as computers relay information. But, then again, computers can't pull your hand away from a fire.

The information passed from neuron to neuron travels like electrical current. When the nerve current reaches the end of one neuron it must somehow jump over the space—the synapse—to get to the next neuron. To accomplish this, neurons manufacture chemical substances called neurotransmitters. And influencing the way neurotransmitters work is the mechanism of action for most psychiatric drugs.

Different neurons use different neurotransmitters to conduct their messages across the synapse to the next neuron. There are probably at least 100 different neurotransmitters, although scientists have not yet characterized all of them. When the message is conducted to the end of a neuron, it causes the release of one of these chemical neurotransmitters. The neurotransmitter then shoots across the synapse and binds to a receptor on the next neuron. There are specific receptors for specific neurotransmitters. A dopamine receptor binds the neurotransmitter dopamine, for example, and the receptor for serotonin binds only serotonin. Once the neurotransmitter has found its receptor and bound tightly to it, a series of complex signaling and chemical reactions occur inside the new cell. These chemical events then allow the original electrical signal to be transmitted along the axons of the new neuron. In this way, neurotransmitters allow the message traveling along one neuron to be transmitted to the next neuron. One part of the brain communicates with the next. These signals occur in all directions: parts of the brain that control thinking can communicate with parts that control speech; the nerves in the hand that detect the hot flame can communicate with neurons in the spinal cord that make the hand pull away. All of this depends on the efficient use of neurotransmitters binding to receptors on the surface of neurons.

A few more bits of terminology will help make the picture clear enough so that we can explain how the psychiatric drugs work. Figure 1 will also help. The *presynaptic neuron* makes the neurotransmitter that travels across the synapse; its name simply indicates that it comes before the synapse. The cell that receives the neurotransmitter is called the *postsynaptic neuron.* Just try to remember presynaptic neurons make neurotransmitters that bind to specific receptors on postsynaptic neurons and you are practically a neuroscientist.

Once the neurotransmitter has bound to the receptor on the postsynaptic neuron and done its job, it falls off the receptor and floats around in the synapse again. Now, two things can happen. There are chemicals in the synapse—called *enzymes*—that chew up the neurotransmitter. The original neurotransmitter is then turned into other chemical substances and discarded into the spinal fluid that surrounds the brain. A second fate for the neurotransmitter is to be taken back up into the presynaptic neuron that made it in the first place. This is called *reuptake* and is basically a way that neurons recycle neurotransmitters. If the neurotransmitter is neither degraded nor taken back up quickly enough it is possible for it to reattach to the receptor on the postsynaptic neuron and strengthen the original signal traveling down the presynaptic neuron. It is believed, for example, that something must occur in the brain that allows certain memories to be strengthened so that they are retained for long periods of time. If you meet a person once, for example, you will probably only remember his name for a few minutes. But if you meet him several times the name may become permanently engraved in a neuron in your brain. Scientists now think this occurs in a part of the brain called the *hippocampus* and involves chemical processes that strengthen the binding of neurotransmitters to receptors so that the signal is strong.

Interestingly, it has recently been discovered that the gases nitric oxide and carbon monoxide may occur naturally in the human brain and may be responsible for this strengthening of neural signals that causes long-term memory.

Now we can turn to the way psychiatric drugs work in the brain. Each class of psychiatric drugs has a slightly different action, but all of them, as far as we now know, affect neurotransmitters, their receptors, or both.

Antipsychotic Drugs

The antipsychotic drugs—drugs that treat psychotic symptoms like hallucinations and delusions primarily in people with schizophrenia—block the ability of the neurotransmitter dopamine to bind to the dopamine receptor. Therefore, when a nerve signal reaches the end of a neuron that uses dopamine as its neurotransmitter, the presynaptic neuron secretes dopamine into the synapse, but the "keyhole"—the receptor—is blocked by the antipsychotic drug. The dopamine is then degraded by enzymes and some is taken back up into the presynaptic neuron, but it never gets to do its job, and so the neural signal cannot keep traveling from neuron to neuron. Examples of this kind of drug are Thorazine, Haldol, Prolixin, and Mellaril.

Antidepressant Drugs

The antidepressant drugs that treat depression act in a different way. Most of them, like Elavil, Prozac, Tofranil, and Zoloft, block the reuptake of neurotransmitters after they have bound to a postsynaptic receptor and done their job. Most of these antidepressants work on one or both of two neurotransmitters—noradrenaline and serotonin. The newest antidepressants are called selective serotonin reuptake inhibitors—SSRIs for short—because they only block the reuptake of serotonin and don't affect noradrenaline at all. If the neurotransmitter cannot get back into the presynaptic neuron, then it can bind again to the receptor and this will affect the way the receptors respond and increase the strength of the neural signal.

Another type of antidepressant drug, called monoamine oxidase inhibitors—or MAOIs—don't affect reuptake but instead stop one of the enzymes in the synapse from breaking down the neurotransmitters. These drugs, among them Nardil, Parnate, and Aurorix, stop the enzyme MAO from degrading noradrenaline, serotonin, and other neurotransmitters. The net result is the same as seen with the reuptake blocking type of antidepressants— the neurotransmitters have the chance to bind more often and longer to the receptors.

Antianxiety Drugs

Antianxiety drugs of the benzodiazepine class—drugs such as Valium, Librium, Xanax, and Ativan—have yet another interesting action. They affect a neurotransmitter called gamma aminobutyric acid, or GABA. GABA is an "inhibitory" neurotransmitter, meaning that when it binds to a receptor it quiets the postsynaptic neuron down and makes it less likely to conduct a neural impulse any farther. So GABA is used by the brain to quiet things down. The benzodiazepine drugs strengthen the ability of GABA to do this so that drug plus GABA leads to a very sluggish and relaxed neuron. That is the way drugs like Valium and Xanax make anxious people calm down and help insomniacs get some sleep.

Lithium

We don't know much about how lithium works, although there is evidence that it stabilizes neurons by affecting the chemical processes inside postsynaptic neurons after a neurotransmitter has bound to a receptor on that cell. The mechanism of action for lithium—how it can work both to lift a depressed mood and to quiet mania—is a scientific mystery.

Psychiatric Drugs Take Weeks to Work

Many psychiatric drugs take several weeks to work. It usually takes four to six weeks, for example, before a depressed patient taking Zoloft or Tofranil really feels better. Sometimes a patient with schizophrenia will continue to hear voices and insist the CIA is following him for several weeks after starting to take Clozaril or Haldol. This seems to be because it takes several weeks for the receptors in the brain to change the way they respond to changes in neurotransmitter levels. Even though the antidepressant begins blocking reuptake of serotonin very quickly, for example, it takes several weeks for the serotonin receptors on the postsynaptic neurons to change the way they bind serotonin and therefore how they start the process that results in conduction of a neural signal. More and more scientists are coming to think that psychiatric drugs work primarily by changing the way receptors respond to neurotransmitters.

In each chapter on specific illnesses you will find more information on the ways in which drugs for that illness affect the brain. The important thing to understand now is that scientists do understand a great deal about what psychiatric drugs do in the brain. This should help reduce the mystery about them and therefore some of the fear. The drugs do not wash away brain cells or kill them or make new ones grow. No single drug comes anywhere close to affecting every part of the brain or every cell. Psychiatric drugs are medicines that affect particular parts of the body in particular ways.

So far, then, I have stressed what we do know. Psychiatrists who practice the New Psychiatry believe that patients should know as much as possible about these mechanisms. The notion that people should just trust the doctor is no longer acceptable. Understanding what psychiatric drugs do enable a potential patient to know more clearly what is going on in her body when she takes one. From this knowledge many people, including psychiatrists and brain scientists, assume we must know what is wrong with the brain when people are depressed, anxious, or psychotic and how the drugs fix what is wrong. Remember, however, that I have said over and over again that nobody knows exactly what causes psychiatric illness and therefore nobody has the right to say they are "getting to the bottom of things" when they recommend their favorite treatment. This, surprisingly enough, applies in full force to the prescription of drugs for psychiatric illness.

It might seem logical to think that if an antipsychotic drug blocks dopamine from binding to its receptor, and that antipsychotic drug stops a person with schizophrenia from having auditory hallucinations (that is, from hearing voices when no one is talking), then hallucinations must be caused by too much dopamine in the brain. Block dopamine and you "cure" the problem. Sadly, we have reasons to doubt this is true. It seems fairly clear that too much dopamine is not the complete reason people get schizophrenia, even though the drugs that treat schizophrenia decrease the effectiveness of dopamine in the brain. Similarly, it is obvious that antidepressants increase the amount of serotonin and noradrenaline in the synapse. Does that mean that depression is caused by too little serotonin and noradrenaline? Again, for a variety of reasons we now know that this cannot be the complete answer.

We know these drugs work and we know what they do in the brain, but so far we have not been able to "put one and one together to get two." Hence, what we know about how the drugs work has not yet helped us understand what is wrong with the brain in serious psychiatric illness.

Side Effects

Understanding how the drugs work does, however, help us understand the cause of the adverse side effects some of them produce. What are side effects? A side effect is anything a drug does that we don't want it to do. We want antidepressants to relieve depression, antianxiety drugs to reduce anxiety, and antipsychotic drugs to stop psychotic symptoms. Anything else is a side effect. Unfortunately, all medications have side effects because no chemical substance in nature is so specific that it only does one thing to the human body. Think of the food we eat. When we have a steak we want it to taste good and to restore important proteins the body needs to function. All the other things the steak does—such as make us gain weight and increase our cholesterol level—might be called adverse side effects. Most people decide that the risks of eating steak, at least once in a while, are outweighed by the benefits and so they eat steak.

I don't mean to trivialize the side effects caused by psychiatric drugs because, as you will see in this and other chapters, side effects can be serious and sometimes limit the ability of an individual to take a specific medication. Still, it is important to understand that side effects are not "poisonous" effects of drugs as some would have us believe.

What Causes Side Effects

As explained above, psychiatric drugs work by and large by affecting specific neurotransmitters and their receptors. Side effects generally occur when the drugs affect a receptor in the body that has nothing to do with the psychiatric illness. Here are some examples:

The antidepressant drugs work mainly by affecting serotonin and noradrenaline in the brain, but many of them also block receptors for a neurotransmitter called acetylcholine. The technical name for a drug that blocks the acetylcholine receptor is *anticholinergic,* and the anticholinergic side effects of antidepressant drugs are among the most annoying. The result of blocking the acetylcholine receptor is to cause dry mouth, constipation, difficulty in urinating, and sometimes blurry vision.

Many of the antidepressant drugs also block a receptor found on blood vessels called the alpha receptor. This can cause lowering of blood pressure, especially when a person taking them stands up quickly. The result is to make one feel dizzy and lightheaded.

Some psychiatric drugs can make a person feel sleepy, others cause insomnia. Many psychiatric drugs cause weight gain and many also affect sexual function. A few antidepressants can have effects on the way the heart beats, and lithium can affect the function of the kidneys and the thyroid gland. In Table 6 some of the common side effects are listed; much more information is contained in the individual chapters on psychiatric illnesses. The table gives only a summary of side effects. Not all drugs in each class produce all of these side effects, and some side effects are left out. But looking even at this summary, a person might legitimately ask, Why take a chance? Isn't there a better way to get over depression? Aren't these drugs more dangerous than psychosis or panic attacks?

How Dangerous Are Side Effects?

These questions highlight the difficulties doctors have in discussing the potential side effects of medications with their patients. All the side effects listed in the table—and many not included due to space considerations—are possible. A good doctor, one who adheres to the New Psychiatry, wants the patient to be fully informed and aware of all possibilities so she can participate in making treatment decisions. Yet the doctor knows that most of these side effects are very mild; no one gets all of them and some people get none. The side effects are not life threatening and, with the exception of a neurological side effect called *tardive dyskinesia* caused by some of the antipsychotic drugs, never permanent. If a side effect arises and the patient cannot tolerate it, it is always possible to stop the drug and the side effect will go away.

The fact is that most people placed on psychiatric drugs tolerate them very well. Dry mouth is annoying, but hardly an issue when an antidepressant

TABLE 6
COMMON SIDE EFFECTS OF PSYCHIATRIC DRUGS

Drug Category	Side Effect
Tricyclic Antidepressants	dry mouth, constipation, urinary hesitancy, sensitivity to sun, blurry vision, dizziness when changing position; some (Elavil, Sinequan) are sedating; may affect heart rhythm; weight gain possible
Monoamine oxidase inhibitor antidepressants (MAOIs)	high blood pressure, low blood pressure, sexual problems, weight gain, insomnia
Serotonin reuptake inhibitor antidepressants (SSRIs)	insomnia, anxiety, sexual problems
Antipsychotics	low blood pressure, sedation, weight gain; some cause dry mouth, constipation, urinary hesitancy, and blurry vision; neurological side effects (see Chapter 12 on schizophrenia for details)
Antianxiety drugs	sedation; very rarely, confusion and incoordination; physical dependency
Lithium	weight gain, tremors, increased urination, decreased thyroid function; rarely, kidney problems

has brought someone back from a crushing depression in which she thinks she is better off dead. And for many of the side effects there are tricks and antidotes that relieve them. Table 7 lists some of these remedies.

With so many different drugs to choose from and a wide variety of "tricks of the trade," it is usually the case that side effects can be managed.

The important thing to know about side effects is primarily to know that they exist. Make sure the doctor tells you what they can be and don't hesitate to use reference books to learn more. But don't let them scare you. If a side effect occurs when you are on a psychiatric drug, call your doctor immediately and tell her about it. Don't panic and don't stop the medication abruptly until you speak to the doctor. Remember that there are many steps to be taken, ranging from just waiting to see if the side effect goes away to adding

T A B L E 7

STEPS TO TAKE TO REDUCE PSYCHIATRIC DRUG SIDE EFFECTS

Side Effect	Possible Remedies
Dry mouth	Suck on sugarless hard candies
Constipation	Drink six or more glasses of water a day
Urinary hesitancy	A drug called Urecholine (bethanecol) usually reverses this
Blurry vision	Usually goes away on its own, but a change in eyeglass prescription may help
Sensitivity to sun	Use No. 15 sunscreen (you should use this anyway)
Dizziness	Get up slowly from lying or sitting position; drink a lot of fluids and increase intake of salt, especially in hot weather
Sexual problems	These often go away on their own; a drug called yohimbine (Yocon) may help
Sedation	Take the drug right before bedtime; switch to a different drug in the same class that is not sedating
Insomnia	Take the drug in the morning; short-term use of sleeping pills can help; switch to a drug in the same class that does not cause insomnia
Neurological side effects (antipsychotic drugs only)	Antidotes exist—examples are Cogentin, Artane, Symmetril, Kemedrin; may switch to a different drug that causes fewer of these
Thyroid and kidney problems (lithium only)	Avoidable by regular blood tests that monitor thyroid and kidney function

an antidote to changing drugs. Side effects should not be a reason to avoid a psychiatric drug if you need one.

Psychiatric Drugs: What Are They Used For?

The use of psychiatric drugs should always be tied tightly to diagnosis—that is, there are certain specific psychiatric diagnoses known to respond to medications. In no area of psychiatric treatment is making the diagnosis more important than in the use of drugs.

TABLE 8

PSYCHIATRIC ILLNESSES THAT RESPOND TO MEDICATION

Illness	Drug Used
Major depression	Tricyclic antidepressants, SSRIs, ECT
Atypical depression	SSRIs, MAOIs
Psychotic depression	Tricyclic antidepressants plus antipsychotic medications, ECT
Seasonal depression	Light therapy
Bipolar mood disorder	Lithium, Tegretol, Depakote
Panic disorder	Tricyclics, high-potency benzodiazepines, SSRIs
Generalized anxiety disorder	Benzodiazepines, BuSpar
Obsessive compulsive disorder (OCD)	SSRIs, Anafranil
Social phobia	MAOIs, beta blockers
Schizophrenia	Antipsychotic medications

Key to abbreviations: SSRIs—selective serotonin reuptake inhibitors (e.g., Prozac, Zoloft); MAOIs—Monoamine oxidase inhibitors (e.g., Nardil); ECT—Electroconvulsive therapy.

In Table 8 I list specific psychiatric syndromes that are known to be medication-responsive and the class of drug generally recommended for these syndromes. Readers should refer to the specific chapters on individual illnesses for further information.

There are other conditions, like bulimia, alcoholism, and posttraumatic stress disorder, for which medications may be useful, but the table lists only those illnesses for which there is abundant evidence that medication works.

Does this mean that if an individual has one of the conditions in Table 8 that he or she must take medication? Not necessarily, as the chapters on the individual conditions will attest. For example, while a person with schizophrenia or bipolar mood disorder (formerly called manic depressive illness) will almost always take medication, a patient with panic disorder or social phobia may receive medication, psychotherapy, or both. But medication should always at least be considered in a treatment recommendation for anyone with an illness listed in Table 8.

How We Prove Drugs Work

How do we know that medications work for these conditions? Unlike the case with psychotherapy, it is possible to prove scientifically whether a medication works or not for an illness. The way to do this is to conduct something called a randomized, placebo-controlled, double-blind trial.

A doctor may have an idea that a drug works, let's say for depression. So he gives the drug to ten of his depressed patients and eight of them get better. He reasons that eight out of ten depressed people probably wouldn't get better on their own, so he writes a paper claiming the new drug is an antidepressant and sends it to a scientific journal.

The doctor is surprised when he receives a letter of rejection back from the journal. He shouldn't be, because there is a grave flaw in his thinking. There are several reasons why it may seem the drug is effective but really isn't. First, some people with depression respond very well to a kind, considerate person listening to their problems. The doctor probably didn't just give his depressed patients the new drug, but also talked to them and maybe counseled them. That, rather than the medicine, may have been the effective ingredient in getting them better. Second, we have only the doctor's word for it that the patients got better. It is not that we think he would lie but rather that improvement is always in the eye of the beholder. The doctor—and his patients as well for that matter—may have been so hopeful that the drug would work that he convinced himself there was a response. For these reasons, the journal editors were correctly reluctant to publish the paper.

In order to prove a drug works there must be what we call placebo control. That means that one half of the patients are given a sugar pill that looks and tastes just like the real medicine. Second, there must be randomization, meaning that a patient has an equal chance of getting the real drug or placebo. Third, there must be a double-blind study, meaning that neither the doctor nor the patient know whether an individual in the study is getting the active drug or the placebo until the study is completed. Presumably, patients will get the same amount of attention from the doctor regardless of whether they are taking the drug or the placebo, so if the patients who are taking the real drug turn out to get better more often than those taking the placebo we can be sure the drug really worked.

An Example of a Drug Study

So the doctor took our advice and, working with several other doctors, entered 100 patients into his study. Fifty got the new drug, and 50 were given placebo. At the end of the study, the results were tabulated. Of the 50 patients on drug, 40 (or 80 percent) got better. Of the 50 on placebo, 10 (or 20 percent) got better. A statistical test of these results shows clearly that it couldn't be chance—the drug really is better than placebo. Using this methodology, the doctor gets his paper published and is on his way to introducing a new antidepressant medication. The figure shows the steps in performing a drug study.

The United States Food and Drug Administration requires much more work that one experiment to prove that a drug works, but the hallmark of their decision to approve a new drug is review of randomized, placebo-controlled, double-blind trials. Many, many times a drug studied without this design will look good, only to prove no more effective than placebo when the proper study is finally done.

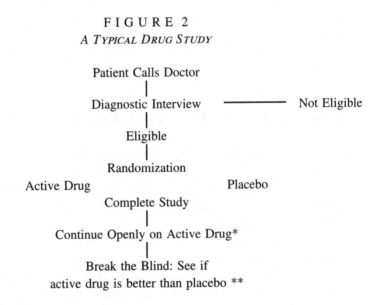

FIGURE 2

A TYPICAL DRUG STUDY

Patient Calls Doctor

Diagnostic Interview ———————— Not Eligible

Eligible

Randomization

Active Drug   Placebo

Complete Study

Continue Openly on Active Drug*

Break the Blind: See if
active drug is better than placebo **

*This is not always an available option. Sometimes, when the study is over, the patient must then be treated with conventional medications.
**The blind is broken by the investigators, usually the company that makes the experimental drugs, after all the patients have completed the study.

Some forms of psychiatric treatment are difficult to study with the standard placebo-controlled, double-blind design. Psychotherapy is an example. First, what is a "placebo" psychotherapy? How could we design something that looks and feels like psychotherapy, but isn't? And how can a psychotherapy trial ever be done with double-blind conditions? A patient and the therapist have to know they are doing psychotherapy. These problems have made it more difficult to prove that psychotherapy works, although in the chapters on psychotherapy you will see that important attempts have been made that come close to studying psychotherapy under appropriate, controlled conditions. It is easier to study drugs under these conditions than psychotherapy. This doesn't mean that drugs are better; it does mean, however, that it is easier to provide acceptable scientific evidence that a drug is useful for a medical condition than it is to prove that psychotherapy is effective. The New Psychiatry demands that reasonable attempts be made to study all psychiatric treatments scientifically. Patients must be informed about the degree to which this has been done, or is even possible, for any treatments recommended for them to try.

For each illness, then, in Table 8 (on page 87), there have been an adequate number of scientific studies using rigorous methods to show that a drug is effective. You and your doctor may decide not to employ a medication even if you have one of these conditions, or a knowledgeable psychiatrist may recommend something not on this list. That is okay as long as you have been given a good reason for the recommendation. The important message is that medication should never be discounted or dismissed without careful consideration.

Psychiatric Drugs: How Do I Know If I Need Them?

It is commonly thought that drugs are reserved for people with very severe illnesses and psychotherapy for people with milder illnesses. This is partially true. Very severe psychiatric illnesses should almost always be treated with psychiatric drugs. Table 9 lists the situations in which medication is usually included in the treatment recommendation.

The situations listed in Table 9 usually occur in people with severe depression, schizophrenia, mania, or obsessive compulsive disorder. Such people should take medication. The risk of not doing so can be severe to catastrophic, including getting fired or arrested, contracting sexually transmitted diseases (e.g., HIV infection), hurting someone, becoming ill from lack of food intake, and dying by suicide. Psychotherapies have a role in these situations, but in my opinion, it is too risky to rely on them alone. Medication is virtually required.

Next, we must consider less severe situations. There are many conditions for which evidence suggests that both psychotherapy and medication are effective. Here, patient and doctors have a choice. These conditions are listed in Table 10.

In the situations listed in Table 10—mild depression, panic disorder, generalized anxiety disorder, social phobia, and bulimia—there are studies that indicate medication to be effective. Indeed, for mild depression, panic disorder, and generalized anxiety disorder, these studies are fairly conclusive:

TABLE 9

SITUATIONS IN WHICH MEDICATIONS ARE USUALLY NEEDED

1. Suicidal thinking
2. Hallucinations or delusions
3. Inability to sleep or eat
4. Marked decrease in ability to function: can't work, can't care for children, can't attend to personal hygiene
5. Self-destructive behavior: wild spending sprees, inability to control sexual impulses, belligerent behavior leading to trouble at work
6. Uncontrollable ritualistic compulsions: constant washing or checking

TABLE 10

SITUATIONS IN WHICH EITHER MEDICATION OR PSYCHOTHERAPY MAY WORK

1. Depression without suicidal thinking, marked loss of function, or inability to eat or sleep
2. Panic disorder
3. Generalized anxiety disorder
4. Social phobia
5. Bulimia

most patients with depression, regardless of the type or severity, respond to antidepressants; most patients with panic disorder respond to one of the antipanic medications; and most patients with generalized anxiety disorder respond to either a benzodiazepine (such as Valium or Xanax) or BuSpar (buspirone). At the same time, there is excellent evidence that mild depression responds just as well to cognitive and behavioral treatment as it does to antidepressants; very good evidence that panic disorder responds to cognitive/ behavioral treatment; and some evidence that generalized anxiety disorder also responds to psychotherapy. There are similar, although somewhat more limited, sets of data for drug and psychotherapy effects with social phobia and bulimia.

In these cases it is not a question of psychotherapy working and drugs not working; rather, patients have a choice. The basic differences are fairly simple to detail. Medications work faster but have adverse side effects;

psychotherapy takes longer but doesn't have side effects (at least physical ones).

Some people make the choice very quickly. There are those who think that medication is always a last resort and opt for the behavioral psychotherapies, and there are those who just cannot accept the idea of talking about problems, prefer more medical explanations for psychiatric illness, and decide to take medication. At this point in our understanding of the illnesses in Table 10 neither approach is incorrect. In the future, research may tell us how to predict beforehand which individual patient will respond best to either drug or psychotherapy, but for now we really can't tell who is most suited for which treatment.

My best advice for the general patient is as follows: If you and your doctor feel you can wait a few months to get better and you have the time and resources for a once-a-week treatment, it is a reasonable approach to start with a cognitive/behavioral therapy for the conditions listed in Table 10. If the psychotherapy does not work, then medication can always be started. Medication can also be started at any time if the condition becomes more severe and more immediate relief is needed.

Finally, there are conditions for which medication may play a role but can never be the whole answer. Some form of psychotherapy is always needed for the conditions listed in Table 11.

TABLE 11

*SITUATIONS IN WHICH MEDICATION IS ONLY PART OR
NO PART OF THE SOLUTION*

1. Alcohol and drug addiction
2. Specific phobia
3. Marital problems
4. Problems of living
5. Personality problems (neuroses)
6. Sexual problems
7. Insomnia

As always in this book, each of the conditions listed in Table 11 is discussed in more detail in the sections on individual illnesses. These disorders require some type of nonmedication intervention as part of the total treatment package.

It is important to emphasize that there are exceptions to every rule in the medication treatment of psychiatric illness. There may be a patient with bipolar mood disorder somewhere who actually does okay without taking medication; I have seen an occasional person with specific phobia who did well on antianxiety medication; and there are times that an antianxiety medication works best for someone with schizophrenia. Hence, don't insist to your doctor that he is wrong if he recommends something different than what is written in this book. The important principle—the one that is in accord with the New Psychiatry—is to insist on getting a good reason that makes sense to you. Don't fall for "In my experience the drug works for what you have" or "It is too complicated for you to understand why you must take this drug." Insist on a rational explanation before you swallow even one pill.

Psychiatric Medication: How Do You Know It Is Working?

It is always very disappointing when I see a new patient who has been taking a psychiatric medication for many months without any sense it is helping. The one advantage of medication over other forms of psychiatric treatment is that an effect is usually discernible in a matter of weeks; no one should ever continue to take medication unless it is clear there is a benefit.

The effectiveness of a medication in an individual patient is usually not subtle. Most of the time, if the drug is helping everyone knows it. The critical thing is that reasonable and well-defined expectations about what drug treatment can accomplish must be spelled out before starting medication.

The goals of psychiatric medication treatment are fairly concrete. Here is what drugs cannot accomplish:

1. They will not improve your basic personality.
2. They cannot give you job success or a better marriage.
3. They will not make you smarter, more athletic, or a better parent.

In other words, medications are not there to alter your personality, control your mind, or work a miracle. They should, however, relieve and often eliminate certain target symptoms. Table 12 gives a quick summary of some of those target symptoms.

Again, the summary in Table 12 should be supplemented by looking at discussions in the chapters dealing with individual disorders. What Table 12 should indicate is that the clinical action of drugs is fairly specific. After four to six weeks on an antidepressant, a patient should recognize that she is sleeping and eating better, crying less, concentrating better, and feeling more cheerful. Some of these things can be objectively measured; for example, the actual number of hours of sleep should increase and weight loss should slow or stop. A patient with panic disorder should see a clear decrease

TABLE 12
TARGET SYMPTOMS THAT MEDICATIONS SHOULD RELIEVE

Condition	Symptoms
Depression	Sadness, excessive guilt, insomnia, poor appetite, hopeless and suicidal thoughts, low energy, poor concentration
Schizophrenia	Hallucinations, delusions, disorganized thinking
Mania	Euphoria, racing thoughts, hyperactivity, hallucinations
Panic disorder	Panic attacks, anticipatory anxiety, phobias
Obsessive compulsive disorder	Obsessions, compulsions
Generalized anxiety disorder	High anxiety level
Social phobia	Anxiety attacks during social and performance situations
Bulimia	Binges

and even elimination of panic attacks while on medication. Bulimics treated with drugs ought to stop bingeing and purging.

Types of Response to Drugs
Drugs can either work, partially work, or fail to work. By "partially work" we mean that target symptoms are reduced but not eliminated, or that some symptoms are eliminated but others remain. A depressed patient may be eating and sleeping better but still feel sad; a panic patient may go from ten attacks a week to one or two; a bulimic patient may binge occasionally but not induce vomiting. In the case of a partial response, the doctor and patient have to decide whether to raise the dose of medication, add another drug to the first drug, change drugs, or abandon drug therapy and try psychotherapy. What is important is that after a reasonable amount of time on a drug— usually about one or two months—there should be a complete evaluation of how well it is working. If it isn't working at all, it should be stopped.

Psychiatric Rating Scale
Some psychiatrists use rating scales to decide if a patient's symptoms are getting better during medication therapy. These are basically checklists of

symptoms that apply to various psychiatric diagnoses. There are rating scales for almost every psychiatric illness, some to be filled out by the patient (self-rating scales) and some that the doctor fills out after interviewing the patient (clinician-rating scales). These usually generate an overall number that indicates how severe the illness is. For example, a score of 18 on the Hamilton Depression Rating Scale (HAMD) signifies fairly severe depression. In the course of treatment, one would want to see that go down to five or six to indicate the depression has improved.

Whether rating scales are used or not, it is critical that a set of target symptoms is identified before starting medication and that this set be evaluated periodically to see if things are changing in the right direction. Never stay on medicine that isn't helping.

Psychiatric Drugs: What Are the Practical Arrangements?

Psychiatric drugs can only be prescribed by a licensed physician. That doctor, however, does not have to be a psychiatrist. In fact, if all the people with psychiatric illness who could benefit from treatment actually sought it out, there would not be nearly enough psychiatrists to take care of them. Hence, it is necessary, especially in rural areas far from cities, for much of the psychiatric drug prescribing to be done by general practitioners, family physicians, and internists.

This can, however, raise problems. Although all doctors take some psychiatry in medical school, most have relatively little experience dealing with serious psychiatric problems. It is really not any easier to treat someone who is depressed than it is to take care of someone who has pneumonia, but while no one asks psychiatrists to treat lung disease, everyone thinks the family doctor is an expert on mental disorders. Studies have noted that non-psychiatric physicians tend to miss psychiatric illness and, when they do treat it, tend to prescribe inadequate doses of drug or sometimes the wrong drug. Antianxiety drugs such as Valium are often incorrectly prescribed for depression, and very low doses of antidepressants are commonly ordered.

Psychiatrist or General Practitioner

Since getting to a psychiatrist may not be possible, it is obviously important for the patient and his/her family to be as knowledgeable as possible about psychiatric problems and their treatments, which is, of course, one reason I wrote this book. Beyond that, it is important not to continue on a course of medication treatment with your family doctor for too long if you are not getting better. General practitioners and family doctors generally know that if an illness they are treating does not get better in a reasonable time they should get a consultation with a specialist. This is done routinely with conditions such as diabetes, high blood pressure, and emphysema: if the patient doesn't improve, the general practitioner calls in an endocrinologist, cardiologist, or pulmonary specialist for advice on further treatment. The same should always be done for psychiatric illness. If depression, panic attacks, or generalized anxiety remain after four to six weeks of medication treatment, the family physician should usually refer you to a psychiatrist for consultation.

Often, psychologists, social workers, or other therapists decide that a patient they have in therapy may have a psychiatric illness that could respond to drugs. The advantages and disadvantages of combining medication and psychotherapy for various conditions are discussed in more detail in Chapter 5. The one thing that should never be done is to have the therapist discuss your situation with a doctor and then have the doctor send you a prescription without seeing you. It is mandatory that you actually see the doctor yourself for a medical evaluation before taking medication. It is also essential that the doctor who prescribes the medication see you for follow-up visits.

What to Cover at the First Visit

When you see the doctor and medication is recommended, there are some essential things to cover. Table 13 lists these and the follow-up care process.

The doctor needs to know your medical history in detail. The doctor should ask you about any medical illnesses you have or have had and about any other medications you are taking. If the doctor doesn't ask, be sure to volunteer the information. Don't ever be afraid you are annoying the doctor by telling him about your medical condition or asking if any drugs you may be taking or might take in the future could interact badly with the psychiatric drug about to be prescribed. If the doctor seems annoyed or abrupt, find another doctor.

It is always helpful if you bring copies of your medical records with you, including results of blood tests and X rays. The more you gather before the first visit with a psychiatrist, the easier it will be for her to determine if there are medical problems that may influence the decision about which, if any, psychiatric medications you should take.

Follow-Up Care

Once a drug is prescribed, follow-up care is mandatory. Psychiatric medication is never a "Take two aspirin and call me in the morning" situation. Nor should a patient ever take medication for protracted periods of time without being in touch with the prescribing doctor. The actual amount of follow-up monitoring varies considerably from illness to illness and drug to drug.

In general, more severe illnesses need more doctor-patient contact, at least in the early part of treatment. A physician must be in close touch with the

TABLE 13
SUGGESTED STEPS FOR MEDICATION MANAGEMENT

STEP ONE: The Initial Visit
- Diagnostic interview
- Careful medical history, including listing all drugs patient is currently taking
- Start medication

STEP TWO: First Follow-up Visit
- About one week after initial visit
- Check on new problems and side effects
- Consider dose adjustments

STEP THREE: Several Phone Calls
- Should be brief (not more than 5 minutes or an appointment should be scheduled)
- Check on progress and side effects

STEP FOUR: Second Follow-up Visit
- About four weeks after initial visit
- Assess if drug is working
- Check on new problems and side effects
- Consider dose adjustment

STEP FIVE: Third Follow-up Visit
- About six weeks after initial visit
- Assess if drug is working; if not, consider change in treatment plan

STEP SIX: Maintenance Follow-up Visits
- Occur as long as medication continues to be prescribed
- May be monthly or at longer intervals, depending on specific illness and medication

patient to be sure the condition is not deteriorating and that no serious side effects have emerged. Also, it is very often necessary to adjust the dose of psychiatric medication in the first few weeks of treatment.

Many patients, unfortunately, do not want to see the doctor after the first visit. Some are in psychotherapy with a psychologist or social worker and feel they already have enough "mental health" visits every week. Others do not want to pay the fee for extra visits. Whatever the reason, refusing to return for follow-up visits is not safe and is inconsiderate.

The fees charged for medication management are important to consider. The main problem, as discussed more in Chapter 16, is that health insurance providers discriminate against psychiatric patients. In New York City, a patient may see his internist because of the flu, spend less than 30 minutes in the office, and walk out with a bill for $600 in doctor's fees, laboratory tests, and X rays. If the man has a job, his health insurance will pay for it; if he is over 65, Medicare will pay some of it and the rest the doctor, by law, will have to forego. An initial consultation by a psychiatrist for a patient complaining of depression will take about 90 minutes and the bill will range from $200 to $400. Most health insurance companies pay almost nothing for this. Understandably, people are reluctant to see the psychiatrist too often.

The system obviously needs to be changed, but it is not appropriate to expect doctors to agree to give substandard care. In general, if a patient is started on a psychiatric drug she should see the doctor about one week after starting it. In the interim, there will often be one or two phone calls to check on side effects. At the first follow-up visit the doctor will make sure the patient's condition is stable—most psychiatric drugs will not have worked in one week, so the psychiatrist will want to make sure things aren't getting worse. The psychiatrist should also review side effects with the patient and answer all questions. Follow-up visits like this usually take 20 to 30 minutes.

There then will be several phone calls between the doctor and patient, but another follow-up visit about four weeks after starting the medication is usually recommended. At that time, the medication may have begun to work, so it is time to assess whether things are improving. If not, some adjustments may be made in dose or other medications may be added. Two weeks later, a third follow-up visit often takes place because by now the drug should be helping considerably.

If the drug is working, most psychiatrists will want to see the patient about once a month as long as he continues to take it. If it is not working by six weeks, it is usually time to consider changing to another drug. In that case, the process may start over and there may be additional follow-up visits required.

If you are considering medication, you should be sure to ask the psychiatrist either before or during the first visit about fees for follow-up visits. If you can't afford the doctor's fees, you should ask for referrals to clinics that charge what you can afford. The thing to avoid is to start medication without the financial ability to return for follow-up. Sometimes patients say—especially when prescribed one of the newer medications such as Prozac or Zoloft, which have relatively few side effects—that they do not see the need for follow-up visits. "What are you going to do," they ask, "that you can't do if I call you up?" There is, however, no substitute for seeing a patient in person. Also, if the point of not coming in to the office is to save money, expecting the doctor to spend 20 minutes on the phone for free is unfair. The public is understandably angry at many aspects of modern medical care, but the system presently demands that doctors charge patients directly in order to earn a living. Don't expect your doctor to bear personal responsibility for our creaking health-care system.

Follow-up visits generally last between 20 and 30 minutes if the only purpose is to monitor medication. If a patient is in psychotherapy with someone else, the psychiatrist prescribing medication will be careful not to interfere by offering more psychotherapy. The follow-up visits should focus mainly on medication response, remaining symptoms, side effects, checks of blood pressure and pulse as needed, and plans for further medication administration.

Patients' and Doctors' Responsibilities

Although medication can be administered without psychotherapy, it is not necessary or acceptable for the psychiatrist doing this to be cold, aloof, or abrupt. The New Psychiatry demands empathic care and respect for the patient regardless of the treatment modality employed. Some psychiatrists think they are adopting a "medical model" and rush patients through their offices, spending only a few minutes with each and acting as if questions are criminal intrusions. That kind of behavior is not "medical"; no one would or should tolerate it from a cardiologist, urologist, or neurosurgeon. Doctors are expected to be considerate, compassionate, kind, and caring. That means they need to be interested in the lives of their patients and ready to answer questions and give advice when needed. This is not psychotherapy; it is simply good medicine.

The patient should also be considerate. An occasional phone call to the doctor is appropriate and should be answered the same day. However, if you are having a lot of trouble with the medicine and have many questions, make an appointment. Some patients believe that they are the doctor's only patient and that they have a right to 20-to-30-minute phone consultations several times a week. Your doctor is not being cruel or dismissive if he asks you to come to the office if things get complicated.

Before you accept a prescription for psychiatric medication, make sure the doctor is available 24 hours a day, seven days a week. Emergencies with psychiatric drugs are rare and you will probably never need to call the doctor in the middle of the night or on Sunday afternoon. Still, a sudden bout of dizziness, a rash, vomiting, and many other side effects warrant a call to the doctor. She should call you back the same day and be prepared to deal with the problem. If you call your doctor and don't get a return call, call again. If the doctor gets mad at you (and you are not someone who calls excessively or tries to get free psychotherapy on the telephone), find a new doctor. Don't expect less from your psychiatrist than you would from your pediatrician or gynecologist. No one would continue to see a pediatrician who failed to return phone calls promptly; psychiatrists should behave the same way.

Psychiatric Drugs: Concluding Remarks

In many ways it is hard to understand why psychiatric drugs are so controversial and garner so much media attention. I suppose that when they were first introduced they threatened many concepts of mental health and illness. At the time, psychiatrists believed that unconscious mental processes governed personality and behavior; disorders of mental life could, therefore, only be treated by a process that uproots those deep-seated emotions. Drugs don't change how we think, feel, or experience life. They don't really change personality. Naturally, depression can make a person irritable, mania causes grandiosity, and psychosis can express itself as suspiciousness and paranoia. Drugs can correct many of those features, but relieving the symptoms of an illness seems vastly different from changing basic personality. Thus, at first psychiatric medication probably seemed a superficial "fix." It also threatened therapists who were used to treating patients for very long periods of time.

But psychiatric drugs have been around now for more than 30 years. It is surprising that they still seem frightening and even sinister to some people. By now it should be clear that they have limited but beneficial effects. In fact, psychiatrists are often disappointed that drugs don't do more. Drugs can make a person with schizophrenia stop hearing voices, but they do not cure schizophrenia. They are miraculously effective in reversing some severe cases of depression, but more than half of all people with an episode of depression get another one unless they keep taking the drug. Antibiotics kill bacteria and eliminate the basic cause of infectious diseases. That is a real cure. Psychiatric drugs seem to work more like insulin for diabetics. They replace something that is either missing or not functioning correctly, but they don't produce a "cure."

Enlightened psychiatrists and psychologists, those who practice the New Psychiatry, know that psychiatric drugs play an important role in combating mental illness. The important thing is to be cautious and informed about psychiatric drugs, not afraid of them. Know exactly what they are used for, their side effects, and the way to judge if they are helping. Don't be afraid to ask questions, to get a second opinion, or to read the *Physicians' Desk Reference (PDR)* and other books. Don't take a drug if it is making you feel worse unless the doctor assures you the situation is temporary. Never take a drug indefinitely if it isn't helping, and always see your doctor for follow-up visits. Above all, remember that you have a right to the best that medical technology has to offer. Psychiatric medication is an ever-developing tool that should be made available to all people suffering from psychiatric illness.

5.
Combining Drugs and Psychotherapy

WHEN MEDICATIONS CAME along in psychiatry in the late 1950s, psycho-analytically trained psychiatrists objected. When cognitive and behavioral therapies started emerging as effective, the psychopharmacologically trained psychiatrists protested. Each camp thought its treatment approach worked and the others were useless.

Today, the New Psychiatry takes a very different approach. Many different types of therapy are good for different illnesses and different individuals. With this broadening of acceptance of diverse approaches, it is natural that psychiatrists now frequently recommend to a given patient that combining medication and psychotherapy might give the best result. The New Psychiatry is only interested in providing safe and effective treatment. If that means borrowing from different points of view to offer a patient a combination of therapies, then that is what must be done.

Combining drugs and psychotherapy has a specific place for specific problems. It also introduces some complexities and unique problems into getting the best psychiatric treatment. Let me start by giving some examples of both appropriate and inappropriate uses of combined medication and psychotherapy.

Some Case Studies
Case Number 1. Mr. B. was suffering from depression. It had taken him more than a year to recognize this, but finally his wife, his children, his friends, even his boss convinced him that something needed to be done. For more than a year he had moped around the house on weekends, complaining that nothing interested him and worrying that a predicted snowstorm would prevent him from getting to work on Monday, that a drought would kill all the grass on his lawn, that he lacked the money to pay his taxes, and that his back pain was getting worse. He slept poorly, had little appetite, and rarely showed any interest in sex. This behavior was in marked contrast to his usual calm and confident demeanor. At first, his wife thought he was just passing through a ''midlife crisis,'' then worried that he was having an affair, and then that her husband had a hidden medical problem. Mr. B. was finally persuaded to see the family doctor, who found nothing wrong physically and recommended a consulta-tion with a psychiatrist. The psychiatrist easily diagnosed depression and

started Mr. B. on an antidepressant. Mr. B. didn't like the idea and kept insisting, "I don't like taking medication, I don't even take aspirin." But five weeks after starting the medication, Mr. B. was better. He was sleeping through the night, eating more, and stopped complaining about his back-aches. Sounds like a clear-cut success, but there is more to the story.

One day, Mr. B. came to see the psychiatrist for a medication follow-up visit. During the whole session he looked as if he wanted to ask the doctor a question, but couldn't. Finally, the doctor asked him if there was anything he wanted to say. "Well, I don't think it has anything to do with the medicine," Mr. B. began, "because it's something that has been going on for a long time." "That's okay," the doctor reassured him, "you can ask me anyway." Reluctantly, Mr. B. continued. "Well, actually, it has to do with my wife, well really it is me. I keep thinking I want to have an affair. I didn't think about it so much when I was depressed. I realize now how depressed I must have been because I never thought about sex at all then. But when I'm not depressed, you know, doc, I have a pretty normal sex drive, only I keep thinking I should sleep with other women. Actually, the problem is I didn't have that much experience before we got married. My wife did. We went to the same college and she had a lot of guys interested in her. I don't mean she slept around or anything, but I was kind of shy and I, well this is kind of embarrassing, I really only slept with one other woman before I got married. Maybe I should have had a few more experiences before I got married."

It is important to remember that Mr. B. made these revelations to his psychiatrist *after* his depression had resolved. Hence, his ruminations about having an affair, his self-doubts, and his embarrassment are not attributable to the hopelessness, anxiety, and self-denigration characteristic of patients suffering from depression. Rather, Mr. B. has longstanding worries about his relationships with women, about his social skills, and about his standing as a man. He revealed that he was a shy adolescent and found it difficult to talk to women, that he feels competitive with other people—including his wife—who had more sexual experience, that he feels cheated, and that there is some standard of sexual experience he feels he has failed to meet.

There are no drugs that solve these problems and Mr. B. will need psy-chotherapy to resolve them. Importantly, his psychiatrist did not decide that his depression was *caused* by his self-doubts but instead recommended psychotherapy in addition to medication. In this case, the medication resolved a depression that permitted the patient to reveal other life prob-lems that otherwise would have remained buried. Mr. B. should remain on his antidepressant for at least six months to be sure his depression does not recur. At the same time, he should begin psychotherapy to make him feel more comfortable with who he is and the choices he has made in life.

The above example represents a case in which a mixture of medication and psychotherapy should work well, but things do not always turn out so well as the next example reveals.

Case Number 2. Dr. Q. had been in therapy with a psychologist for four months. Her original complaints involved feelings of inadequacy as a mother. Dr. Q. was a successful physician with two young children. She felt she was a good doctor but not a good parent. She related to the therapist many instances in which she felt she was irritable with her children, scolding them instead of listening to them. She even revealed that at times she believed she would have been better off never having children. The therapist established that Dr. Q.'s husband was not much help; he was a businessman who spent most of his time at work and little time with his family. Dr. Q. was really not as bad a parent as she believed; rather, she was excessively hard on herself, unable to insist that her husband share the responsibility, and guilt-ridden. The therapy began with attempts to help Dr. Q. understand the realities of her situation and substitute a plan for improvement for guilt and self-recrimination.

Despite the fact that Dr. Q. liked the therapist and felt the therapy was helpful, she developed more anxiety and depression after the therapy began. Dr. Q. developed sleep difficulties, decreased concentration, low energy, and generalized anxiety. The therapist believed he was on the right track with Dr. Q., but also wondered whether she should be placed on an antidepressant as well. He referred her, therefore, to a psychiatrist who specialized in medication treatment.

The psychiatrist scheduled a one-hour consultation, but he kept Dr. Q. waiting for 40 minutes. He seemed rushed and gave Dr. Q. very little time to ask questions. His formulation was: "You are obviously depressed and I think you have had several depressions in the past. The only thing that is going to help you is an antidepressant. The psychotherapy is really a waste of your time. You feel inadequate as a mother because you are depressed and you are intimidated by your husband because you are depressed. Take the medication and all of those feelings will go away."

Sensibly, Dr. Q. did not follow the psychiatrist's advice. She recognized that her self-effacement and her marital problems were not entirely products of depressed mood. Perhaps if she were not so depressed she would handle those things better, but no antidepressant would make her husband change his behavior and improve the couple's domestic situation. But, unfortunately, Dr. Q. rejected the idea of taking medication entirely. The consultant had been so abrupt that she felt abused and rejected the medication approach as arrogant and superficial. Clearly, however, Dr. Q. was suffering from a treatable depression. Medication could have been combined with psychotherapy and she would have felt better and probably more able to benefit from the therapy and handle her life problems. In this case, a psychiatrist specializing in psychiatric medication discouraged a patient from taking medication that would probably have helped.

The situation can also work in reverse, as the following example shows.

Case Number 3. Ms. P. went to a psychiatrist because of phobias. She had a job that required traveling, but recently she found herself besieged with anxiety every time she even thought about getting on a plane. A few times she had terrible anxiety attacks in the air: her heart would suddenly start to pound, she hyperventilated, and felt as if she were about to die. One time she just could not got on the plane and had to cancel an important business trip at the last minute. For many years she had experienced similar anxiety attacks in cars, trains, and on buses, but the problem with flying was really significant because it was having a clear impact on her career. If she couldn't get on a plane, she would eventually have to find a different job.

The psychiatrist came to the conclusion that Ms. P. was afraid of success and that her phobias were the manifestation of an unconscious wish to fail. He believed these fears of success came from ongoing conflicts between Ms. P. and her mother. He recommended psychoanalytic therapy.

In fact, the psychiatrist was on to something. Ms. P. did have a very complicated relationship with her mother that included a great deal of competition. Furthermore, Ms. P. was not sure she liked her job and often felt she was either not good enough or that the job was unimportant and a waste of her talent. These kinds of issues are, of course, amenable to psychotherapy.

But the psychiatrist did not recognize that Ms. P. was also having classical panic attacks. A more careful history would have revealed that for more than five years Ms. P. had been having panic attacks that came on unexpectedly in a variety of very ordinary circumstances, like walking down the street or sitting in a movie theater. Later, the attacks began occurring whenever she was in a car and only recently during airplane rides. She easily met all of the criteria for panic disorder. An antipanic medication would have probably blocked the attacks within four weeks and Ms. P. would then have been able to fly comfortably. The kind of psychotherapy she was in, however, could take years to work and might never stop panic; Ms. P. felt she could not even wait a few months to get her symptoms under control.

In this case, a psychotherapist did not pick up on the need for medication. Ms. P. should have continued the psychotherapy, but antipanic medication should have been added.

These three examples are all situations in which the patient probably would have gotten the most benefit from a combination of medication and psychotherapy, but only one patient received both treatments while the other two only had psychotherapy. I could have given many examples of patients who receive medication only, when psychotherapy would have helped them as well. Such situations clearly violate the tenets of the New Psychiatry because they represent an unwillingness to provide the patients with tailor-made treatment approaches. In the above examples, clinicians adhered to rigid points of view that ignored what the patient needed. There are two main reasons why the combination may be more beneficial than either treatment alone. First, psychotherapy and medication may treat two different aspects of a person's problem and therefore be complementary. In the example above of the depressed man who was contemplating having an extramarital affair, Mr. B., it is clear that medication was the proper treatment for his current and fairly acute depression, while psychotherapy was the correct approach for his longstanding shyness and sexual preoccupations. Second, there is some reason to believe that for some conditions medication and psychotherapy work better together than either alone.

Practical Aspects of Combined Treatments

The practical aspects of conducting simultaneous drug treatment and psychotherapy vary. Only physicians can prescribe medication, so a doctor has to be involved. Almost anyone thinks he can give psychotherapy, but we will limit our discussion to qualified mental-health professionals who are either psychiatrists, psychologists, social workers, or psychiatric nurses. Psychiatrists generally prescribe medication and give psychotherapy, but even here there are exceptions. Some psychiatrists, called psychopharmacologists, specialize in medication treatment only and do not generally offer psychotherapy, while there are psychiatrists who primarily work as psychoanalysts and avoid prescribing medication.

Often the decision about who to pick for both drug and psychotherapy treatment is made on the basis of who is available and what can be afforded. Psychiatrists are one of the very few medical specialists in short supply in the United States, and there are many communities, particularly in rural and inner-city areas, that do not have any. In such a case, psychiatric medication is prescribed by a general practitioner, pediatrician, family doctor, or internist and psychotherapy is conducted by a social worker, psychologist, or nurse.

Psychiatrists generally charge the highest fees among mental health professionals. Many people can afford to see a psychiatrist to get medication because of the limited number of visits required but cannot afford a psychiatrist's fees for psychotherapy. Such people often see the psychiatrist only for medication and get psychotherapy from a less expensive type of therapist.

Finally, it is common for a patient in psychotherapy with a nonphysician therapist to find the therapy very helpful and still believe medication might be needed. Such a patient need not discontinue a valuable therapy but should ask to see a psychiatrist only for medication while the therapy continues.

There are advantages and disadvantages to seeing one person for therapy and another to get medication. The most obvious advantage, as mentioned above, is that it can save money because psychologists, social workers, and nurses generally charge less than psychiatrists for psychotherapy sessions. The main disadvantage is that it often becomes difficult to figure out which treatment is helping which problems. Let's say a patient with depression and a history of involvement in bad romantic relationships is seeing a psychiatric social worker for psychotherapy and a psychiatrist for antidepressant medication. The therapy seems to be going well because the patient is getting more understanding about why she picks men who are unavailable even though she is looking for a long-term relationship. The medication is helping because her previous symptoms of sadness, suicidal thinking, weight loss, and insomnia are mostly gone since the drug was started.

But after seeing the therapist for six months and being on medication for three months she has another romantic disappointment. The man she is seeing tells her he loves her but is not ready for a committed relationship and has decided to break up. She is plunged into despair and thinks her life is hopeless. She cannot sleep for several days but does not contemplate suicide. She is angry at her psychotherapist; why, after all this time, isn't she able to avoid this kind of relationship? The therapist decides the patient is unconsciously trying to sabotage the therapy by reinitiating maladaptive behavior patterns. The patient also questions whether the medication is still working? How could she get so depressed if she is taking an antidepressant? So the therapist approaches this apparent relapse as a psychotherapeutic issue while the psychiatrist recommends changing antidepressants.

It would be better, of course, to make one change at a time. If the patient improves it will be hard to tell whether the change in medication or new psychotherapeutic intervention is the reason. Both the social worker and the psychiatrist want to do something to help. Both think that if the patient relapses it must mean that it is something for which each is specifically responsible. Splitting the treatment like this may therefore not always generate the best outcome.

My own feeling is that if you can afford it and are not presently in an otherwise useful psychotherapy it is generally best to see one person for both therapy and medication. That means, in most cases, that a psychiatrist is preferable. If that is not possible, the next best thing is to be sure that the therapist and the doctor know each other and talk to each other about your case.

Most non-MD therapists know psychiatrists with whom they have worked in the past. If you think medication should be given in addition to therapy and your therapist isn't a psychiatrist, ask your therapist if he or she regularly refers patients to someone for medication consultations. The therapist should first call the doctor, make sure he is willing to accept a referral, and then describe the situation. After you have seen the doctor, he should then call your therapist and review the consultation and his recommendations. At several intervals, the therapist and psychiatrist should speak to each other to be sure they know what the other is doing. This is especially true if a crisis arises or if there is felt to be some need to change the treatment.

This procedure also follows when a physician prescribing psychiatric medication refers a patient to a non-MD therapist. Again, it is best if the doctor has a therapist she frequently refers to, trusts, and with whom she can work.

Three Pitfalls of Combined Therapy

There are several pitfalls to be avoided if you see a different person for therapy and medication. Occasionally, a non-MD therapist decides that a patient needs medication, calls a doctor and describes the case, and then has the doctor send the patient a prescription. The doctor never actually sees or talks to the patient. This is never to be done. Some people are under the misconception that prescribing psychiatric medication is a trivial function that anyone can do, hence there is no need to actually see a doctor. This is nonsense, as I hope Chapter 4 about psychiatric medications makes clear. The need to see a doctor to get a psychiatric medication is not just because state laws mandate that only doctors can prescribe medication; it is because psychiatric drugs are not toys and need to be monitored by someone who has training and experience with them.

The above is relevant to a second, more common pitfall. Often, a patient in therapy will see a doctor to get medication, begin the drug, and then feel there is no need to see the doctor again. This is both dangerous and unfair. It is dangerous because psychiatric drugs, while safe, have a number of adverse side effects. It is unfair because the doctor who prescribes the medication must take responsibility for what happens; that doctor should be able to see the patient for follow-up visits to be sure the drug is working properly and not causing serious side effects.

A third pitfall occurs when the patient gets the doctor prescribing the medication involved in the psychotherapy. If the doctor is a psychiatrist, he may also be a psychotherapist in addition to treating patients with medication. In the case in which a patient has a non-MD therapist, however, the psychiatrist is asked only to prescribe and monitor the medication. Nevertheless, during follow-up visits or over the phone the patient may begin to talk about issues that are not relevant to medication management with the psychiatrist. Here is an example of how this may be a problem:

Communication Is Essential

Case Study. Ms. T. was in therapy for a little more than a year with a psychologist when she had her first child. The therapy began when Ms. T. was still trying to decide if it was time to start a family. She had been married for four years, but was not sure how strongly in love she was with her husband. She had a good job and could not decide if she wanted to try to combine it with motherhood, wait longer to have a baby, or quit the job and stay home with a new child. She became paralyzed with indecision and sought out psychological help. The therapy went well and Ms. T. resolved conflicts with her husband and then made the decision to get pregnant.

About two weeks after delivering a healthy daughter, Ms. T. developed a fairly classic postpartum depression. She stopped eating and wandered around the house all night, unable to sleep. She told her husband that she felt she was not really ready to be a mother, that she would never be able to handle the responsibility, and that she felt guilty because she knew she would ruin the child's life. Her husband tried to reassure her, but after several days he called her therapist and described what was happening. At first, the therapist believed that Ms. T. was having a renewal of the kind of self-doubts that brought her into therapy in the first place. But after several sessions, the therapist became alarmed that Ms. T. was increasingly distracted and morose. She recommended that Ms. T. be evaluated for medication. So Ms. T. called her obstetrician, who gave her an appointment for the next morning. The obstetrician examined her and obtained some blood tests. He asked Ms. T. to describe what was wrong and she told him she was feeling depressed. The obstetrician asked Ms. T. if she wanted to see a psychiatrist, but she told him she already had a therapist and simply wanted to know if she should take antidepressants. The obstetrician prescribed Elavil, one of the oldest antidepressant medications, and told Ms. T. to take one pill, 50 mg, at bedtime.

The antidepressant seemed to help at first. Ms. T. slept through the night for the first time after starting Elavil, and her husband noted that she seemed to have a little more appetite. The therapist thought that Ms. T. seemed to be a bit more animated and more able to discuss her fears of raising a child in therapy sessions. But after the first week Ms. T. began complaining about a series of new physical problems: constipation, dry mouth, and fatigue. She was still finding it hard to cope with the newborn and even asked her husband if he thought they should put the baby up for adoption. Ms. T.'s therapist, reasoning that since she was taking an antidepressant the problems must be psychological, redoubled her efforts at getting to the bottom of Ms. T. worries and fears. She urged Ms. T. to continue taking the dose of Elavil every night and to come to therapy twice instead of once a week. Nevertheless, Ms. T. continued to become more depressed and three weeks after beginning to take Elavil she swallowed the remaining ten pills in the bottle at once in a suicide attempt. Fortunately, when she could not be aroused the next morning her husband called an ambulance and she was taken to the emergency room, where her condition was stabilized. She was admitted to the hospital and on the second day a psychiatrist was called to consult.

Here is a situation of a patient clearly "falling through the cracks." Ms. T. had a therapist whom she saw every week, a physician prescribing medication, and a concerned spouse. Despite all of this attention, she almost died. We worry about depressed people who live alone and have no therapists or doctors, but how could Ms. T.'s condition been allowed to deteriorate to this point?

The problem in Ms. T.'s case is the complete lack of communication. Ms. T.'s therapist should have spoken to the obstetrician and presented the case to him. If the obstetrician refused to talk to her, then Ms. T. should have been sent to a different doctor for medication. The obstetrician in this case should have called the therapist to get more information and to tell the therapist why he had prescribed Elavil. It is also not clear how comfortable this particular obstetrician was with treating depression. He asked Ms. T. if she wanted to see a psychiatrist, perhaps indicating that he would have preferred her to do that. Had she seen a psychiatrist it is very unlikely she would have been given Elavil. Elavil is one of the oldest antidepressants, and although it is effective, it has more side effects than newer drugs for depression. The drug is very sedating and that is why Ms. T. felt a little better at first—Elavil allowed her to get some sleep. But the dose of 50 mg is rarely enough to treat depression; most patients need closer to 200 mg to recover. Apparently, the obstetrician did not warn her in advance about such potential side effects as dry mouth and constipation, nor did he arrange for follow-up visits to see how she was doing. The therapist was under the mistaken belief that the "medication" aspect of things was under control and assumed, therefore, that all the remaining problems must be due to psychological issues. The obstetrician probably believed that someone would call him if things were not going well, but depressed patients usually do not take that kind of initiative. Ms. T.'s husband felt that there were experts involved and they should be on top of things.

THERE ARE many lessons to be learned from this near tragedy. First, if the treatment is going to be split between a non-MD therapist and a physician, one giving psychotherapy and the other medication, then the two professionals must speak with each other at the time of referral and at several points thereafter. Second, before a patient takes psychiatric medication from any doctor, she should be sure the doctor is comfortable and experienced with treating psychiatric problems and has the time and inclination to make a full assessment of the situation and see the patient for follow-up visits. Third, family members should not be shy with therapists or physicians. Mr. T. was in a better position than anyone to know that his wife was not doing well and he should have called the therapist, the obstetrician, and anyone else involved to tell them what was going on. Interestingly, Ms. T. was transferred to the psychiatric ward of the hospital, placed on another antidepressant (Norpramin) and the dose was raised to 200 mg. Four weeks later her depression was completely resolved. She went on to be an excellent mother and, when the baby was six months old, she returned to work as well. This story had a happy ending, but had Ms. T. had 30 or 40 Elavil pills left in the bottle when she took the overdose, she would have died.

The combination of medication and psychotherapy is often a highly effective way of resolving multiple aspects of a psychiatric problem. I do not want the example of Ms. T. to frighten anyone from trying both. Furthermore, there are many examples in which non-MD therapists and physicians work well together so that the patient gets optimal psychotherapy and medication treatment. As with any other aspect of medical care, the more patients and their families know about good procedure, the better able they will be to make sure the treatments they are getting are safe and effective.

6.
Couples and Family Therapies

IN PREVIOUS CHAPTERS on medication and psychotherapy treatments it is assumed that there are only two people present: a doctor and a patient. We now turn to treatments involving three or more people.

There are three broad ways to look at the indications for couples and family therapy, two that I endorse and one that I do not. Bear in mind that these comments apply only to patients. When a child is the patient, family therapy plays a different, and usually central, role in the treatment plan. The first will seem obvious. When a married (or significantly attached) couple do not get along or when a family is fraught with fighting and dissension, marital and family therapy is the obvious choice. More on this later.

The second indication revolves around helping families cope with severe mental illness. This applies to such conditions as schizophrenia and drug abuse in which an ill family member inevitably impacts on the lives of everyone else in the household. In many ways this is no different from teaching families how to cope with diabetes or AIDS. Family members need to be educated about the illness and instructed about how to be most helpful. They also frequently need an outlet for their frustration and they benefit from the insights and support of other people who have to cope with serious mental illness.

The third set of indications really comes from something called the "family therapy movement." Right away, the discerning mental-health consumer should be wary, because treatments are supposed to be based on their scientifically established effectiveness and safety; the word *movement* implies some kind of political statement. And that, in essence, is what the family therapy movement is. Devotees of this school feel that the family is at the root of most psychiatric problems, including depression, anxiety, and schizophrenia. Whether or not there are obvious family problems, these family therapists believe the entire family must be treated. I would like to deal with this third idea now by giving an example of a case conference I once witnessed.

The case involved a young man with schizophrenia. There was no question about his diagnosis. When he was 18, Carl first began hearing voices telling him that men from other planets were developing a special method of communicating with him. He believed that characters on television were transmitting special messages from outer space people to him. Sometimes

Carl appeared to be talking to himself and doctors were able to elicit the information that Carl believed he was actually speaking to outer space people. They told him not to eat green or yellow foods, to collect garbage for rocket fuel, and to only wear clothing that was blue, orange, or red. At several points in his life, Carl had to be hospitalized after refusing to eat or come out of his room for days on end while he sorted through piles of rubbish he had collected from neighborhood garbage cans. Carl was arrested three times for trespassing in order to collect the garbage and twice for undressing in public when he discovered that some of his clothes were not the "permissible color." Carl had been placed three years earlier on an antipsychotic medication called Haldol and had not required hospitalization since then. He had been eating and dressing normally, but his parents were concerned that he still showed little motivation to do anything more than read science fiction comic books and watch television.

Psychiatric residents at the clinic where Carl received his treatment were interested in family therapy and invited a family therapist to do a case conference. Carl and his parents came to the conference. Carl's father was a factory worker and his mother a clerk at a bank. They had no children other than Carl. They had been married for 32 years, worked hard, and earned a modest but sufficient income; they could afford a small house and one vacation a year. Neither of them had ever suffered from psychiatric illness. Carl's father had mild high blood pressure and his mother suffered from occasional migraine headaches, but they were both very responsible and followed their doctors' instructions so that both conditions were under control. They were the kind of people who were used to trusting doctors. Naturally, Carl represented a tremendous burden, both financially and emotionally.

The consultant interviewed the family together for 20 minutes, then saw Carl's parents alone for ten minutes, and then Carl for another ten minutes. During this time Carl's parents spoke about how upset they were that their son had not gone to college, as he once seemed fully capable of doing, and now showed no inclination to work. They expressed the fear that the medication might be making him sluggish and "dull." While they talked, Carl became visibly agitated, fidgeting and moving about in his seat. When interviewed alone, Carl would tell the consultant almost nothing except that he liked television and didn't feel "ready" to have a job. When the parents were alone, the consultant asked them, "Are there any problems between the two of you?" "Of course," Carl's father answered, "we fight sometimes, but it's nothing serious." The consultant then asked how often they had sex together, which turned out to be infrequently. Carl's parents were clearly not the sort of people to feel comfortable discussing this kind of thing with a stranger. The consultant asked whether either parent had ever had an affair. Carl's mother looked shocked and his father vigorously denied ever being unfaithful. The consultant wondered, "Since you don't have sex often, don't you ever think about having sex with other women?'' Carl's father acknowledged that the thought crossed his mind sometimes, but ''after 32 years I am not about to do it. I love my wife and we have enough trouble with Carl not to go making more problems. We rely on each other a great deal to handle him.'' Carl's mother added, ''I couldn't deal with Carl without my husband. He's bigger than I am and before he started the Haldol he used to get violent sometimes.''

From this information, the consultant came to a startling conclusion. With Carl and his parents present she declared, ''I want to congratulate Carl for devising a very effective method of keeping his parents together. It is obvious that Carl's parents have serious marital problems. By acting in a sick way, Carl forces his parents to divert their attention away from their own problems and on to Carl. In this way, Carl maintains the family intact. It is very important that Carl not do anything too quickly that might destabilize this delicate balance because it could result in his parents separating or getting divorced. Therefore, I recommend that Carl continue for now to live at home, refuse to work, and occasionally hear voices. He should only change these behaviors when there is evidence that his parents are working out their own problems and can stand for Carl to get better.''

Family therapists call this kind of thing *paradoxical intention*. Essentially, you tell the patient to do exactly the opposite of what you really want him to do. You can imagine the impact on Carl's parents. These people who were used to trusting doctors were now being told that they were responsible for Carl's behavior. Instead of an illness, Carl's problems were framed as a reaction to a family situation. Carl's parents had no idea they had serious marital problems. Actually, they had sex a good deal more frequently than they were willing to tell the consultant.

There are many reasons why this is a perversion of family therapy. First, there is evidence strongly contradicting the belief that family patterns cause psychotic illnesses such as schizophrenia. As discussed in Chapter 12 our best scientific evidence today indicates that schizophrenia is a brain disease that may be inherited. Second, this formulation merely makes an already stressed family feel further burdened by guilt, the last thing they need to function properly. Third, this kind of approach will never make a person with schizophrenia better. In effect, it is useless.

Family therapy of this sort becomes even more suspect in today's world of so many nontraditional families. What explanation would this consultant have if Carl was raised by his mother alone, as is the case for so many American children today?

I raise this example early in our discussion of couples and family therapy to make an important point: psychiatric illnesses, as the New Psychiatry insists, are not universally, or even usually, caused by bad marriages or bad families and should not be treated automatically with marital or family therapy. A depressed patient needs psychotherapy and antidepressants; a psychotic patient needs antipsychotic medication; and an alcoholic should go to Alcoholics Anonymous. Marital and family therapy should be reserved for two cases: when there is a clear marital or family problem or for the purposes of helping a family cope with a serious psychiatric problem in one of its members.

Because family therapy is usually employed when there is a problem with a child, and psychiatric problems of children is an area about which I profess little expertise, I will deal mainly in this chapter with couples therapy. I will focus attention at the end, however, on the use of family therapy as a coping strategy for serious mental illness.

Couples Therapy: When Should It Be Considered

By using the phrase "couples therapy" instead of "marital therapy," I am clearly emphasizing the point that in modern American society there are many significant relationships between two people that do not involve legal marriage. But I also want to emphasize that couples therapy usually should be devoted to people in serious, long-term relationships who have developed difficulties getting along. I have been asked occasionally to see "couples" who had been dating for only a few months but felt there was something "psychologically wrong" that prevented them from enjoying their relationships. There is a danger in submitting such tenuous relationships to a psychotherapy; often what happens is that a terrible relationship gets artificially stabilized by the therapy and is needlessly prolonged. Also, a "couple" of just a few months is really two individuals trying to form a relationship, not a relationship that has a life and psychology of its own.

So my first point is that only serious relationships involving commitments should be the focus of a couples therapy. Whether the couple is married or of different sexes is irrelevant.

When to Get Couples Therapy

People have different thresholds for deciding they need to get help for a relationship problem. The old-fashioned idea is that couples stay together no matter what. Sometimes this takes patience and forbearance—I have a certain sympathy for people who stay in less than optimal marriages for the sake of raising children free of the trauma of divorce. Other times, it makes little sense to maintain a destructive relationship—we all cringe when we hear of women who have stayed in marriages with physically abusive husbands for years and years.

At the opposite extreme is the "modern" notion that anything less than the ideal relationship should be abandoned. A cartoon I saw depicts a couple discovering they use different brands of toothpaste and rushing to their respective lawyers to initiate a separation. People like that should probably not get married in the first place; certainly, I would advise them against involving children in this kind of narcissistic quest for perfection.

Obviously, then, I do not advocate entering couples treatment after a few disagreements or even some serious blowups. Most couples can use their own resources to resolve routine conflicts.

On the other hand, it is a serious mistake to wait to see a therapist until a couple have lawyers or are physically separated. While many married people, especially in the midst of a big fight with their spouse, entertain the passing thought that they might be better off divorced, a good rule of thumb is to consider therapy at the point that conflicts are severe enough to raise the question of whether the relationship is worth preserving.

If you are in a relationship and things are not going well, ask yourself: "Is this a relatively recent problem that has only been bothering us for a few weeks? Have I tried everything I can to resolve it?" Don't leap to catastrophic conclusions about the quality of your relationship based on a few weeks of discord. Most relationships go through periods that last as long as several months in which there is conflict and decreased warmth and communication.

On the other hand, if you recognize that the conflicts are not only lasting longer than a few months but that there appears to be something fundamentally wrong with the relationship that you and your partner cannot seem to resolve, you should consider getting help. Here are two scenarios that illustrate these points:

Two Opposite Cases

Herb and Alice.   Herb and Alice were married for five years and had an eight-month-old child. They were in their late twenties. They were extremely excited to have their first child, but after a few months began quarreling about various household responsibilities. Alice had taken a leave of absence from her job to take care of the baby while Herb continued to work as an insurance agent. Herb felt compelled to work extra hours to make up the lost income while Alice was on leave from her job. When he arrived home at seven or eight every night, he felt it was time for him to have dinner and relax. Alice was happy with the baby, but missed her work as a personnel manager and often found herself bored and stressed taking care of an infant. When Herb would come home, she felt it was his turn to take care of the baby and give her a break so she could relax. Inevitably, the couple began fighting about who should change diapers, give the baby her bath, and play with her until her bedtime. In the course of this, Alice began wondering if Herb wasn't really a selfish person after all and not the kind, giving man she had married. Herb started feeling his wife was too demanding and wondered if he could continue working 60 hours a week for the rest of his life. During one of their fights, Herb declared to Alice, "I am sorry I ever married you," and Alice replied, "Then just get a divorce."

Some would say that Herb and Alice were in pretty bad shape and on the verge of divorce. There are plenty of marital therapists who would be delighted to engage this bright, financially stable couple in a long therapy. Such therapists would readily agree with Herb and Alice that they were not communicating and had "deep" differences about how to manage their relationship.

But there also might be a simpler solution. First of all, Herb and Alice had been quite happily married for five years, before the baby was born. Neither had ever thought about a divorce. Clearly, their difficulties were related to assumptions each was making about how to arrange their life with a child. If you asked either of them at a calmer moment, they would quickly admit to loving their spouse and to dreading the idea of a divorce. I would recommend against couples therapy for Herb and Alice until they tried a simpler solution. Here is what they did:

Alice called her obstetrician to ask for the name of a couples therapist. Instead of merely passing on a referral, this enlightened doctor asked Alice what the problem was. Alice briefly related the conflict and the doctor advised that Alice tell Herb that their problem was not a serious marital conflict but rather a reaction to caring for a baby. They should try to figure out a better way to divide up the work and see if that helped.

So Alice confronted Herb with this information and, with a sigh of relief (because the last thing he wanted was to enter therapy or get a divorce). Alice explained that taking care of a baby all day constituted a very hard job. Herb reviewed his anxiety that he had to work like a maniac to keep the family's finances afloat. They devised a plan to share the work of caring for their daughter in the evenings. Although they still had fights, neither again contemplated dissolving the marriage.

The story of Herb and Alice has a good ending. It would have had the same ending if the couple had entered couples therapy. This situation raises a classic problem in evaluating such therapies. If Herb and Alice had entered treatment, they would have ultimately reached the same conclusion about how to fix their relationship. I am sure they would also have gained insight into a number of other aspects of their relationship and personalities as well. They, and the therapist, would conclude that the therapy had helped them, perhaps even saved the marriage. In fact, a far less intense, expensive, and prolonged solution worked just as well. No one has yet done a head-to-head comparison of "simple" versus "complicated" treatment for relationship problems that meets scientific criteria for being a real study. Hence, couples should carefully evaluate the nature of their problems and decide if they might not fit into the Herb-and-Alice category before entering a couples therapy.

On the other hand, the following case illustrates the opposite end of the spectrum from Herb and Alice.

Sylvia and John. Sylvia and John were married for three years and had no children. They had known each other since high school and, after a few years apart following graduation while John was in the Navy, married when they were both in their early twenties. During the time he was away in the Navy, Sylvia dated a few men and had a sexual relationship with one of them. All the while, however, she expected that ultimately she would marry John and never got emotionally involved with anyone else. John had a few brief sexual encounters while in the service. Later, he admitted that he never thought about life after the Navy, but once out it seemed that everyone assumed he would enter his uncle's farm supply business and marry Sylvia. Their wedding was festive and served equally as a homecoming party for John. Both John and Sylvia got fairly drunk during the reception and, like a surprisingly large number of newlyweds, did not have sex on their wedding night. In fact, in the first few months of their marriage they had sex only a handful of times; each time it seemed to Sylvia that John was simply fulfilling some kind of obligation. Sex was quick and without emotion, but neither of them complained.

A year after their marriage, John began drinking. At first, Sylvia thought it was merely the stress of his job—John's uncle was a difficult boss— but she quickly realized the drinking was becoming a serious problem. John began going to bars after work instead of coming home, staying out late drinking, and missing work.

To the observer the problem here is clearly John's alcoholism, and there is no question this had to be dealt with first. In this case, fortunately, it was dealt with. John was stopped by a policeman for speeding, found to be drunk, and ordered to attend an alcohol treatment program to get his license back. He did this and was successful in becoming abstinent from alcohol. Unfortunately, nothing got better in Sylvia and John's marriage. At first Sylvia was delighted that her husband had stopped drinking, but now instead of falling asleep on the couch at night he picked fights with her about trivial things.

Sylvia developed headaches and saw her family doctor. He asked her in the course of taking a medical history if she was under any particular stress and she broke down in tears, explaining that she spent all the time fighting with her husband and that they hardly ever had sex. The doctor seemed embarrassed and gave her a prescription for Valium, which she never filled. John told his alcohol counselor on several occasions that he was worried his marriage wasn't working out, but the counselor told him that people with alcohol problems usually have trouble with close relationships and that the important thing was to stay away from alcohol.

After three years of marriage, Sylvia noticed lipstick stains on one of

John's shirts. She confronted him and he tearfully confessed to having an affair for the previous month, then left the house. Sylvia and John remained married for two more years, but he then had another affair and left for good.

ONE GETS THE feeling in reading Sylvia and John's case that they had virtually pleaded for help but got none. Could couples therapy have helped them? That is quite possible. There seem to be two major problems. Sylvia found John unexciting. John could only see Sylvia as part of a life he did not really want to lead. But it is also possible that the two had serious differences in personality and outlook that would make a successful marriage impossible. People should have urged them to seek help. A good therapist would have permitted each to air out their complaints. John would have had to become a more exciting lover. Perhaps the couple would have had to move to another town or city and John would have needed to start a new career. Or perhaps these young people, who did not have children, were better off getting divorced. In any event, I regard this kind of situation as a tragedy because simple suggestions, like the kind that benefited Herb and Alice, do not work in situations like this. Telling Sylvia to "make the best" of a marriage without sex and constant bickering or blaming the whole situation on a drinking problem in remission were facile and useless. A trained therapist might have been able to help Sylvia and John understand the dynamics of their relationship and at least give them tools and options to fix things.

Let me reinforce, then, my basic advice on couples therapy. Try simple solutions first, but don't permit a deeply ingrained set of differences and continued unrest to go unchecked. The worst that can happen if you see a couples therapist is that you will waste time and get divorced anyway.

Couples Therapy: How to Get Started

A couple has decided that their problems cannot be resolved alone. Each partner has made an effort to talk with the other and both have tried a few simple solutions, like rearranging schedules, making an effort to do things together, sharing household responsibilities. Some of these suggestions are listed in Table 14.

Despite sincere efforts, the things in Table 14 haven't helped the couple. They are still fighting and neither person is happy. How do they find a therapist?

TABLE 14

SOME SIMPLE THINGS TO TRY BEFORE STARTING COUPLES THERAPY

1. See if you and your spouse agree that there are problems.
2. Try to define those problems.
3. Agree to discuss them on a regular basis; leave some time free a few times a week to talk.
4. Review your schedules and try to spend more time together.
5. Discuss the assignment of household responsibilities and be sure it is fair.
6. Try to do enjoyable things together more often, even if they are simple, like going for a walk or exercising together.
7. Have a frank discussion about your sex life.
8. See if you can both give up on old grudges and focus on the current status of your relationship and the future.

How to Find a Couples Therapist

As with all other forms of psychotherapy, finding a good and appropriate couples therapist can be perilous. Many people from a variety of disciplines believe they are good at couples therapy. Some are psychiatrists, psychologists, or psychiatric social workers; others have no real degrees or special training. Remember that in some states in the United States anyone can call himself a therapist without any training or certification. On the other hand, there are plenty of high-powered, very skillful psychiatrists and psychologists who are terrible at couples therapy. I believe that couples therapy requires special talent, which cannot be taught, some training, and a lot of experience. And those three aspects form my advice about how to find a couples therapist.

To get a referral, ask as many people as you can. If you are already seeing a psychiatrist or other mental health professional, that is one place to get a referral (I will come back later to the case in which one or both people in a couple is already seeing a therapist and decide to add couples therapy). Of course, a very good source of referral is always a couple who has had a good experience, but people are sadly reluctant to divulge that a therapist has helped their marriage. Family doctors sometimes know of couples therapists, but often they simply know therapists in general who may or may not be good at couples therapy.

The best bet for most people is to get three or four names from several different sources and interview them. I strongly advise against starting a couples therapy before seeing several different therapists. Most people nowadays get second and even third opinions before having a surgeon repair torn cartilage in a knee or remove a gall bladder. I like to think that people believe marriage and other long-term relationships are just as important and therefore will be equally willing to take the same care before selecting a particular treatment.

There are several important things to look for in a couples therapist. I will go out on a limb and say that only therapists who have therapy training and a degree in psychiatry, psychology, or social work should be considered. I am sure there are plenty of couples therapists without these credentials who are helpful, but I think it is reasonable to require therapists to undergo formal training before taking on the responsibility of tampering with people's lives. Pastoral counselors, by the way, often undergo as extensive training as other therapists and may also be very skilled. Most religious organizations do provide for special training in various kinds of therapy for interested clergy. It is wrong, however, to think that priests, ministers, or rabbis automatically have special abilities to help couples resolve their problems. They know how to marry people and generally operate under some bias that breaking up marriages is not the optimal solution, but religious training by itself does not qualify someone to be a therapist.

After ascertaining that the therapist has had training and a degree, the next thing to ask about is experience. Do not be afraid to ask the therapist how many couples she has actually treated. A therapist may have many patients and do a good job, but only rarely see couples. As I will discuss below, couples therapy is very different form individual psychotherapy and requires special talent and skills. The therapist should be able to reassure you that he or she treats couples on a fairly regular basis and considers this to be a specific area of her expertise. You might even ask what usually happens to these couples. Remember that many people seek out couples therapy when it is already too late or when they have a relationship that is best dissolved; hence, every couples therapist should have cases that end up in divorce and cases that stay together.

Experience and training are fairly easy to assess. Less clear is whether the therapist has the special talent necessary to conduct a couples therapy. It is difficult to deal with two people who are angry with each other. Some couples are fully capable of fighting with each other through an entire therapy session, seeming to show little interest in what the therapist has to say. There is also always the threat of a seriously adverse outcome occurring. People generally come to couples therapists because they have some hope that their relationship can be saved. While perhaps not as dramatic as the case of the surgeon who has to perform an operation precisely right or the patient will die, the pressures on a couples therapist are often severe. And unlike the situation confronting the surgeon who may have performed the operation many times before, every couple presents a unique set of circumstances so that the therapist is always forced to come up with new strategies and ideas.

It is absolutely critical that *both* people in a couple feel comfortable with the therapist. There are therapists who, sometimes unconsciously, have difficulty understanding the viewpoint of one member of the couple and inevitably take sides. This is a prescription for failure. Some therapists carry a bias that women in marriages are always victimized by their husbands. They will see everything in these terms and believe that the solutions always rest in making men more communicative and emotionally open, and having them take more responsibility for doing the dishes and cleaning the house. There are some therapists who instinctively identify with men in relationships; they always find women to be too demanding and emotional and believe the solutions lie in getting the wife to stop complaining and picking fights. Interestingly, the sex of the therapist is not always the determining factor in these biases. I know female therapists, for example, who seem to have great difficulty understanding the pressures and concerns that women have in troubled marriages and always side with the husband. Obviously, in many marital situations it will be important for the husband to become more communicative and the wife to stop complaining. In others it is the woman who fails to make her needs known clearly and the husband who is too critical. The point is that a relationship problem is never the fault of one person. (Of course, I am not considering the special case in which a wife is physically abused by her husband; no woman is ever to be blamed for that.)

Sometimes the reason a person does not feel comfortable with a particular therapist during an initial consultation is not so logical. As I said in the chapters about individual psychotherapy, such feelings should usually be honored. Even if there is a "neurotic" reason for not liking a therapist, there is enough to do in a couples therapy without having to first deal with not liking the therapist. Try a different therapist.

Basically, then, I think both members of the couple must feel that the therapist understands them, appeals to them, and seems empathic. The therapist should be open about his or her training and experience and should offer some kind of formulation at the end of the first meeting that indicates an understanding of the problem and some idea about how to proceed.

Many people wonder if it is necessary for a couples therapist to be married or have children in order to fully grasp what goes on in a marriage. Similarly, people wonder if gay therapists are the only ones qualified to treat gay couples having difficulties. These are difficult questions to answer. Theoretically, it is not necessary for someone to have personal experience with a situation to be a competent therapist. A cardiologist does not have to have had a heart attack herself to know what to do when a patient has one. Many of the issues that confront couples are fairly universal issues that everyone experiences in relationships.

But these are theoretical considerations. While being married is probably not a prerequisite for doing couples therapy with married people, and straight therapists can undoubtedly help gay couples, having those experiences undoubtedly enrich a therapist's ability to help. I have treated married couples with problems raising their children before and after having children of my own. There is no question in my mind that only after three or four weeks of having to get up for the 3:00 A.M. feeding did the stress this can impose on a marriage become clear to me. It is easy to say that husbands and wives should share that responsibility and if they don't it has to be negotiated, but I can now appreciate that even a very happily married person will do almost anything to convince his spouse to do the feeding. Similarly, I don't know to what extent straight people fully appreciate the special stresses gay couples labor under. Although many people will disagree with this, I believe it is fair game to ask a couples therapist some personal questions that would not be appropriate when choosing an individual therapist. I do not think it is wrong or improper to ask a couples therapist if he is married or, in the case of a gay couple, if he is gay. Catholic couples for whom divorce is not an option may find a Catholic therapist most able to appreciate this special constraint. Because, as I will explain below, couples therapists are generally more personally involved in therapy than are individual therapists, their own personal experience is sometimes relevant to the success of the therapy.

What to Expect in the First Meeting

Couples therapists have different ways of handling the initial contact. Most will want to see the couple together and then each person separately at first. If you are following my advice and interviewing several therapists, this can make for an awful lot of "consultation" sessions. Therefore, I favor an initial meeting of at least an hour with both people in the couple present. At that time, the therapist should encourage each person to explain their version of the problems—and the strengths—of the relationship. The therapist should watch carefully for signs of how the couple relate to each other. When I interview a couple (or probably more accurately, when a couple interviews me), I always watch to see if they ever look at each other when they talk, how they refer to each other, and whether they seem emotionally involved. It is not necessarily a good sign if the couple gets through the initial meeting without fighting. After all, they are in the office because they are not getting along and the therapist should want to see "where it hurts," just like a cardiologist wants to hear the heart murmur or the ophthalmologist looks for the redness in the eye. A couple that gets through an initial session without quarreling is either being unnecessarily polite or, more likely, they have developed a cold and distant way of relating to each other.

Just as in any other psychotherapy consultation, at the end of the first meeting the therapist should make some statements about what she thinks the problems are. Obviously, the therapist cannot be expected to know exactly what is wrong and all the steps necessary to fix the relationship. Nevertheless, a skillful couples therapist should already have some ideas about what needs to be fixed.

Couples Therapy: How Does It Work?

While there are a number of "theories" about couples therapy, my suspicion is that good couples therapists mainly do what they have found works. The New Psychiatry is less interested in fanciful and unproven theories than in practical outcomes. Hence, in discussing how couples therapy works, I will stay away from complicated theoretical ideas and concentrate on broad categories of technique.

A first decision a couples therapist has to make in dealing with a couple in trouble is whether the relationship is worth saving. This should not be a moral judgment—that is, regardless of one's view about the "sanctity of marriage," a couples therapist should make an assessment about whether there is a reasonable chance that the relationship can be repaired in such a way that both members of the couple can be reasonably happy.

Notice that I keep using words like "reasonable" in describing the goals of couples therapy. A major problem has become the unrealistic expectations people have about what marriage is supposed to be like. The wild infatuation that couples often experience in the first few months of a relationship is not always sustained through the ups and downs of ordinary life. This is not merely because people get used to each other as the relationship lasts; rather, at some point a couple has to integrate its relationship into a variety of other life demands. Jobs, ambitions, children, other friends, disappointments, illnesses, and aging all impinge on the early euphoria experienced by couples as they fall in love. There are three things a couple can do with these facts. (1) They can silently suffer as the relationship seems to take one turn for the worse after another, but do absolutely nothing to make things better; (2) they can recognize that there is nothing critically wrong with the relationship, but that it must change in order to maintain its vitality; (3) or they can split up and try to find a new infatuation.

Sometimes, therefore, a couple may present its problem as desperate and seemingly irreversible. The therapist, on the other hand, may recognize that the couple has unrealistic expectations for marriage and therefore decide that the marriage might survive and the couple live a happy life if they can be brought to endorse more reasonable ideas of what marriage should be like. It is important to recognize that I am not advocating a blanket approach that divorce is always the wrong outcome and a marriage must be saved at all costs. Rather, in this situation, the therapist is willing to try to help the couple rearrange its thinking and then see if the marriage is viable.

When the Relationship Cannot Be Saved

Other times, however, it may be quite obvious to the therapist that the marriage is doomed. I am rarely optimistic about the chances for survival in the following kind of situation:

Jim and Marjorie had been married for twelve years. On two occasions Jim had affairs with other women. The first occurred a year after they were married, when the couple was struggling with serious financial pressures and Marjorie's father developed a terminal illness. When Marjorie discovered the affair she was enraged, but she was also distraught over her father's impending death and felt that perhaps she had not been a ''good'' wife. Jim agreed to end the affair and Marjorie forgave him. For at least a year after this, however, Marjorie could not get the fear that Jim was having another affair out of her head. Anytime Jim came home late from work or said he was going out with friends she became suspicious and depressed. Gradually, these fears subsided, but a few years later Jim was caught in another affair. He was dramatic in his apologies and swore he would never have another affair. Once again, Marjorie forgave him, but she also became anxious and fearful that he would cheat. She found it difficult to enjoy sex with Jim and often snapped at him.

Now, the couple is in a couples therapist's office because Jim has again confessed to having an affair. This time, however, he is not readily agreeing to stop. He insists that he is ''justified'' because his wife has not been sexually compatible with him for several years and, in fact, often gets nasty and criticizes him too much. Marjorie says this is because after his second affair she has never really felt she could trust Jim.

Infidelity, as I discuss below, does not always mean the end of a marriage, but in the case of Jim and Marjorie it would take a minor miracle to ever get Marjorie to trust Jim again. Furthermore, it is very difficult, if not impossible, to conduct a successful couples therapy when one member of the couple continues to engage in extramarital relations. Jim in reality feels entirely justified in having an affair and gives little indication he will readily stop. Marjorie has been living for twelve years with a man she cannot trust, with whom she feels chronically angry. This one is not going to work.

Unless, of course, children are involved. Some couples therapists and many lay people endorse the concept that children are better off when a loveless, contentious marriage is dissolved. According to this view, it is more damaging for children to witness their parents constantly embroiled in fights than to settle into life with divorced parents. Given the high divorce rate, approaching 50 percent in some parts of the country, there are plenty of children from broken homes around who seem to grow up more or less intact.

Unfortunately, while this view is very convenient for people who want to get divorced, it is not necessarily true. Very few studies have properly examined the adjustment made by children when their parents get divorced or their ultimate outcome as adults, but the few reports approaching scientific quality that exist suggest that children do not fair well when their parents get divorced. My own feeling is that whatever a couple without children is willing to put up with for the sake of maintaining the relationship, a couple with children should probably be willing to put up with more. The therapist should lay out for the couple the potential risks to the children of a divorce and expect the couple to factor these risks into its decision. In other words, when the therapist helps the couple come up with a list of reasons for and against staying together, one of the reasons in favor of maintaining the relationship is legitimately because that is usually best for the children.

Let us suppose that a couples therapist has decided a relationship has a chance for improvement and survival. The therapist should be very clear about this, while at the same time noting that couples therapy does not guarantee a good outcome. Next, the therapist should outline for the couple what the major problem areas seem to be and what her approach will be to solving them.

Three Types of Couples Therapy

There are, as I said above, many different approaches to couples therapy. Guided by the work and writings of one of my teachers, Dr. Christian Beels, I think there are three broad categories of approach which are usually combined: (1) behavioral, (2) cognitive, and (3) insight-oriented.

The behavioral approach to couples therapy is a problem-solving approach that aims at getting couples to do things differently. Spending more time together, sharing responsibilities, altering sexual patterns, and changing the way fights are conducted are examples of behavioral interventions. In this mode, the therapist listens carefully to what the couple does and makes active suggestions for changes. Often, the therapist introduces these changes gradually over several weeks in the form of ''homework'' assignments. The couple may be expected to keep notes of what they do and how they feel as each change is incorporated.

For example, one couple complained about infrequent sexual relations, although they were clearly attracted to each other after several years of marriage. One of the problems had to do with their schedules. The wife worked late, wanted to have sex at night, and sleep late in the mornings. The husband wanted to have sex in the morning, but his wife could not bear getting up so early. Rather than figure out a solution, they stopped having sex except on vacation. A therapist explained that each should be willing to make compromises to accommodate the other and designed a program in which the couple would have sex two mornings and two nights a week. She helped the couple figure out ways to make this maximally enjoyable, including getting the husband to agree to make breakfast on the mornings they had sex so that his wife could stay in bed longer. The program was introduced in parts over several months, but resulted in a vast improvement in the couple's sexual relationship.

A cognitive approach to couples therapy focuses on the thoughts, attitudes, and expectations that people have for each other. Relationships generally get into serious difficulty when each partner harbors a set of expectations for the relationship that the other member either does not know about or can't meet. A simple example is a couple in which the husband washed the dishes after dinner every night for two weeks, then had a fit when his wife told him she would not be able to pick up his shirts from the cleaner one day because she had an appointment downtown. The husband had been washing the dishes with the secret belief that this behavior would lead his wife to do things for him in return. There were several problems with this belief, however. First, the wife did not consider washing dishes as a favor for her; the dishes had to be washed, both of them used them, and, as far as she was concerned, her husband should do his share. Second, her husband had never made it clear that he wanted something in return for washing the dishes every night. Third, the wife had a legitimate reason for not being able to pick up the shirts. The basic problem here is that the husband had symbolically written and signed a contract that his wife knew nothing about.

This is clearly a very simple example, but it represents a significant cause of marital distrust and difficulty. Sometimes, it takes a therapist to recognize and untangle all of these thoughts and beliefs, articulate them, and then help the couple decide which are mutually compatible and which are hopelessly unilateral. In this mode, then, the therapist is constantly trying to readjust thoughts and expectations so that both members of a couple feel comfortable with each other.

Insight-oriented approaches borrow from psychoanalytic theory and usually deal with differences in personality that can hinder a couple's relationship. Here we are dealing with the deeply rooted aspects of character and personality that psychoanalysts believe are formed in early childhood and endure throughout life. The motivations for these aspects of character and personality are largely unconscious, but psychoanalytic theory explains that they have powerful impact and influence on how people behave and experience the world. In the first flushes of love, aspects of personality may be obscured and people can overlook profound differences between themselves and new partners. Only with time do these differences emerge and cause problems in the relationship. Because they are so ingrained, behavioral and cognitive approaches may not be sufficient to address them.

Some Gender-Specific Differences

Some of these differences may be gender-specific in certain situations. I am about to make a few sweeping generalizations that will undoubtedly disturb some people. My only defense is my insistence that these should be regarded as generalizations, with many exceptions possible. A good place to learn more about this is from an outstanding book by Dr. Deborah Tanner called *You Just Don't Understand.* I don't know if Dr. Tanner, a linguist by training, realized this, but her book is a primer that should be read by couples in difficulty (and probably by couples not in difficulty as well) and by couples therapists. More about this later.

The "gender-specific" differences I am referring to are virtual clichés, but they have some truth. Women tend to be far better at expressing their feelings and putting their emotions into words than men. Men tend to react to conflict by becoming angry and aggressive, while women become hurt and anxious. Dr. Tanner synthesizes this in her book by carefully noting the ways in which men and women use language and communicate. Let me give an illustration of this in a case example.

Allison and Robert were married for seven years and had no children when they came to see a couples therapist. It was clear that Robert was reluctant to be in the therapist's office. He was a busy investment banker who constantly looked at his watch through the first session, clearly worried that he would be late for his next appointment. His speech was short and clipped; he offered few details beyond what was absolutely necessary to describe an event. Allison, an advertising executive, seemed distraught. Often during the first meeting she appeared on the verge of tears, but seemed to make nearly heroic efforts to hold them back. She acted as if she wished the session could go on forever, as if this was her one big chance to have a serious conversation with her husband.

It was clear that the couple's relationship was strained, although not on the verge of breaking up. Allison had consulted a psychiatrist about one year prior to the couples therapy consultation because she felt listless, confused, anxious, and unhappy. She was suffering from a mild depression that responded to brief psychotherapy, but the psychiatrist noted that she had many misgivings about her marriage. Allison complained frequently that she could not talk to her husband, that he seemed increasingly distant, preoccupied about money and work, and dismissive of her feelings. The psychiatrist had recommended that she and her husband see someone together.

At the first meeting, the couples therapist asked what the problem was; Allison began haltingly. "Basically, I don't feel that Robert and I are as close as we used to be. He always seems mad at me but he won't admit it. I feel our whole life revolves around his work and how the markets are doing. When he has a good day he smiles and when the market goes down he is grumpy. We have some important decisions to make, like starting a family, and I want things to be all right for us before we make a step like that."

The therapist noted that Robert looked like he was about to choke when Allison mentioned starting a family. He asked Robert what he thought about Allison's description of their relationship. "I really don't see any problem here," he replied. "I have to work hard and Allison has to accept that. That's the kind of job I have. It's a lot different from listening to people talking all day."

The therapist noted Robert's obvious dig at him. Robert was already establishing the fact that he was a more important person than the therapist; here is where training and experience are important because the worst thing would be for the therapist to become defensive or attack Robert back. Rather, the therapist noted that Robert had a sense of self-importance that might also extend to his feelings about his wife. The therapist turned to Allison and asked, "You work also, isn't that correct?"

Allison then explained that she also had a full-time job and earned a substantial income. Her job was pressured and insecure; the advertising industry is not the place for people who cannot tolerate job insecurities. She did not think that Robert's job was really the problem. "He thinks I want to restrict his work and make him spend more time with me. First of all, I never say a word to him about how many hours he spends at work. I like the money he makes too."

"You spend more of it than I do," Robert inserted, but the therapist ignored this comment for the time being. Allison continued. "Second, I don't want to have to beg him to spend time with me."

Allison became tearful. Robert, obviously uncomfortable, looked away from her. The therapist asked him if he had any comments. "I think it is really all just not true. I have told her a million times that I do want to spend time with her."

Robert and Allison's interaction illustrates some classical difficulties between married couples. Notice that Robert does not say anything about how he feels about Allison or make any attempt to address her rather poignant descriptions of her feelings. Rather, he argues the facts and criticizes her. He insists her feelings are "not true," as if feelings are facts that can be validated, and accuses her of making unreasonable demands.

A good couples therapist will probably apply some aspects of behavioral and cognitive therapy in trying to help Robert and Allison. For example, one problem is that Robert consistently refuses to spend any time talking about the marriage with Allison, so one homework assignment might be that the couple has to spend at least 30 minutes three times a week—to start—talking about their relationship. The therapist would probably add some rules and regulations. Neither person would be permitted to answer the phone or end the discussion prematurely. These discussions should be conducted at a time convenient for both partners and every effort should be made not to turn them into fights.

Cognitively, the therapist might try to train Allison not to automatically regard Robert's going to work as a rejection of her. The therapist would also try to show Robert that Allison's insistence on a better relationship should not be automatically interpreted as a threat to his ability to conduct his business and earn a living.

But these techniques might well fall short of the mark for Robert and Allison. I think that in this situation a successful couples therapy would have to demonstrate to them the very basic differences in their personalities and the way these differences impair their ability to get along with each other. Allison will have to become a less sensitive, more independent person, while Robert will have to become a far more sensitive and less driven individual.

Can Marital Therapy Work?

There is controversy about whether couples therapy can actually accomplish goals like this. Some would say that Allison and Robert should be in individual therapy to work on their personalities and in couples therapy also. There are practical and theoretical reasons to oppose this view, however. Practically, there are few people who have the time or the money for all of those psychotherapy sessions. Even with the different proposals to reform health care, my guess is that no plan would pay for two individual and one couples therapy session a week for very long. Theoretically, there are also problems. What tends to happen is that each person in the couple goes off into ''their corner'' and complains about the other person. The individual therapist usually supports his own patient and often things get even more polarized between the couple.

It is hard to say whether Allison and Robert can be happy together. In many ways they are a mismatch and, given that they have no children, it might be best for them to try again with new partners. I would recommend six months to a year of couples therapy in which they try to learn how to accept each other, recognize each other's strengths and weaknesses, and stop attacking each other. If their marriage gets on track, each might then consider individual therapy to work on their own personality deficiencies.

Couples Therapy: What Are the Practical Arrangements?

Couples sessions generally last longer than individual sessions, simply because more people are involved and everybody has to have a chance to talk. In the beginning the therapist will probably interview the couple together a few times and then ask to see each person individually one or two times. This should not become an individual psychotherapy, however, and the couples therapist should not start treating one member of the couple individually while the couples treatment is going on. Generally, the therapy sessions last between an hour and an hour and a half and are scheduled weekly. Often, the therapist assigns the couple a variety of assignments for the days between the sessions.

Costs vary a great deal for couples sessions. As with any type of psychotherapy, psychiatrists tend to charge more than psychologists, who in turn charge more than social workers. As I stated earlier, the most important thing is to pick a therapist you feel comfortable with, who comes highly recommended, and who has experience specifically doing couples therapy. It is not wrong to enter cost into that equation. More expensive couples therapy isn't necessarily better couples therapy.

One important practical consideration is confidentiality. Ordinarily, of course, a therapist pledges not to discuss anything a patient says with anyone, even the patient's spouse. This doesn't work in couples therapy since both people obviously know what is being said. The trick is handling communications that occur between only one member of the couple and the therapist. These may occur during the few individual sessions the therapist has with each member or during telephone conversations that sometimes occur with the therapist. What should the therapist do if, for example, a wife confides that she is having an extramarital affair that her husband doesn't know about? In almost all cases the therapist should honor this confidence. The therapist should tell the couple at the beginning that as much openness as possible is desirable. Furthermore, the therapist should point out that she will be placed in a difficult and uncomfortable position trying to keep secrets while also attempting to maintain a neutral stance toward the couple. Nevertheless, confidentiality should be honored. The only exception is if the therapist believes someone is going to be physically harmed as, for example, could be the case if a wife reveals she is afraid she might lose control and shoot her husband. In this case the courts have indicated that confidentiality should not be honored by therapists, and indeed if violence occurs the therapist can be held accountable.

Couples Therapy: Summary

I have indicated that couples therapy is a legitimate psychotherapeutic enterprise, although there is little scientific evidence telling us exactly how often it actually proves effective. Because of this, the New Psychiatry demands that both clinicians and patients constantly question whether a particular couples therapy is actually working. There are many ways to describe different types of couples therapy, but one useful way is to break it down into the broad categories of behavioral, cognitive, and insight-oriented.

One always has to take a practical approach to couples therapy. It is better to get help before you are anywhere near the divorce lawyer's office, but don't allow a protracted therapy to merely stabilize a terrible relationship.

Pick a couples therapist carefully, define the goals of the therapy in the early sessions, and keep expectations realistic. Couples therapy will not make your marriage resemble that of the Stones in the *Donna Reed Show,* but it should help you to avoid a situation like that encountered by the couple in the movie *War of the Roses.*

A Brief Discussion of Family Therapy

Most family therapy in the United States is actually couples therapy. What remains to be discussed are situations in which children and their parents are involved in therapy.

I call this a "brief discussion" because there is an entire, crucial role of family therapy that I will not say much about, the application of family therapy to psychiatric problems involving children. Anytime a child requires psychiatric care, the entire family, including siblings, is involved. Minimally, the child psychiatrist will interview the parents extensively and in most cases see the parents frequently during the course of the treatment. I am aware that some children are enrolled in individual psychotherapy that extends for prolonged periods (that is, for years) during which time the therapist has little contact with the parents. I think this is almost always not only a waste of time but an ineffective treatment approach and potentially destructive. Children do not need to spend their time in psychotherapy if it can be avoided. The object of psychiatric treatment for children is to get them better as quickly as possible with the least amount of intervention. This almost always means involving the family.

Thus, when children present with behavioral problems like fighting in school, stealing, or disobeying teachers, or when they develop phobias, depression, or attention deficit disorder, the psychiatric evaluation and treatment should be a family treatment. I want to stress that anytime a child needs treatment, the family should be involved.

Psychiatric Illness Affects the Family

This leaves one other important use of family therapy to discuss. Serious psychiatric illnesses such as schizophrenia, bipolar mood disorder, and severe recurrent depression have profound effects on family life. In the past this has been ignored, and, in some circles, as the example I gave at the very beginning of this chapter shows, families have even been blamed for these illnesses. The New Psychiatry takes a very different view: families often suffer almost as much as the patient and therefore they need two kinds of help. First, families need reassurance and support; they need to be told that they are not the cause of the illness and that they should not feel guilty. Second, families need information about the best ways to handle a variety of situations that arise when a family member has a serious psychiatric illness.

When someone is depressed, is it best to leave them alone or should they be urged by family members to get out of bed and join in family activities? When do you tell a son, daughter, or parent that she appears manic and should call the doctor? Is it best to let a patient with schizophrenia sit in his room all day mumbling to himself, or should he be pressured to come out and go for a walk? What constitutes helpful cajoling as opposed to intrusiveness?

These are questions that plague families and that deserve addressing. A few studies have shown that when families are involved in treating patients with schizophrenia who also take antipsychotic medication, the rate of rehospitalization can be reduced. The kind of family treatment involved, however, is very special. It does not involve trying to find a cause for the illness within the family dynamics; rather, it is focused on teaching the family how to recognize the earliest signs of relapse so that medication can be adjusted, when to leave the patient alone and when to urge more activity, and which things are good to point out to a patient and which may make her feel worse.

Gerard Hogarty, a great but sometimes overlooked researcher at the University of Pittsburgh, has produced the most impressive scientific data showing the value of family therapy toward the well-being of patients with schizophrenia. It is important to stress that Hogarty is an advocate of antipsychotic medication; he is completely realistic about schizophrenia and does not believe it is a social disease or a disease caused by bad family ''vibes'' or ''vectors.'' Rather, he has repeatedly shown that careful family intervention increases the chances that a patient with schizophrenia who takes antipsychotic medication will be able to stay out of the hospital and lead a more productive life. Other researchers are trying to find out to what extent these family treatments also improve the mental health and functioning of the people in the patient's family who do not have schizophrenia.

Family Therapy in a Group Setting

Family treatments aimed at helping people cope with serious mental illnesses are often done in groups. For example, four or five families who all have a person with schizophrenia in them may get together regularly with a therapist. Some of these groups include the patient and some do not. The therapists may come from any discipline—psychiatry, psychology, or social work—but should be experienced both with treating the illness itself and with family therapy. More and more these treatments are limited to a fixed number of sessions, often around ten, with a manual-driven agenda. The sessions include basic information on particular mental illnesses, such as schizophrenia or bipolar mood disorder, opportunities for family members to share their difficulties in dealing with an ill relative, and strategies that group members have found effective. It is extremely helpful for people to learn that they are not the only ones who sometimes get frustrated with and even angry at a son, daughter, parent, or sibling who has schizophrenia or bipolar mood disorder. Further, families are often quite resourceful in finding clever solutions and coping mechanisms that can be tried by other families.

There is a theory that families with too much "expressed emotion" contribute to relapse among patients with schizophrenia. Some studies suggest that such families in which there tends to be a lot of passionate communication, argument, and intrusiveness produce an environment that is too stimulating for people with schizophrenia. Family treatments have been devised to attempt to reduce expressed emotion and produce a calmer, less intrusive background for the patient. The advantage of this work is that it rests on some experimental investigation in which scientists have attempted to use appropriate research methods to determine if the theory is correct and if treatment intervention is helpful. It must be emphasized, however, that not all studies agree that levels of expressed emotion really do contribute to the outcome of people with schizophrenia. Further, it is not at all clear that treatments aimed at expressed emotion change have any positive effects.

For now, I strongly recommend that families that include a patient with schizophrenia or bipolar mood disorder attempt to find at least a short-term family therapy. These can usually be located by contacting one of the advocacy groups in your community, especially local chapters of the National Alliance for the Mentally Ill (NAMI), the National Depressive and Manic Depressive Association, and the Mental Health Association.

7.
Group Therapy

GROUP PSYCHOTHERAPY RAISES a lot of eyebrows. It should. This is one of the modalities that is easy to misuse and potential group therapy patients need to be forewarned.

To be sure, there are important instances in which groups make a lot of sense. In this chapter I will try to list these and explain how group therapy can be compatible with the New Psychiatry. Addiction treatment, for example, has long relied on a group format. Alcoholics Anonymous is still the most effective way to combat alcoholism and it is always conducted in group format. In the chapter on Family and Couples Therapy, I discussed groups of families who gather with a therapist to learn how to cope with a seriously ill relative. Some of these specific uses of group therapy will be discussed a little later in this chapter.

But group therapy has so many obvious economic advantages that it has been used to treat problems for which there is little evidence that it works. Group therapy appeals to patients because it usually costs less per session than individual therapy. It appeals to therapists because they can usually make more per hour treating a group than an individual. And it appeals to third-party payers—insurance companies—because treating a bunch of patients at the same is obviously cost-effective (although in reality, as I've noted before, insurance companies never pay much for any type of mental health treatment, including group therapy).

Many people suffering from neurotic or personality disorders—those enduring character traits that cause unhappiness and interpersonal stress—are convinced to enter group therapy by therapists. It is not always easy to figure out why this recommendation is made to such patients. Often, it seems that the therapist just happens to be interested in group therapy and believes that this is a useful modality to treat people who are not happy with their lives. The groups may include people with a wide variety of problems. Some are obsessive compulsive, others histrionic, others phobic or shy. Some of the people in the group may even be suffering from such psychiatric syndromes as depression, panic disorder, and bulimia. They get together once or twice a week, usually for between 60 and 90 minutes, and talk about their problems.

Books and articles have been written explaining the theory behind this kind of group psychotherapy. I will have more to say about this later, but for now let me summarize how this is supposed to work. Like family therapy, group therapy has been promoted by therapists who form a kind of "group therapy movement." They point out that people do not live in isolation and therefore that therapy in a social context makes sense. By being in a group, a patient supposedly has the opportunity to learn that others also suffer from emotional pain, which may reduce isolation. Further, other patients may share methods of coping with problems and may be able to point out to a patient the kind of things he or she does wrong in social situations. The therapist also has the opportunity to observe how a patient interacts with other people: Does he get angry too quickly or sound sarcastic and dismissive? Is he overly sensitive and unable to take a joke? This may guide the therapist in figuring out what kinds of problems the patient really has and what kind of intervention is necessary. For all of these reasons, group therapy *sounds* like a good idea.

But does it work? Group therapists are quick to point to some research studies that do indicate that group therapy works as well as individual therapy for some people. Closer inspection indicates, however, that these studies are few and far between and raise more questions than answers. Essentially, we do not know whether group therapy is as or more effective than individual therapy, or whether it is effective at all.

Dangers of Group Therapy

A real danger of group therapy, in my opinion, is that it becomes a substitute for real-life social interaction. Some people get very used to the group and feel more comfortable talking to fellow group members than to "outsiders." Rather than using the group as a platform to go on to other social interactions, they become overly dependent on it. Further, therapists sometimes exert subtle (and sometimes not so subtle) pressure on group members to stay in the group. If a group dwindles to three or four members it ceases to be a "group" for therapeutic purposes and the therapist will have to either recruit new members or start all over again. To keep the group at a critical number, usually a minimum of five people, the therapist may be reluctant to let people quit. Sometimes, patients seem to stay in groups for years without any obvious benefit. It merely becomes habit.

I think it is useful and consistent with the principles of the New Psychiatry to divide group therapy into two broad categories: task-oriented, diagnosis-specific groups and open-ended, diagnosis-nonspecific groups. I will argue that the former can indeed be very useful and certainly cost-effective. The latter should be approached with caution, although some people will benefit.

Task-Oriented, Diagnosis-Specific Groups

There are many reasons why it may be useful to treat people who have the same psychiatric problems in groups. Foremost among them is the chance it gives patients to learn that other people have the same problems. Because of the stigma attached to mental illness, an incredible number of patients believe they are alone in their suffering. Many specific illnesses impose an additional burden of isolation. Depression causes social withdrawal, phobias restrict a person's ability to travel, and schizophrenia makes communication with others difficult. Many psychiatric patients think of themselves as "oddballs" and believe the only hope is to maintain as low a profile as possible, hoping no one will notice their illness.

In a group, however, patients quickly learn that their own condition is common. It is also not exotic; although all people are unique individuals, a patient with agoraphobia can quickly realize from a group therapy setting that there are a lot of people in the world with agoraphobia, the illness is very similar from person to person, and treatment is usually successful.

A second advantage of the group format is that it increases the number of "helpers" available. By offering support and often examples of how they handle difficult situations, members of a group help each other. This broadens the ability of the therapist to produce change.

Finally, as mentioned earlier, groups that focus on a particular illness are usually very cost-effective. A patient with agoraphobia may require a type of behavioral therapy called *in vivo* desensitization. This means that such a patient, who is generally afraid to leave home unless accompanied by a trusted companion, will benefit from a therapy program in which she is gradually "exposed" to increasing challenges. This may start with walking around the block and then progress to driving five blocks away from home, to taking a short train ride, and to flying to a nearby city. The treatment can be done with an individual therapist, who first draws up with the patient what is called a "hierarchy"—a series of steps the patient will take to increase the amount of time she is alone and the distance she travels away from home. The therapist usually then accompanies the patient for the first few exposures, allowing the patient to be alone more and more with later steps in the hierarchy. The patient does not advance to the next step until she has mastered the present level, able to complete a task with minimal anxiety. Studies have shown that this kind of treatment is highly effective for phobics.

But the treatment can also be accomplished in a group and studies suggest—although do not yet prove—that desensitization in group format is just as successful for phobias as individual treatment. In this case, because most people with agoraphobia have more or less the same travel restrictions, the group and the therapist decide together what steps will be taken in the hierarchy and then the group goes together for the first few outings. For future steps group members pair off, then go alone. One therapist is able to treat as many as a dozen people at the same time. The cost is low and the outcome usually beneficial.

There are, again, two distinguishing features of such a group. First, all the people have the same diagnosis. Second, the group has a very clearly defined task. Groups of phobics exist to get people to overcome their phobias.

Alcoholics Anonymous groups focus on abstinence from alcohol. Bulimia groups stress cessation of binge eating. While group members may gain in other ways—their self-esteem may improve, for example, by seeing that other people who they respect suffer from the same illness—the group measures its success solely on how many members accomplish the primary task.

TABLE 15
*CONDITIONS THAT MAY RESPOND TO TASK-ORIENTED,
DIAGNOSIS-SPECIFIC GROUP THERAPY*

- Agoraphobia
- Social phobia
- Eating disorders
- Alcoholism
- Drug abuse
- Compulsive gambling
- Sexual behavioral abnormalities

In Table 15 I list some conditions that may be suited for task-oriented, diagnosis-specific groups. Note that each of these conditions involves an easily identifiable behavior that needs to be changed. Agoraphobics avoid travel, social phobics avoid social situations, eating disorder patients binge and purge, etc. The sexual behavioral abnormalities I am referring to, incidentally, include voyeurism, exhibitionism, and pedophilia. In each situation, there is either something the patient should be doing or should stop doing. Groups can be successful in helping people accomplish that goal. It is generally not helpful to mix diagnoses; voyeurs are not put in groups with cocaine addicts. The therapist is generally a specialist in the diagnosis targeted by the group and the goal is set during the first session. The group works together to accomplish the goal, then either disbands or goes into a kind of maintenance phase.

Some Examples of Useful Group Therapy
Here are a few examples of patients who might benefit from group treatment.

Agoraphobia.   Majorie is a 36-year-old nurse with agoraphobia, a condition described in more detail in Chapter 11. Marjorie began having panic attacks when she was 22, and about a year later became so afraid of having attacks in ''dangerous'' situations that she stopped leaving home unless her mother or sister went with her. After nearly three years of being homebound, Marjorie was placed on medication and her panic attacks ceased. She became able to walk from home to a nearby commercial street and go shopping, to travel in a car if someone else drove and it wasn't rush hour, and to sit in church or a movie theater without eyeing the exit nervously every five minutes. But Marjorie still could not drive in a car alone, take a bus or train ride, or even contemplate getting on a plane.

Then she read of an organization called Anxiety Disorders Association of America, called the national office, and got the name of a therapist who conducted group treatment for people with agoraphobia. The therapist interviewed Marjorie individually, confirming the diagnosis of agoraphobia and noting that while medication had eliminated her panic attacks she still feared having one if she engaged in what she firmly believed were dangerous activities. The therapist recommended she join a newly forming group. The group was composed of six other people with agoraphobia. Although the severity of illness differed—one member was still homebound while another could drive by himself for limited distances—every member identified getting over phobic avoidance as the goal.

The therapist used the first session to explain the way the group would work. First, she described herself. She herself had once suffered from agoraphobia, had a successful treatment, and then become a social worker with the idea of helping other agoraphobics. She had run groups for phobic people for six years. She regularly attended meetings and seminars about phobias, anxiety disorders, and behavioral treatment. This group would meet for 12 sessions. In the first session the group members would introduce themselves, explain their condition, and briefly review their personal situations. Then the therapist would give them information about agoraphobia. In the second session the group would design a hierarchy of activities to gradually expose themselves to phobic situations. They would then meet together eight times and actually carry out these tasks. There would be homework and practice for group members to complete between meetings. In the last two meetings the group would get together again in the therapist's office to discuss their progress and plans for the future.

As in all groups, the members were cautioned about confidentiality. This is always a tricky issue in group therapy. Individual therapists pledge never to reveal anything a patient tells them and, with a very few exceptions, it is considered highly unethical to breach this promise. Members of a group do not have that kind of professional obligation and must be trusted not to reveal each other's secrets. At the start of most groups the leader will usually insist that members agree not to talk about what goes on in the group to outsiders.

Marjorie's group started at the level of the most severely affected member, who had difficulty leaving her house alone. The group actually went to her home for the first ''field'' session and walked with her about one mile. The therapist went with the group and made sure that each member rated his or her anxiety level during the walk. In subsequent sessions, the group went in smaller and smaller subgroups to shopping malls, on municipal buses, and on car rides. In one session they formed a caravan of cars and drove across a bridge during rush hour.

At the final sessions, it was clear that five of the seven group members had made substantial progress and were now able to accomplish previously terrifying tasks. One member felt he had made some progress, but still complained of a number of restrictions. The final member actually felt she was getting worse and had gone from limited ability to travel to almost none. The group leader recommended that these two treatment "failures" try an individual therapy. The group agreed to meet again in one month so that they could discuss the maintenance of their progress and even plan further group trips to help overcome lingering phobic avoidance.

THIS FORMAT obviously has drawbacks and risks. Some people do not appreciate having to share their therapy with a group and feel they are not getting sufficient attention for their unique problems. That is, I believe, a legitimate objection and such people should still seek individual therapy. A risk is that the group will become a crutch for some patients, who become dependent on it to maintain any progress. This is not different from the risk of becoming dependent on an individual therapist or a drug, but in the case of group therapy some relatively withdrawn and isolated individuals may find that the group is a substitute for regular social interactions. Rather than overcome their targeted problem, like agoraphobia, they show little interest in getting better and great interest in keeping the group going forever. For that reason, I think it is usually a good idea to limit the number of times a group for phobics meets.

Addiction therapy. A second example needs little elaboration. Allen, a 52-year-old accountant, finally agreed he would have to stop drinking. His internist had found abnormal liver tests on his last examination, he had smashed up his car while drunk (miraculously, he suffered only minor injuries and no one else was hurt), and his wife threatened to leave him if he didn't sober up. Reluctantly, Allen picked up the phone and dialed the number for Alcoholics Anonymous. Begun by two men, one a physician with alcohol problems, AA remains the most effective mechanism we have to combat alcoholism. It is not foolproof and plenty of people who start AA do not remain sober. But AA has helped millions of people stop drinking. It relies heavily on a group format. It is diagnosis-specific because everyone at an AA meeting has a drinking problem. It is task-oriented because the main goal is to stop drinking.

AA was the first so-called Twelve-Step program, a method now used by groups that treat a variety of addictions. AA makes explicit what the

TABLE 16
The Twelve Steps

1. Our common welfare should come first; personal recovery depends upon AA unity.
2. For our group purpose there is but one ultimate authority—a loving God as He may express Himself in our group conscience. Our leaders are but trusted servants, they do not govern.
3. The only requirement for AA membership is a desire to stop drinking.
4. Each group should be autonomous, except in matters affecting other groups, or AA as a whole.
5. Each group has but one primary purpose—to carry its message to the alcoholic who still suffers.
6. An AA group ought never endorse, finance, or lend the AA name to any related facility or outside enterprise, lest problems of money, property, or prestige divert us from our primary purpose.
7. Every AA group ought to be fully self-supporting, declining outside contributions.
8. Alcoholics Anonymous should remain forever nonprofessional, but our service centers may employ special workers.
9. AA, as such, ought never be organized; but we may create service boards or committees directly responsible to those they serve.
10. Alcoholics Anonymous has no opinion on outside issues; hence the AA name ought never be drawn into public controversy.
11. Our public relations policy is based on attraction rather than promotion; we need always maintain personal anonymity at the level of press, radio, and films.
12. Anonymity is the spiritual foundation of our Traditions, ever reminding us to place principles before personalities.

Twelve Steps are (see Table 16 above) so the treatment is focused. The first step is to publicly admit that one is an alcoholic. This was the hardest part for Allen, who still harbored the idea that he could control his drinking by himself, even though he had been drinking himself into near oblivion for more than 20 years without any obvious ability to stop. The group therapy format is critical to AA's success; members of AA groups actively assist each other in stopping drinking, including making themselves available 24 hours a day to fellow members who may be about to slip and have a drink. Group members pressure each other to stop, discuss their own tricks for remaining abstinent, and make the alcoholic patient feel part of a team working toward a victory.

There is a subtle religious aspect to AA that offends some people. For that reason, alternative group therapy formats have developed that tend to focus less on the inspirational aspects of abstinence. But group treatment seems ideally suited for most addiction therapy, hence the creation of organizations like Narcotics Anonymous and Gamblers Anonymous. All of them take the attitude that group cohesiveness and pressure is extremely useful in battling weak impulse control.

Sexual Behavioral Disorders.   My third example involves a 26-year-old man with a sexual disorder. Craig, a seemingly ordinary, law-abiding citizen with a good job, is a voyeur, popularly known as a "peeping Tom." There are about two million theories on what causes this behavior, but there is no proof for any of them. Craig has spent his adult life hating himself for his compulsion to peep, but he has never been able to control it. He has seen therapists, some of whom have treated him with intensive psychoanalytic therapy and some who prescribed drugs for obsessional thinking, but nothing has stopped him from hiding in the bushes looking into people's windows. He often considered killing himself as the only way to stop, but after years of voyeurism, Craig eventually accepted his perversion as just part of his life, not different from going to work or going to the movies. Then he got caught, arrested, and convicted of a crime. As a condition of his sentence he was ordered by the judge to attend a special program for "sex offenders." Fortunately for Craig, the one chosen was a respectable clinic at a university medical school. Craig was interviewed by a psychologist who was conducting research on treatment of sexual compulsions and Craig was placed in a group of men who were all voyeurs. This group operated on principles of behavior therapy applied to a group situation. In the first session, the group members introduced themselves and one by one revealed their compulsions. For some, it was the first time they told anyone about their secret behavior. Then the psychologist explained the rules of confidentiality. Voyeurism is illegal and therefore no one would come to treatment if he risked being exposed.

In subsequent sessions, each member of the group was asked to explain in detail all of his thoughts and feelings in the moments before peeping. He was asked to reveal how he felt before, during, and after each act of voyeurism. Members of the group were encouraged to comment on one another's revelations by noting things that they had themselves felt or experienced. For most of the members of the group it became clear that there was always a period of anxiety and tension leading up to peeping that was only relieved by actually doing it. Once the peeping was completed, all the group members acknowledged a period of remorse and self-hatred, often vowing never to do it again. The psychologist in this and future sessions designed exercises to help break this pattern. Group members were encouraged to call each other the moment the urge to peep began, to have a plan for an alternative activity (a "way out") each time they felt compelled to peep, and to focus only on the post-peeping period of remorse in their minds.

The group met weekly for three months, then every other week for two months, then once a month for the remainder of the year. Half of the group members were able to stop peeping entirely, another quarter reduced the amount of voyeurism, and the rest were treatment failures. This is actually a very high success rate for an otherwise difficult to treat condition.

In Table 17, I stress some of the key features of diagnosis-specific, task-oriented groups.

TABLE 17
KEY FEATURES OF DIAGNOSIS-SPECIFIC, TASK-ORIENTED GROUP THERAPY

- All members have the same psychiatric diagnosis.
- The leader is an expert in that particular diagnosis.
- There is a clear goal that all members want to reach.
- The goal is usually to start or stop a particular behavior.
- The sessions are focused on the goal.
- The therapy is time limited.

Groups like these are sometimes conducted by therapists in private practice. In deciding if you want to join one, apply the principles in Table 17. Question the therapist carefully about the nature of the group, the therapist's credentials, and how long the group will last.

Practical Aspects of Group Therapy
Practically speaking, most group therapy sessions last about 90 minutes and are conducted weekly. In a private practice group each member is expected to pay a fee for each session; some therapists require that members agree to pay a fee in advance for a block of sessions. Don't start group therapy if you don't think you will probably go to all of the sessions. Groups get a kind of cohesiveness that helps them progress and can be seriously undermined if members drop out in the middle. On the other hand, never feel that you are trapped in a group if it is clear to you it isn't working out for you. After a few sessions you may feel that the other members are too different from

you or that the way the group is going won't help you. Tell this to the group leader and, if a resolution doesn't seem possible, quit. Don't let the therapist or the other group members pressure you into wasting several months watching other people get help.

Understand also that confidentiality can never be maintained by a group the way it is by an individual therapist. At very least, the other group members are, of course, going to know a lot of personal information about you. Beyond that, remember that members of a group may promise not to blab your secrets around town, but you are stuck taking their word for it. Psychiatrists have been successfully sued for breaching a patient's confidentiality, but I do not think there is any legal solution if a fellow group member tells people about the things you say in a group. In actual practice this does not seem a terrible problem because most people in groups adhere to confidentiality rules. It is, however, something to keep in mind.

Many groups are run by clinics, both private and public. Sometimes this is because the clinic does not have the money to pay for therapists to treat everybody individually. It is important to remember, however, that diagnosis-specific, task-oriented groups are often first-rate treatment. If you have a phobia, for example, the clinic may want to put you into a group for treatment. You should feel that you have a choice in this, but consider the group as a reasonable option.

Medication Groups

Some clinics have "medication" groups in which people taking psychiatric drugs meet together with a psychiatrist for adjustment of medication and side-effect checks. Essentially, the doctor goes around the room and asks each patient to state how he is doing and what side effects he has. The doctor then adjusts the medication of each. Patients may have an opportunity to discuss their symptoms with one another, but these "medication" groups are really designed to save money by conserving psychiatrist time. They may work fairly well for some patients, but do not be fooled into thinking there is anything particularly therapeutic about them. We will probably see much more of this kind of approach under proposed managed care systems. I doubt that patients' medical care will suffer much, but it does seem less than desirable to be denied a few private minutes with your doctor.

Diagnosis- But Not Task-Specific Groups

Some groups are diagnosis-specific but not really task-oriented. Usually these are support groups for patients with a variety of illnesses. There are support groups for survivors of childhood sexual abuse, families of alcoholics, and patients with bipolar mood disorder. I have mixed feelings about these. On the one hand, I think it is critical for people to be able to meet with similarly afflicted individuals. This cuts down on the loneliness and isolation they experience. On the other hand, I worry that some of these groups do not actively encourage people to get better, but rather encourage them to incessantly vent their rage, anger, and disappointment. A group of patients with bulimia should focus on how to stop binge eating, for example, not on how terrible it is that society treats obese people unfairly or on how bad parents cause bulimia. While society is unfair to obese people and many bulimics have had awful childhood experiences, groups that do not try to get people better often go on forever. Make sure, therefore, that your support group encourages members to do everything they can to overcome their disabilities and live a happy life.

Open-Ended, Diagnosis-Nonspecific Groups

This is not a treatment method in which I have a great deal of faith. Nor do I believe that open-ended, diagnosis-nonspecific groups play a role within the New Psychiatry. These statements will undoubtedly raise the ire of the many adherents of the group therapy "movement," hence I feel compelled to make such a disclosure at the beginning. That way, some readers may decide to consult other sources that take a more positive attitude.

In diagnosis-nonspecific groups, patients will have a variety of complaints. Usually, social and demographic features link the members more than type of illness. These groups tend to include people of similar economic and social demographics, such as ones with all middle-class people, all wealthy people, all women, all professional people. They usually do not mix people with extremely severe and active psychiatric illnesses—such as schizophrenia—with people with less severe, more chronic illness—such as dysthymia (chronic depression), personality disorder, and generalized anxiety disorder. Hence, there is a kind of homogeneity to them, but this has nothing to do with the psychiatric problems under discussion.

A very common mode of entry into such a group is the recommendation (sometimes the very strong recommendation) of an individual therapist who also happens to run groups. The exact reason for these recommendations is not always made clear to the patient. Sometimes patients with a variety of psychiatric problems have the common difficulty of poor interpersonal relationships. They may be shy and unable to meet or talk to people or, at the other extreme, they may be arrogant and overbearing and irritate people. The group psychotherapy setting may be one way for the therapist to observe a patient exhibiting these deficiencies in a social situation. Group members, theoretically, can be more blunt than ordinary acquaintances in pointing out bad or obnoxious behavior and in helping the patient to change. This is a fairly concrete reason for recommending group therapy. The problem is that most open-ended groups never define a task as specific as helping members improve their social skills; hence, it is up for grabs whether that particular problem will be addressed in any systematic way.

Beyond helping with socialization, open-ended groups are supposed to help by bringing to bear something called *group process*. This poorly defined concept comes from much better articulated theories from other fields, like anthropology, sociology, and social psychology. There is a fascinating literature about how groups of people work together, but its application to group psychotherapy is not well defined.

I have seen too many patients start a group psychotherapy for very ill-defined reasons and then keep going every week (sometimes twice a week) for years. They often get very attached to fellow group members and may even socialize with them outside of the group, although there is usually an explicit prohibition against sexual relationships among group members. During the sessions group members talk about their lives, their relationships, and their problems and other group members make comments. Somehow, this is supposed to relieve the suffering of the group members.

Group therapy proponents will cite "studies" that supposedly show this kind of thing works, but those studies are neither rigorous nor convincing. In fact, there is no good evidence that open-ended groups help; in addition, they can be expensive, time-consuming, and lead to unnecessary dependence.

Obviously, there are exceptions. If you are in a good psychotherapy with a therapist you trust and respect and the therapist is able to give you a clear, cogent, and believable explanation for why group therapy would be helpful, such advice may take precedence over all of my cautions. Also, low-cost group therapy may be preferable to no therapy at all if you cannot afford an individual therapist, although it is painful to recommend a therapy merely because it is cheaper.

In general, however, I think it is appropriate to be very wary of open-ended groups. In most cases, alternative therapy, either a task-specific group or an individual therapy, is a more reliable method of treatment.

Group Therapy: Concluding Remarks

It is, as I have continuously stressed in this book about the New Psychiatry, no longer acceptable to recommend a treatment only because the idea behind it *seems* interesting or because that is what the therapist likes to do. Some forms of group therapy, the ones I have called task-oriented, diagnosis specific, seem to have fairly good and tested track records. Other forms, the ones I have called open-ended, diagnosis-nonspecific, are to my mind lacking in empirical support and need to be approached cautiously. This could change tomorrow. Ten new, well-designed studies could be published in the next editions of high-quality scientific journals attesting to the benefits of open-ended group therapy. As an adherent of the New Psychiatry that would mean I would immediately change my recommendation. Without more evidence, however, I will stay with these opinions for now.

8.
Hospitalization

PSYCHIATRIC HOSPITALIZATION RAISES the specter in many people's minds of the snake pit, a "lunatic asylum" from which there is no escape. Images of straitjackets, locked doors, forced medication, painful electroshock, and violence are conjured. It is never easy to suggest hospitalization to a psychiatric patient.

Indeed, psychiatric hospitalization is becoming increasingly less common and less necessary. Fortunately, the New Psychiatry offers a range of effective treatments that can safely be accomplished on an outpatient basis. Fortunately, then, most psychiatric patients will never face the need to be hospitalized.

Sometimes, however, hospitalization is necessary. It is very important for patients and families to know when hospitalization is beneficial and what kinds of hospitals are best. Sadly, there are still psychiatric hospitalizations that approach the "snake pit" version, but this is clearly avoidable. Rather than having a knee-jerk response to the word "hospitalization," it is important to know the facts so that this sometimes lifesaving step can be accomplished properly.

Psychiatric Hospitalization: When Is It Indicated?

Psychiatric hospitalization is generally indicated for the following two broad reasons: (1) when it is too dangerous to allow the patient to remain at home or (2) when there are specific things that can be accomplished in a hospital which the patient needs and cannot get as an outpatient. Before agreeing to a hospitalization, the patient and family should be sure one of these two criteria is met.

The Dangerousness Criteria
How much danger is enough to warrant a psychiatric hospitalization? This is obviously a very subjective question and one that psychiatrists are notoriously bad at answering. Studies have shown that the ability of psychiatrists—or anyone else—to predict future violence is very poor. The most powerful predictor is a past history of violence, a fact not very helpful in trying to determine if someone who has never made a suicide attempt but is now threatening to should be admitted to the hospital. Many years ago there was a fear that psychiatrists were hospitalizing patients too casually and perhaps

exaggerating the seriousness of suicidal or homicidal threats. Today, most states have very strict laws limiting a psychiatrist's ability to hospitalize someone against his will. The standard is that there must be imminent danger that the patient will do physical harm to himself or someone else. In many cases, unfortunately, this has swung the pendulum too far in the opposite direction, with people at risk for committing violent acts being allowed to leave hospital emergency rooms because the psychiatrist is afraid of violating their civil rights.

Anyone at serious risk for suicide or committing a violent act against another person because of psychiatric illness should be immediately hospitalized. There are certain conditions that increase the risk of violent acts. Psychotic depression, described in more detail in Chapter 10, has a very high suicide rate, for example, and often requires hospitalization. Although people with schizophrenia are not more likely to commit violent acts than the general population, patients who are acutely psychotic may lose impulse control and normal ability to monitor their behavior. This is particularly true of people with paranoid psychoses in which they fear that others are trying to harm them. When such a person appears violent or talks about hurting others, it is almost always best to hospitalize him. Thus, if there is any fear that a patient will commit a violent act, he or she should be hospitalized.

There are other dangerous situations that may require hospitalization. Patients with severe depression or with anorexia nervosa may eat so little as to jeopardize their lives. Sometimes they need to be fed against their will until treatment can clear up the psychiatric illness. This is often best done in the hospital.

Involuntary Commitment

Quite frequently, patients who are potentially dangerous to themselves or others don't agree that there is a need for hospitalization. A suicidal patient may want to die and hence refuse to be hospitalized. A patient under the influence of a paranoid psychosis may really believe he has enemies who need to be destroyed. In such cases, the law provides for a mechanism to hospitalize the patient against his will. This is called involuntary or civil commitment. Next to giving shock treatment, civil commitment has probably been the most controversial aspect of psychiatry. Books and movies are full of horror stories in which people who are political dissidents get trapped in hospitals against their will. Sometimes these stories focus on a completely normal person who is forced into the hospital while unscrupulous family members or business partners steal all their assets. Psychiatrists are often conspirators in these tales. We now know, unfortunately, that things like this were fairly routine in the former Soviet Union, where psychiatric hospitalization was used for political reasons. Later in this chapter I will discuss situations in which it has been charged—and may well be true—that some teenagers in this country were improperly hospitalized against their will for the financial gain of certain private hospitals.

Indeed, it once was fairly easy for psychiatrists to hospitalize patients involuntarily in many parts of the country. All that was required was for a doctor, perhaps with the corroboration of a second, "independent" doctor, to sign a certificate asserting that the patient needed involuntary hospitalization and the patient was shipped off. Today, I still sometimes get calls from distraught families asking me to sign papers ordering the police to take their son or daughter directly to the hospital for commitment. They are shocked to learn that in my state (New York), and in most others in the country, such a thing has not been possible for many years.

With few exceptions, a patient can only be involuntarily admitted these days if he or she is first brought to a hospital emergency room. This is usually done by police or an ambulance. In the emergency room, a doctor must determine that the danger presented by the patient is serious and imminent—that is, the doctor has to have very good reason to believe that if he doesn't put the patient into the hospital the patient will either die or kill someone right away. A second doctor has to examine the patient and agree. Then they sign what in New York is called a "two physicians certificate." A family member must also sign, indicating that they also take responsibility for the commitment. Once the patient is in the hospital, most states mandate that he be seen within the first few days by an attorney who represents committed patients and that the patient have the opportunity to go before a judge to argue that he should be released.

These regulations were put in place to protect people from losing their civil rights in commitment proceedings. It is clear that some people need to be hospitalized whether they agree or not, but it is also clear that this situation could lead to abuse and certainly no single psychiatrist should have the power to incarcerate someone.

Some say, however, that these rules are now so stringent that patients in need of inpatient care are being denied potentially beneficial treatment. A mother of a 30-year-old man, living at home with her, called me recently to ask me to have her son "committed." What could he be doing that would motivate a mother to make such a request? Her son, in fact, had barricaded himself in his room and was refusing to come out or eat. This had gone on for several days. She was afraid to go in because her son had been making angry and violent noises and had screamed several times, "If you come in here I will kill you!"

The best I could do was advise her to call the police. She thought I might have some magical words to say to her son that would calm him, but in fact there is very little anyone can say to an acutely psychotic person barricaded in his home and not responding to common sense. If the person refuses to come out, the police have to be called to get him out and bring him to the emergency room. So the woman reluctantly called the police. The police came and banged on the door. The patient opened the door and told the police he would come out and eat. They asked him if he would go to the hospital and he refused. The police left. The man slammed the door and continued his hold-out. The police were not wrong in this case. Their instructions are that they cannot force someone to go the hospital unless they see something that is unarguably convincing that a disaster is about to occur. The patient answered their questions in a way that made it difficult for them under existing law to take any further action. I believe he should have been hospitalized and treated with antipsychotic medication. So did his mother, who had to live with him. But civil rights law took precedence. The patient ultimately committed suicide.

There is not much more I can say about this situation. Somehow, legal scholars, doctors, and families will probably have to come up with a better system that simultaneously protects civil liberties and gets very ill people treatment that will help them. Some will argue that people should have the right to commit suicide. Here, I am restricting myself to the case in which a person with a serious mental illness needs treatment that would reduce the risk of violence. In my opinion, existing law is going to have to bend somewhat to accommodate this situation.

When Therapy Requires Hospitalization

As mentioned above, the second reason to hospitalize a patient is to accomplish a therapeutic goal that cannot be done as an outpatient. In these cases the patient is admitted to the hospital voluntarily and has the right to sign out whenever he or she wishes. No immediate emergency is discerned, but there is agreement among the doctor, patient, and family that there is no other way to effect a positive treatment outcome without hospitalization.

An important instance of this is the case in which a medical problem makes outpatient treatment of a psychiatric illness difficult. Here is an example.

Avery: A Case of Major Depression. Avery, a 69-year-old retired steamfitter, developed severe depression following cardiac bypass surgery. The surgery itself was uneventful and from the cardiologist's point of view Avery was doing fine. But two weeks after leaving the hospital his wife called the cardiologist and asked if it was usual for patients following such surgery to refuse to get out of bed or eat. The cardiologist suspected depression and asked to see Avery. In the doctor's office, Avery appeared tired, listless, and sad. He did not talk very much and tears welled in his eyes at one point. He had lost six pounds since being discharged from the hospital, a situation that alarmed the doctor. A psychiatric consultation was requested and the diagnosis of major depression made.

Avery was started on a type of antidepressant called fluoxetine (Prozac), which has very few medical side effects and is generally safe for patients with heart problems. However, after six weeks on this drug he was still depressed and had lost an additional five pounds. The psychiatrist wanted to try an antidepressant from a completely different class, called nortriptyline (Pamelor). However, there were aspects of Avery's heart condition that could make such treatment risky. At very least, Avery would need careful medical monitoring, including several electrocardiograms. The cardiologist, psychiatrist, Avery, and his wife agreed that hospitalization would be the safest and quickest way to accomplish this. Fortunately, Avery did well on nortriptyline and after a four-week hospitalization was discharged. He quickly gained weight and remained free of depression.

Sometimes it is necessary to remove a patient from his usual environment in order to effect a good treatment outcome. This is often the case with drug and alcohol addiction problems. While some people are able to remain abstinent from addicting substances while in outpatient therapy, others find the temptations inherent in their daily lives too overwhelming and cannot stop. Many addiction experts believe that there are ''cues'' in the environment that trigger addicts to seek and take the abused substance. For example, an alcoholic may routinely associate all business dealings with high anxiety and a need to drink. Unless the alcoholic is temporarily removed from business situations, he may not be able to break the cycle and stop drinking long enough to start a treatment program. In such cases, hospitalization may be useful. There is currently quite a bit of research trying to figure out whether hospitalization, which is expensive, offers advantages over outpatient treatment for substance abuse and, if it does, whether there are particular patients who benefit from inpatient treatment. Right now, it is fair advice to say that a person who has tried to detoxify from an abused substance as an outpatient and fails should probably consider an inpatient treatment program.

Hospitalization for ECT

Patients who require electroconvulsive therapy (ECT) usually, but not always, require hospitalization. More can be read about ECT in Chapter 10. ECT is generally reserved nowadays for severely depressed patients who have failed to respond to other antidepressant treatments, including medication and psychotherapy. It is quite frequently given to elderly depressed patients or patients with other medical conditions because it is relatively safe. Still, the patient is anesthetized during the treatment and many clinicians prefer to do it only on inpatients. While outpatient ECT is becoming increasingly common and appears to be quite safe, the need for ECT is often a legitimate reason for hospitalization.

Hospitalization for Severe Personality Disorder

There are other instances, although more controversial, in which some experts continue to recommend hospitalization. A prime example is the treatment of a severe personality disorder called borderline personality disorder. More can be read about borderline personality disorder in Chapter 15. Briefly, this syndrome got its name because it was originally believed that such patients were on the "border" between neurosis and psychosis. They usually do not have much in the way of frank psychotic symptoms, such as hallucinations (hearing and seeing things that aren't there) or delusions (fixed, false beliefs, such as the conviction that Martians are following them around). Nevertheless, these patients have severe difficulty functioning, often suffering from tremendous levels of anger, depression, and anxiety. They have trouble forming friendships and relationships, alienate people because of incessant demands and hostility, and frequently make suicide attempts. Therapists generally do not like treating these patients and psychopharmacologists argue about which, if any, medications should be used.

Sometimes, often after the borderline patient makes a suicide gesture by superficially scratching her wrist or taking a small overdose of sleeping pills, hospitalization is recommended. It is not always clear, however, what purpose the hospitalization is going to serve. Personality disorders are, by definition, enduring traits that do not change in a matter of weeks or even months. Hence, hospitalizing a borderline patient for a few weeks or even two months will rarely result in a dramatic change. Sometimes, a short hospitalization results in less acute suicidal behavior and thus serves to avert a tragedy. In that case it is obviously fully justified as an emergency procedure.

More questionable, however, are long-term hospitalizations that sometimes last a year or more. Here, the idea is that intense and very frequent therapy in a highly structured environment for a long period of time can make a real change in the borderline personality syndrome. There is very little scientific evidence to prove that prolonged hospitalization really accomplishes that goal, although proponents of the practice can point to successful cases. Opponents say the patients would do just as well being treated as outpatients and that long-term hospitalization merely makes the borderline patient more infantile and dependent. Gradually, the controversy is becoming increasingly moot as fewer and fewer insurance companies will pay for long-term hospitalization and very few families can afford it.

Recently, scandals have been reported in the media involving unnecessary hospitalization of psychiatric patients, particularly adolescents. In these cases, patients were apparently coerced into admission to the hospital for unclear reasons and kept only until their health insurance ran out. Then, seemingly miraculously, the patient was dubbed cured and ready to be discharged. It is hard to know how extensive this practice has been, but even were it to be rare, it is outrageous. Just at the time when we feel we are making some headway in reassuring the world that psychiatric treatment is useful, safe, and humane, we have evidence of incarceration for profit under the disguise of psychiatric care. I am concerned that when patients truly need to be admitted to the hospital they will now become frightened that they are being conned and will have trouble getting out of the hospital. Here are some questions to ask before you (or a family member) are admitted to a psychiatric hospital:

---

1. Why is hospitalization needed? Is it absolutely clear that outpatient treatment would not be equally successful?
2. Who will take care of me while I am hospitalized? My regular doctor or a doctor assigned by the hospital? Will my outpatient doctor still be able to have influence over what treatment I receive?
3. What happens if I change my mind and want to get out of the hospital? Can I sign out the same day or is there a waiting period?
4. How long is it likely, given my condition and expected treatment, that I will remain in the hospital?
5. Who will take care of me when I leave the hospital?

There are clear reasons that psychiatric hospitalization can be necessary and beneficial; some are listed in Tables 18 and 19. It is very important, however, to ask as many questions as you wish before agreeing to go in.

TABLE 18
EMERGENCIES THAT MAY REQUIRE PSYCHIATRIC HOSPITALIZATION

- Active suicidal thinking with a plan for doing it
- Hearing voices (''command auditory hallucinations'') ordering the patient to commit a violent act
- Refusal to eat to the point that health is seriously jeopardized
- Any threat to physically harm another person

Types of Psychiatric Hospitals

From the movies, one gets the idea that there are two types of psychiatric hospitals. On one extreme are the kind of horrible, degrading hospitals depicted in movies like *The Snake Pit* and *One Flew Over the Cuckoo's Nest.* At the other extreme are the gorgeous sanitariums for very wealthy people as seen in the movie *Harvey.*

TABLE 19
SOME NONEMERGENCY REASONS FOR PSYCHIATRIC HOSPITALIZATION

- Coexisting medical problems make psychiatric treatment more risky for an outpatient.
- ECT is needed.
- Drug or alcohol treatment has not worked on an outpatient basis.
- The patient has a severe personality disorder that completely interferes with the ability to function and has not been amenable to outpatient therapy.

State Hospitals

Most states have psychiatric hospitals that are generally responsible for taking care of patients with schizophrenia and other very severe psychiatric illnesses. Before antipsychotic medications were introduced in the late 1950s, there was very little treatment that worked for patients with schizophrenia and some spent entire lifetimes in state psychiatric hospitals. Depending on how much money the taxpayers were willing to spend, these hospitals could either be horrible or quite acceptable. With the introduction of medications for schizophrenia, the population of patients with schizophrenia requiring lifelong hospitalization has drastically decreased. Today, only a handful of patients spend years in state hospitals; most remain for about a month when they have a psychotic decompensation (that is, the symptoms of a psychotic illness like schizophrenia flare up) and are then discharged for outpatient care. There is woefully too little provision of outpatient and rehabilitation services for patients discharged from state hospitals. Some enter a "revolving door" of continous readmission and discharge; others become homeless. In general (although this varies from state to state), state psychiatric hospitals do not charge patients but are an entitlement to citizens of the state who require hospitalization. There has been great difficulty attracting doctors, nurses, and social workers to work in state hospitals, usually because of relatively low salaries. Hence, in some situations the standard of care for psychotic patients in state hospitals is subpar, although many attempts are now made to ensure that these hospitals, while generally not fancy, provide adequate medical care and are safe.

General Hospitals

General hospitals often have a psychiatric unit. Such general hospitals may be municipal (usually owned by cities or counties), voluntary (private but not-for-profit), or for-profit institutions. Patients are usually admitted to these hospitals with a variety of diagnoses for relatively brief periods of time, usually less than one month. Commonly, patients with acute psychotic illnesses, serious life-threatening depression, and substance abuse are admitted to psychiatric units of general hospitals. In many cases, the patient must have health insurance that provides for psychiatric care. Many health insurance policies restrict the number of days of psychiatric hospitalization, even when they do not place such restrictions on other medical hospitalizations. This policy understandably enrages people who care about mental health and is constantly under attack.

Private Psychiatric Hospitals

Private, free-standing psychiatric hospitals are usually institutions that exist to make a profit. Many offer excellent care but they can be quite expensive, sometimes requiring payment above and beyond what health insurance will pay. Some of these private hospitals are famous, like Austin Riggs, Silver Hill, the Menninger Foundation, Paine Whitney, and Shepard Enoch Pratt. One of them, McLean's, is a major teaching hospital of Harvard Medical School. These hospitals usually have programs for a wide range of psychiatric problems.

The decision of which hospital to go to depends on many factors. These include the ability to pay, which one's personal physician has admitting privileges to, and which has an available bed. If you are going into the hospital electively, you can usually visit the hospital before deciding if you want to be admitted there. Also, extensively question your doctor about the hospital and hospitalization, including whether you have a choice as to which hospital to go to.

How, ultimately, should the choice of hospital be made? Do not pick a hospital merely because it is the most expensive, has the prettiest rooms, or the best swimming pool. You are not going into the hospital for a vacation, and some hospitals that advertise beautiful living conditions neglect the most up-to-date medical care that you need. On the other hand, do not pick a hospital that is an underfunded, municipal orphan that has trouble keeping its nurses and has a shortage of doctors. Pick one, if possible, that has an affiliation with a medical school department of psychiatry, that appears clean and well-appointed, and that promises you regular meetings with your own physician. Some state-operated psychiatric hospitals will actually fit this picture, so do not automatically rule out a nonprivate hospital.

Psychiatrists don't take psychiatric hospitalization lightly. It disrupts a person's life and can be frightening. But it is better to have a patient in the hospital than risk a suicide or miss the chance to finally end a drug addiction. Hospitalization should be considered carefully and used only when a clear benefit to the patient is foreseen.

PART III The
ILLNESSES

9.
How Psychiatric Diagnoses Are Made

THROUGHOUT THIS BOOK, I make a big deal about diagnosis. In the rest of medicine, this would seem like much ado about nothing. Making a diagnosis is considered the obvious first step in treating a patient with a complaint. Doctors are supposed to start off by asking a lot of questions, running tests, and then telling the patient what is wrong.

But for psychiatrists the idea of making a diagnosis was once actually controversial. Even today, there are some psychiatrists and psychologists who think too much emphasis is being placed on psychiatric diagnosis. They are wrong, but it is important to understand what the fuss is about in order to understand how psychiatric diagnoses are properly made. Diagnosis is the centerpiece of the New Psychiatry.

For psychoanalysts, who dominated American psychiatry through the 1960s, all emotional problems arise from unconscious conflicts. Although Freud used diagnostic terms like *depression, anxiety,* and *obsessive compulsive neuroses,* he was mainly interested in how psychological drives and defenses in the patient's unconscious mind produce emotional symptoms. It was more important to him to understand what lay deep beneath the surface of the patient's conscious mind than to derive distinct categories of observable psychiatric illnesses.

A German psychiatrist, Emil Kraeplin (1856–1926), is far less famous than Freud to the general public, but today many psychiatrists regard him as the first modern psychiatrist. Certainly, he placed great emphasis on trying to describe and distinguish different kinds of psychiatric disorders. One of his most important contributions was to describe the illness *dementia praecox,* which we today call *schizophrenia,* and to differentiate it from *manic depressive psychosis,* which we now call *bipolar mood disorder.*

But because the Freudians were much more influential than Kraeplin and his followers, psychiatric diagnosis was not given much importance throughout most of the twentieth century. Imagine medicine without diagnoses like diabetes, hypertension, gout, or cancer. That is essentially how psychiatrists operated—rather than concentrating on a diagnosis, the psychiatrist only attempted to understand how the patient's early childhood produced unconscious conflicts that lead to emotional symptoms.

Turning the Diagnostic Tide

There are many things that turned the tide on this, but one always sticks in my mind as an important turning point. Somebody noticed in the 1960s that American psychiatrists were far more likely to give patients with psychotic symptoms (such as hallucinations and delusions) the diagnosis of schizophrenia, while British psychiatrists were more likely to give them the diagnosis of manic depressive illness (today called bipolar mood disorder). Could it be that psychiatric illness varied so much between the two developed, English-speaking countries? Or were psychiatrists in America and Britain calling the same thing by a different name?

This wouldn't have mattered so much if there were no treatments for either or both illnesses. However, scientists had begun to test a new drug called lithium that seemed to work particularly well for manic depressive patients but was not terribly helpful for patients with schizophrenia. If there is a drug that treats a particular disorder, it becomes extremely important to correctly identify all the people who have that disorder.

The "U.S.–U.K. Study," published in the 1960s and 1970s, looked at the discrepancy between English and American doctors and essentially found that the British were more often correct. American psychiatrists tended to call all patients with psychotic symptoms schizophrenic, but more careful history-taking revealed that these patient actually suffered from alternating states of depression and mania. When manic, the bipolar patient can become psychotic and act very much like a patient with schizophrenia. But the mania is usually followed by a period of normal mood and then by a period of depression.

Another issue was also crucial in turning our attention to diagnosis. Through the 1970s, it was the official policy of the American Psychiatric Association to regard homosexuality as a mental illness. Gay people often bought this and thought of themselves as mentally disordered; therapists believed it was their proper role to attempt to change homosexual people to heterosexual.

But in the 1970s many people began to object. No one had any idea what makes some people gay and some people straight. Certainly, the designation of homosexuality as a psychiatric illness was not based on any scientific rationale. It would make equal sense to say people with brown eyes are mentally disordered. A huge fight broke out among psychiatrists. Out of this fight emerged a new leader in American psychiatry and an advocate of the importance of psychiatric diagnosis, Dr. Robert Spitzer. In 1973, Spitzer took the side of those who felt there should be scientific evidence before calling a condition a psychiatric illness. His side won and the American Psychiatric Association now holds a completely different position to its original one; homosexuality is no longer regarded as a diagnosis and it is considered unethical to influence a gay person to change his or her sexual orientation.

DSM-III *Changes Psychiatry Forever*

Spitzer became the world's leading psychiatric "nosologist"—the branch of medicine that deals with classification of illnesses and syndromes. He was named chairman of a task force to develop a new system of psychiatric diagnosis. When this system—called the *Diagnostic and Statistical Manual, Third Edition* (or *DSM-III*)—was released in 1980 it changed psychiatry forever.

DSM-III included a list of all psychiatric disorders and the criteria for making each diagnosis. It has since been revised twice—the so-called *DSM-III-R,* and now *DSM-IV.* But the real break came between *DSM-II*—the pre-Spitzer era—and *DSM-III.*

In 1952 the American Psychiatric Association first published a *DSM.* It listed various psychiatric disorders, but gave no criteria for making the diagnoses. It was largely ignored. *DSM-II* was published in 1968, again simply listing disorders without any real definitions. This left psychiatric diagnosis in the eye of the beholder—one clinician's obsessive neurosis was another's depression. The joke was that if you put a patient in a room with 50 psychiatrists and asked each to come up with a diagnosis you would get 51 different diagnoses—the patient would have one too.

DSM-III included two very controversial things. First, and foremost, it gave explicit criteria for making each of the diagnoses. A sample, for panic disorder, is given in Table 20 (taken actually from the most recent *DSM-IV* edition). As you can see, the disorder is explicitly defined and differentiated from other conditions. Most important, a patient must have at least a minimum number of symptoms to meet the criteria for the disorder. Some people have likened this to a Chinese menu method of making a psychiatric diagnosis—one from column A and one from column B (of course, Chinese restaurants don't seem to use that system much anymore).

Axis One and Axis Two

The second controversial aspect of *DSM-III* was to de-emphasize the word *neurosis.* Neurosis had been an important feature of psychoanalytic theory, defining a state of psychological disability produced by unconscious conflict but was not as severe as psychosis. The *DSM-III* eliminated this difference, focusing on individual syndromes, some of which—like schizophrenia—have psychotic symptoms and others—like panic disorder—do not. What was once called "neurosis" was renamed "personality disorder" and moved out of the main classification. The major psychiatric disorders are listed in the new *DSM* system in what is called "Axis I." The personality disorders are listed, with criteria for them, in "Axis II." A person with a major psychiatric illness, like bipolar mood disorder or social phobia, may or may not also have one of the Axis II personality disorders.

TABLE 20
*Diagnostic Criteria for Panic Disorder**

A. Both (1) and (2)
  (1) recurrent unexpected Panic Attacks
  (2) at least one of the attacks has been followed by 1 month (or more) of one (or more) of the following:
      (a) persistent concern about having additional attacks
      (b) worry about the implications of the attacks or its consequences (e.g., losing control, having a heart attack, "going crazy")
      (c) a significant change in behavior related to the attacks
B. Absence of Agoraphobia
C. The Panic Attacks are not due to the direct physiological effects of a substance (e.g., a drug of abuse, a medication) or a general medical condition (e.g., hyperthyroidism).
D. The Panic Attacks are not better accounted for by another mental disorder, such as Social Phobia (e.g., occurring on exposure to feared social situation), Specific Phobia (e.g., on exposure to a specific phobic situation), Obsessive-Compulsive Disorder (e.g., on exposure to dirt in someone with an obsession about contamination), Posttraumatic Stress Disorder (e.g., in response to stimuli associated with a severe stressor), or Separation Anxiety Disorder (e.g., in response to being away from home or close relatives).

*Reprinted with permission from the *Diagnostic and Statistical Manual of Mental Disorders, Fourth Edition,* Copyright 1994 American Psychiatric Association.

Controversies About DSM-III

Why were these things so controversial? First, the list of criteria for making each diagnosis is supposed to be "atheoretical." This means that the list includes only symptoms that are observable or that the patient reports. *DSM-III* supposedly does not involve any of the competing theories about what causes or "underlies" these different disorders. For example, to get the diagnosis of panic disorder listed in Table 20, the patient has to report having recurrent panic attacks. Each attack must have a certain minimum number of symptoms from the list (four), and the attacks must interfere with the patient's ability to function. Further, the attacks cannot be regularly provoked by the same stimulus—that would be a different psychiatric condition (phobia)—and they cannot be caused by another medical condition, like thyroid disease or epilepsy. Using these criteria it becomes fairly easy for clinicians seeing the same patient to agree whether or not the diagnosis is actually panic disorder. When a diagnosis is clear enough that clinicians can agree in most cases whether a patient does or does not have it, the diagnosis is technically said to be "reliable." Now, when the patient sits in the room with 50 psychiatrists and tells her story, most of them agree on the diagnosis.

But psychobiologists believe that panic attacks are caused by random firing of abnormally sensitive cells in the brain; cognitive and behavioral psychologists believe that panic attacks arise because patients have learned to entertain a pathological set of catastrophic thoughts; and psychoanalysts insist that panic attacks are produced by unconscious anger and fear that the anger will drive loved ones away. The psychobiologist wants *DSM-IV* to say that the panic attacks come out of the blue, without any provocation; the behaviorist wants *DSM-IV* to say the patients must have catastrophic thoughts and to list them; and the psychoanalyst wants the psychological defense mechanisms and unconscious conflicts to be listed.

In general, the psychoanalytic community was the most distressed by *DSM-III*. While biologically and behaviorally oriented psychiatrists generally think in terms of diagnoses, the psychoanalysts found *DSM-III* to be a sterile enterprise. Many complained that it reduces human personality to mere lists of symptoms and loses the richness of human experience. Further, the psychoanalysts argued that by focusing only on discrete syndromes and not on early rearing experiences, defenses, or the unconscious, *DSM-III* would encourage clinicians to treat only the superficial manifestations of psychiatric illness and not what they believe are the underlying causes.

To give you an example of how vituperative these debates became, I cannot resist telling a personal anecdote. Once, on vacation, I was waiting with my family on line at a barbecue to get my dinner. The man behind me struck up a conversation and told me he was a psychiatrist from the Boston area. It was shortly after the *DSM-III* had been published. He asked me what I did and I told him I was a psychiatrist from New York City. When he found out I worked at the same medical school as Robert Spitzer—Columbia University—he yelled so that everyone else on the line could hear: "That miserable Spitzer! He has ruined American psychiatry!" It didn't exactly make my dinner pleasant.

The DSM system is now so well entrenched that it rarely evokes that kind of passion among American psychiatrists any longer, although there are still a few who detest it. Given its widespread acceptance, it is very important for consumers of psychiatric care to understand exactly how it works. After explaining that I will review some of its important advantages and then its problems.

The Multiaxial System

Somewhere in the development of the *DSM* system it became apparent that all the information necessary to characterize a patient's illness could not be communicated by making a diagnosis based on the criteria given for each condition. First, there was the issue discussed above about what to do about the personality disorders. Remember that personality disorders are considered to be enduring traits a person exhibits that cause difficulty in living a successful and enjoyable life. Patients with the major psychiatric illnesses may or may not have personality disorders, and personality disorders may or may not influence the course of the major psychiatric illnesses. It seemed important to have criteria for the personality disorders, but the *DSM-III* committee wanted to make them separate from the major psychiatric illnesses. Thus, Axis Two.

Next, there was the question of coexisting medical problems. Psychiatrists are medical doctors and they wanted to make it clear that no psychiatric diagnosis could be complete without considering the physical health of the patient. Then, it was felt important by some to note whether any significant life stress had occurred in close proximity to the psychiatric illness. This is also somewhat controversial because increasingly many psychobiologists believe that genetics and biological factors are more important than life experiences in determining whether an individual will develop a psychiatric illness. Hence, the decision was made to list the existence and severity of life stressors separately when making a diagnosis.

Finally, many of the criteria sets for the various psychiatric illnesses require that, in order to make the diagnosis, the illness have a clear negative impact on the ability of the patient to function. Obsessive compulsive disorder is an example of an illness in which this is important. At its worse, a patient with obsessive compulsive disorder may spend his entire day carrying out compulsive rituals, like washing his hands hundreds of times and checking to be sure no dirt exists anywhere in the house. Obviously, this patient is severely functionally impaired. On the other hand, however, many people have a relatively benign compulsive ritual or two. How many people set the alarm clock before going to bed, turn off the light, and then feel compelled to check the clock one more time to be sure they have set it correctly? This is generally irrational behavior because the clock is always set correctly and the individual ought to learn after a while that the checks are unnecessary. Yet it should not be classified as a psychiatric illness because merely checking the alarm clock once a night does not result in any serious disruption of one's ability to function in life and certainly should not motivate anyone to see a psychiatrist. Hence, the degree to which a person's life is impaired is important and it was decided that that too should be considered separately when making a psychiatric diagnosis.

The result of this is what is called the "multiaxial system" for *DSM-III*

TABLE 21
THE AXES OF DSM-IV

Axis I	The major psychiatric diagnosis. Examples are depression, schizophrenia, alcoholism, anorexia nervosa.
Axis II	The personality disorders. Examples are obsessive compulsive, histrionic, antisocial, and borderline personality disorders. A patient can have an Axis I diagnosis and no Axis II diagnosis, an Axis II diagnosis and no Axis I diagnosis, or both.
Axis III	Nonpsychiatric, medical conditions that may be present.
Axis IV	Any life stresses that the patient may have experienced.
Axis V	The Global Assessment of Functioning (GAF) Scale. This scale rates the patient's overall ability to function on a scale from 100 (no problems, perfect functioning) down to 0 (imminent danger of committing suicide or complete inability to function).

and its successors. The "Axes" are listed in Table 21. Axis I is the major psychiatric illness; Axis II is the personality disorder; Axis III is the medical condition the patient may have; Axis IV is the life stress and its severity; and Axis V is called the "Global Assessment of Functioning" (GAF), which is a scale from 0 to 100, with 100 representing excellent functioning (which nobody has) and 0 complete inability to function (for someone, for example, who is so ill they remain institutionalized and bedridden).

In actual practice, psychiatrists tend to use Axis I and ignore the rest in many situations, but insurance companies and government agencies often insist that all five axes are listed when giving a complete psychiatric diagnosis. Naturally, patients may have no Axis II, III, or IV diagnoses and it is acceptable to say that.

Psychiatrists in the United States and in many countries around the world are now well trained in the *DSM* system. Typically, the psychiatrist will ask a patient questions attempting to find out which *DSM-III* Axis I disorder the patient has. Once the psychiatrist has the right combination of symptoms that meet the criteria for an illness in *DSM,* the diagnosis is made.

DSM-III and *IV:* What Are the Advantages?

The biggest advantage of the current *DSM* system is that it standardizes diagnoses. Because each diagnosis has a set of fairly straightforward criteria, each diagnosis now means the same thing to most people. When I say a patient has major depression, another doctor will be able to understand what I mean. Before the *DSM-III,* psychiatrists used many different names to describe the same thing. Now there is some consistency and reliability for diagnoses.

For the patient, this means that specific treatments can now be directed at specific illnesses. This makes it much easier to understand why a particular treatment is being recommended and also possible for the patient to recognize when specific symptoms are—or aren't—getting better.

This also has major advantages for scientists. Imagine what would have happened to scientists trying to find out the cause of diabetes if the term "diabetes" meant a blood sugar problem to some doctors, a heart problem to others, and a problem with vision to still others. In fact, some patients with diabetes do have problems with all three. If there was no general agreement about what defined diabetes, I can imagine one scientific group publishing a paper titled "Diabetes Is Caused by High Blood Sugar," another group publishing a paper called "Diabetes Is Caused by Poor Blood Supply to the Heart," and a third group publishing a paper called "Diabetes Is Caused by Narrowing of the Small Vessels in the Retina."

Similarly, psychiatric illnesses often involve abnormalities in many different areas of mental function. Patients with schizophrenia may feel sad, patients with depression may sometimes hear voices (hallucinations), and patients with anorexia nervosa can be very anxious. With this much overlap among different illnesses, it is clear that scientists need some criteria to establish which condition they are studying. Otherwise, they might inadvertently include a hodgepodge of patients with many different problems in a study and get very weird results. Unquestionably, therefore, *DSM-III* and its successors have made psychiatric research far more possible.

Now for the complaints about *DSM-IV.*

DSM-III and *IV:* What Are the Disadvantages?

A reasonable complaint about *DSM-III* and its successors is that they are regarded by many clinicians and scientists as being more definitive than its framers ever intended. When *DSM-III* was devised (and similarly when each of its successors was created), experts, gathered together in the various committees and subcommittees, reviewed all of the available scientific evidence in deciding which diagnoses should be included and what criteria would be laid out for making each diagnosis. But in many areas the data was not that good, it was just the best available. Hence, Spitzer and everyone else insisted that *DSM-III* diagnoses should not be considered to have biblical status. If someone did a research study on patients with "schizophrenia," for example, and found that some but not all of them seemed to have a particular abnormality, it could mean that there are subgroups among patients with schizophrenia that *DSM-III* doesn't know about. The researchers should not just throw their data away. If some patients with a mood disorder turn out to respond to a new antianxiety drug, it could mean that those "depressed" patients represent some category not yet recognized by *DSM-III*. It does not automatically mean that it is wrong to treat a depressed patient with an antianxiety drug if that is what good research shows might work.

Unfortunately, and perhaps predictably, *DSM-III* and its successors have been regarded as an absolute system of truth by some clinicians and scientists. Remember that it is rarely the case that we know what causes any psychiatric disorder and hence most of our diagnoses are based on what symptoms seem logical to group together; most of our treatments are based on what works. Although *DSM-III* is a powerful and well-researched system, it should not inhibit clinicians or scientists faced with difficult clinical situations from exercising their own judgment and creativity.

A second disadvantage is also felt to be an advantage by many: the atheoretical nature of *DSM-III*. Although I do not personally agree with this criticism, in fairness I will lay it out. Many people feel that psychiatrists have a special mission to regard all people as individuals and recognize the complexities of human experience. To them, the *DSM-III* is "reductionistic." It takes a human being with a life story and reduces him or her to a mere diagnosis based on a menu of symptoms. These critics complain about making "checklist" diagnoses and fret that careful interviews of patients will become obsolete in favor of sterile interactions between automaton-like clinicians and patients.

It is true that some clinicians do take the "checklist" approach to psychiatric diagnosis and this is wrong. But interestingly, I have watched Dr. Spitzer, the prime mover behind *DSM-III*, interview patients many times and seen him conduct thorough, personable interviews. Only after the interview is concluded does he use the *DSM-III* guidelines to organize the information collected. Nevertheless, if *DSM-III* does encourage clinicians to merely read from a checklist of symptoms and encourage "yes/no" answers only to each item, that is a bad thing.

The New Psychiatry and Diagnosis

According to the New Psychiatry, psychiatrists must act like doctors, and a critical part of this is to make a careful and specific diagnosis for each patient. Psychiatrists should not be held to any different standard than other physicians in making a diagnosis. All doctors should be careful to regard their patients as individuals and not as mere collections of symptoms. We encourage young surgeons, internists, and gynecologists to think of a patient's medical complaints in the context of the total life situation. But a heart attack is a heart attack whether it strikes a 50-year-old woman with three children, a 75-year-old man who once lived in Albania, or a 24-year-old woman who just received a big but stressful promotion at work. Similarly, depression is an awful illness that usually needs rapid treatment. In order to adhere to the New Psychiatry, psychiatrists must be sensitive to all of the individual nuances, but they also have to recognize a responsibility to make a diagnosis and start treatment.

In the end, then, I think *DSM-III* and *DSM-IV* have been among the most positive things to happen in psychiatry. The system forces psychiatrists and other mental health professionals to think logically about what patients have, to design rational treatment plans, and to approach research in a systematic way. It permits patients to understand more about their conditions and why certain treatment options are recommended. It may seem sterile, but in fact it is a useful tool that, in the hands of an appropriately warm and concerned clinician, can help turn a confusing muddle of symptoms into a coherent entity. As long as clinicians do not regard it as holy writ, I think it serves patients and their doctors very well.

How Is a Psychiatric Diagnosis Made?

In trying to make a diagnosis, psychiatrists rely on exactly the same bulwark as any other physician: the history. It may surprise many people to learn that despite all of our incredible modern biomedical technology, a medical history is still the cornerstone of all diagnoses. All the tools at the disposal of today's physician are used to confirm or rule out the diagnostic impression a doctor gets from asking the patient what is wrong.

To illustrate, let me give an example of a nonpsychiatric medical diagnosis that may at first seem to rely solely on the use of complex technology. A 34-year-old man has been having headaches. He sees his doctor. His doctor refers him to a neurologist. The neurologist sends him for a magnetic resonance imaging (MRI) scan of the head. The MRI scan shows a cyst in part of his brain. He has surgery, the cyst (fortunately not cancerous) is removed and he lives happily ever after.

It sounds from this story as if the diagnosis was based entirely on the MRI scan. You might imagine that no medical history-taking ever took place. In fact, by the time the neurologist ordered the MRI scan, she was already fairly certain that the patient had something growing in his brain and, moreover, was reasonably certain that it was not cancer. The MRI served to confirm her impression and gave additional information that permitted the surgeons to know where to cut. How did the neurologist arrive at this conclusion? By carefully questioning the patient, she ascertained a number of key factors about the type of pain he was having, how long he had experienced headaches, whether aspirin or other painkillers made it better, whether there was any family history of headaches, and so forth. Piecing together these bits of information directed the neurologist's attention toward the possibility of a tumor of some kind. This is almost always the way medical diagnoses are made. Otherwise, everyone who ever has a headache would wind up getting an MRI scan, which costs about $800. Usually, doctors order tests only after they have a pretty good idea what the problem is.

The Key Questions

Psychiatrists are no different. A psychiatric diagnosis is arrived at by asking questions in key categories. First, there is the "present illness." The psychiatrist will ask what problems the patient is having at the time of the first consultation and when they started. Sometimes the problems will be of recent origin and sometimes they may go back months or years in time. In cases in which the history of the present illness seems very long, the psychiatrist will try to figure out if there has been some recent change or worsening. Often in such cases the doctor will ask, "You have had these problems for a long time, but you only recently decided to see a psychiatrist, so what has happened recently that made you decide you might need psychiatric help?"

In completing the present-illness portion of getting the history, the psychiatrist will often conduct a review of psychiatric problems that the patient has not mentioned to be sure nothing has been missed. For example, if a patient is complaining of depression, after learning about the depression and how it has affected the patient's ability to function, the doctor will find out if the patient has had other psychiatric symptoms lately, such as severe anxiety, panic attacks, hallucinations, or obsessive thoughts. At the end of the present-illness section of the history the psychiatrist should have a detailed idea of all of the patient's current symptoms and complaints.

Next, the psychiatrist will inquire about the "past history." This will mean asking about all previous bouts of psychiatric illness. Has the patient been depressed before? Did she ever seek counseling in the past? Has she ever taken psychiatric drugs in the past? Is there a history of drug or alcohol abuse? In some situations the past history can dramatically change the diagnosis that might have been made if only the present illness had been elicited. For example, a patient may complain of depression and currently have all the features of a depressive illness. But in getting the history the psychiatrist may find out that not only did the patient have several other periods of similar depression in the past, he has also had episodes of mania in which he experienced a euphoric mood, boundless energy, and unrealistic optimism for prolonged periods of time. Now the diagnosis will be changed from depression to bipolar mood disorder (formerly called manic depressive illness).

Looking at the Family

The psychiatrist will also want to take a detailed family history of psychiatric illness before deciding on a diagnosis. There is very good evidence that some psychiatric illnesses tend to run in families. These include schizophrenia, bipolar mood disorder, major depression, panic disorder, obsessive compulsive disorder, and alcoholism. Also, there is some evidence that suicide can be familial. Hence, finding out that one or more blood relatives had a specific psychiatric illness can be an important clue in determining what the patient has. The use of family history information must be approached cautiously, however, because we do not yet know exactly how psychiatric illness is transmitted from one generation to the next. Some of it may actually involve abnormal genes, while other aspects of transmission of psychiatric illness may involve children learning certain abnormal patterns of behavior from their parents. Hence, it is always possible that a child and parent may both have psychiatric illness, but the illness may be different.

Nevertheless, family history can help, as it did in the following example.

Mary, a 23-year-old woman, was brought by her parents to see a psychiatrist. She had dropped out of college at the age of 19, worked as a store clerk for a year, then tried to return to college on two occasions but dropped out each time. Now she was living in her parents' house, spending most of her time watching television, eating to excess, and complaining that her head hurt. She looked glum and sometimes irritated during the psychiatric consultation and spoke as little as possible. She acknowledged having a great deal of anxiety, sometimes hearing voices that told her she was a terrible and ugly person, and wanting to sleep as much as possible. During two previous episodes in her life her parents reported that she was extremely excited, talked incoherently, and believed she was a special disciple of God. Those episodes lasted about a month each. Every time Mary would then return to her current glum and listless self.

This is a difficult diagnosis to make. At first glance, the diagnosis of schizophrenia seems logical. The patient has had a progressively downhill course since age 19. She has several psychotic symptoms, including auditory hallucinations (hearing voices) and delusions (believing she has special religious powers). She is isolated, withdrawn, and apathetic.

But in taking the complete history the psychiatrist learned that the patient's maternal grandmother and an uncle both had clearly defined bipolar mood disorder (formerly known as manic depressive illness) and both were successfully treated with lithium. Knowing this information the psychiatrist decided to consider more carefully the possibility that Mary was suffering from a severe form of bipolar disorder herself. He was able to establish that Mary currently felt very sad and guilty and had active suicidal thoughts. On the other hand, during the two more excited episodes she felt powerful, energetic, and euphoric. There were in fact periods of fairly normal functioning between these episodes. During these times Mary attempted to return to college. When she was high, she had grandiose delusions; when she was down, she had depressing hallucinations. The psychiatrist decided to diagnose bipolar mood disorder and considered that Mary currently had psychotic depression as part of this bipolar disorder. He initiated treatment with three medications: an antidepressant to relieve the depression, an antipsychotic to stop the hallucinations, and lithium to prevent future mood swings. In two weeks the voices stopped and four weeks later Mary's mood improved to the point that she was talking, sleeping, and eating less, and thinking about trying to return to school. Both the antipsychotic and antidepressant medications were gradually discontinued and Mary has been maintained on lithium for several years without disabling symptoms. In this situation, the family history was clearly of great benefit in establishing the psychiatric diagnosis.

Taking a Medical History

Another critical part of the history that needs to be taken before establishing a psychiatric diagnosis is the medical history. Many psychiatrists object to the term ''medical'' history because they feel that a psychiatric history is also a ''medical'' history, but most of us understand that by ''medical'' history we mean finding out if the patient has any physical illnesses or is taking any medications that might be responsible for the psychiatric complaints.

Sometimes, medical illness masquerades as psychiatric disorder. All that is apparent to the patient and doctor are the psychiatric symptoms. It is probably every psychiatrist's nightmare to miss a brain tumor or metabolic condition in a patient complaining of depression, anxiety, or other psychiatric condition. Hence, the psychiatrist must be very careful to assess the possibility of an underlying medical condition. Some psychiatrists will conduct their own physical examination, while others ask the patient to see an internist or general practitioner for this. Sometimes, the psychiatrist will want to have lab tests done, not because they are particularly helpful in establishing a psychiatric diagnosis but because they can help rule out a medical problem. Here is an example:

Jasmine, a 36-year-old telephone company employee, saw a psychiatrist for a complaint of depression. She never actually used the term to describe how she felt until her family doctor told her he thought that was what she was suffering from. Jasmine complained of having absolutely no energy and of feeling tired and fatigued all the time. She looked very slowed down to the psychiatrist, talking haltingly and even moving slowly. She said she had also been feeling very anxious and, despite the fact that she did not believe she was eating all that much more, that she had gained weight over the last few months. She also complained that she had no sex drive, that she had missed her period for several months, and that she had a lot of aches and pains. Something also seemed wrong with her hair.

The psychiatrist completed the consultation and told Jasmine she wanted to get one more medical test done before agreeing that depression was the proper diagnosis. As any first-year medical school student reading this has already probably guessed, Jasmine turned out to have an extremely low level of thyroid hormone in her blood. In fact, she was suffering from almost complete thyroid gland failure. All her symptoms could be explained by thyroid disease and all went away almost immediately after she was placed on thyroid hormone medication.

It is important to note, however, that such dramatic cases in which the psychiatrist plays Sherlock Holmes and uncovers a medical condition causing psychiatric symptoms are very uncommon. In the vast majority of cases no medical problem is found. Unfortunately, all too many patients see one doctor after another and undergo many tests—some of them incurring some health risks themselves—before finally accepting the fact that they have a psychiatric problem. It is crucial to be sure there are no serious medical problems before making a psychiatric diagnosis but equally important not to go on a medical adventure while delaying getting treatment for a psychiatric problem.

Getting back to the discussion of taking a history, by this point in interviewing a patient the psychiatrist should have a fairly good idea if there is an "Axis I" disorder according to *DSM-IV*. There is now probably enough information to determine if a major psychiatric illness such as depression, schizophrenia, or panic disorder is present. Also, an Axis III code can be made; this is merely the presence and severity of medical problems. But more information is going to be needed in order to decide if the patient has a personality disorder (Axis II), if there have been any important life stresses (Axis IV), and how well the patient has been functioning (Axis V). Although not all psychiatrists specifically think in terms of these axes, all should now turn their attention to a fuller understanding of the patient's life circumstances.

The Psychosocial History

Sometimes called the "psychosocial history," this part of the diagnostic interview begins at birth and extends to the present. The psychiatrist will be interested in learning some details about the patient's parents and siblings, what her childhood was like, whether she was a good student and had many friends, and whether there were psychological problems in childhood. The psychiatrist will ask about the patient's education, sexual history, hobbies, work history, and about current relationships. During this time, the psychiatrist will be trying to understand what stresses the patient has experienced that might have a bearing on her current complaints and how well she functions in personal and work situations. Often merely by listening to the patient talk the psychiatrist will get some feeling about what she is like.

Does the patient tend to make many self-disparaging comments or does she seem grandiose and self-involved? Does she talk about people in her life or seem isolated and lonely? A sense of the patient's personality will often come through during the diagnostic interview.

What the Psychiatrist Should Not Do

There are some things the psychiatrist is not (or at least should not be) doing during the interview. Psychiatrists are not here to judge whether a patient is right or wrong or good or bad. They also do not read hidden and perverse meanings into everything the patient is saying. The idea of the diagnostic interview is simply to establish a diagnosis and formulate a treatment plan. Patients should feel free and comfortable to tell the doctor the truth about everything.

The Mental Status Exam

Medical students and psychiatric residents are taught that at some point in the diagnostic interview they should conduct what is called "the mental status examination." When psychiatrists take the examination for board certification, they interview a patient and must do a mental status exam in order to pass. In actual practice, however, as psychiatrists become more and more experienced the mental status exam tends to become less and less formal.

The mental status exam is supposed to be the psychiatric version of a physical examination. Usually, after a doctor takes a medical history she whips out her stethoscope and begins to examine the patient. So, too, after getting the psychiatric history the psychiatrist is supposed to do the mental status exam. First, the psychiatrist notes the patient's physical appearance. Does he look sad, disheveled, or smell bad? Is he calm or agitated? Does he make eye contact? Next, the psychiatrist assesses the patient's mood and level of emotion by noting things like rate of speech, facial expression, tearfulness, and whether the patient reacts to happy and sad events with the appropriate emotion. Depressed patients will look glum, talk slowly, cry, and respond to every question with expressions of hopelessness and guilt. Manic patients seem irritable and euphoric, talk very fast, laugh a lot, and act as if everything is good news. Some patients with schizophrenia show very little emotion or react to sad news with inappropriate smiles. All of these observations are taken into account in determining mood for the mental status exam.

The next part of the mental status exam is usually a description of how the patient thinks. The psychiatrist notes whether the patient entertains psychotic thoughts and ideas (called delusions), whether he describes hallucinations, if what he says makes logical sense, or if he has obsessive ruminations. These observations help to indicate if the patient has a psychotic illness, like schizophrenia. After this, there is usually a notation about whether the patient appears to have any propensity for violence, such as entertaining suicidal thoughts or having an actual plan for committing suicide, or thinking about harming or even killing someone else. Then the psychiatrist usually decides if the patient seems to have any insight into his illness. Some patients with mania or schizophrenia, for example, do not think anything is wrong with them, while patients with depression or panic disorder often are acutely aware that they have a problem.

Finally, the psychiatrist assesses the possibility that the patient has an underlying neurological disorder by testing memory, the ability to do simple calculations, and whether the patient is oriented. To do this the psychiatrist is taught to first ask the patient if he knows the date and time, where he is, and whether he knows some basic facts like who the President of the United States is. Then, the psychiatrist will see if the patient can do simple arithmetic, remember the names of three objects in five minutes, and repeat a seven-digit number from memory. These are very gross tests of brain function and will only identify rather serious dementia or delirium states. Nevertheless, psychiatrists want to be sure that the patient is not suffering from a dementing illness, such as Alzheimer's disease, or a disease that can cause delirium, such as acute liver failure.

Medical students and residents often conduct the mental status examination as a separate part of the diagnostic interview, going through each step sequentially. Typically, more experienced psychiatrists get the information at various times during the interview. For example, they may ask about suicidal ideas during the present-illness part of the interview when the patient is talking about problems with depression and ask again later when inquiring about reasons for a previous hospitalization. Some psychiatrists will omit the memory and orientation questions in patients who are obviously alert and cognitively intact. Hence, it may not always be obvious that the psychiatrist is doing a mental status examination, but all competent psychiatrists can write one down about the patient when the interview is completed.

The elements of the diagnostic interview are listed in Table 22. It is important to remember that the order given in the table is only one possible way of proceeding and in some cases it is not necessary to ask questions in every category. If a patient starts off by saying, "I have never had a problem until last month when I had an anxiety attack," it is doubtful that the psychiatrist will spend much time on past psychiatric history. It is a good idea to review the table before seeing a psychiatrist, however, because it may help you remember important information. Be prepared to give a full explanation about your current symptoms and past history. Try to remember if any of your relatives ever suffered from psychiatric problems. Write down all the therapists and psychiatrists you ever saw and the names and doses of psychiatric medications you have taken. Try to obtain copies of medical records if you have recently seen doctors or have been hospitalized. The more information you can provide, the easier it will be to make the correct diagnosis and get treatment started.

TABLE 22
PARTS OF THE PSYCHIATRIC DIAGNOSTIC INTERVIEW

1. *The Present Illness:* All of the current symptoms and problems—essentially, the main reason the patient is coming to see the doctor. This will also usually include an inquiry about alcohol and drug use.
2. *Past Psychiatric History:* A complete and detailed list of all previous episodes of psychiatric difficulties, including any hospitalizations, previous therapies, and prior use of psychiatric drugs.
3. *Medical History:* A review of nonpsychiatric medical problems, allergies, hospitalizations, accidents, operations, and medications used.
4. *Family History:* Review of psychiatric illnesses in first-degree relatives, including history of suicide, substance abuse, and psychiatric hospitalization.
5. *Psychosocial History:* This portion is a review of the highlights of the patient's life, including characteristics of parents and siblings, early childhood experiences, education, relationships, marital and work history, hobbies and interests, sexual experience, and children.
6. *The Mental Status Examination:* This may be interspersed among the other parts of the diagnostic interview and includes an assessment of appearance, mood, thinking process, suicidal and violent ideas and plans, insight, intelligence, and memory.

Note that psychiatrists may get this information in different order and in some cases will not need to elicit information in all of these categories.

When More Information Is Needed

The psychiatric diagnostic interview is the basis for establishing a psychiatric diagnosis. At the conclusion of the interview the psychiatrist and patient may be able to agree on a *DSM-IV* diagnosis. In some cases, however, more information will be needed, as follows:

1. Some patients are unable to give enough information themselves to make a diagnosis possible, perhaps because they are too depressed to talk much or because they have a memory problem and cannot recall all the facts. Other patients may distort the history, often because of a psychotic illness such as schizophrenia or some forms of mania in which the illness itself creates a disturbance in the way the patient perceives and reports facts and information. In these cases the psychiatrist may need to obtain information from other sources, such as family members, other doctors and therapists, and old hospital records. Any time the psychiatrist discusses the

patient with a third party he must always be sure he does so with the full understanding and permission of the patient. It is optimal, however, if patients and families cooperate with the doctor and provide as much information as possible.

2. Sometimes it is difficult to decide if there is an underlying nonpsychiatric medical or neurological problem that is causing the apparent psychiatric disturbance. In this case the psychiatrist may ask for medical tests and/ or consultations with specialists in other medical areas. It is important to understand that there are, at present, no diagnostic tests for psychiatric illnesses themselves. Blood, urine, and X-ray tests may be requested to rule out other problems that may cause or complicate the psychiatric problem.

3. Personality disorders can be hard to diagnose. Patients do not come to the psychiatrist's office with complaints like ''I think I have borderline personality disorder'' or ''I have the following characteristics of an antisocial personality.'' Although we have criteria for making personality disorder diagnoses in *DSM-IV,* it often takes time for a psychiatrist to get the feeling and flavor of the way a patient behaves, thinks, and interacts with others to know for sure what the personality disorder problem is. For example, in the middle of a severe depression it may not be obvious that for most of a patient's life he has been self-involved, cold to others, grandiose, and unable to accept any criticism—all signs of a narcissistic personality disorder. Only after the depression has been treated do these personality traits become more apparent. On the other hand, a patient may seem shy, withdrawn, and afraid to engage in relationships: signs of what *DSM-IV* calls the ''avoidant personality disorder.'' In some cases, but not at all, the patient might also have the Axis I disorder called social phobia in which she experiences severe anxiety attacks in certain social situations. Once treated, the patient no longer avoids anything and the ''avoidant personality disorder'' mysteriously disappears.

For these reasons, it is sometimes necessary to extend the diagnostic interview to include further visits while more information is gathered. The psychiatrist may want to wait until past medical and psychiatric records can be obtained and may want to get the patient's permission to interview other caretakers and family members. Sometimes, it is necessary to see the patient himself several more times before being sure of the diagnosis. It is important, however, for the psychiatrist to be clear with the patient about what is going on. The patient should be told that more information is needed in order to get a firm diagnosis. Until that is done, treatment can only be symptomatic. That is, the psychiatrist can offer some therapeutic interventions to try and relieve immediate symptoms and problems. If a patient is having trouble making a critical life decision, for example, the psychiatrist need not wait to establish a firm diagnosis before trying to help the patient figure out what to do. If there are psychotic symptoms but it is hard to know if the patient has schizophrenia, mania, or Alzheimer's disease, the psychiatrist may decide to give antipsychotic medication to relieve those symptoms while still trying to make the definitive diagnosis. Nevertheless, no complete treatment plan is made until patient and doctor agree on the diagnosis.

Psychiatric Diagnosis: Concluding Remarks

The hallmarks, then, of making a psychiatric diagnosis are the careful, detailed psychiatric history and the use of rigorous diagnostic criteria. Our current diagnostic system, *DSM-IV,* isn't perfect by any means; it represents a compromise among many factors. But the *DSM* system forces the clinician to make a diagnosis and to think about treatment in a rational way. There is absolutely no reason why this has to be a sterile or dehumanizing approach. Just as a doctor can treat a person with diabetes either compassionately or coldly, a psychiatrist can treat a patient with depression as either a whole person or just a collection of symptoms that fit a set of criteria. Once the diagnosis is made, the psychiatrist has available a wide variety of treatment techniques and options that should be tailored not only to the patient's diagnosis but all the circumstances of his or her life situation. But without a diagnosis, treatment is usually idiosyncratic, blind, and inefficient. A diagnosis is a necessary, but not always sufficient, condition for proceeding with treatment. In the next several chapters I will review the main psychiatric illnesses and how they are treated.

10.
Depression

MORE THAN ONE out of every ten people will suffer a serious depression some time in their lives, yet depressed people feel no one is like them. They often think they deserve to feel depressed, as if they should be punished for some horrible crime they cannot even name. The idea that they ought to get help for their depression, that it is perfectly okay to be happy and look forward to the next day, seems a completely foreign notion.

It is true that everyone feels sad from time to time. Obviously, humans are programmed to feel down when sad things happen. Only a very callous person would smile during a real tragedy. The death of a loved one almost universally leads to prolonged melancholy. This is all part of normal human life and psychiatrists are not expected to change the real life adversities that naturally lead to sad feelings.

The New Psychiatry is firm that depression is an illness. At times in the past there has been a tendency to consider depression either as a personality trait, a "rite-of-passage" through various stages of development, or as a collection of bad mental habits. In fact, depression is a fairly easily recognized and diagnosed condition with a very high response to therapy. The New Psychiatry is also adamant that a variety of treatment approaches must be considered individually for each patient and then carefully and compassionately applied. These approaches will include, in varying degrees for each individual with depression, elements of psychoanalysis, cognitive and behavioral treatment, and medication.

Depression may or may not seem to begin after a real tragedy, but it is actually not all that important in making the diagnosis of depression to assess right away whether a real-life event was the immediate trigger. The important thing to know about "clinical depression," the kind of depression that psychiatrists are expected to treat, it that is takes on a life of its own. Most often, there does not seem to be any obvious reason why a patient became depressed; even when there is, the depression lasts longer and is more severe than the triggering event warrants. Just as we are programmed to react with sadness to sad events, we also have a tremendous capacity to recover from adversity and renew our interest in life. When this becomes impossible, it is likely that depression has set in.

Like many medical conditions—cancer, pneumonia, heart disease— depression covers a lot of ground and is not a single clinical entity. People who come to see a psychiatrist and say they are depressed are sometimes surprised when the doctor asks, "What exactly do you mean by depressed? What are you actually experiencing?" But there are numerous forms of depression, each with different characteristics and different courses. Depending on the type of depression, the treatment will vary. In addition to pure depression, there is also another main form of mood disorder called bipolar mood disorder. Formerly called "manic depressive illness," bipolar patients get both periods of depression and periods of elevated mood. So first let me describe five main types of depression that are summarized in Table 23. Bipolar mood disorder will be covered in the next chapter.

Depression: The Main Kinds

Major Depression

The hallmark of *major depression* is the complete inability of the patient to be cheered up by anything. Psychiatrists refer to this as a "nonreactive" mood. In major depression, regardless of how a person got to be depressed, there are no external events that provide relief. A person with major depression may get the most incredibly good news, but her mood will not budge an inch. Everything that happens, good or bad, is greeted with either indifference or dismay.

Along with the nonreactive mood, there are certain very common features of major depression. Here are the symptoms:

Symptoms of Major Depression
- The patient usually feels worse in the morning than at any other time of day. This is called "diurnal mood variation."
- The patient may fall asleep but then awaken many times during the night. Often, the patient wakes up many hours before he needs to and then cannot fall back to sleep. This is called "early morning awakening" or "terminal insomnia."
- The patient loses his appetite, has no interest in eating, and loses weight. Such weight loss can occasionally become life-threatening.
- The patient cannot concentrate. Typically, patients with major depression complain that they find themselves merely staring at the television set or words on a page but have no idea what is going on. Reading comprehension suffers, so do test scores.
- The patient feels tired and fatigued, with very little energy.
- The patient blames himself for things no one else would ever hold him responsible for and spends hours submerged in guilty ruminations.
- The patient feels that life is not worth living, that others would be better off if he was dead, and fantasizes about dying or being killed. Some patients actively contemplate suicide and make concrete plans for how they will kill themselves.

Major depression is a very serious illness. Often, a patient with major depression is someone in his or her forties, fifties, or older who has been relatively well all along until a sad and despondent mood slowly begins overcoming him. It may take several months before the full picture of major depression is obvious, but a patient with major depression usually seems to most people to have undergone a clear and obvious change. To the observer, the patient with major depression rarely smiles, looks pained, and moves and talks very slowly. This slowed-down appearance is called "psychomotor retardation." It simply means that the patient's mind and body seem at a relative standstill.

If it is not treated, major depression can be fatal. It is the leading cause of suicide. Indeed, every patient with major depression should be considered at risk. Sometimes major depression goes away by itself, but this is not to be counted on; treatment should almost always be initiated as quickly as possible. Because patients with major depression feel so terrible about themselves they may not think they deserve help and secretly believe that they should just be left to die. That is why psychiatrists always want the assistance of family members and friends in treating a patient with major depression.

Unfortunately, major depression tends to be a recurrent illness, so that when it is resolved—even with good treatment—it can recur. For that reason, once a person has suffered an episode of major depression he and his family should be vigilant for the warning signs that it is occurring again.

Bipolar Depression

Bipolar depression is essentially a major depression that occurs in a patient with *bipolar mood disorder* (formerly called manic depressive illness). That means the patient has alternating periods of manic highs and depression, usually separated by periods of normal mood. A person with bipolar illness usually starts out with an episode of depression. Sometimes this first episode of depression will end with a sudden swing to the high side and the diagnosis of bipolar mood disorder rather than major depression is made. Other patients may have several episodes of pure depression before experiencing their first mania.

Bipolar illness usually begins earlier in life than pure major depression, with the typical onset in the early twenties. The depressions that bipolar patients get are often extremely severe and there is a high risk for suicide if untreated. The features of bipolar depression are fairly similar to those of pure major depression, although some patients with bipolar depression become so lethargic that they sleep all of the time and do not experience the insomnia that is common to major depression.

Psychotic Depression

This is really a variant of major depression. In addition to most of the features of major depression, however, a patient with *psychotic depression* develops what are called "psychotic symptoms," usually hallucinations, delusions, or both. Psychotic symptoms are common to several psychiatric illnesses, including schizophrenia, mania, and some types of drug and alcohol intoxication. They are sometimes described as a "break with reality."

Hallucinations are usually auditory—that is, the patient hears voices when no one is talking. These voices are not loud noises or the patient's own thoughts, but seem to the patient as if someone is actually talking to him. Patients are often surprised that others cannot hear these auditory hallucinations. Visual hallucinations (seeing things) are less common than auditory hallucinations and olfactory hallucinations (smelling things), and tactile hallucinations (feeling things, usually crawling on the skin) are rare.

Delusions are fixed, false beliefs held by the patient. They have absolutely no basis in reality, but the patient cannot be talked out of them. One example is paranoid delusions, in which the patient believes that people are watching him, talking derisively about him, or forming plots to hurt him. People often misuse the term "paranoid" when they say things like, "I am paranoid about my boss" or "I am paranoid about going into that dangerous neighborhood." In this case, what they really mean is "afraid," not "paranoid." There are many other kinds of delusions, such as religious delusions (believing that one is a special messenger of God), delusions of responsibility (believing that one is responsible for events that actually have nothing to do with him, such as starting World War II or causing a famine in Africa), and somatic delusions (believing that one has things growing inside the body or that a body part is misshapen, for example). Again, it is important to stress that these are not simply exaggerations or fears and are not amenable to reason. A person with a somatic delusion is not simply a hypochondriac who frequently and wrongly believes she has a medical illness. The patient with a somatic delusion may believe there is a gigantic tumor growing in his stomach and that he can feel it, even though he looks fine and no one else can feel it. If an X ray is taken that is negative, the patient usually thinks the X ray was done incorrectly or that the doctors are lying and have switched the X rays.

When these psychotic symptoms occur as part of depression they have a characteristic quality. The hallucinations and delusions are in keeping with a depressed theme: the voices usually tell the patient he is a terrible person and should die and the delusions usually involve beliefs that the patient has done awful things and that people are planning to punish him. Depressed patients do not hear voices telling them they are God or have delusions that they are rich and famous and brilliant. Psychiatrists say that the hallucinations and delusions of psychotically depressed patients are "mood syntonic" or "mood congruent" to indicate that they are themselves depressing in nature.

Usually psychotic symptoms develop after the depression is already in place, although in some cases the first indication of a disturbance is hallucinations and delusions. Here is an example of psychotic depression.

TABLE 23
THE FIVE MAIN KINDS OF DEPRESSION

Features	Major	Bipolar
Sleep	Insomnia	Insomnia
Appetite	Decreased	Decreased
Worst time of day	Morning	Morning
Energy	Diminished	Diminished
Onset	Abrupt	Fluctuates with mania
Common age of onset	All, but can be any	Young adults
Ability to function	Impaired	Very impaired
Suicidal	Sometimes	Often
Mood reactive to external events	No	No
Loss of interest	Yes	Yes

An Example of Psychotic Depression. Mr. M. is a 52-year-old factory worker whose father committed suicide at the age of 59. He is married and has two children who are doing well in school. Mr. M. had been satisfied with his job and life circumstances, but six months prior to seeing a psychiatrist he began worrying about his job security, even though there had been absolutely no mention of a problem at work. Every time he saw a story about factory layoffs or hard economic times on the news he became despondent. His wife noticed that he looked worried all the time and seemed to be losing his appetite. He started complaining of various aches and pains and missed several Sunday morning bowling games, something he would never ordinarily do. His interest in sex diminished and he seemed listless and distracted.

One day his boss called him into the office and gently asked him if everything was all right because he looked ''pale and worried'' all the time. Mr. M. interpreted this to mean he was about to be fired and came home and burst into tears at the dinner table. He started waking up at three every morning and lost almost 20 pounds. One day there was an accident in the factory and one of his coworkers broke his arm. Mr. M. was actually in the lunchroom when it happened, but he became convinced that the accident was his fault. Several days later he told his wife that he had killed another worker and would soon be arrested. He stopped going to work and ordered his wife to stop answering the phone or the door, insisting each time it was the police coming to get him for murdering his coworker. One morning, Mr. M.'s wife woke up at five and noticed her

T A B L E 23 (CONT.)

Psychotic	Dysthymic	Atypical
Insomnia	Increased	Increased
Decreased	Increased or decreased	Increased
Morning	Evening	Evening
Diminished	Diminished	Diminished
Abrupt	Chronic	Chronic
Adults	Adolescent	Adolescent
None	Usually preserved	Usually preserved
Usually	Infrequent	Infrequent
No	Yes	Yes
Complete	No	No

husband was not in bed or in their room. She looked all over the house for him and then went outside. She found him sitting in the car in their garage with the motor running and a hose leading from the exhaust through a crack in a car window. Fortunately, Mr. M. was still conscious. His wife screamed and he jumped out of the car. She called the police, who promptly brought Mr. M. to the nearest hospital emergency room.

The case of Mr. M., dramatic as it may sound, is altogether too common. Of all the forms of depression, psychotic depression is the most dangerous and the most lethal. Notice that Mr. M. had no prior psychiatric history himself, but that his father had committed suicide, indicating a family history of serious depression.

The most tragic thing about Mr. M.'s case is that it was allowed to go to the point that a fatality almost occurred. Even before he tried to commit suicide, many people noticed that something was wrong; after all, he had lost 20 pounds, couldn't sleep, and looked sick. Yet, as often happens, no one dared suggest he see a doctor, let alone a psychiatrist. As a postscript to the story, let me say that Mr. M. was admitted to the hospital and treated with two different medications. Four weeks after the suicide attempt he was again smiling, eating, sleeping well, and enjoying himself. Fortunately, he lived to get the appropriate treatment.

Atypical Depression

The term *atypical depression* was originally coined to distinguish a fairly common illness from major depression. Foremost among the differences with major depression is the fact that the atypical depressed patient can usually be cheered up, at least temporarily, by positive events. Unlike patients with major depression, then, the atypical patient is said to have a "reactive mood." This does not mean that the cause of her depression is more likely to be an external, adverse life event or that the depression she experiences is mild. Patients with atypical depression usually do not have a clue how they got depressed in the first place and their depression can be very severe. "Reactive mood" simply means that the patient retains the capacity to experience happiness when something good happens. Usually, the relief from depression is brief and the patient slumps back into depression in a few hours or days.

In addition to reactive mood, other important features of atypical depression are:

- Extreme sensitivity to rejection and criticism
- A tendency to overeat, especially carbohydrates, when depressed
- A tendency to oversleep when depressed
- Extreme lethargy, often bordering on a feeling of physical paralysis
- Mood often worse in the evening than in the morning
- Anxiety symptoms, including anxiety attacks, are common

Notice again how some of these symptoms are different from those observed in major depression. For example, while patients with major depression tend to suffer from insomnia and lose their appetite, patients with atypical depression tend to oversleep and overeat. Patients with atypical depression usually do not get hospitalized because the illness is chronic and rarely reaches the crisis proportions that can occur with major depression. Nevertheless, atypical depression is serious, as can be seen from the following example.

An Example of Atypical Depression. Ms. T. is a 34-year-old investment analyst who came to see a psychiatrist only after her closest friend told her that she had recently been put on an antidepressant and felt better than she had in her whole life. Ms. T. never really considered herself to be a depressed person, but on questioning by the psychiatrist she was unable to remember any time in her life when she really felt happy. As a child she was shy and inhibited, although she did well in school. She started gaining weight in high school and this made her feel very unpopular. Because of this, she spent most of her free time studying and watching television and by college she was pretty much a loner. Ms. T. still did well in college, majoring in economics, then worked at a bank for two years, and obtained an M.B.A. degree. She became a fairly successful investment analyst, able to make a good living, and did make a friend at work.

However, she was so sensitive to criticism and so afraid of making mistakes that she rarely took even small risks at work and therefore was not seen as one of the top analysts at work, even though she was clearly one of the most intelligent. Romantically, Ms. T. was even less successful. She generally dressed in drab, poorly fitting clothes and rarely smiled. She often felt tired and preferred to sleep on weekends rather than go out. Occasionally she would get interested in a man, but if he did not call her a second time she would become severely despondent, spending days or even weeks crying and overeating. The psychiatrist diagnosed atypical depression and recommended psychotherapy and medication. These made a substantial difference in Ms. T.'s life, especially in her overall mood, which became much more consistently cheerful and optimistic.

Again, the contrast of this case with the case of Mr. M. who had psychotic major depression is obvious. Mr. M.'s depression had a relatively abrupt onset and rapidly became nearly catastrophic; Ms. T.'s depression lingered for years and although it disrupted her life a great deal it never threatened it. Nevertheless, both these cases of depression deserved evaluation and treatment. In Mr. M.'s case, the need for help became all too obvious when he nearly died; in Ms. T.'s case, the need for help became apparent only when she realized that a friend with a similar problem had been helped. Patients with atypical depression frequently fail to realize that there is much wrong with them; their depression becomes paradoxically like a comfortable companion. No one can or should force such a person to get help. Ms. T.'s decision to try and change her life was entirely voluntary, but to me it would be tragic for a person to live her entire life in a chronically depressed state and never even attempt to take advantage of treatment technologies that can help.

Dysthymia

Some people do not get well-delineated periods of depression but remain more or less depressed all the time. This is referred to as *dysthymia,* and it affects about 6 percent of the population during their lifetime. Some people refer to dysthymia as "low-grade" depression or "chronic" depression. People with dysthymia feel blue or "down in the dumps" more often than not, but usually are able to function. Hence, they may be so used to feeling depressed that they do not even recognize that anything is wrong. There is no sudden onset of symptoms or development of severe functional incapacitation as there is with major depression.

In the *DSM-IV,* a person with major depression or a person with dysthymia can also have atypical features. In this book, however, I have discussed atypical depression as if it is a separate condition. This is because the concept of atypical depression was originally created as specifically different from major depression, and dysthymia was created to convey the idea of a somewhat less serious but very lingering type of depression. To my mind, *DSM-IV* has gotten these things a bit mixed up. For the patient's perspective, it is important to understand that the treatment of atypical depression and of dysthymia is virtually identical and that in many cases dysthymia and atypical depression overlap in a given patient. You have atypical depression if you are able to maintain some reactivity of mood and have specific symptoms like increased sleep, increased appetite, rejection sensitivity, and extreme fatigue. You have dysthymia if you are almost always depressed but still are able to work or care for your family and still eat enough to stay healthy.

Depression: Are There Other Categories?

The five categories of depression—major, bipolar, psychotic, atypical, and dysthymia—which were just discussed in detail, were highlighted because they are the classifications that most psychiatrists currently use. Furthermore, dividing types of depression this way is important when deciding upon treatment plans. There are a number of other categories of depression that have been proposed and written about in the past. Some of them are:

Postpartum depression. There is actually considerable controversy about whether depression in a woman following the delivery of a child is really more common than depression in general. That is, depression is such a common illness—more than one in ten Americans get it in their lifetime—that it is bound to occur by chance after childbirth. Large epidemiological studies have generally failed to show any significant increase in depression in the postpartum period, but clinicians and new mothers have long suspected that this time is an especially vulnerable one for developing depression. Depression in the postpartum period must be distinguished from "the blues." Many women feel a bit let down after the baby is finally born and may experience sad, listless, and bored feelings. These are especially troubling to the new mother because everybody tells her that she should be ecstatic. Actually the people who usually say this are either men, or women who have had babies many years before and have forgotten that they themselves once had "the blues." Indeed, no one likes to be told how to feel.

One theory to explain "the blues" is that the new mother feels neglected once the baby is born; during pregnancy she was the center of attention, but once the baby has arrived she may feel she has been relegated to second place by her husband and family. Another theory—and the one I think is far more plausible—is that the tremendous hormonal changes that occur during labor and delivery have an effect on energy, concentration levels, and mood. All of this is different from a true depression. The "blues" usually do not impair the ability to function and last only a few days.

When depression does occur in the postpartum period it generally resembles major depression in most aspects. Infrequently, major depression in this period can become psychotic depression leading to such delusions as the mother believing the baby is not really hers or that it has not even been born. This fortunately is very rare, but psychotic postpartum depressions must be treated as a medical emergency. Both psychotic and nonpsychotic depressions in the postpartum period require vigorous psychiatric treatment, usually with both antidepressant medication and psychotherapy.

Involutional melancholia. This is a kind of depression that is supposed to be unique to elderly patients. The term is rarely used anymore because it is now clear that all it represents is the fact that major depression is very common in elderly people.

Secondary depression. Patients with other medical and psychiatric conditions may sometimes develop depression. For example, patients with cancer, diabetes, or AIDS can become depressed; so can patients suffering from alcohol abuse or bulimia. For theoretical reasons, some psychiatrists refer to depression that occurs after another illness as "secondary." The scientific value of this distinction is unclear. The depression still exists and may be no less severe despite its onset as a "secondary depression." In terms of treatment, it is obviously important when conducting a psychotherapy to know and use information about prior conditions that may have predisposed the patient to becoming depressed. When using antidepressant medication, however, it is less important to categorize depression as primary or secondary because both respond in about the same way to medications.

Depression: Is It Ever Normal?

To answer this question, we must first distinguish sadness from depression. It is, as I have stated above, normal to become sad when bad things or disappointments occur. In such cases, there is an obvious reason for feeling sad, the depressed mood clearly begins at the time of the adverse experience, and the sadness is time-limited. There are none of the so-called vegetative symptoms of depression, like prolonged insomnia, loss of appetite, or curtailed sex drive and no suicidal thoughts. This does not require treatment; the best thing is to have someone cheer you up.

Another common situation that must be distinguished from depression is what my mentor Donald F. Klein of Columbia University calls "demoralization." People who suffer from psychiatric conditions other than depression may eventually become so weary of living with their problems that they become discouraged and feel hopeless. For example, there are patients suffering from severe phobias who fear traveling even very short distances from home. These patients, described in more detail in Chapter 11, become virtual prisoners in their own homes and after years of this, especially if they have tried and failed to find relief through treatment, feel that life as a phobic person is too difficult and restricted to be worthwhile. This does require treatment, but is not the same situation as depression. Here, the patient would readily tell us that if the phobias were lifted she would feel deliriously happy. Such people usually do not suffer from vegetative signs of depression even though they may be very unhappy.

Finally, there are situations in which depression with all of its common clinical symptoms is expected and normal. The most obvious is after the death of a spouse, parent, or child (the last of which is believed to be the most serious loss a person can suffer emotionally). A bereaved person commonly develops a depression that is virtually indistinguishable from major depression. A person in this situation has a persistently depressed mood and is almost impossible to cheer up. He or she usually has no appetite, no energy, no interest in anything, and no idea what life is about. Insomnia is common. Interestingly, many people have observed that the depression following a loss is often worse if the relationship between the bereaved and the deceased was not good; somehow, a good marriage often prevents a widow or widower from protracted grieving.

Psychiatrists generally try not to treat bereavement too aggressively. There is an old myth that if you do anything to ease the symptoms of depression in a bereaved person you will only make the mourning period longer, as if the full experience of depression is necessary to complete the grieving process. This is basically nonsense and there is nothing wrong with, for example, giving a widow a sleeping pill if she cannot sleep after the death of her husband. Still, given the fact that the depression following bereavement is a normal reaction that usually goes away by itself and generally does not reach life-threatening proportions we typically do not intervene. It is important, however, not to turn our clinical back on bereaved people. Sometimes the depression does get serious enough to warrant attention when, for example, a widower stops eating or begins to contemplate suicide or if the depression lasts more than a few months without any signs of abatement. At this point, psychiatric consultation may be necessary.

Aside from the examples cited above, depression is really not normal and should not be merely accommodated. Rather, every attempt should be made to encourage a depressed person to get help as quickly as possible.

Depression: What Causes It

The Three Schools
Just as there are always three main ways to approach the treatment of a psychiatric illness, there are usually three main theoretical approaches to the cause of a psychiatric illness—psychoanalytic, cognitive/behavioral, and biological. These do not have to be mutually exclusive systems and the important thing is to attempt to explain an individual's illness so that she

can get the best possible treatment. It is important, however, to understand how different theoretical camps view the origins of depression.

Psychoanalytic Theories

Freud articulated the psychoanalytic idea of the origin of depression in his famous and brilliantly reasoned paper "Mourning and Melancholia." This has become the basis of psychoanalytic approaches to the cause of depression. Here, Freud explains that although both the mourning process and depression (melancholia) might come in response to a terrible loss, such as the death of a loved one, and share certain clinical features, such as profound sadness and loss of interest in the outside world, the two conditions are very different. Mourning is a natural and even necessary grieving process that resolves in a reasonable time. The melancholic, or depressed person as we now say, feels that his own self-regard and self-image have been massively lowered by the loss. Not only is the world poorer to this person, he too feels empty and worthless.

Freud then explains that the theory can be generalized to depressions that are not the result of an actual death, but rather of a loss that is entirely unconscious. According to Freud, we all carry around an idea of what we are supposed to be like and how we think we should perform. Hence, when we feel we have not lived up to our own standards, we feel we will be left, and the experience is as if someone we love has died. The result is, once again, depression.

There have been many modifications of this theory by psychoanalysts over the years, but it remains a powerful and compelling way to look at depression. The key concepts are the sense of a loss, ambivalence, anger directed inward against oneself, and the feeling of failing to live up to one's internal standards. Remember that most of this occurs outside of the conscious awareness of the patient with depression.

A Psychoanalytic Approach: The Case of John. John, the manager of the men's clothing department in a small department store in the Midwest, was born during the Depression. His father was a salesman and his mother a housewife. John has a younger brother and sister, another sister died in infancy four days after birth when John was six years old. He vaguely remembers that his mother stayed in her room for several weeks after the infant died, and that even when she came out of her room, she seemed tired and sad all of the time for months. Because she was in mourning, his mother was not available to respond to him as before. Like any normal child, John was angry that this baby had taken his mother away, but he also felt guilty about his angry feelings and worried that these feelings might have caused the baby to die. During that time John's father was often in a bad mood and repeatedly snapped at John for what seemed like minor infractions. When John's brother and later his sister were born in the next few years, he feared what might happen. Would his mother stay in her room and his father be mean to him again? Each time he tried his best to be especially good and do everything he possibly could around the house to help. He cleaned the kitchen, took out the garbage, and did all of the shopping.

In time, John became an especially organized and efficient young man and was often praised for the way he helped his parents and took care of his siblings. In school his teachers loved to have him around because he would always be the one to volunteer to erase the blackboards or to help pass out cookies at snacktime. John worked hard, but his grades were not always good and he did not get into college as he had hoped. Instead, he took a job after high school similar to his father's as a salesman and slowly worked his way up until at the age of 56 he was running his own department in a store. John married and had two sons of his own.

Recently, however, a 34-year-old man was appointed to a managerial position and became John's boss. John had hoped to be promoted to this position, but the younger man was a college graduate, which seemed to be a prerequisite for the job. One day, the already demoralized John came home and one of his sons asked him for a loan to help buy a new car. John really wanted to help, but knew he didn't have the money handy. Instead of saying this to his son, who would have been disappointed but not angry, he lectured him on the need to make his own way in the world and not depend on his parents anymore. This led to a big argument and for days father and son did not speak to each other. Over the next several weeks John became increasingly irritable over minor things and soon lapsed into a depression. He lost his appetite, could not sleep, and stopped having sex with his wife. At the urging of his wife, he finally went to see their family doctor who recognized immediately that John was suffering from major depression.

The features of John's case may seem very obvious to the reader, but in reality psychoanalysts have to search with their patients for clues that reveal what happened during their childhoods. Hence, the case of John should enable us to see how the theories of psychoanalysis operate to explain the cause of depression:

It is clear that when John's infant sister died at four days of age, his mother became depressed. John's father, already stressed by difficult financial times during the Depression, became even more tense and irritable with the family tragedy. The six-year-old John was unable to fathom all of the nuances of these events. He felt his father was criticizing him for not being a good boy and that to win back the affection of his parents his only hope was to be as good as possible. John developed the unconscious idea that complete devotion to duty is necessary to maintain the love of one's parents. His goal in life was to work hard and be as successful as possible in serving the boss so that the boss would always love him.

Hence, he was the apple of the teacher's eye as a child and a perfect employee as an adult. In real life, however, merely being good does not guarantee success. It did not get John good grades in high school, for example. And it could not ensure that he would always get the promotion he wanted. Hence, John's unconscious view of the world was shattered when his boss not only failed to promote him but gave the managerial job to a younger man with less experience. John's unconscious interpreted all of this as a failure to live up to his internal standards and a loss of love. According to psychoanalytic theory, depression was the natural sequelae (aftereffect).

I AM GOING to use the same case of John in the next two sections to show how cognitive/behavioral and biological theorists would see things completely differently. The main problem with the psychoanalytic theory for the cause of depression is that it is hard to prove. It makes a compelling story, one that is full of drama and compassion. And contrary to popular belief, it does not apply only to intellectuals living in Northeastern cities but to a working man living in the Midwest as well. But, as scientists and doctors we must always ask ourselves—"Is it true?" What seems obvious in the world of science and behavior may not always be correct. One might say that it seems obvious that the early life experience of John led to his depression when he was confronted by significant stress and disappointment in his adult life. Still, how do we know for sure if "A"—what happened to John at age six—really led to "B"—the depression he developed at age 56?

The fact is that we cannot be sure the theory is true. There are really no large-scale studies in which hundreds of patients with depression have been carefully studied from a psychoanalytic perspective and the theory proven correct. Often, psychoanalysts will attempt to argue that their theories are correct on the basis of one or two very compelling cases like John's. If it turns out that a psychoanalytic psychotherapy works in the case they feel further justified to assert that the theory is correct. But we must always be very careful not to argue from single case reports. Every doctor can tell a story of some theory or other of hers coming true, only to find that when many of the cases are studied the theory proves only inconsistently true. I cannot tell you how many times I have read a report in which a drug is given to a patient with a psychiatric condition and the patient gets all better. There was an elegant theoretical reason why the doctor thought the drug would work in the first place and finding that it did work made the doctor feel certain that his theory was ready for recognition by the Nobel Prize committee. Then, other people try the same drug on the same condition and it doesn't work. And I confess that from time to time I myself have been that doctor left holding the bag with what seemed to be a brilliant theory. Hence, I state again that what seems obvious and emotionally compelling may simply not be true as the sole explanation.

Should we believe the psychoanalytic theories at all? It is hard to turn our back on such a huge body of literature that has captured the attention of so many psychiatrists and psychologists for over 100 years. Still, we must be quite cautious in our acceptance of psychoanalytic theories for depression. As we will see in the next few pages, however, the situation is not all that much better with cognitive/behavioral and biological theories.

Cognitive/Behavioral Theories

Cognitive and behavioral theorists assert that depressions arise from a series of bad mental habits. This may sound at first like a ridiculously simple notion, but reflection will make it appear more serious. As we progress through life we learn an enormous number of things, some of which become routine. Few adults get into a car and carefully think through the steps of driving. We don't say to ourselves, "Insert the key into the ignition, step on the gas gently while turning the key, now release the key and step on the brake, check your rearview mirror. . . ." Rather, we have started a car so many times that it is almost like second nature, we do it automatically and without thinking. If we observe different people getting into their cars, however, we will notice many small, individual differences. Some people adjust the rearview mirror immediately after getting behind the wheel, others pump the accelerator once, twice, or three times. I always reach for the handle that moves the seat back, even though if I thought about it I would realize that no one else has driven the car since the last time I did.

There are lots of different factors that go into determining the series of steps an individual takes before starting the car. Some have to do with the habits of whoever taught us to drive; these are likely to be influential and we probably copy many of them. Copying the behaviors of others is called "modeling" by behaviorists and is a type of learning. Other behaviors may have perfectly rational explanations. My wife is shorter than I am and when she drives the car she always moves the seat up. It has therefore become a habit of mine to reach for the lever every time I get into the car.

If there can be so much complexity involved in a simple process like starting the car, imagine how complicated must be the various thoughts and actions a person characteristically develops when facing a stressful situation. We are likely to have modeled many reactions on those of people close to us, including parents, siblings, teachers, and friends. The movies we watch and books we read are all going to influence us. The specific events that occur to us as we live life will also teach us a number of lessons and from them we will learn to act in certain ways.

Patients with depression, according to the cognitive/behavioral school of thought, have learned a series of maladaptive ways of reacting to the world, both in thought and in deed, that make them feel depressed. In some ways, as described in Chapter 3, cognitive/behavioral theorists are not all that interested in how a patient developed the thoughts and behaviors that they have. In this school of thought, lengthy searches for how things got to be the way they are rarely take place. Hence, while a psychoanalyst spends enormous amounts of time attempting to figure out what happened in a patient's early childhood that led him to become depressed, the behaviorist is more interested in identifying the current, distorted thoughts and actions that keep the depression going.

What kinds of maladaptive thoughts and actions do depressed patients have? One of the nice things about cognitive/behavioral theories is that they attempt to be quite specific and based on data. Hence, behaviorists have attempted to collect data on how depressed people actually react, think, and behave. In general, depressed patients tend to have automatic thoughts that cast the worst possible light on every possible event. Even when there are several alternative explanations, depressed people have a penchant for picking the one interpretation that is guaranteed to make them feel bad. Often, they are not directly aware of this. They are convinced that their interpretation is the only possible one. Hence, the depressed person has a selective way of viewing the world. She is prone to "all or nothing" ways of thinking in which she tells herself that if she is not able to accomplish every aspect of a task then she has failed completely. In this way, a depressed patient always sets herself up for failure. Depressed people also exaggerate the consequences of bad events. If a bad thing happens, or if they predict a bad thing will happen, they are always convinced that the implications are far more serious than another person might. Finally, the actual behavior of depressed people serves to maintain their depression; they do none of the things that most of us do to get satisfaction and joy out of life. Nor do they make attempts to find out if their negative predictions and interpretations are actually accurate.

Behaviorists believe that these bad mental habits make a person prone to develop depression and, once depressed, to remain depressed. It is important to recognize that such ways of thinking and acting are deeply ingrained—they are very longstanding habits. You cannot simply tell a person who is depressed: "Stop thinking that way, don't have such depressed thoughts, and get out and enjoy yourself." Rather, cognitive therapy for depression is seen as a precise method of reeducating a depressed person so that she entertains fewer depressed thoughts. Although many people worked to develop these ideas, the most prominent cognitive theorist has been Professor Aaron Beck, whose book *The Cognitive Therapy of Depression* is a classic. One of Beck's students, Dr. David Burns, has written a version of Beck's work for the general audience called *Feeling Good,* which should be read by every person with depression.

Let us turn now to the case of John, described above in the section on psychoanalytic theories, and see how a cognitive/behavioral theorist would view his situation:

A Cognitive/Behavioral Approach: John Revisited.   John entered the office of a cognitive/behavioral therapist for a consultation and immediately stated, "I am sorry I am late, but I always have difficulty getting places on time." In fact, he was exactly two minutes late for his appointment, which was good for the doctor, who was actually five minutes behind schedule himself. When the doctor asked John to begin describing his problem, he first explained, "It is always hard for me to explain these things, I am not very good about talking about this kind of thing. That's why I get in so much trouble with my son. I really yelled at him about the car for nothing and screwed everything up. He is probably going to need you more than I do with a father like me coming down so hard on him. And now that I will probably lose my job, things are going to be terrible for him and my wife and my other kid. I guess I am here because my wife wants me to come, but there really isn't much you can do for me because I've messed everything up so badly already."

The consultant noted that within the span of just a few minutes John had made numerous self-critical statements and accused himself of things, like being late for the appointment and not being good at talking to a psychiatrist, that were unreasonable to feel guilty about. In taking the history, the consultant focused on John's constant penchant for negative self-appraisal. He berated himself for not getting better grades in high school, even though he had worked hard and tried his best. The therapist pointed out that it wasn't as if he spent his high school years taking drugs and shoplifting; he tried to get good grades and when it appeared he wasn't going to get into college, something that happens to millions of Americans, he made sure to get a good job. The consultant also examined John's belief that he was a failure at work and about to get fired. This was an example of "all or nothing thinking."

Because John was not going to get promoted, he leaped to the conclusion that he was a complete failure. In fact, John had done much better than most other men in managerial positions in small department stores. His income was solid and he was well liked by bosses, coworkers, and those who reported to him. John assumed that the reason he was not promoted was that his superiors were dissatisfied with him, but upon careful scrutiny it became obvious that there was absolutely no evidence of this. In fact, the president of the company had recently singled him out for praise as a valued employee and he had received a raise! There were lots of alternative reasons why John had not been given the promotion, one of which was that management was simply making a terrible mistake by going outside of the company. John had a right to be disappointed if he had hoped to be promoted, but his insistence that all of this represented evidence of major failure and shortcoming on his part was way off the mark. Furthermore, the consultant was able to discern that John had always been a very loving and attentive father and that his son, while annoyed at getting yelled at for wanting help buying a car, did not immediately come to despise his father. In fact, the son chalked the incident up to the fact that his father had been depressed and was already planning a strategy to convince John to give him the money at a later date.

This line of inquiry is clearly different from that taken by the psychoanalyst. The cognitive therapist is only minimally interested in early childhood events and disinterested in unconscious motivations. What interests the cognitive therapist is the actual thoughts and actions of the patient. Clearly, John is prone to incessant negative evaluations and these promote depression. He also takes no action to solve his problems, such as discussing his failure to get a promotion with his boss who has known him for more than a decade. Rather, he insulates himself with his self-criticisms and feels awful. The cognitive therapist comes to the same conclusion as the psychoanalyst about John: he is suffering from depression. But the cognitive therapist has an entirely different idea about why John is depressed. To the cognitive therapist, the depression is caused by John's bad habit of entertaining only catastrophic thoughts ("I am sure I am going to be fired," or "My son is going to hate me") and negative self-evaluations ("I am stupid and couldn't get into college" or "They won't promote me because I stink at what I do").

IN THE NEXT section we will discuss whether cognitive and behavioral therapy is likely to work for depression; now, the question arises whether the theory has any basis in fact. Do all the bad cognitions a man like John demonstrates actually cause his depression?

As was the case in trying to decide whether psychoanalytic theory is correct, we must honestly answer that there is precious little evidence that cognitive theories really explain how depression starts in the first place. Many clinicians argue that negative cognitions, like those John had, are merely symptoms of the depression. Like poor appetite and insomnia, depression clouds a person's mind and makes him focus only on bad thoughts and catastrophic predictions. This is obviously a chicken-and-egg controversy—does depression cause maladaptive cognitions or do maladaptive cognitions cause depression?

Furthermore, even if it is true that depressed people have negative cognitions first and then become depressed, we are still left with the thorny problem of what caused the negative cognitions in the first place. Do people learn to have negative cognitions by copying their parents?—a theory that would appeal to the cognitive/behavioral theorist; or because there are unconscious conflicts that manifest themselves as depressing thoughts?—the kind of theory psychoanalysts like; or because there is something wrong with the chemistry of the brain?—the psychobiologists' answer. It is impossible to answer these questions with certainty because to do so we would need to gather a rather large group of individuals who are not depressed but do have a clear tendency to entertain negative cognitions. Then, we would have to follow these individuals for many years to see if they get depressed at any greater rate than a matched group of nondepressed individuals who generally focus on optimistic, positive thoughts.

There is one way, however, that we might determine if cognitive theory of depression is correct and that is to see if the theory reliably predicts a good response to a particular treatment intervention—that is, cognitive therapists have designed a treatment strategy specifically based on the theory that depression is generated by negative cognitions. The therapy, as we will see shortly, is specifically designed to correct these negative cognitions. If the treatment works, scientists would say the theory it is based on has gained some validity. And, in fact, there is reasonably good evidence that, at least for mild depression, cognitive/behavioral therapy is quite successful for treating depression. This evidence is different from the "evidence" psycho-analysts offer in support of their treatment approaches. While psychoanalytic theorists generally produce individual case reports of depressed patients who have improved, cognitive theorists are able to point to more scientifically designed studies in which groups of patients undergo cognitive therapy in comparison to other forms of treatment. In these studies, cognitive therapy appears to work. Hence, there is scientific evidence that cognitive therapy may to some degree correctly describe the basis of some forms of depression.

Psychobiological Theories

Biological theories about psychiatric illness are based on the belief that malfunctions in the way the brain works cause the problem. These theories gained great attention during the 1960s when medications were introduced that successfully treat many psychiatric illnesses. In the case of depression, the antidepressant medications are unquestionably effective in relieving illness. Even before these medications were available, it was known for many years that producing a very brief convulsion in a depressed person could produce, in many cases, a dramatic result. Electroconvulsive therapy (ECT) is still the single most successful treatment for major depression, working in more than 80 percent of cases. The fact that physical therapies like antidepressant medication and ECT work led scientists to wonder if a physical malfunction in the brain might not be the cause of depression.

No one really knows, even today, exactly what ECT does in the brain, but the effects on the nervous system of antidepressant medications are better understood. The first group of antidepressant medications introduced in the

1960s—and many introduced since then—all had the property of increasing the brain levels of chemicals called neurotransmitters. Neurotransmitters are responsible for allowing brain signals to be transmitted from one brain cell—called a neuron—to the next. The antidepressant drugs increase the levels of two neurotransmitters in particular, one called noradrenaline and the other called serotonin. It was natural for scientists to wonder if a deficiency in noradrenaline or in serotonin or both might not be the cause of depression.

Years of research were spent trying to prove that neurotransmitter levels are reduced in depressed patients. We can now conclude that this hypothesis is probably wrong, for several reasons. One reason is that while the antidepressant drugs increase the levels of neurotransmitters in the brain after just a few days, they take many weeks to work in actually reversing depression. Another reason is that no one has convincingly shown that the levels of neurotransmitters are actually low in any of the bodily fluids available for study in depressed patients. This last objection must be tempered by the fact that neurotransmitter levels in blood, urine, or even in the spinal fluid are probably very poor reflections of what is actually going on in the brain. A final objection is that some antidepressants have been introduced in very recent years that do not seem to have much effect in raising the level of either serotonin or noradrenaline, but work in treating depression. For these reasons, the simple hypothesis that low levels of neurotransmitters cause depression and that increasing them with the antidepressant drugs cures depression is no longer entertained by most scientists. Instead, much more complex theories involving the way brain cells communicate are now being considered.

The Genetic Component in Depression

Another biological theory, which will come up over and over again as we discuss each psychiatric illness, is that depression may be genetic. There is, in fact, evidence that depression runs in families. A person with depression is more likely to have a first-degree relative who is depressed than is a person without depression. For most medical illnesses, this would be taken as fairly convincing evidence that genetics are at work, but for a psychiatric illness like depression, we cannot be sure how much is actually inherited and how much is learned by being around depressed parents or siblings for many years. We have already seen that psychoanalytic and cognitive/behavioral theorists believe that parental influences, either in the form of early childhood experiences or in transmitting learned behaviors, are important in shaping the tendency to become depressed. The work to tease apart nature from nurture in depression has not been done yet, and so the simple fact that one's parents were depressed does not necessarily mean that the depression was inherited.

Evidence for a Biology of Depression

There are, however, two fairly hard pieces of evidence that at least some forms of severe depression have a biological basis. One is the finding that severely depressed patients have an abnormality in the secretion of a hormone called cortisol. The other is the finding that people who attempt or complete suicide by violent means have low levels of the neurotransmitter serotonin in their brains.

Cortisol is a hormone secreted by the adrenal gland, which sits right on top of the kidney. It has many important biological functions, including participating in the regulation of the immunological response to infection and the way the body handles nutrients. In normal people, the secretion of cortisol by the adrenal gland peaks at the end of sleep and then falls through the day, reaching its nadir in early sleep. But almost 20 years ago, scientists, including the late Dr. Edward Sachar, discovered that patients with major depression and psychotic depression—but probably not dysthymia—do not shut off cortisol secretion appropriately and therefore secrete an excess amount over a period of 24 hours. More recently, a number of scientists, including Dr. Philip Gold of the National Institute of Mental Health, have shown that the problem with cortisol probably originates in the part of the brain called the hypothalamus, which is responsible for secreting regulatory hormones. One of these regulatory hormones, called cortisol-releasing hormone (CRH), appears to be produced in greater amounts by depressed patients than normal. Excessive amounts of CRH probably stimulate the hypersecretion of cortisol by the adrenal gland, which is seen in patients with major depression. Furthermore, it is known from animal studies that CRH by itself can produce many of the physical symptoms of depression, such as loss of appetite, sleeplessness, anxiety, and decreased sex drive.

The second finding has also been reproduced (what scientists call "replicated") by several different groups. Investigators, among them Dr. John Mann and the late Dr. Michael Stanley, have examined the brains of people who have died by violent suicide—that is by jumping out of a window or shooting themselves instead of taking a pill overdose—and found a clear decrease in the amount of brain serotonin compared to the normal brain. Most of these unfortunate patients had severe depressions before killing themselves, suggesting that low serotonin may indeed occur in the brains of severely depressed patients. Remember, however, that this low level of serotonin probably does not fully explain how antidepressant drugs work.

Psychobiologists now use some incredibly sophisticated technologies to study brain function in depression. This often leads to the impression that they are the "real" scientists and others, like the behaviorists, are the "soft" scientists. It is correct to believe that psychobiology is a very promising avenue to try to uncover what causes depression, but it must be acknowledged that no psychobiological theory of the cause of depression has yet been proven. One could even level the same criticism at the psychobiologists that is leveled at the cognitive/behavioral theorists: perhaps hypersecretion of cortisol and cortisol-releasing hormone and decreased brain serotonin are only artifacts, things that occur after depression sets in. At present, we have no way of knowing if this is, in fact, the case.

Let us now turn to the way in which a psychobiologist might view the case of John:

A Psychobiological Approach: John Once Again. For several months prior to seeing a psychiatrist, John had become noticeably moody and temperamental. According to his wife, and to John himself, he always had a tendency to be down on himself and somewhat pessimistic. Nevertheless, he had always been able to enjoy himself, had a healthy appetite, slept through the night, and had a good sex drive. His wife believed that the impending decision about who would be promoted at work might have been bothering John, but it was not obvious whether this was related to his depression because John seemed to be getting increasingly "blue" and "down" even before it was clear that a position was opening up at work.

By the time John saw a psychiatrist he was a sad-appearing, almost anguished man who wrung his hands when discussing his job and seemed visibly agitated. He had lost ten pounds and not slept more than four hours a night for over three weeks. It was hard for John to think of anything that could cheer him up and his wife confirmed that he had not smiled or laughed for quite some time. The consultant ascertained that John did not have any psychotic symptoms and that although he felt miserable and sometimes thought it would be just as well if he died, he had no intention of harming himself. The psychiatrist also reviewed John's medical history and learned that he had had a complete medical evaluation at work only two months before the consultation. Finally, the psychiatrist was interested to learn that both of John's parents had histories of depression. His mother became depressed after each of her pregnancies and required psychiatric treatment on two occasions for depression, including a time after she lost a newborn infant. John's father, although never treated for depression, apparently had several episodes of "black moods" when he had difficulty going to work and was noted to increase his alcohol intake. The psychiatrist considered the possibility that the disappointment about not getting promoted was an important contributing factor to John's depression, but nevertheless noted that although he might have had a longstanding tendency to be morose from time to time, John had never had a serious depression before that affected his performance at work or interfered with basic functions like eating and sleeping. The psychiatrist therefore diagnosed major depressive disorder and prescribed an antide-pressant medication.

ONCE AGAIN, the differences between the biologically oriented approach and the other approaches to depression are quite clear, although I have deliberately exaggerated these differences to make the point. Notice that the biologically oriented psychiatrist takes a history but is primarily interested in what is called "phenomenology"—that is, what the symptoms are and in what order they occurred. Essentially, this kind of psychiatrist takes a history like any physician, starting by asking, "Where does it hurt?" and "What is the pain like?" The psychiatrist is interested in this case in John's parents only insofar as there may or may not be a family history of depression. The psychiatrist considers negative cognitions to be purely the symptoms of the depression, not its cause, and is mainly interested in knowing at what point in the development of the current episode of depression these thoughts began.

This approach may seem coldhearted. After all, psychiatrists are supposed to be interested in a patient's life, dreams, and aspirations. Indeed, all too many biologically oriented psychiatrists do conduct consultations in a business-like manner, really becoming caricatures of surgeons and internists. They can sound like a *Dragnet* version of psychiatry—"Just the facts, ma'am." On the other hand, the approach can be just as warm as the cognitive or psychoanalyti-cally oriented approach, depending on the personality of the doctor. If you go to your family doctor with a sore throat, you can be treated coldly or warmly depending on the physician's attitude, not depending on whether he asks you about your parents or how you feel about having a sore throat.

The biological approach to depression is often criticized as being "super-ficial"—that is, psychoanalytically oriented and cognitive/behavioral thera-pists insist that approaching depression as an illness with a course and symptoms does not get "to the bottom of things." But as we have seen above, no one knows at this point what the "bottom" of depression really is, and so it is entirely disingenuous for anyone to claim that his approach offers the only true, bottom-to-top, once-and-for-all cure. Like the case with cognitive theory, the main point in favor of biological theory is the overwhelming body of good scientific evidence showing that antidepressant medication works. At present, therefore, our best indication of how good a theory of what causes depression is depends mainly on whether it predicts a good treatment response to a specific therapy. Both cognitive and medication treatments have been validated scientifically; psychoanalytic therapy for depression has not been so validated, although this is more because of lack of effort than because studies have shown that psychoanalytical therapy does *not* work.

A patient with depression, armed with some knowledge about what the different theoretical approaches are, must now decide what kind or kinds of treatment to accept. Once again, therefore, I will describe treatment of depression according to the three main psychiatric approaches.

Depression: What Are the Treatments?

All three of the main psychiatric treatments have been applied to depression.

Psychodynamic Psychotherapy

Psychodynamic psychotherapy is a long-term treatment that attempts to uncover the unconscious conflicts that cause the person to be depressed. Guided by psychoanalytic principles, this approach is based on the idea that depression stems from a sense of failing to live up to one's own ideals, unconscious fears of losing love and respect from others, and deep-rooted anger that the patient's conscious mind would find unacceptable if it knew about it in detail. The anger is therefore turned against the patient's own self and results in depression.

Because it takes many months to years to work, psychodynamic therapy can be recommended only for fairly mild depressions. A depression that threatens a person's life—that is, if the patient is suicidal or unable to eat—or even a depression that makes it acutely difficult for the patient to function in his expected roles is not appropriate for psychodynamic treatment. The kind of depression that may respond to psychodynamic psychotherapy is usually chronic and occurs in someone who is generally unhappy and confused but still able to work and form some relationships. Here is an example of a patient with depression who might benefit from psychodynamic psychotherapy:

Psychotherapy as a Treatment for Depression: An Example. Joan, a 36-year-old magazine editor, complained to a psychiatrist that all the men she goes out with are only interested in sex and cannot make commitments to longer-term relationships. She has a history of getting quickly infatuated with very handsome and successful men, becoming sexually involved with them after one or two dates, and then finding herself rejected after two or three months of a stormy courtship. She also complains that her female friends are mostly married and having children and therefore not "interested" in her. Finally, she thinks she is not fully appreciated at work for all of her "great talents." Joan thinks she should be offered a promotion at the magazine. As it is, she barely makes enough money to pay all her expenses and is frequently in debt. Despite these complaints, which have been ongoing for years, Joan makes it to work every day and enjoys several hobbies, including playing tennis and going to art galleries. When she gets most depressed over her life problems she tends to eat to great excess, often gaining ten pounds in slightly over one month, and sleeps most of the time when she is not at work. During these periods she often wishes she would just die, but has never contemplated actually killing herself.

Her psychiatrist learned that Joan's father was a very dashing, self-involved, and successful man who doted on Joan, despite the fact that he divorced her mother when Joan was a young girl and had two more marriages and many affairs after the first divorce. The psychiatrist gradually concluded, after several meetings with Joan, that she had a fixation on superficially attractive men who were clearly not interested in marriage. It was, in fact, quite neurotic for Joan to continually fall for men like that. It also turned out that Joan actually made little effort to engage her friends and did not push herself very much at work either. From her father she had internalized the idea that she was special and that all things should be presented to her in life with little effort on her part. Only when this unconscious view of life was threatened—as when she was rejected by a boyfriend or not doted upon at work—did she lapse into depression and, unconsciously, bitter anger that her omnipotent father was not taking better care of her.

Given the fact that Joan is not in any acute danger from her periodic depressions and that there are a number of unconscious conflicts, she might begin a course of psychodynamic psychotherapy. As described in Chapter 2, this will involve her coming to see the psychiatrist at least once—and usually two or more times—every week for a period of at least one year. The treatment will actually probably require at least three to five years. During this period of time, Joan will be assisted by the psychiatrist to explore her early childhood relationships with her parents, to recognize the sources of her narcissism and anger, and to learn to link these unconscious sources of conflict with the malfunctioning patterns of her everyday life. She will have to understand that no scientific studies have proven that psychodynamic psychotherapy is actually effective in treating depression, but that this approach has been recommended and used for nearly 100 years with many testimonials to its success. It is probably the only treatment approach that can deal with the relationship of early childhood events to adult life.

Cognitive Psychotherapy

Cognitive psychotherapy is a much briefer form of treatment than psychoanalytic psychotherapy and can be applied to more serious and acute depressions. Here, the therapist attempts to rapidly identify the maladaptive and negative thoughts, or cognitions, that the patient entertains and that maintain the depressed state. Most cognitive therapy includes *behavioral therapy,* so that the therapist also designs exercises and homework that will help the patient change his behavior in a direction that will help alleviate depression. These assignments include directing the patient to get out of bed every morning, force himself to eat, shower and dress neatly, do things that formerly were enjoyable even if the depression now makes them seem empty gestures, and avoid doing things that are clearly going to make him feel more depressed. A therapy that is somewhat related to cognitive/behavioral psychotherapy is called *interpersonal psychotherapy,* designed by Dr. Gerald Klerman and Dr. Myrna Weissman. This therapy specifically attempts to restore and improve relationships in the life of a depressed patient. Here is an example of the application of cognitive/behavioral psychotherapy to a depressed patient.

Cognitive Therapy as a Treatment for Depression: An Example. Allen, a 44-year-old insurance executive, began feeling depressed about one year ago. His symptoms included decreased enjoyment from most activities, insomnia, loss of appetite, and very consistent depressed mood. He had been fighting constantly with his wife of almost 15 years to the point that the couple considered separating. His business was doing poorly and he had to face the prospect of shutting it down. He had two sons, one of whom was doing only average work in school. The psychiatrist noted that Allen constantly referred to the fact that he had almost become a millionaire in his business, but now was facing losing everything. He also complained that his wife was too hard on him and criticized him for everything, including his business problems. He expressed disappointment over his son's performance at school and blamed himself, insisting that he was a "terrible father." Allen devoted all of his time, including weekends, to the office, trying to fix the business. He spent a small amount of time talking to an old friend, who had a very successful insurance business in another city. The psychiatrist quickly assembled the "facts" of Allen's situation, partly by meeting with his wife. First, Allen's business was probably not going to fail completely but, because of a few turns of bad luck and one or two less-than-perfect decisions, was indeed facing hard times. Second, Allen's wife was in fact a very understanding woman who made only one or two critical comments about Allen, mostly involving the fact that he seemed to be spending too much time in the office. Third, Allen's son was not failing in school, was a fairly happy and well-adjusted young man, and had a passion for sports. He was clearly not as intellectually gifted as his brother but was by no means a failure. Finally, the friend whom Allen spoke to about his business problems had always been very competitive with Allen and after the conversations Allen usually felt, if anything, worse.

The psychiatrist then began to systematically address every one of Allen's mistaken ideas and predictions. He helped Allen understand that his belief that his business was going to fail was an example of "all or nothing thinking," in this case, Allen believed that either he made a million dollars a years or he was bankrupt. He helped Allen correct his hypersensitive reactions to every comment his wife made, showing him that most of the time he misinterpreted what she said. The psychiatrist also directed Allen to think about his son more realistically: not everyone is a scholar, lots of people get Cs and Bs in grade school and go on to lead perfectly happy lives, and Allen was not responsible for his son's grades, although it would not hurt him to spend more time helping his son with his schoolwork. Finally, the therapist encouraged Allen to limit his conversations with his competitive friend and seek out a wider range of confidantes, including people who might be more supportive.

A recent study by the National Institute of Mental Health indicated that both cognitive/behavioral and interpersonal psychotherapy are effective for depressions in the mild range. This means that patients suffering from dysthymia and major depression may respond to cognitive/behavioral therapy. Patients with very severe major depression that involves suicidal intentions or significant weight loss or with either psychotic or bipolar depression should not be treated with cognitive/behavioral psychotherapy as the only approach.

Antidepressant Medication

Antidepressant medication is the fastest way to resolve a depression, usually working in two to six weeks. There are essentially three categories of antidepressant medication—heterocyclic, monoamine oxidase inhibitors (MAOIs), and selective serotonin reuptake inhibitors (SSRIs).

The traditional medications for major depression are the *heterocyclic antidepressants*, which include such brand names (generic names in parentheses) as Elavil (amitriptyline), Tofranil (imipramine), Norpramin (desimipramine), Sinequan (doxepin), Pamelor (nortriptyline), Ludiomil (maprotiline), Vivactil (protriptyline) and Desyrel (trazodone). These drugs generally take about four weeks to work. They are well tolerated by most patients but are problematic for people with certain heart conditions, with a rare form of glaucoma called narrow-angle glaucoma, and men with enlarged prostate glands. They have a number of mostly annoying and not dangerous adverse side effects, including causing dry mouth, constipation, urinary hesitancy, and dizziness when moving quickly from the sitting to standing position. Most of these drugs can cause weight gain. They are generally the first line of medication treatment for patients with severe major depression, psychotic depression, and bipolar depression (but see below for additional considerations in treating psychotic and bipolar depression).

Monoamine oxidase inhibitors (MAOIs) are the most potent antidepressants. The MAOIs include (generic names in parentheses) Nardil (phenelzine) and Parnate (tranylcypromine). They are tricky to administer, however, because patients who take them must be on a special diet that eliminates certain tyramine-containing foods—most notably cheese, aged meats, and several kinds of alcoholic beverages—and many other medications. They also have a number of side effects, including causing weight gain, insomnia, dizziness, and sometimes fluid in the joints (edema). Some patients get slightly high from them, a condition called hypomania. Because of the dietary restrictions and side effects, MAOIs are generally reserved for patients with dysthymia, atypical depression, or major depression who fail to respond to other classes of antidepressants. They should almost always be prescribed by a doctor with special expertise in psychopharmacology. Two additional MAOIs are Eldepryl (selegiline) and Aurorix (moclobemide). These medications appear to have fewer side effects than the traditional MAOIs and, in the case of Aurorix, no dietary restrictions are necessary. Eldepryl is actually sold in the U.S. for treatment of Parkinson's disease, while Aurorix is available only in Europe and Canada. It is likely that neither drug will prove as effective for depression as Nardil or Parnate.

The *selective serotonin reuptake inhibitors* (SSRIs) are the newest class of antidepressant and include Prozac (fluoxetine), Zoloft (sertraline), and Paxil (paroxetine). Luvox (fluvoxamine) is also an SSRI but is mainly marketed for treatment of an anxiety disorder called obsessive compulsive disorder. The two newest antidepressants, Effexor (venlafaxine) and Serzone (nefazodone) also have strong effects on the serotonin system, but each also has other features that make them novel. Wellbutrin (buproprion) is not an SSRI but seems to have the same clinical profile as the SSRIs. All of these drugs have far fewer side effects than either heterocyclics or MAOIs. A recent campaign by several cults to discredit Prozac has proven to be entirely fraudulent; these drugs do not increase the risk of suicide or violent behavior and in fact can be administered to almost all patients with depression. The side effects from Prozac, Zoloft, Paxil, Luvox, and Effexor seem limited to gastrointestinal upset (stomachaches, cramps, and diarrhea), sexual problems, and insomnia. Serzone may cause drowsiness. These usually go way after a week or two of taking them. Hypomania can occur, but is less common than with MAOIs. SSRIs take four to six weeks to work. They are now the drug treatment of choice for dysthymia and atypical depression and are often prescribed as the first drug for patients with major depression.

There are a few more drug treatments for depression that need to be discussed that do not fit neatly into the categories of heterocylic, MAOI, or SSRI.

Boosting the Antidepressant Response

Sometimes, a patient will have only a partial response to an antidepressant medication, even after a good four-to-six-week trial at an adequate dose. Before moving on to another medication or alternative therapy, many psychiatrists now try to boost the effectiveness of the antidepressant drug by adding a second medication. There are combinations of SSRIs and heterocyclic antidepressants that appear to work more effectively for some patients than either drug alone. Such combinations are tricky and can cause serious side effects, so they should only be attempted under the care of an experienced psychopharmacologist. Thyroid medication can sometimes be added to an antidepressant to yield a better response. The patient does not need to have any obvious disease of the thyroid gland for this to work. Finally, lithium, described in more detail in the next chapter for the treatment of bipolar mood disorder, is used to augment the effectiveness of antidepressants.

Anxiety Drugs and Depression

Patients with depression are often very anxious and sometimes the anxiety is more prominent than the depressed mood. For this reason, some clinicians, particularly nonpsychiatric physicians, prescribe antianxiety medications for depression. When depressed patients are given one of these drugs, like Valium or Xanax, they may actually feel better because they will sleep better and be calmer, but it is unlikely the depression will respond. Xanax, unlike other antianxiety medications in the benzodiazepine class (like Valium, Librium, and Ativan), has been said to have antidepressant properties, but these are weak and not to be relied upon. In general, antianxiety medications should never be the main treatment for depression. They may be given as adjunctive treatment to antidepressants to reduce agitation and improve sleep.

Light Therapy

Some patients with depression routinely become ill in the winter when the length of the day shortens. This is called seasonal affective disorder (SAD). There is evidence that treatment with bright light may be helpful. The first thing is to be sure there really is a seasonal aspect to the depression. Some patients think there is, but careful questioning and review of their history reveals that there have been periods of depression during the summer and winters when they felt fine. If SAD is really the diagnosis, light treatment is appropriate. There are differences of opinion among experts about how much light is needed and what time of day is best for treatment. Currently, one recommendation is to be in the room for 30 minutes with a source of 10,000 lux every morning from late fall to early spring. Gaze at the light occasionally, but do not look directly at it for sustained periods of time. I recommend that patients considering this see an ophthalmologist first because bright light theoretically could harm a person's retina if there is already disease there. The lights can be bought or rented from several companies. The patient should be followed regularly by a psychiatrist during the light treatment because some patients develop manic or hypomanic symptoms during it or at the end of the winter season.

Electroconvulsive Therapy

Electroconvulsive therapy (ECT)—sometimes called shock treatment—is the most effective antidepressant treatment, working in about 80 to 90 percent of patients with major, psychotic, and bipolar depression. Contrary to the image of ECT presented in the movie *One Flew Over the Cuckoos's Nest,* ECT is very safe. The patient is anesthetized for the procedure and does not actually have a physically obvious convulsion. There is no pain involved and memory is only temporarily disrupted; patients who have had ECT generally have completely normal memory function several weeks after the treatment, although they never remember the events on the actual day of the treatments. ECT is generally given in a series of 6 to 12, or sometimes more, treatments, usually administered every other day. The patient's consent is required. Because of the bad publicity given to ECT, severely depressed patients are generally deprived of this highly effective therapy; studies have shown that poor people are less likely to receive ECT than wealthy people with the same degree of depression. ECT is usually reserved for severely depressed patients who fail to respond to antidepressant medication and psychotherapy.

Treatment of Depression: The New Psychiatry Approach

We have now reviewed three theoretical approaches to understanding the cause of depression and the three corresponding treatment approaches. The following tables, 24–27, represent the New Psychiatry approach. Here, we take each of the five main types of depression and attempt to provide a treatment plan that integrates all of these theories and treatments. As the New Psychiatry dictates, the guiding principle is always what will work to provide the best result for the individual patient. Remember that these treatment plans are rough guidelines because there are thousands of individual variations that will best suit a particular person, but they should be useful as guides to getting the best therapy for depression.

Bipolar Mood Disorder

In the last chapter we discussed bipolar depression and noted that this is a kind of depression that occurs in people who also get the opposite kind of mood—mania. Now we turn to a fuller discussion of bipolar disorder.

Nearly one percent of the population suffers from "mood swings." This does not mean going from ordinary happiness to sadness, but experiencing

T A B L E 24
New Psychiatry Treatment for Major Depression

1. Begin one of the newer antidepressant medications—Prozac, Zoloft, Paxil, Lurox, Effexor, or Serzone. The choice will depend on individual factors. A few patients will do better starting with a heterocyclic, usually desipramine (Norpramin, Pertofrane) or nortriptyline (Aventyl, Pamelor).
2. Decide with the psychiatrist whether a course of cognitive psychotherapy would be helpful. This usually requires weekly sessions for 10 to 24 weeks.
3. Adjust the dose of medication and deal with adverse side effects over the next four to six weeks. Expect a significant relief from depression by then.
4. If response is good to medication, stay on it for at least six months. If there have been previous episodes of major depression, stay on the medication longer. At this point, consider with the psychiatrist whether psychodynamic psychotherapy might be helpful.
5. If response to medication is not good by six weeks, consider augmentation with another medication or change in antidepressant drug. Continue to consider various psychotherapies.
6. If response to several medications is inadequate and depression remains severe, consider ECT.

T A B L E 25
New Psychiatry Treatment for Bipolar Depression

1. We assume patient has already been diagnosed with bipolar mood disorder (see next chapter) and is having a breakthrough depression. Consider adjusting dose of primary medication for bipolar mood disorder, which is usually lithium or Depakote.
2. If step one fails or the doses of lithium or Depakote are already at maximum, check the thyroid level. If abnormal, treat with thyroid replacement. If normal and depression is significant, an antidepressant can be started. Wellbutrin is an excellent choice because it may have a lower potential to cause mania than other antidepressants. Other choices are Paxil, Zoloft, and Effexor. Some patients may need an MAO inhibitor.
3. Once depression resolves, taper off the antidepressant and continue lithium or Depakote.

TABLE 26

NEW PSYCHIATRY TREATMENT FOR PSYCHOTIC DEPRESSION

1. Consider emergency hospitalization. Patient is probably a very high risk to commit suicide.
2. Begin a heterocyclic antidepressant, usually either desipramine (Norpramin, Pertofrane) or nortriptyline (Aventyl, Pamelor), and an antipsychotic medication such as Haldol, Trilafon, or Risperdal. Advance the dose of both drugs to therapeutic levels.
3. The psychotic part of the psychotic depression should begin to resolve first over the next days to two weeks. If the depression component does not lift, lithium might be added.
4. If medication treatment fails, or if the patient is so depressed that he refuses to eat and may starve to death, ECT should be started.
5. After remission, antipsychotic medication can be tapered off, but antidepressant medication should be continued indefinitely.

TABLE 27

NEW PSYCHIATRY TREATMENT FOR DYSTHYMIA AND ATYPICAL DEPRESSION

1. Consider psychotherapy as a first option. This may be either psychodynamic or cognitive or a combination of techniques depending on the patient's individual situation, personality, and wish.
2. Medication can be considered as a first option as well, or can be reserved if patient does not respond to psychotherapy. Good first-line medications for dysthymia are Prozac, Zoloft, and Paxil. Effexor may also be effective.
3. Psychotherapy should demonstrate some effectiveness after several months. See the chapters in this book on psychotherapy for more information on how to judge if it is working.
4. If medication is used and it works, it is often possible to discontinue it after about six months, particularly if the patient is engaged in a useful psychotherapy.
5. A few patients with very severe dysthymia or atypical depression need to take medication for longer periods of time. Some will not respond to SSRIs and will need to take an MAO inhibitor like Nardil or Parnate.

discrete periods of both severe depression and abnormally elevated mood. There are two kinds of elevated mood that psychiatrists are concerned with, mania and the milder hypomania.

When a patient is manic he feels on top of the world. His self-esteem is at its highest and he feels confident and optimistic. This might sound like a good thing, except that the patient also talks so fast that no one can really follow what he is saying. His own thoughts race through his mind and the patient will often describe not being able to keep track of them himself. He seems to jump from one idea to another. He does not need to sleep, often going for days with just a few hours' sleep, and may be extremely irritable and nasty. The manic patient becomes hyperactive to an extraordinary degree, often spending wild amounts of money, making many long-distance phone calls, and engaging in reckless behavior. Entire life fortunes and businesses have been lost by manic patients. The patient may also engage in indiscriminate sexual behavior.

Sometimes the symptoms become psychotic in proportion. The patient's overconfidence becomes delusional and he starts believing he is God or Jesus or some other variant or that he has special magical powers. He may even begin having auditory hallucinations—hearing voices—telling him how great he is.

Hypomania is a mild form of mania. The patient is clearly suffering from an elevated mood and is irritable and expansive, but the condition is more subtle and less dangerous. A manic patient may go bankrupt in a matter of days, get arrested, or become infected with HIV because of promiscuous, unprotected sex; a hypomanic patient is not going to get into this degree of trouble but will usually manage to irritate almost everyone around him. He will be irritable and aggressive, interrupt everyone, and dominate every conversation. He will brag, talk fast, and spend too much money.

Neither of these conditions is desirable and both need treatment. Except in very rare cases, a patient who gets manic or hypomanic will always have corresponding periods of depression (the so-called bipolar depression mentioned earlier in this chapter). Typically, a bipolar patient alternates between being manic and being depressed. Each episode may last a week or longer, with periods of normal mood (called "euthymia") in between. A patient with four or more episodes of mania or depression per year is called a "rapid cycler." Patients who have had both full-blown mania and depression are said to have bipolar I disorder; those who have had depression and hypomania but never mania are said to have bipolar II disorder. Men and women have bipolar I disorder at an equal rate; bipolar II disorder is more common in women and more often also involves the personality disorders described in Chapter 15.

Bipolar Disorder: A Genetic Illness

There is a general consensus that bipolar disorder is a genetic illness. It clearly runs in families and almost certainly involves a biologically based abnormality in mood regulation. Illness usually begins in the early twenties and rarely disappears without treatment. Mania is often mistaken for schizophrenia and frequently requires hospitalization to control.

Lithium Therapy

The treatment of bipolar disorder almost always involves medication, and lithium is the mainstay of therapy. Discovered by an Australian physician, John Cade, and perfected by a Danish psychiatrist, Mogens Schou, lithium is a naturally occurring salt that unquestionably prevents both highs and lows in bipolar patients. All patients with bipolar illness should be treated first with lithium, unless special considerations (see below) apply.

Lithium comes in 300-mg pills and capsules (and a 450-mg extended-release preparation). The only way to know how much to take is to obtain a lithium blood level, that is, a blood test that tells the actual level of lithium in the body. The amount of lithium taken is adjusted to get a target blood level, usually around 0.8 mEg/1. If the level is too low, the drug will not work; if too high, serious side effects can occur.

Typically, the patient is started on 300 or 600 mg per day for the first few days and then a lithium level is obtained. If the level is too low, say 0.3, the dose is raised and then another level obtained a few days later. This is repeated until the target blood level is achieved.

Lithium can have a number of side effects. Many patients get an upset stomach from it at first, so it is best taken on a full stomach. It can increase urination and give a very fine hand tremor (which can be treated). If the lithium level gets too high, above 1.2, serious side effects become apparent including vomiting, diarrhea, confusion, and somnolence. This is a medical emergency and must be reported to the doctor immediately. However, lithium toxicity can almost always be avoided by carefully monitoring the lithium level. For the most part, patients do not mind taking lithium except for the almost inevitable weight gain it produces.

Routine blood tests are required before starting lithium and at approximate six-month intervals thereafter. This is because lithium can often interfere with thyroid hormone production (an easily treatable situation) and rarely impair kidney function (which mandates stopping the drug). As a precaution, blood tests are checked in these areas.

It will take a while to know if lithium is working. Without treatment, episodes of mania and depression may be spread apart by months, so the success of lithium therapy cannot be determined until enough time has elapsed to be sure that acute episodes of either have stopped occurring.

Occasionally, depression will occur even during relatively successful lithium therapy. The first thing to determine is if the patient has been faithfully taking her medication. A low lithium blood level will show that noncompliance is the problem. Sometimes, low thyroid levels caused by lithium can produce a state that looks like depression. This is usually quickly remedied by the addition of thyroid hormone medication. If the depression is not due to noncompliance or a thyroid problem, however, it may be necessary to add an antidepressant to the lithium.

Unfortunately, antidepressant medications have been accused of producing rapid cycling in bipolar patients—that is, the patient's depression initially responds, but then the patient goes in and out of mania and or depression even more rapidly than before. Although the risk of antidepressant-induced rapid cycling has probably been exaggerated, it is still wise to be cautious when giving a bipolar patient an antidepressant drug. Wellbutrin (buproprion) has been found by some psychiatrists to be less likely to produce mania in bipolar patients, so this is one good choice. No matter which antidepressant is selected, however, it is best to use it for a short time—that is, only as long as it takes for the depression to resolve. Then lithium alone should be relied on to prevent future episodes.

When Lithium Fails

Lithium only works in about 70 percent of bipolar patients. When it fails, there are two other drugs that are effective. Both are anticonvulsants. One is called Tegretol (carbamazepine) and the other is Depakote (divalproex sodium). Tegretol is often added to lithium when lithium has failed alone. It is a relatively safe and well-tolerated drug, but can cause visual disturbance and lightheadedness in some patients. Very rarely there is a suppression of the production of blood cells, called lymphocytes, that are necessary to fight infection. Therefore, it is necessary to do a blood test called the CBC (complete blood count) as well as the Tegretol blood level at several points during Tegretol treatment.

Increasingly, clinicians are using Depakote to treat bipolar patients. The Food and Drug Administration recently granted the manufacturer of Depakote the right to market it for the specific treatment of bipolar disorder. It is perhaps the best tolerated of the three medications for bipolar disorder, although weight gain, hair loss, and sedation can be problems. When Depakote was first introduced as an anticonvulsant several years ago, a few very seriously ill newborn infants who were on it and other medications died of liver failure. Because of this there are warnings about Depakote to watch for liver problems. In fact, to my knowledge no adult treated with Depakote has ever developed a serious liver problem from the drug. We do perform blood tests to check on liver function on a regular basis, as well as the CBC and Depakote blood level. Nevertheless, Depakote is increasingly proving to be a safe and effective drug for bipolar illness.

When acute mania occurs, lithium may take too long to settle things down. In this case, patients can be treated with a benzodiazepine drug (usually lorazepam—brand name Ativan) or with one of the antipsychotic drugs described in the chapter about schizophrenia. These drugs work quickly to calm the patient and the antipsychotic drugs also stop delusions and hallucinations. The antipsychotic drugs (such as Haldol, Thorazine, Risperdal, and Trilafon) should be given only until the patient has achieved control over her symptoms. Then, lithium, Tegretol, or Depakote should be relied on to prevent future symptoms.

It is often asked how long a patient with bipolar illness should remain on lithium. The answer is that we honestly do not know. Bipolar illness can be a lifetime problem and for some patients lithium therapy may be necessary for that long. Occasionally, a patient goes for a decade without the slightest hint of a mood disturbance, either up or down. If that patient is in a very stable life situation and is involved with people (usually family or very close friends) who will watch over her and call the doctor at the first sign of trouble, it may be worth the risk to try to discontinue medication. Otherwise, it is sensible to remain on lithium indefinitely, with regular visits to the doctor for checkups.

11.
The Anxiety Disorders

PERHAPS BECAUSE ANXIETY disorders are the most common psychiatric illnesses, they are sometimes treated as trivial nuisances rather than serious conditions. According to the National Institute of Mental Health's Epidemiological Catchment Area Survey, 27 percent of the adult American population has an anxiety disorder, according to the *DSM-III-R* criteria, during their lifetime.

How can so common a group of conditions be serious? Doesn't everybody get anxious? Isn't anxiety a good thing in many situations? Is this anything more than the psychiatric equivalent of the common cold?

Anxiety disorders, as I will explain, are indeed very serious and sometimes even completely incapacitating. It is, however, absolutely true that everyone gets anxious sometimes and that anxiety is often a very good thing.

Anxiety is a very primitive emotion in many ways; unlike depression or psychosis, it is quite obvious that species from the lowest parts of the animal kingdom get nervous. Believe it or not, goldfish respond to Valium with a reduction in anxiety level. Anxiety and its close relative, fear, alert us to dangerous situations and help us avoid harm. If you open the door to your home and smell smoke, you feel anxious almost before you know why; thanks to that anxiety you quickly check the kitchen, find the fire, and call the fire department. Imagine if you treated the smell of smoke casually and took your time! Anxiety makes students study, married people think twice about having affairs, and taxpayers pay their taxes. We fear the consequences of not studying, having extramarital relationships, and being tax delinquents. Most would agree that without anxiety we would have a society in which no one followed any rules. In fact, there is experimental evidence suggesting that sociopathic people actually have a defect in the ability to feel anxious during threatening situations. Without anxiety, there is little to prevent them from breaking the rules.

Interestingly, a small amount of anxiety appears to have a beneficial effect on brain function. If we measure the amount of blood that flows through the brain using modern brain-imaging techniques it can be shown that low levels of anxiety cause an increase in brain activity. The student who is a little worried she may not get a good grade if she doesn't study for a test actually has an improvement in the ability to concentrate and retain information.

But large amounts of anxiety have the opposite effect. Brain activity seems to decrease when people become excessively anxious, making it harder to pay attention and memorize things. The student who is beside himself with anxiety usually finds his worst fears come true: he does poorly on the test.

When we talk about anxiety disorders we absolutely do not mean the day-to-day anxieties and worries that are not only normal but positively beneficial; rather, we mean excessive amounts of anxiety that seem generated for no rhyme nor reason. It is fine to be a little worried about the grade on a test, that makes us study. But what is the point of wringing our hands and being paralyzed by fear?

One simple way, then, to think of anxiety disorders is that they involve anxiety for which there is no reasonable stimulus. If you are told you have a tumor, you are normal if you worry that it might be cancer. If you are worried that you have cancer after the doctor tells you there is nothing to be found, you might be suffering from an anxiety disorder.

Beyond this simple definition, however, is a more important set of distinctions: we now recognize several different kinds of anxiety disorders. Some of these can be fairly mild, while others may be very severe. The idea that anxiety disorders are like a cold, however, is patently incorrect. We now know that patients with some anxiety disorders can become severely limited in their ability to function or enjoy life. Also, anxiety disorders seem to increase the risk of developing alcohol and other drug addictions and of committing suicide. There is some evidence, although very shaky, that people with anxiety disorders may be more likely to develop a variety of serious nonpsychiatric medical problems, including heart disease. But even without these dire outcomes, it is clear that anxiety disorders cause a substantial amount of suffering and should never be ignored or trivialized.

The Six Types of Anxiety Disorder

There are six different anxiety disorders that I will discuss in detail. These are: *generalized anxiety disorder* (GAD), *panic disorder* (with or without agoraphobia), *social phobia, specific phobia, obsessive compulsive disorder* (OCD), and *posttraumatic stress disorder* (PTSD). In addition, I will review a particularly difficult situation in which a patient has both depression and an anxiety disorder at the same time. All these conditions have in common the basic definition of an anxiety disorder: anxiety out of proportion to the realistic threat. After that, however, each has its own set of specific criteria and special treatment considerations.

Anxiety Disorders: What Are the Different Kinds?

Table 28 lists the different types of anxiety disorder and basic criteria for each.

TABLE 28

THE ANXIETY DISORDERS

Disorder	Description
GENERALIZED ANXIETY DISORDER	Continuous anxiety for at least six months with needless worry, physical complaints, and tension.
PANIC DISORDER	Discrete panic attacks lasting 10 to 30 minutes, each characterized by severe physical symptoms and fear and occurring repetitively; often leads to phobias, including agoraphobia (fear of being alone).
SOCIAL PHOBIA	Anxiety attacks in social and/or performance situations; leads to avoidance or either specific situations or more generalized avoidance of most social interactions.
SPECIFIC PHOBIA	Irrational fear of a specific thing, situation or place—examples include arachnophobia (spiders), astrophobia (heights), claustrophobia (closed-in spaces); often normal in early childhood.
OBSESSIVE COMPULSIVE DISORDER	Need to complete repetitive, ritualistic behaviors that serve no rational purpose, such as washing over and over again and/or need to entertain persistent, senseless thoughts or images such as having to perform useless mathematical caulations or seeing an image of a dead person over and over again; although the patient realizes these obsessions and compulsions are useless, there is an inability to resist them without experiencing severe anxiety.
POSTTRAUMATIC STRESS DISORDER	A characteristic set of psychological symptoms following a real and terrible traumatic life experience that would be expected to produce symptoms in almost anyone. Such stresses include being a concentration camp survivor, being in an automobile accident in which many people are killed, or living through a violent crime. Ordinarily

adverse life experiences are not
included. The characteristic symptoms are
persistently reliving the experience (in
dreams or while awake or both), avoiding
situations reminiscent of the traumatic
event, losing the ability to experience
events with a full range of emotion, and
generalized anxiety.

Generalized Anxiety Disorder: Description

A person with generalized anxiety disorder (GAD) is more or less always anxious. The *DSM* criteria say this has to be the case for at least six months, but many patients with GAD have this problem from early childhood through adult life. The *DSM* criteria also say that to have GAD a patient must have ''excessive anxiety and worry . . . about a number of events or activities.'' Patients with GAD usually worry unrealistically about almost everything. Finally, the anxiety must interfere with the person's ability to function or enjoy life in order for it to be considered serious enough to warrant a diagnosis of GAD.

It is important to be clear about the terms *excessive* and *unrealistic*. An example of a patient with GAD will help.

A Case Study of Generalized Anxiety Disorder. Until he started having trouble at his job, Jim never really thought he had a psychiatric problem. But about one year before he came to see a psychiatrist for the first time, he had been promoted to vice-president at his company. At first he felt proud and excited to be recognized by his boss for his hard work and talents, but within a few days of getting the promotion he started worrying about all the new responsibilities he was going to have. He was afraid that other people at work would resent his promotion and undermine his efforts. He wondered if he really knew the business well enough to be a vice-president. He started brooding about all the times in the past that he didn't do a good job and wondered if the boss had taken them into account before deciding to promote him. Maybe he had merely ''pulled the wool'' over everybody's eyes.

Once in place as vice-president, Jim generally felt miserable all the time. He worried constantly that something would go wrong, that he would be fired, that he would become homeless and destitute. He had trouble falling asleep every night, lying in bed rehearsing every one of the day's events and anticipating tomorrow's stresses with dread. He began suffering from constant stomachaches, probably because he gulped down his food, and a variety of back and muscle aches. Sometimes he found other things to worry about besides his job, and in some ways this was a relief—worrying about what kind of report card his son was going to get, whether his car would pass inspection, or whether the consumer price index was going up at least gave him time off from worrying about work.

After several months of this he became convinced that he wasn't doing an adequate job at work and that it wasn't worth all the anxiety. He resolved to ask his boss for a demotion. In his mind this would be the safest thing to do—go back to an easier job before he completely screwed things up and got fired altogether. At least that way he would be sure his wife and child would be provided for. How would he ever get health insurance if he didn't work? Because he began complaining regularly of headaches and fatigue, his wife insisted that he see the family doctor. When writing his notes about Jim the doctor began: "Extremely tense 41-year-old man who talks very fast and seems to be worried about everything." The doctor examined Jim and did some tests. He found mild hypertension but nothing of a physical nature. Mostly, he found that Jim was anxious. The doctor and Jim's wife persuaded him that he should see a psychiatrist before voluntarily giving up his job.

With careful questioning, Jim revealed to the psychiatrist an almost lifelong history of worry, tension, and anxiety. Even in elementary school he would throw up on the day of tests and he could never bring himself to try out for sports because the anxiety made him quiver. From time to time Jim would get mildly depressed and stop worrying, but usually his mood improved enough to revivify his anxiety.

The striking thing about Jim was that almost none of his worries ever bore fruit. He did well on tests, went to college, and obviously was successful at work. His son got good report cards, his cars always passed inspection, and he always had enough money to pay the rent and buy food for his family. He knew this was the case; Jim understood that his worrying was excessive and rarely based on reality, but he insisted that the relatively good outcomes only applied to his *past* worries. The current worries seemed more serious and he could not be reassured that these too were excessive and unrealistic.

Clearly, Jim suffered from generalized anxiety disorder. His worry and anxiety were excessive, almost leading to his giving up his promotion, producing all kinds of physical disturbances, and lasting for more than six months. Because worrying had become such a way of life for him, he did not recognize that something was wrong. Only gradually, with treatment, did Jim come to understand that most people do not spend all their time worrying and that most people are able to recognize when their anxieties are getting out of hand. Some people like Jim resort to alcohol or other drugs to stay calm; others lapse into more serious bouts of depression. The latter patients with GAD seem to periodically decide that their worries are so terrible that everything is simply hopeless. Instead of worrying that things *might* turn out badly, they decide things are already awful and depression replaces anxiety. Improvement for them sometimes only means that their mood brightens sufficiently that they are able to resume worrying.

We don't really have enough research information about GAD, probably because most patients who have it either never get help or else are treated by nonpsychiatric physicians with such antianxiety drugs as Valium. Relatively few have made it into research studies. Consequently, we are not entirely sure at which age GAD starts, although it clearly can start in school-aged children and rarely begins for the first time after age 50. Males and females seem to be affected about as often.

In order to make the diagnosis *DSM-IV* requires, in addition to excessive worry and a minimum six-month course, the patient must also have three of the six symptoms listed in Table 29.

T A B L E 29
SIX SYMPTOMS OF GENERALIZED ANXIETY DISORDER

1. Restlessness or feeling keyed-up and on edge
2. Easy fatigability
3. Difficulty concentrating or "mind going blank" because of anxiety
4. Irritability
5. Muscle tension
6. Trouble falling or staying asleep

Hence, if you worry too much about nothing—or someone says you do who knows you well—and you have some of these six symptoms, you deserve a check-up by a psychiatrist. In the next section you will see that there are very good and successful treatments for GAD.

Generalized Anxiety Disorder: Treatment

Compared to most of the other anxiety disorders there is a clear lack of good research studies about the treatment of GAD. We know some things about which drugs work, a little about behavioral and cognitive psychotherapy, and almost nothing about psychodynamic or psychoanalytic psychotherapy. This may seem surprising because, after all, anxiety has been around for a long time and one would think that by now scientists from all the different treatment approaches would have tried to prove that their specific treatments are effective. The problem has been that very few studies have been done exclusively focused on the diagnosis of GAD. Studies merely involving "anxious patients" are not that helpful because this is a grabbag term that might include people with panic disorder or people who very recently had an adverse life event that made them worry, or even people with posttraumatic stress disorder. When we talk about GAD we want to know what treatments specifically work for people with at least six months of continuous anxiety and worry who are not depressed and have some of the six symptoms listed in Table 29. Here, unfortunately, there are gaps in our current scientific knowledge.

Medication for General Anxiety Disorder

We do know with great confidence that a class of antianxiety medication called the benzodiazepines is almost always an effective treatment for GAD. Some of the drugs in this class are almost household words—Valium, Librium, and Xanax. You can read more about them in Chapter 4 or in *The Essential Guide to Psychiatric Drugs*. After one or two doses of a benzodiazepine like Valium (diazepam), a patient with GAD will begin to feel less nervous, tense, and anxious. Physical symptoms of anxiety, such as headache and palpitations, will respond and after one week of taking them the GAD patient may be immensely improved.

Thus the quickest and surest way to control symptoms of GAD is to give a benzodiazepine. Why continue the discussion? The reason is that benzodiazepines have become among the most controversial medications in all of clinical medicine. In 1973 approximately 80 million prescriptions were written in the United States for these drugs; today, they are often maligned and although still frequently prescribed, benzodiazpines seem to induce almost as much anxiety in doctors and therapists as the anxiety in patients with GAD that the drugs relieve.

The problem is not usually side effects because benzodiazepines are fairly safe. They can cause sleepiness (many are prescribed as sleeping pills) and they interact with alcohol, so that the combination of Valium or Librium with a drink can really be a knockout. Occasionally a person can become disinhibited or confused with them, but this is rare. Basically, the benzodiazepines are very safe medically.

The Problem with Benzodiazepines

The problem is that benzodiazepines are hard to stop taking. Here is an example of the problem.

The Case of Mary. Mary, a 36-year-old nurse, has GAD. Her family doctor makes the diagnosis and prescribes one of the benzodiazepines, let us say Valium. He tells Mary to take a 5-mg pill twice a day, a very standard dose. Mary takes a Valium the next morning and notices that for the first time in years she feels calm about going to work. She is a little sleepy during the day, but actually feels she is working better and concentrating harder because her mind is not clogged with extraneous worries. She takes another Valium at bedtime and falls right off to sleep, something she has been unable to do for a long time. Mary continues to take the Valium twice daily and continues to feel better and better. After a week of this, the drug does not even make her feel sleepy during the day and she finds she can have a glass of wine at a party without an adverse consequence. After two weeks of this Mary thinks the drug is nearly a miracle, but her doctor has told her she should stop taking it after 14 days. She is fine without it for a day, but then Mary notices that her old worries, headaches, and stomach cramps are coming back. And for the first time in two weeks she tosses and turns for hours in bed, entertaining one needless concern after another, unable to fall asleep. After two days of this, Mary calls her doctor, who is in a hurry and tells her to go back on the Valium for another two weeks. Mary does and again almost immediately feels better. After two more weeks she calls the doctor and asks for a refill. At this point she remembers how hard it was to stop the first time and doesn't even raise the question of discontinuing the Valium with her doctor.

And so Mary keeps getting refills every month until she has been on the drug for six months, all the time not seeing the doctor but feeling well. She never takes more than two 5-mg pills a day (in fact, some days she forgets to take the bedtime dose and doesn't miss it). But after six months her doctor realizes how much time has elapsed and asks Mary to come in. He tells her that she should be better by now and that it is not good to take Valium for such a long time. Mary is instructed to stop the Valium. After a few days she begins feeling more anxious than she had before even starting the Valium. She goes through three nights of not sleeping at all, feels nauseated all day, and can barely concentrate on anything. She calls her doctor, but he refuses to give her anymore Valium. At this point, Mary calls a psychiatrist, who tells her she is suffering from a withdrawal reaction. Mary is put back on Valium and almost immediately feels better.

This is a somewhat extreme and dramatic example, but it nicely illustrates the main problem with the benzodiazepines when treating GAD. Although Mary got relief from her symptoms, she soon found herself unable to stop taking the medication. It is unclear if what she experienced at two weeks actually represented a withdrawal reaction; more likely, it was the return of the original anxiety disorder symptoms. But at the six-month point Mary clearly had a withdrawal reaction; her anxiety was worse than it had been before even starting medication and she had a new symptom—nausea. Such withdrawal reactions are not life-threatening, but Mary's was made worse by the fact that the doctor abruptly withdrew the medication instead of slowing tapering her off Valium over several weeks. If the patient remains off the benzodiazepine for several weeks, the withdrawal response usually subsides. Nevertheless, benzodiazepine withdrawal reactions are often very uncomfortable and may prompt the patient to go right back on the drug. Notice that, like most GAD patients treated with a benzodiazepine like Valium, Mary never needed to increase her dose of medication to get a therapeutic effect. The idea, promulgated in some people's minds by the book and movie *I'm Dancing As Fast As I Can,* that people who take drugs like Valium or Xanax wind up having to take continuously more and more drug to get the same antianxiety effect is incorrect. The problem with benzodiazepines is that it is often hard to get off them.

The withdrawal problem has raised an intense debate about the benzodiazepines. Opponents of them say that patients wind up hooked on them and that is a terrible thing. It is better, they say, to be anxious than to find yourself needing to take a drug all the time to avoid a withdrawal reaction. They have gone so far as to call the drugs "addicting," which is a technically incorrect use of the term, but their point is that an anxious person may so crave relief that he or she will do anything to feel better without considering the long-term consequences.

Proponents of benzodiazepines insist that GAD is a disabling and painful illness that rarely goes away without treatment. Benzodiazepines are medically safe and effective, so why worry if the patient needs to take them for a long time? Diabetics take insulin every day for a lifetime without anyone complaining.

Alternatives to Benzodiazepines

Before I give my own recommendation on using benzodiazepines, let me point out that there are medication alternatives. Several years ago an antianxiety drug that works entirely differently from the benzodiazepines was introduced; it is called BuSpar (buspirone). Exactly how buspirone works remains a mystery; it clearly does not bind to the receptor in the brain that benzodiazepines bind to and it does not affect the action of the brain's inhibitory neurotransmitter GABA they way benzodiazepines do. Possibly, BuSpar works by decreasing the action of the neurotransmitter serotonin, but this has not yet been proven. In any event, unlike the benzodiazepine antianxiety drugs, BuSpar is not sedating (that is, it does not cause sleepiness), is not an anticonvulsant, is not a muscle relaxant, and does not interact with alcohol. BuSpar actually has very few side effects, occasionally causing a mild headache or dizziness (but usually not). Perhaps of greatest importance, BuSpar can be stopped without any withdrawal syndrome.

In head-to-head comparisons with a standard benzodiazepine antianxiety drug, studies have shown that BuSpar works about as well. All of this makes BuSpar sound like a miracle drug for patients with GAD. Unfortunately, there is a catch. It takes at least two weeks, and probably closer to four, before BuSpar works. Patients started on BuSpar must take it three times a day for weeks before realizing an antianxiety effect. That can feel like a very long time to get relief from severe anxiety. Furthermore, no matter what the official drug studies showed, most clinicians have found that BuSpar is really not as potent as benzodiazepines such as Valium or Xanax; it works but it doesn't have the calming effect of the older drugs. Patients who have been successfully treated for GAD with benzodiazepines in the past usually find BuSpar to be a weak alternative.

Recently, another medication possibility has been introduced for the treatment of GAD—antidepressants. For many years anxiety experts insisted that antidepressant drugs worked for many forms of anxiety disorder but not for GAD. But in the last few years, some very well performed scientific studies find that antidepressants of the tricyclic class seem to be as, and possibly more, effective in treating nondepressed GAD patients than the benzodiazepines. Drugs in the tricyclic class include Tofranil (imipramine) and Elavil (amitriptyline). Once again, the benzodiazepines work faster than tricyclics, but after a few weeks recent studies find that GAD patients actually feel better with tricyclics than with benzodiazepines. As discussed in Chapter 4, however, tricyclics such as Tofranil have a number of unpleasant side effects—including dry mouth, constipation, weight gain, and blurry vision. Patients with certain heart rhythm problems often cannot take them.

A Medication Plan for Generalized Anxiety Disorder

At the present time, therefore, we have three types of medications that can be prescribed for generalized anxiety disorder (GAD): benzodiazepines (e.g., Valium, Librium, Xanax), BuSpar, and tricyclics such as Tofranil.

Here is my own specific recommendation. For a patient with GAD who has never received treatment with medication before, I would start with BuSpar at a dose of 5 mg three times daily. After several days this should be increased to a total of 20 mg a day, then to 25 mg three days later, and then another three days later to 30 mg a day (always in three equal doses of 10 mg each). This dose should be continued for a total of four weeks from the time BuSpar was first started. Patients who do not respond should then have the dose increased to 40 mg for a few days, then 50 mg if there is still no response, and then after several more days, if there is still no response, to 60 mg. As the dose is increased above 30 mg the chances of getting side effects increases, including nausea, dizziness, and headache, but in the great majority of cases there are no side effects to BuSpar.

If the patient does not respond at all to BuSpar, I would then try one of the tricyclic drugs. At this point our best evidence recommends the tricyclic drug Tofranil. Patients with a type of glaucoma called narrow-angle glaucoma, those with enlarged prostates, and some with heart problems may not be able to take Tofranil. The dose of Tofranil varies, but is usually started at 10 or 25 mg a day for anxious patients and then slowly raised to between 100 and 200 mg per day. Doses up to 300 mg are sometimes prescribed if necessary. There will be side effects, including dry mouth, constipation, and often dizziness upon standing. Patients may also experience weight gain, some urinary hesitancy, and increased sweating from Tofranil. It will take four to six weeks for the drug to work.

Finally, if the tricyclic does not work, and medication is still considered an important part of the treatment, a benzodiazepine should be prescribed. For most patients, the choice of which benzodiazepine does not really matter; elderly patients should generally only be prescribed the "short half-life" benzodiazepines—Xanax (alprazolam), Serax (oxazepam), or Ativan (lorazepam). The "long half-life" benzodiazepines—Valium (diazepam), Librium (chlordiazepoxide), and Tranxene (clorazepate) are just as good for non-elderly patients. These drugs will work quickly for almost all patients. Although the patient is often warned to be careful driving or operating machinery while taking benzodiazepines because they can make the patient sleepy, most people take benzodiazepines with little trouble. The interaction between benzodiazepines and alcohol means that a person taking benzodiazepines must be very careful with how much they drink; a little alcohol will go a much longer way toward causing intoxication and sedation when someone is also taking a benzodiazepine.

Of course, this plan of trying BuSpar, then Tofranil, then a benzodiazepine assumes that the patient can wait weeks for relief from anxiety. If the first two drugs don't work the patient may have to wait more than two months before getting on the benzodiazepine. Some patients can wait and prefer to try this route rather than jump right to the benzodiazepines with all of their withdrawal problems. Other patients need to get better faster; their anxiety may be so severe that they can't sleep at night or concentrate on anything during the day. In these cases it is prudent to go right to a benzodiazepine first.

Minimizing Benzodiazepine Problems

If a benzodiazepine is prescribed, there are several things that can be done to minimize withdrawal symptoms when it is time to stop it. These are summarized in Table 31. First, the lowest possible dose should be used. That means starting at a low dose (about 5 mg per day of Valium, 0.5 mg of Xanax, 25 mg of Librium, or 1 mg of Ativan) and waiting to see if that

TABLE 30

DRUGS USED TO TREAT GENERALIZED ANXIETY DISORDER
(Generic Names in Parentheses)

• BENZODIAZEPINES	Valium (diazepam), Librium (chlordiazepoxide), Xanax (alprazolam), Tranxene (clorazepate), Serax (oxazepam), Ativan (lorazepam)
• BUSPAR	(buspirone)
• TRICYCLICS	Tofranil (imipramine)

TABLE 31

STEPS TO MINIMIZE THE BENZODIAZEPINE WITHDRAWAL SYMPTOMS

1. Use the lowest *effective* dose.
2. Give the medication for the shortest possible time.
3. Do not take benzodiazepine if there is also an alcohol or other drug abuse problem.
4. Most important—*taper off the medication slowly.*

works. If not, higher doses can be given, but it is important not to overshoot. Make small increases in the dose and wait several days before the next dose increment. If a relatively high dose of a benzodiazepine does not work (about 15 mg per day of Valium, 3 mg of Xanax, 75 mg of Librium, or 3 mg of Ativan), it is reasonable to redo the initial consultation and make sure the illness is really generalized anxiety disorder. It is important to give enough drug to control the symptoms, but withdrawal symptoms are less severe the lower the dose. The key, then, is to prescribe the lowest *effective* dose.

It is also a good idea to keep the amount of time you take the benzodiazepine as short as possible. After taking a benzodiazepine for a few weeks, try lowering the dose or even stopping the drug and see if you can get by without it for a while. Perhaps by this point some of the psychotherapeutic techniques described in the next section of this chapter will have begun to work and less—or even no—drug can be used. There is good evidence that the shorter the period a benzodiazepine is taken, the less severe will be the withdrawal symptoms. On the other hand, for patients whose GAD is severe and whose symptoms can only be controlled with the medication, it is not fair or medically reasonable to insist on discontinuing the medication over and over again. Obviously, the patient and doctor must use careful judgment and decide together how long the benzodiazepine trial should be.

People who have alcohol or other drug problems usually have the most difficulty getting off benzodiazepines. Such patients should probably be prescribed benzodiazepines only if it is absolutely necessary and nothing else works.

Ultimately, the most important maneuver to minimize the benzodiazepine withdrawal syndrome is to taper off the medication slowly. Abrupt discontinuation causes the most severe symptoms, including the relatively dangerous ones like withdrawal seizures. After taking a benzodiazepine for several months, it is prudent to slowly lower the dose over another period of months. For example, Xanax is best discontinued by lowering the dose in very small weekly amounts, perhaps as slowly as 0.25 mg per week. There are studies indicating that adding certain medications during the withdrawal period may minimize the withdrawal symptoms, but most patients are able to get off benzodiazepines if the drug is tapered off slowly. Remember not to find yourself on a boat in the middle of the ocean without your benzodiazepine medication. When you are ready to stop, you and your doctor should make a reasonable tapering off schedule.

Medications have been well studied in the treatment of GAD, but there is evidence that some forms of psychotherapy may also be effective. In the next sections I will review these alternative methods and, finally, give the New Psychiatry recommendations.

Generalized Anxiety Disorder: Behavioral and Cognitive Therapies

As I explained earlier, there has been a remarkable lack of specific treatment research for GAD, especially using psychotherapies. We can make some statements, however, about some behavioral and cognitive therapy techniques. The basic format of cognitive and behavioral psychotherapy is discussed in more detail in Chapter 3.

Stress Management

Table 32 lists some of the behavioral and cognitive techniques that have been used for GAD. A technique called *stress management* should probably be applied to all patients with GAD, regardless of whether they decide to take medication or not.

We do not know to what degree stress actually produces GAD; psychobiologists believe GAD is an inherited disorder involving brain chemicals. Nevertheless, it is intuitively clear that stress cannot be good for a person suffering from GAD and probably makes the condition worse. Interestingly, many people with GAD do not recognize that their lives are filled with too much stress or that there are many things they do that actually increases the level of stress. Here is an example of one such patient.

T A B L E 32
BEHAVIORAL AND COGNITIVE THERAPIES FOR GAD

Stress management	Identifies stressful situations in patient's life and methods of eliminating them
Relaxation training	Progressive tightening and relaxing of individual muscle groups; alerts patient to one of the main physical events that occurs during anxiety (muscle tension), produces relaxation, and relieves anxiety-provoked muscle aches
Biofeedback	Uses physiological monitoring equipment to train patient to reduce physical arousal by controlling anxiety; of doubtful usefulness
Cognitive therapy	Identifies patient's automatic anxious thoughts and teaches methods of challenging them by adopting more realistic approaches

The Case of Roger.   Roger, a 42-year-old computer software developer for a midsize company, clearly had GAD when he sought psychiatric attention. His life was an anxious tumult with constant worry. He worried that he would be yelled at by his boss, that his reports would be flawed, that his ideas wouldn't work. He worried that his wife was angry at him, that he wasn't spending enough time with his children, that he would not be able to pay all his bills. He worried that his vacation wouldn't be fun. It was difficult for him to confront reality about these things: he had held the same job for 15 years, his boss rarely acted displeased with him, no one ever criticized his reports. Roger's wife had no more than the usual complaints about her husband and loved him very much, his children were doing fine, and he never missed paying a bill in his life. The psychiatrist ascertained that Roger had been an extremely anxious individual since at least early adult life, so that it was unlikely that anything in his current life was causing the condition. Still, there were a number of things that Roger had overlooked that clearly contributed to his anxiety. He habitually overslept, resulting in his getting to work a little late everyday. This resulted in constant worry that he would not have enough time to get his work done. In addition to this he did not have an answering machine at work, even though most of his coworkers had them, and therefore his day was constantly interrupted by phone calls. At home he was so fearful of neglecting his children that he virtually refused to spend any free time without them. Hence, he never relaxed on his own. He also turned vacation planning into a nightmare, assuming he was totally responsible for the whole family's good time.

Whether or not these habits caused Roger's generalized anxiety disorder is beside the point; the psychiatrist correctly assessed that Roger needed help identifying sources of stress in his life and minimizing them. Roger was instructed to put two alarm clocks in his room, set ten minutes apart, to make sure he did not oversleep. He bought an answering machine and restricted phone calls to discrete parts of the day. He scheduled, with great reluctance, reasonable periods of relaxation without the children during the week (his children were actually relieved to be free of their father for a few minutes here and there) and he agreed to share the planning of vacations with the rest of his family. All of this may sound easy, but it required a great deal of effort to show Roger that he had heaped demands on himself that other people found ways to avoid. Roger needed to go through a process of first recognizing the stress he provoked in his life and then agreeing to change some longstanding habits.

Relaxation Training

A technique that seems beneficial is *relaxation training*. One of the clear physiological manifestations of anxiety is a tightening of muscle groups throughout the body. This is the key reason anxious people get headaches: it actually has nothing to do with the brain but rather is caused by tightening of the temporalis muscle that surrounds the skull, causing both sharp stabbing and chronic dull pain. Relaxation training teaches patients how to relax muscles. Patients are usually instructed to sit in a comfortable chair in a quiet room and tense one muscle group after another in a regular sequence. First, for example, the muscles of the feet and lower leg are tensed as tight as possible, almost to the point of hurting, and then they are relaxed. Next, the same procedure is followed for upper leg muscles, then abdomen, chest, hands, arms, shoulders, neck, and finally head and facial muscles. Patients are told to go through this procedure at least once, and often twice, a day for several weeks. This accomplishes three things. First, it teaches patients to know when they are tense. Often, patients do not realize they are suffering from chronic muscle tension, but after practicing the relaxation technique they have a physical cue that alerts them to acute increases in anxiety. Second, the technique is relaxing. Patients can use it as one way of calming themselves during particularly anxious moments. Finally, relaxation training can result in a reduction in physical pain, especially headaches and backaches, that patients with GAD frequently experience.

Biofeedback

Biofeedback is sometimes advocated for anxious patients, but it is not a method I find particularly compelling. In the usual biofeedback procedure the patient is hooked up to physiological recording devices by small skin electrodes (they do not deliver any shocks) that are connected to machines that record heart rate, blood pressure, breathing, skin conductance (the amount of sweat produced by glands just under the skin), and muscle tension. The idea is to train the patient to relax sufficiently so that heart rate and blood pressure are lowered, breathing is slowed, skin conductance reduced, and muscle tension decreased. This is supposed to help the patient break the cycle of anxiety-producing physical discomfort and arousal that lead to anxiety. Very impressive equipment is sometimes used, with lots of whirring dials and bleeps. In actual fact, there is very little evidence that the machines help very much. Relaxation training without biofeedback appears to be simpler to deliver and at least as effective.

Cognitive Therapy

Stress management and relaxation training can be accomplished in just a few sessions. A more extended treatment involves cognitive therapy. As described in Chapter 3, cognitive therapy attempts to reorganize a patient's maladaptive thinking and approach to life. According to the cognitive theory, patients with generalized anxiety have the bad habit of entertaining anxious thoughts without critically evaluating them. In essence, they come to believe their own worries to the point that they sometimes don't even realize they are actually worrying. Here is an example of how one patient with generalized anxiety disorder described her thinking about a situation:

"I know that they would have sent me the results by now if there was good news. It's obviously bad news. I thought about calling but when you call they get annoyed and they can take it out on you so I didn't call, mostly because I am afraid of the results, but obviously it's bad. That is probably it for me at that place. I think it's pretty clear that if I didn't do well this time they were going to lose interest in me, so I'm going to have to move on, but I am very worried about where I will move on to, because with this kind of a result, who is going to be interested in me?"

It almost doesn't matter what this patient is actually referring to. These kinds of thoughts are generically characteristic of people who have GAD. Notice how the patient has decided that because results she was expecting did not come by mail the results must be bad. She also has leaped to the conclusion that she will get in trouble if she calls for the results, even though it is not clear why, if she is so convinced she is going to get bad news, she cares so much if the people giving it are going to "take it out" on her. Does that mean there is still some hope the result won't be bad? From the conclusion that the result must be bad, she has jumped to the further, more general conclusion that everything is bad, that she is ruined. In the space of seconds this anxious woman has decided that because something has not arrived in the mail her life is in disarray!

Cognitive therapy of anxiety first aims to make the patient with GAD aware of this litany of unchallenged worried thoughts and then to enable the patient to challenge them. This patient would first be asked to consider the evidence that not receiving news in the mail automatically means the news is bad. How many days has it been? Do the results always arrive in the same amount of time? Has anyone ever received good news after this amount of time? If the patient can even move from believing it is absolutely, 100 percent certain the news will be bad to giving it a 50–50 chance this will be enormous progress. Similarly, she will be taught to challenge automatic convictions about people being mad at her simply because she makes a phone call and to admit that she is engaging in a kind of magical thinking: "Maybe if I don't call the results will somehow improve."

Anxious patients often seem to feel that worrying somehow protects them from harm. In fact, whether we worry endlessly or not about something rarely has a bearing on the outcome. Strikingly, anxious people often worry rather than take an action that might really prevent a bad outcome. I can worry all I want about having a heart attack to the point that I have little energy left to exercise, which might really prevent a heart attack. Yet anxious people live under the mistaken idea that if they don't worry about something, it will happen.

Cognitive therapy of GAD will take at least 10 weekly sessions and possibly as many as 20. No attempt is made to "uncover" the supposed causes of the anxiety and little exploration of childhood is undertaken. The focus is almost entirely on the patient's conscious thoughts. We still need to discuss one more therapy for anxiety, psychodynamic psychotherapy, before developing an approach to treatment.

Generalized Anxiety Disorder: Psychodynamic Psychotherapy

In formulating his psychoanalytic theories, Freud paid particular attention to anxiety. His classification of anxiety changed over the years, with the final version articulated in his ground-breaking monograph *Inhibitions, Symptoms and Anxiety*. Freud came to believe that anxiety was the result of a clash of powerful forces in the unconscious. He had divided the unconscious mind into three parts, the id (seat of the most primitive passions), the superego (the conscience), and the ego (essentially the mediator between the two, the part of the mind that makes living in the real world possible). Conflicts among the different parts of the mind, always out of the patient's direct awareness, can result in the symptom of anxiety. Hence anxiety was seen as a "signal" of deeper emotional conflict.

This leads naturally to the psychoanalytic idea that unseating these unconscious conflicts—making them conscious—should lead to a relief from anxiety. Because powerful forces are at work to keep the conflict unconscious, however, this process is slow and arduous. Mental defenses that prevent conscious awareness of the conflict must first be carefully stripped away. They do not dissolve easily, however. Merely telling the patient "this is the conflict that is causing you to be anxious" has no effect. The patient will be indifferent to such an abrupt instruction. Rather, a slow process is undertaken whereby the unconscious material is exposed bit by bit. This process is called psychoanalysis, described in more detail in Chapter 2, and is the longest of all the psychotherapies.

A shorter version of psychoanalysis is called *psychoanalytic psychotherapy,* also described in Chapter 2. Here the psychoanalytic principle is still used—the cause of the anxiety is still held to be unconscious conflict—but the therapist tries to speed the process along by offering more direct instruction to the patient. Most classical psychoanalysts believe that only a real psychoanalysis in which the patient sees the therapist four or more times a week for years and lies on a couch during sessions can ultimately completely uproot the unconscious conflict that causes the generalized anxiety. Modern realities, especially the almost universal refusal of health insurance companies to reimburse people for psychoanalysis, have forced most psychoanalysts to treat patients with the shortened version in which the patient sees the therapist only once or twice a week for a few years and sits up during sessions.

The theory behind the psychoanalytic treatment of generalized anxiety disorder is intellectually one of the most satisfying parts of Freud's work. The image of anxiety forming as the result of titanic clashes between opposing unconscious forces is dramatic and fascinating. Indeed, we see many patients who seem to fit this picture, for whom anxiety appears to be the tip of the iceberg of emotional difficulties. They worry about relatively unimportant aspects of daily life, while we are convinced as therapists that more important and compelling issues are beneath the surface. Certainly, these unconscious dynamics are of more interest to therapists than the constant worries of patients with GAD. Hence, it is more attractive to some therapists to deal with unconscious problems than conscious ones.

The question is, of course, do psychoanalytic therapies work? Here there can be no firm answer. No scientific study has ever been done that either proves they work or indicates that they do not. It is understandably extremely difficult to do valid scientific studies on psychoanalytic therapies, as discussed in Chapter 2. What could possibly serve as the placebo control for psychoanalysis? In recommending psychoanalytic therapy to patients with GAD, some therapists are guided by their firm belief that this is the best kind of treatment, others by their experience that they can get patients better.

Sometimes it just seems clear that a particular patient does have conflicts out of awareness that might benefit from a psychoanalytic treatment. Such patients usually complain of a number of difficulties in life in addition to generalized anxiety, such as problems with work and relationships and self-esteem. Of course, severe chronic anxiety can also cause such difficulties, so this is no guarantee that unconscious conflicts are operating. At very least, patients need to be informed consumers when considering all their options before agreeing to a psychoanalytic therapy. It will be very interesting but also costly and time-consuming and there is no guarantee it will work any better than the shorter medication or cognitive and behavioral therapies.

Generalized Anxiety Disorder: The Integrated New Psychiatry Approach

I have now described three treatment approaches to GAD: medication, cognitive/behavioral therapy, and psychoanalytic therapy. The New Psychiatry approach to generalized anxiety disorder, as to all conditions, is to use all three to the extent that they can help in an integrated way. From this, as summarized in Table 33, we can give a general idea of how to approach treatment.

For the patient with GAD who has never had treatment before and who has relatively mild symptoms, the first treatment approach should be behavioral and cognitive therapy. Such a patient is suffering from chronic anxiety but is able to function at work and in social settings and can sleep through the night most of the time. She is also able to tolerate the physical discomforts of GAD, including headaches, backaches, and gastrointestinal upset, without taking painkillers (including aspirin and Tylenol) or making frequent visits to the doctor. A patient like this may be able to get over many of her symptoms with a combination of stress management and relaxation training. Some cognitive therapy may also be helpful. The number of sessions needed will vary but should not exceed a two- or three-month course of weekly meetings with the therapist. The target should be a marked and noticeable decrease in anxiety level, less worry, and the elimination of physical discomfort.

If psychotherapy does not work alone I recommend trying BuSpar (buspirone). This has the fewest side effects of any of the antianxiety medications and is easy to stop taking. The patient should be started at 5 mg of BuSpar three times daily. This is increased by 5-mg increments every three days until 30 mg is reached. It is then important to wait until the patient has been on the drug for a total of four weeks before deciding if it is working. If it is working, the patient can be kept on the medication for several weeks without any problem. Tapering off is not technically necessary for BuSpar, that is, the drug can be stopped abruptly, but I generally discontinue it by 5 mg every two or three days. If 30 mg is not effective, the dose can be raised by 10-mg increments every week to a total of 60 mg. At the higher

TABLE 33
A TREATMENT PLAN FOR GAD

If the symptoms are relatively mild and the patient has never received treatment before:

1. Begin cognitive/behavioral therapy, including stress management, relaxation training, and cognitive techniques.
2. Consider psychoanalytic psychotherapy only if there is compelling evidence that unconscious conflicts of childhood origin are at work.
3. If psychotherapy alone is not helpful, begin BuSpar, 5 mg three times daily, and gradually increase the dose (see text). Wait four weeks for a response.
4. If psychotherapy plus BuSpar is not helpful, stop it and begin imipramine at 10 mg daily, and gradually increase the dose (see text). Wait four weeks for a result.
5. If imipramine plus psychotherapy is not helpful, begin a short half-life benzodiazepine (Xanax, Ativan, or Serax) with intermittent use only when anxiety symptoms are severe.

If the symptoms are severe or the patient has failed to respond to treatments in the past:

1. Begin cognitive/behavioral therapy as above

and

If the patient can wait four weeks for symptom relief, begin BuSpar as above. If patient cannot wait or has been treated with benzodiazepine successfully in the past, begin intermittent use of short half-life benzodiazepine as above.

2. If the patient does not respond, begin benzodiazepine medication on a regular basis with doses two to three times per day.
3. Keep the benzodiazepine dose as low as possible and attempt to discontinue it at periodic intervals. Never stop a benzodiazepine abruptly—always taper off the dose.

---

dose more side effects can occur, including headache, nausea, and dizziness, but in general BuSpar side effects are very mild and transient.

If BuSpar does not work, and the patient is still in the relatively mild category, it is appropriate to try a tricyclic drug, probably imipramine (Tofranil), because at this time it is the only tricyclic that has been reasonably well studied for GAD. The patient is started at a very low dose, usually 10 mg at bedtime, and this is raised by 10 mg every other night to a total of 50 mg, then to 75 mg in three days, and then to 100 mg in three more days. After a few days at 100 mg, the dose is raised to 150 mg and the patient is kept on the drug for a total of four weeks before a decision is made about how well it is working. If it is not working, the dose can be raised to 200 mg, then 250 mg a week later, and finally one week later to 300 mg. There will be side effects to almost any dose of imipramine and these include dry mouth, constipation, and urinary hesitancy. Some people will gain weight and experience dizziness when moving quickly from lying or sitting to standing. More information on these side effects and on certain medical conditions that limit the use of imipramine can be found in Chapter 4.

It is assumed that during these medication trials, the behavioral and cognitive therapy is continuing. More cognitive therapy is indicated if initial attempts with stress management and relaxation training are not sufficient. If all of this fails, however, it is reasonable to try a benzodiazepine. The patient should be informed that it is possible that it will be difficult to discontinue a benzodiazepine and that it will be important to use it sparingly if possible. Patients with a history of alcohol or other drug abuse should probably not be given benzodiazepines for the treatment of relatively mild GAD, although there is disagreement on this point.

In the case of mild GAD, when benzodiazepines are used it is a good idea to start with one of the short half-life drugs (brand names for these are Xanax, Serax, and Ativan) and tell the patient to take a very low dose when the anxiety symptoms are most bothersome. Problems with withdrawal usually only occur after the patient has taken a benzodiazepine at regular intervals throughout the day on a daily basis for several weeks and then decides to stop the medication. By using the drug intermittently there is less of a chance that this will occur. A reasonable approach, then, is to give the patient a prescription for Xanax or Ativan, both in 0.5 mg strength, and tell her to try to use it only once a day at most and to skip days when possible. The benzodiazepine can be prescribed along with BuSpar or imipramine if it is felt that either of these drugs has helped but not enough. Some behavioral and cognitive psychotherapists insist that benzodiazepines impede the psychotherapy, but there is absolutely no evidence for this point of view and I see no reason why a patient whose anxiety has not responded to initial psychotherapeutic attempts should be denied symptom relief with benzodiazepines.

Psychoanalytic psychotherapy can work for patients with GAD, but it is a lengthy process that may not seem worthwhile to all patients. Remember not to be persuaded by the claim that "only psychoanalysis really gets to the bottom of the problem." This is mere wishful thinking. Rather, consider psychoanalytic therapies if you and your therapist reach the conclusion that you are in the grip of important unconscious conflicts that arise from childhood problems. Although not all psychoanalytic therapists agree, it is perfectly appropriate to administer antianxiety medication while in psycho-analytic psychotherapy.

If the GAD is more severe or the patient has had previous treatment for GAD, the recommendations made so far may need modification. Such patients may already have had extensive psychotherapy or found that neither BuSpar nor a tricyclic like imipramine were effective. Patients who have previously been treated successfully with a benzodiazepine usually do not find BuSpar to be nearly as effective, and current recommendation is to skip BuSpar altogether in such situations. In cases of severe anxiety, the patient may be facing a crisis at work, school, or home such that they absolutely need to function quickly. For example, a patient with severe GAD may repeatedly fail examinations in college because of his extreme nervousness. Now the patient is about to take another, critical test which he simply cannot afford to fail. In such an instance it may not be reasonable to wait for weeks until either psychotherapy or BuSpar or imipramine take effect. It is prudent, therefore, to begin a benzodiazepine immediately because this gives the patient the best chance to get better.

For some patients it may become necessary to give benzodiazepines on a regular basis. Such patients are usually suffering from severe GAD and have failed to respond to other treatments. Although this is not the optimal situation, it should not be regarded as a disaster or improper medical procedure. Although the risk of having difficulty stopping a benzodiazepine should never be taken lightly, there are also substantial risks to untreated anxiety. First, and foremost, of these risks is continued, unabated suffering. GAD is not just a little nervousness, and people who have it may find themselves totally unable to function or enjoy life. Other risks of not treating GAD include development of depression and use of alcohol as a self-medication tool. There is some evidence that GAD may predispose to some medical problems, including high blood pressure, and thereby indirectly increasing the risk of heart attack or stroke.

If benzodiazepines are used on a regular basis it is still best to keep the dose as low as possible, as long as the anxiety symptoms are under control. The patient who has taken a short half-life benzodiazepine may begin to take the drug several times a day. A reasonable starting point is Xanax or Ativan in a dose of 0.5 mg two or three times daily. This should only be increased if there is a continuation of symptoms. Doses of either drug around 3 mg a day are usually sufficient to control GAD. Some clinicians feel that long half-life benzodiazepines, like Valium, Klonopin (clonazepam), or Tranxene (clorazepate), are better for regular use because they produce a steady blood level throughout the day. Patients taking short half-life benzodiazepines, like Xanax, Serax, or Ativan, sometimes find that the effect of the drug wears off before the next dose and they begin having some withdrawal symptoms in the middle of the day.

Once the benzodiazepine taken regularly has become helpful, it is important to renew attempts to control anxiety symptoms with psychotherapy. It is often true that patients benefit from psychotherapy more when their most acute symptoms are relieved by medication. Behavioral and cognitive therapies may actually enable the patient to ultimately stop taking the benzodiazepine more quickly and easily.

A few patients with severe and tenacious GAD will find themselves unable to discontinue benzodiazepine because every time they try their symptoms immediately relapse. Such patients should be permitted to continue to take benzodiazepines indefinitely. It is assumed that valiant attempts have been made to find alternatives to the benzodiazepine in such cases, but that they have failed. To insist that such a patient suffer from anxiety because of some dictum that benzodiazepines should not be given on a long-term basis is pure nonsense. Benzodiazepines have never been associated with any long-term health risk, and as long as the dose is kept as low as possible to control symptoms, it is clear that patients function much better—not worse—while taking them.

Panic Disorder: Description

Unlike generalized anxiety disorder, panic disorder has been extensively studied by scientists. In fact, during the 1980s panic disorder seemed to be the ''psychiatric illness of the decade,'' attracting substantial amounts of research attention and research funding from both the government and the drug industry.

Looking back, it is hard to figure out exactly why panic disorder suddenly interested everyone. Credit for first describing panic disorder as a unique anxiety syndrome goes to Donald Klein, who first reported in the early 1960s that there is something of particular interest about anxiety attacks. Since then the various features of panic disorder have been very well described and a variety of well-tested treatment options have been provided. We even have some intriguing ideas about what causes panic disorder.

The Panic Attack
The most important part of panic disorder is the panic attack itself. Panic attacks are very discrete and relatively sudden bursts of physical symptoms that convince someone having one that he or she is in the midst of a catastrophic event. In the beginning of the illness the attacks are almost entirely unexpected—that is, the patient is going about usual daily routine and has not just received bad news or been frightened or had an argument with someone. Then, seemingly out of the blue, it suddenly becomes difficult to catch one's breath, the heart begins to race with chest discomfort and palpitations, there are tingling feelings in the hands and feet, and feelings of dizziness, lightheadedness, and nausea begin. A list of the common physical

symptoms of a panic attack is given in Table 35, taken from the *DSM-IV*. The suddenness and severity of these physical symptoms terrifies the person having a panic attack into having one or more of three immediate psychological reactions: (1) I am going to die, (2) I am going crazy, (3) I am going to do something completely out of control like drive my car off this bridge.

These attacks usually last 10 to 30 minutes. Many people (perhaps as many as 30 percent of the general population) will have a single panic attack sometime in their life. People with panic disorder, however, get them repetitively, often daily or even several times a day. Some people need only experience one attack in order to develop a persistent and unremitting fear that another attack is just about to happen. There are currently controversies about whether it is sufficient to make the diagnosis of panic disorder after having only one such attack leading to persistent dread and disruption of life or whether multiple and ongoing attacks should be required. The former definition is favored by cognitive and behavioral therapists who believe that the real problem in panic disorder is not so much the attack itself but the fear of having an attack. The latter definition is preferred by psychopharmacologists and biologically oriented psychiatrists who think that the panic attack is largely a biologically based, medical event that is central to the panic disorder syndrome. *DSM-IV* compromises by requiring both to make the diagnosis. I'll come back to the implications of this difference of opinion later. At this point, it is most important to recognize that all theorists agree that the panic attack itself starts and drives the illness.

Typically, a person having a panic attack is so frightened that she rushes to the nearest hospital emergency room and insists she is having a heart attack. Indeed, she has many physical symptoms reminiscent of a heart attack: chest pain, tingling sensations, nausea, difficulty breathing or catching her breath. The catch is, however, that the usual patient first presenting to the emergency room under these conditions is young with no previous medical history and few risk factors for a heart attack. Panic disorder seems to affect woman about twice as often as men. It may begin anytime from puberty on, although it usually comes to clinical attention in the early to mid-twenties. It is rare for panic disorder to begin for the first time in someone over 50, although this can occasionally happen.

So we now have in our busy emergency room a 24-year-old woman insisting she is having a heart attack. The nurse who admits her to the ER is skeptical. Although the woman appears to be very frightened and tense, she does not seem to be in the kind of pain usual for people with heart attacks. She is young, not particularly overweight, and tells the nurse she does not smoke and that none of her relatives had heart attacks at such an early age. Still, it is possible for a young woman to have a heart attack without experiencing terrible chest pain (although this is very uncommon).

Appropriately, the nurse takes the young woman's vital signs. She finds that her pulse rate is a little fast, let's say 100 beats per minute. (Normal is about 80, although people in good physical condition usually have much lower pulse rates, around 60 to 70 beats per minute.) This is fast, but far from dangerous. Walking up a flight of stairs will get the heart beating at least this fast. The patient's blood pressure is 130 over 85, perhaps a tad high but again not dangerous. (Normal blood pressure is usually given as 120/80, but again people in very good physical condition will have lower blood pressure. Doctors do not usually recommend treating people for high blood pressure until the lower number, called the diastolic blood pressure, gets to 90. It takes much higher blood pressures than this to produce any immediate, life-threatening danger.) Interestingly, the patient is breathing fast, about 20 breaths a minute (we usually breathe about half that rate unless we are exercising).

On the basis of these vital signs, the nurse tells the patient that things seem to be okay, but just to be on the safe side a doctor is called over to ask some questions and perform a physical examination. The doctor learns that the patient was having dinner in a restaurant with friends when the symptoms began. She had a fairly ordinary day at work and had not been feeling particularly nervous or worried recently. There was no history of other psychiatric problems such as depression. Medically, she had always been in good health. She did not drink alcohol to excess, exercised on a regular basis, and did not use drugs. She had never been pregnant or taken birth control pills, but she was sexually active. On physical examination her temperature was 98.6°F and everything else was normal. Blood tests, including a pregnancy test and a test to measure the amount of thyroid hormone, were normal and an electrocardiogram (EKG) showed a heart that was beating a little bit fast but was otherwise completely normal.

In other words, our young woman in the emergency room has no identifiable medical problem. She certainly is not having a heart attack or stroke. The doctor tells her she seems to be fine, maybe something she ate in the restaurant upset her system or maybe she is really under more stress recently than she thought. There really doesn't seem to be any explanation for her symptoms. The patient is reassured that she, in fact, is not about to die, but she is a little perplexed. She is certain that for at least 30 minutes she was in the grip of an overwhelming and terrifying physical force. She still remembers feeling as if she was going to suffocate or faint. How could there be no medical basis? Was she ''losing her mind''?

Like most people early stages of panic disorder, our example patient tries to put the events leading up to her emergency room visit out of her mind. She goes home and goes to sleep. The next morning she feels a little shaky, but basically normal. She goes to work and has a reasonably good day. By the end of the week the whole episode is forgotten.

Anticipatory Anxiety

But the following week, while sitting at her desk at work, our patient starts to feel her heart rate pick up, she begins to perspire, and she starts breathing fast. In a few moments she is in the middle of another, very frightening, attack. She looks pale and shaky to her coworkers, who call an ambulance and have her rushed to the hospital. Once again, doctors and nurses find nothing wrong with her physically. One nurse recognizes her from the previous week's visit and makes a comment like, "Oh, it's you again." Our patient not only feels frightened and perplexed, now she also feels embarrassed. If there is nothing wrong with her, what is going on? The emergency room doctor insists it is just "an anxiety attack, nothing is wrong," and gives her a prescription for a benzodiazepine-type antianxiety drug, in this case Valium. He tells her to take one every day for the next three days, then go to see her family doctor.

Our patient takes the Valium, but she has another attack the next day and goes home from work. Now she knows something is wrong and that the attacks can come on at any time. She also recognizes they will last about 20 minutes. The Valium makes her a little sleepy and somewhat calmer, but has no effect in stopping the attacks. She spends a great deal of time worrying about when the next attack will occur. This is called anticipatory anxiety.

A few days after her second trip to the hospital emergency room, our patient visits her regular medical doctor. He takes a careful medical history, does a physical examination, and runs some more blood tests. He is unable to make a diagnosis. Because of the chest pain that occurs during the attacks, he sends the patient to a cardiologist. The cardiologist also cannot find any abnormalities on physical examination, but because the attacks disturb the patient so much, he also orders a number of diagnostic tests. These include another electrocardiogram, a stress test, and a 24-hour monitoring of heart rhythm. All tests are normal.

Phobic Avoidance

Now our patient is once again told there are no medical problems, but she continues to have anxiety attacks every day and to worry about the attacks most of the time. As the panic and anticipatory anxiety continue, a third problem arises—phobic avoidance. Even though the patient has been told by several doctors that she is healthy, she still fears for her life. When the attacks occur she continues to believe that a medical catastrophe is about to occur. Because of this, she becomes increasingly afraid to be in any place or situation from which a rapid exit is not possible. Essentially, the patient needs to be sure that she can always get to an emergency room in the event of an attack. At first, this means avoiding driving in the car over a bridge during rush hour. What if she has an attack and is unable to continue to drive? Suppose there is a traffic jam and the route to a hospital is blocked? In time, she becomes afraid to drive any place and then starts giving up on long bus rides as well. Airplane rides are clearly out. Malls become frightening because it is often hard to find the exit on a crowded day. When she goes to the theater or church, she finds she must sit on the aisle near the door. Otherwise, it might be embarrassing to have to disrupt many people in a row of seats when she has to rush out to get into an ambulance. Some people with panic disorder become so frightened about getting an attack in a situation in which they cannot get help that they refuse to go anywhere alone. They must always be accompanied by a trusted companion—sometimes called the phobic partner—who can be counted on to call an ambulance and administer life-saving assistance. In this worst case scenario it is said that the patient has *agoraphobia*.

T A B L E 34
COMPONENTS OF PANIC DISORDER

Panic attacks	Sudden, short-lived (10- to 30-minute) outbursts of severe physical symptoms (see Table 35) and fear that one is about to die, go crazy, or do something out of control
Anticipatory anxiety	Constant worry about when the next panic attack will occur
Phobic avoidance	Fear of getting a panic attack in a situation where help is not immediately available; called agoraphobia when patient is afraid to leave the house at all unless accompanied by a trusted companion

As noted in Table 34, then, there are three parts to the panic disorder syndrome—the panic attack itself, anticipatory anxiety, and phobic avoidance. All patients get the first two; about two-thirds develop some significant amount of phobic avoidance. There are many theories about why some people do not develop phobic avoidance, but no satisfactory answer.

Complications of Panic Disorder
What is striking, and typical, about the case presented here is that doctors often don't seem to recognize what is going on. Patients with panic disorder

go from one emergency room to the next, always being told nothing is wrong, sometimes being giving a handful of antianxiety pills, usually Valium. But something is wrong. Studies have shown that during panic attacks heart and breathing rates really do accelerate, although not to medically dangerous levels, and patients with panic disorder are absolutely correct in insisting that physical events occur during their attacks. The attacks themselves are bad enough, but the complications are sometimes even worse. Phobic avoidance can drastically restrict a person's ability to function in any meaningful way. When travel restrictions make it virtually impossible to get out of the house, parenting, work, and social life go down the drain. Some people with panic attacks resort to alcohol to try and block the attacks. In fact, alcohol usually does stop an incipient attack, but its effects wear off in a matter of hours and often the patient has an even worse panic attack at that point. Furthermore, it is believed by some that panic attacks are a cause of some cases of alcoholism.

Many patients with panic disorder, perhaps as many as half, develop serious depression at some point in their lives. There is also an association between panic and suicide attempts. Hence, there is abundant reason to treat panic disorder aggressively. Fortunately, there are very effective therapies for panic and we can say with confidence at this point that the great majority of patients with panic disorder should be able to obtain substantial relief if they receive the proper treatment.

If you have recurrent panic attacks with symptoms like those described in Table 35, you should tell your doctor you think you have panic disorder. If the doctor has never heard of panic disorder, find one who has. You can even call an 800 number sponsored by the National Institute of Mental Health for help in finding someone to provide you with a diagnosis and treatment (1-800-64-PANIC).

Before turning to the treatment of panic disorder, I will review some of the ideas scientists now have about what causes it.

Panic Disorder: What Causes It

Once again, there are basically three schools of thought on what causes panic disorder: psychodynamic, behavioral, and biological. There are few illnesses, however, that seem to provoke as much fighting among the groups as panic disorder. Perhaps this is because different treatments are successful, thus prompting everybody to come up with a pet theory about what causes panic disorder in the first place.

TABLE 35
SYMPTOMS OF A PANIC ATTACK
(From the DSM-IV)

1. Palpitations, pounding heart, or accelerated heart rate
2. Sweating
3. Trembling or shaking
4. Sensations of shortness of breath or smothering
5. Feeling of choking
6. Chest pain or discomfort
7. Nausea or abdominal distress
8. Feeling dizzy, unsteady, lightheaded, or faint
9. Derealization (feelings of unreality) or depersonalization (being detached from oneself)
10. Fear of losing control or going crazy
11. Fear of dying
12. Paresthesias (numbness or tingling sensations)
13. Chills or hot flushes

Psychoanalytic Views

The psychoanalytic theorists, of course, view panic as the conscious manifestation of unconscious conflict. Recently, they have argued that repressed anger may generate panic. That is, in their view a person who harbors anger that the unconscious believes is unacceptable may have panic attacks rather than experience the anger. For example, let us say that a father has unconscious anger toward his son, who lives in another city, perhaps because the son has done better in his career than the father has. Such competitive aggression will seem unacceptable to the father; society tells us that parents are supposed to be proud of their children's accomplishments, not angry and resentful. So repugnant is such anger to the father's superego, that it represses it. Rather than experience anger, he has a panic attack every time he contemplates visiting his son. The father believes that he has the panic attacks because he is anxious about flying in a plane to see his son. In fact, this is just conscious rationalization. The real problem is unconscious anger.

Obviously, such a concept remains unproven. I must say that it is frequently the case when interviewing panic disorder patients that the possibility of such conflict being associated with panic attacks occurs to me. Could panic really be the expression of unconscious anger and aggression? The theory is plausible but hard to prove. The main problem with it is that it lacks practical value because it is entirely possible to treat panic disorder successfully without ever revealing any such unconscious conflicts. Psychoanalytic theorists will insist that unless these conflicts are uprooted by a psychotherapeutic process the patient will never fully recover, but here again they lack the evidence to make such an assertion. There is evidence that panic disorder patients can fully recover without psychoanalytic treatments, and there is no evidence that psychoanalytic treatments are specifically useful for panic disorder.

Behavioral and Cognitive Views

The behavioral and cognitively oriented theorists believe that panic arises from conditioned fear and from anxiety-producing thoughts. Behaviorally, they believe that patients who experience anxiety during ordinarily innocuous situations essentially become conditioned to panic whenever in those situations. For example, a father is driving the car over the bridge trying to get home from work. His children's baby-sitter has a doctor's appointment and must, therefore, leave earlier than usual; hence, the father is in a special rush. He hits a traffic jam on the bridge and begins to worry about whether he will get home in time. It even crosses his mind that the baby-sitter might leave before he gets there. His heart starts to race and his breathing becomes labored. He gets a feeling that he must get off that bridge. Soon he feels as if he is going to suffocate and die. He is having a panic attack. Fortunately, the traffic breaks and he gets home in time. But now, whenever he has to go over the bridge he experiences the same panic attack. He has become conditioned to pair danger with the bridge.

Cognitively, it has been observed that patients with panic disorder seem to entertain a specific set of anxiety-producing thoughts. Two kinds of such thoughts predominate: overestimating the probability of bad outcomes and catastrophizing. In the former mode, the panic disorder patient assumes automatically that the worst possible outcome will occur with absolute certainty. For example, the 24-year-old woman discussed earlier believes without a doubt that every time she has a pain in her chest it must be a heart attack. She never even entertains the possibility that it might be a muscle twinge or an upset stomach. In the second mode, the patient leaps to the conclusion that an outcome will have the worst possible consequences. A panic disorder patient assumes without any room for argument that if he has one more panic attack at work he will be fired, become destitute, and live homeless forever. Now, it is possible that chest pain may represent a heart attack and that having a panic attack at work could lead an unusually insensitive boss to fire an employee, but there are alternative possibilities as well, some with far greater likelihood than these. The panic patient, say the cognitive theorists, causes the attack to occur by dwelling on all of these anxiety-producing thoughts. Obviously, thinking about heart attacks and getting fired is not going to relax anyone, so until the "bad habits" of probability overestimation and catastrophizing are broken, the panic patient's thoughts are his own worst enemy.

Behavioral and cognitive therapists have turned these ideas directly into a therapeutic approach that appears to work. This gives their ideas merit. On the other hand, one may ask the simple question, "Why do panic patients get conditioned to panic so easily and why do they have bad mental habits?" Further, many have argued that panic attacks do not always begin in an anxious situation, such as trying to drive home through a traffic jam. Sometimes it is impossible to figure out what caused the first panic attacks; they simply seem to come out of the blue. Also, it has been argued that panic patients may start making cognitive errors like probability overestimation only after the panic attacks have started. In this scenario, rather than causing the attacks, the anxiety-producing thoughts are caused by the attacks. That is, after suffering from a series of panic attacks and getting no clear answer about what is happening, the panic patient loses his optimism and begins to fear that bad things are inevitable. These are all legitimate criticisms of the cognitive and behavioral theories.

Psychobiological Views

Psychobiologists believe that panic attacks are caused by misfiring of brain cells (called neurons). One prominent theory is that cells in the brain that contain a chemical called noradrenaline fire excessively to cause a panic attack. Evidence for this is that drugs that are known to increase the fire rate of these noradrenaline-containing neurons actually cause patients with panic attacks, but not people without panic disorder, to have a panic attack in the laboratory. Patients with panic disorder also seem to have a variety of abnormal responses to drugs that interact with the noradrenaline system. Another prominent biological theory involves the respiratory system. Laboratory studies have shown that patients with panic disorder hyperventilate under conditions that do not cause respiratory stimulation in normal volunteers without panic disorder. Giving panic patients an injection of a usually benign substance called sodium lactate not only makes them panic but also causes them to breathe very deeply and at a very fast rate. Panic disorder patients are also unusually sensitive to the effects of breathing small amounts of carbon dioxide, a gas not normally found in the air we breathe. Finally, there is some evidence that panic attacks may be hereditary. Panic disorder certainly runs in families and may, according to some analyses, involve an abnormal gene.

All of this biological theory is very satisfying to those who want to see psychiatric illnesses as no different from other medical conditions. That would certainly reduce the stigma attached to these conditions and hopefully decrease the reluctance patients and doctors seem to have to treat them. However, none of the biological theories, however compelling and even plausible they may seem, have yet been proven. They remain theories. Many think it most likely that scientists will ultimately prove that panic disorder occurs when someone with a biological vulnerability is subjected to a particularly adverse pattern of life circumstances—that is, biology and psychology interact. For now, however, we should maintain our interest in the scientific research being conducted on panic disorder but not lose sight of the fact that all we have yet is a series of very interesting hypotheses looking for proof.

Panic Disorder: What Are the Treatment Options?

Medication Treatments

There is an interesting history to treatment of panic disorder. When the condition was first described in the 1960s, most attention to it was paid by biological psychiatrists. Lead by Donald Klein, the first approach was to test medications. It was quickly, and unequivocally, shown that several different kinds of psychiatric drugs do in fact block panic attacks. After taking one of these medications for about four weeks, most patients with panic disorder can expect to stop having the attacks. Once the attacks stop, the patient gradually ceases to worry about having attacks and anticipatory anxiety resolves. Then the patient becomes confident that she can go places without having an attack and phobic avoidance also diminishes. Klein first showed that one of the antidepressant drugs, called Tofranil (imipramine), has this property of stopping panic attacks. Interestingly, the antipanic effect seems to have nothing to do with the drug's antidepressant effect: patients stop having panic attacks after taking Tofranil even if they are not depressed.

Tofranil (imipramine) belongs to the class of antidepressant drugs called tricyclics. Almost any one of the tricyclic drugs can block panic; imipramine is still the gold standard against which all other medications are measured, but other tricyclics including desipramine (Norpramin, Pertofrane) and nortriptyline (Aventyl, Pamelor) are also effective and probably have fewer side effects than imipramine. It is important to remember that the tricyclic drugs must be taken every day in relatively high doses for at least four weeks before they work. These drugs have several adverse side effects, which are discussed in more detail in Chapter 4. But chief among them is that for unclear reasons, patients with panic disorder sometimes react paradoxically to tricyclics at first; they actually get more jittery and nervous and have trouble sleeping. It appears that patients with panic disorder are particularly sensitive to some of the properties of tricyclics and get an initial hypersensitivity reaction. For that reason, we start patients on very small doses and slowly work our way up to therapeutic doses. A typical regimen is to start a patient on 10 mg a day of imipramine and slowly work up to 150 to 200 mg a day over the next two weeks.

Even with this slow increase in dose, many patients with panic disorder (unlike those with depression) find the side effects of tricyclic medications unacceptable. They complain about nausea, dizziness, headache, and jitteriness in addition to the usual tricyclic side effects of dry mouth, constipation, and weight gain. For patients who do stay on the medication, most of these side effects disappear by four weeks or at least become easily tolerated. About 70 percent of patients who remain on imipramine for four to six weeks will have a good clinical response.

Antidepressant drugs of the monoamine oxidase inhibitor (MAOI) class, like Nardil (phenelzine) and Parnate (tranylcypromine), are also effective in blocking panic attacks. They are probably even more effective than tricyclics but because of dietary restrictions placed on patients who take them and their many side effects (see Chapter 4), they are reserved for patients who fail to respond to other treatment interventions.

After the tricyclic drugs, the next major innovation in treating panic disorder was the introduction of Xanax (alprazolam). Xanax has a slightly different chemical structure than the other benzodiazepine-type antianxiety drugs. It surprised many scientists, however, to learn that Xanax can also block panic because they believed that benzodiazepines were effective for generalized anxiety disorder but not panic. But Xanax has been shown in appropriate scientific experiments to block panic attacks just like Tofranil. In fact, Xanax is now the only drug officially designated for use in panic disorder by the Food and Drug Administration (FDA). This must not, however, lead people to think that Xanax is the only drug that works for panic or that doctors are making a mistake not to prescribe Xanax for panic disorder. The Food and Drug Administration can grant an official "indication" to a company for one of their drugs if the company wants to spend the money and take the time to do all the necessary studies and complete all the paperwork. Imipramine has been used for 30 years for panic and obviously works, but no drug company is currently interested in spending the money to get the FDA to give them the official indication. This means that no company can advertise imipramine for use in panic disorder, but doctors who know the scientific literature and read the textbooks are comfortable and absolutely correct in prescribing it for panic disorder.

Xanax has some advantages over the tricyclics. It may work faster (some patients start getting a reduction in panic attacks after one or two weeks) and its only real side effect for most people is mild sedation, which usually goes away in time. Hence most patients with panic disorder are able to tolerate Xanax.

The main problem with Xanax is getting the patient off it. Tricyclics must be tapered off when discontinued, but this is usually very straightforward and the patient does not suffer any withdrawal reaction. Because it is usually necessary to keep someone on an antipanic drug for six months after their last panic attack to prevent immediate relapse, patients treated with Xanax almost always get withdrawal symptoms when they try to stop taking it and many of them insist on going back on the drug. Xanax is a very safe and effective antipanic medication and in many situations is the best drug to prescribe. But because of concerns about withdrawal symptoms some doctors are now trying other remedies before prescribing Xanax.

It should also be noted that other benzodiazepines have now been shown to work for panic disorder. Ativan (lorazepam) is very similar to Xanax in most ways. Klonopin (clonazepam) is longer-acting than Xanax or Ativan. For some patients who start to experience breakthrough anxiety in between doses of Xanax or Ativan, Klonopin is often a better choice because a more steady drug blood level is maintained.

Most recently, the antidepressants of the selective serotonin reuptake inhibitor (SSRI) class have been prescribed as first-line treatments for panic. These drugs currently include Prozac (fluoxetine), Zoloft (sertraline), Paxil (paroxetine), and Luvox (fluvoxamine) and a related drug, Effexor (venlafaxine). There are now a number of good studies published in the scientific literature indicating that these drugs are effective antipanic drugs. Like the tricyclics, they must be started in very low doses for panic patients to avoid hypersensitivity reactions (about 5 mg of Prozac or 25 mg of Zoloft or 10 mg of Paxil a day, for example) and then slowly raised to therapeutic doses (usually 20 mg of Prozac, 100 mg of Zoloft, or 20 mg of Paxil). Patients seem to tolerate the SSRI drugs much better than the tricyclics, and from a medical viewpoint they are safer. Further, they can be relatively easily discontinued with almost no withdrawal reaction in most cases.

At this time, then, most physicians start panic patients on a low dose of either an SSRI (like Paxil) or a tricyclic (like Tofranil or Norpramin) and then work the dose up. The patient should take the medication every day for at least six weeks. If the panic attacks go away, the patient should then stay on the medication for at least six more months before trying to discontinue it. If they don't work, or the patient cannot stand the side effects, switching to Xanax or an MAOI (like Nardil) may be necessary.

Cognitive/Behavioral Treatments

The use of medication for panic disorder is fairly standard and well worked out. Until about ten years ago, most psychiatrists would have insisted that medication is the only reasonable treatment. But now there may be a nonmedication alternative.

Behavioral and cognitive therapists have recently developed specific psychotherapies for panic disorder that appear to be effective. Some have now been studied in fairly rigorous scientific designs, although exactly how to come up with a control treatment is always difficult when studying psychotherapy. How can we design a "placebo" psychotherapy? One of the most publicized of these cognitive/behavioral treatments was developed by Dr. David Barlow at the State University of New York, Albany. His treatment, called Panic Control Therapy, is an 11-session method that focuses on three aspects of the illness: hyperventilation, panic-producing thoughts, and intolerance of minor physical symptoms. Patients are first taught techniques of slow abdominal breathing. This is followed by cognitive therapy aimed at stopping the patient from making probability overestimations and having catastrophic thoughts. Finally, a procedure known as "interoceptive conditioning" is undertaken in which the patient is trained to understand that momentary sensations such as dizziness, fatigue, or heart pounding are not life-threatening.

This procedure seems to work, although there are now fierce debates between biological and cognitive/behavioral therapists about how well it works. Some cognitive/behavioral therapists have cited very suspicious-sounding statistics, claiming that almost 100 percent of their patients respond to cognitive/behavioral therapy. They also tend to dramatize and exaggerate the side effects produced by medications in an attempt to convince the field that cognitive/behavioral therapy is the only safe and effective treatment. The biological psychiatrists are equally strident, often refusing to acknowledge that behavior therapy has clearly been shown to be effective in many studies.

My own opinion is that cognitive/behavioral therapy is effective for about the same number of patients who respond to tricyclic medication therapy: around 70 percent. Cognitive/behavioral therapy has an advantage over medication in that there are no physical side effects and hence most people can get through the whole treatment. A further advantage is that once the cognitive/behavioral therapy is over, there is no need to continue to take a medication. On the other hand, the downside of the psychotherapy is that it takes about three months to work and, at least until we get health-care reform that pays for psychotherapy, can involve considerable out-of-pocket cost for the patient.

There is also a question about how long the effects of a successful cognitive/behavioral therapy last. It is clear that once medication is stopped, the chances of getting panic disorder back again are high; many patients relapse at some point in their lives and need another round of medication therapy. Cognitive/behavioral therapists say that patients learn so much during the treatment that they can stay well forever after the treatment is concluded. This has met with skepticism from the proponents of medication therapy.

The New Psychiatry Approach to Panic Treatment
The tragedy of these debates is that while they may tickle the academic fancy of psychiatrists and psychologists, they leave a patient with panic disorder scratching her head. Should she take a drug or start therapy? Here is the New Psychiatry approach.

Panic attacks are very frightening and there is sometimes some urgency in getting them under control. For very severe illness it may be best to start with medication (and I would usually choose either an SSRI or, in some cases, a tricyclic) because these will work fastest. In less severe situations in which it is felt by doctor and patient that some time can be taken to get the panic attacks under control, I advise trying cognitive/behavioral therapy. Many patients come to me having already made up their mind; they either think medications are dangerous and want therapy or that therapy is useless and they want medications. I don't agree with either position, but in these cases the patient should be permitted to pick the treatment she wants because both are effective. If medication does not work, there is always the option of trying therapy, and vice versa. The key here is to give the patient all the options and permit her to be the key figure in making the initial treatment decision.

What about psychoanalytic psychotherapy? I believe that hardly anyone would recommend this as the first treatment approach anymore. It is critical to stop the panic attacks, especially before phobic avoidance becomes an ingrained way of life for the patient. Psychoanalytic treatments simply take too long to block panic. Hence, it is fair to say that the first-line treatment of panic disorder should be either medication or cognitive/behavioral therapy or a combination of both.

This does not mean, however, that psychoanalysis and psychoanalytic psychotherapy are to be avoided for patients with panic disorder. As discussed in the previous section, psychoanalysts believe that unconscious conflict may be involved in panic. For patients in which such conflicts can be identified, it is reasonable to add a psychoanalytic therapy at some point to the treatment, often after the panic attacks have been blocked.

Phobias: The Three Types

We currently recognize three main types of phobic disorders, *agoraphobia, specific* (formerly called simple) *phobia,* and *social phobia.* Agoraphobia is usually a complication of panic disorder and therefore its treatment is the same as the treatment for panic disorder described in the previous section.

Specific phobias are actually what most lay people think of when we mention the word *phobia.* These are the things that all have Greek names, like claustrophobia (fear of closed-in spaces), arachnophobia (fear of spiders), and triscadekophobia (fear of Friday the thirteenth).

Social phobia is a debilitating and fascinating condition in which patients experience anxiety attacks only in the context of social or performance situations. Unlike the patient with panic disorder and agoraphobia, the patient with social phobia gets relief when alone. I will now discuss approaches to specific and social phobia.

TABLE 36

Suggested Treatment for Panic Disorder

1. For very severe cases in which the fastest relief is necessary:
   - Begin an SSRI (like Paxil) at low dose. If there is a specific reason not to use an SSRI, begin with a tricyclic (like imipramine) at low dose.
   - Increase the dose of medication slowly to a therapeutic level over several weeks.
   - Stay on the medication for six weeks, being careful not to forget to take it.
   - If it works, stay on the medication for at least six more months.
   - Try to do all the things that you became afraid to do while you were having panic attacks. If you still have phobias, ask the doctor to help you by designing an exposure program.
2. For less severe cases in which fast relief is not as critical:
   - Begin cognitive/behavioral therapy. This must be done with a therapist who has been specifically trained in cognitive/behavioral therapy of panic disorder. Do not pick a therapist who cannot convince you that he or she has specific expertise in this area.
   - Complete the therapy, which should last about three months and focus almost entirely on the panic attacks and phobias themselves.
3. If medication does not work:
   - Try a different medication (one of the benzodiazepines like Xanax or Klonopin) or an MAOI (Nardil)
                           OR
   - Try adding cognitive/behavioral therapy to medication.
4. If cognitive/behavioral therapy does not work:
   - Take medication.
5. If it is believed that longstanding, unconscious conflicts are involved in panic attacks, consider a psychoanalytic treatment after your panic attacks have stopped.

Theory and Treatment of Specific Phobias

It is seemingly possible for someone, somewhere to develop a phobia to almost anything. Small-animal phobias are particularly common in which a person experiences intense anxiety and a need to run away from dogs or cats or rodents. I have seen an occasional patient so phobic of dogs, for example, that he had trouble leaving his home for fear of meeting one. Other patients are phobic of heights, swimming, or elevators.

The critical thing in making the diagnosis of specific phobia is that the phobic avoidance have a real and serious impact on the person's life and ability to function. Many people toss around the term *phobic* casually, as in "I am phobic of computers" or "I am phobic of relationships." In the former case, the person probably means that he feels he is having trouble acquiring the skills necessary to use a computer, not that he experiences severe palpitations, racing heart, shaking, and perspiration when he is in the same room as a computer and needs to run away. In the latter, the person probably means that he has difficulty remaining in relationships for long periods of time. A specific phobia must have as its object a single, identifiable thing and it must produce great distress. We also do not include in this category things like "homophobia," which is not a medical illness but rather a bigoted attitude.

No one really knows what causes specific phobias. Sometimes they arise after a traumatic event: a person becomes phobic of dogs after being bitten by one, or of swimming after nearly drowning. Other times, it is hard to pin an actual event on the development of a phobia. Few elevator phobics have actually been stuck in one. The psychoanalysts believe that phobias are a "displacement" of anxiety from one, unconscious object to another, conscious object. Thus, a person with a specific phobia to, for example, dogs might in reality be struggling with an unconscious fear of sexual impulses. Through complex psychological processes, the unacceptable impulse to commit sexual indiscretion is controlled by a conscious phobia that occupies the patient's mind, restricts his ability to function, and reduces his chances of actually committing the "taboo" act. Psychobiologists have generally refrained from theories of the cause of specific phobia.

An exception to the above statement comes with the subtype of specific phobia known as blood-injury phobia. People with blood-injury phobia are terrified of the sight of blood or the prospect of any kind of bodily injury. They are the ones who faint dead away when they have their blood drawn or cut themselves. In my experience, it is generally a six-foot-tall, 200-pound truck driver, who doesn't seem afraid of anything, who passes out cold the minute I go near him with a syringe to give an injection or draw blood. It turns out that blood-injury phobia is found in men and women of all sizes and types and is one of the most highly familial of all psychiatric illnesses. There is little question that it is a biological disorder that involves an abnormality in function of something called the vagus nerve. Most phobic people experience an increase in heart rate when confronted with whatever they are afraid of. Blood-injury phobics have an initial increase in heart rate, but then suddenly their heart rate slows and their blood pressure drops precipitously. This makes them faint. The vagus nerve is responsible for slowing heart rate and it appears that blood-injury phobics inherit an abnormality that makes their vagus nerves fire aberrantly when they see a syringe or blood. The fainting is not dangerous, of course, as long as the patient does not hit his head.

Desensitization Treatment

It is generally agreed that the best treatment for specific phobia is something called *in vivo, hierarchical desensitization.* In gradually increasing doses, the patient is exposed to the phobic object. At each level of exposure there is great anxiety at first, but eventually the patient becomes tolerant of the phobic object at that level of exposure and anxiety diminishes. Eventually, the anxiety is eliminated and the phobia cured.

Let us take, for example, a patient with a terrible fear of heights. I do not mean here a patient who is afraid to go to the top of a skyscraper and hang over the edge—rather, a patient cannot go above the second floor of a building without experiencing overwhelming anxiety. Even the thought of having to go to the third floor provokes total body shaking, heart racing, breathlessness, and terror. This patient can drench his clothes with sweat in moments by standing at the window of the fourth floor of a multi-story building. Obviously, this kind of intense phobia will have an impact on the patient's ability to function and requires treatment.

The treatment might go like this. First, the behavior therapist ascertains what the patient can and cannot do. In this case, for some reason, the patient feels okay on the second floor, so the therapist begins by taking the patient to the second floor and having him look out the window for 15 minutes. Staring down at the ground, even from the second floor, does give him a little anxiety, so this is repeated every day for a week until the patient is completely comfortable. Then the therapist goes with the patient halfway up the stairs to the third floor and stays with him for 15 minutes. This provokes considerable anxiety and so is repeated for several days until he is comfortable. Then up to the third floor itself. Ultimately, the patient spends time on an upper-story floor while the therapist waits downstairs. Finally, the patient is able to go to the twelfth floor and stare out the window for 15 minutes without experiencing any fear. In this way the phobia is extinguished. The treatment is called "in vivo" because it involves the actual confrontation of the phobia rather than, as was formerly done, merely sitting in the doctor's office imagining looking out the window. It is "hierarchical" because there is a graded increase in severity of the exposure. It is called "desensitization" because the patient gradually becomes less and less sensitive to the phobic object.

This treatment method almost always works. By contrast, there is little evidence that medications are effective for specific phobias, and some argue that giving antianxiety drugs actually interferes with the success of desensitization treatments because the drugs interfere with the patient's ability to experience anxiety at each stage of the exposure therapy.

Psychoanalysts argued that behavioral treatments of specific phobias would not be effective because the underlying unconscious fear is not being addressed. They predicted that "symptom substitution" would occur if a specific phobia was simply eliminated by exposure and desensitization; some new phobia would have to take the place of the original one unless the underlying conflict was eliminated.

In fact, there is no evidence that symptom substitution occurs after successful behavioral treatment of specific phobia. Hence, most patients will do fine with exposure and desensitization.

The Theory and Treatment of Social Phobia

Almost anyone placed in front of a large audience of strangers and told to perform will get "stage fright." That is the kind of anxiety reaction that we think is not only normal but probably beneficial. Stage fright is the warning to take presentations seriously, to prepare well and concentrate on doing a good job. If even famous musicians and actors failed to worry about the consequences of doing a sloppy job onstage, we would probably have very few award-winning performances.

It is important, therefore, to distinguish social phobia from stage fright and also from shyness. A person with social phobia gets physical and emotional symptoms of anxiety in performance and social situations that are so severe they cannot be tolerated. Rather than motivating the person to do well, social phobia–related anxiety makes it almost impossible for the patient to perform. Patients with social phobia report that once in the social or performance situation that provokes their anxiety they experience a host of physical reactions very similar to panic attacks: heart pounding, chest pain, sweating, shaking, and blushing. These physical symptoms make them fear that everyone in the audience will see how anxious they are and hence that they will be embarrassed or humiliated. This fear of being humiliated in public produces further physical unrest to the point in which the patient with social phobia absolutely cannot perform. The main difference between panic disorder and social phobia is that panic disorder patients get their attacks more or less at random and feel most comfortable when they are with someone; social phobics only get attacks in the context of social or performance situations and they find relief only when alone.

Social phobia often begins in adolescence and can be extremely debilitating. A high school student with social phobia may find he cannot raise his hand in class for fear of having to answer a question in public. He may not be able to take oral examinations or go to school dances or even have college or job interviews. The result is someone who cannot function either socially or in a work situation. Many social phobics find, unfortunately, that drinking a little alcohol before a performance situation eases their anxiety. The result is often serious alcohol abuse.

It was once thought that men are more likely to have social phobia than women because more men seek treatment for social phobia. Actually, women are more likely to have social phobia but are less likely than men to get help. Some people say this is because in our society it is still more acceptable for women than men to avoid performances and fade into the background. Men, according to this view, are more troubled by the inability to be assertive in public than women.

There are two types of social phobia. Patients with *discrete* social phobia only experience anxiety in specific performance situations. Such patients function normally in most other social situations. For example, a patient who cannot speak in public or who cannot urinate in a public bathroom but who otherwise can talk to people at a party or attend a business meeting will meet criteria for discrete social phobia. On the other hand, patients who experience severe anxiety in all social situations have *generalized* social phobia. Such a patient may be unable to return something to a store, call someone for a date, speak to anyone at a party, or even endorse a check while a bank teller is watching. As will be seen, the distinction has treatment implications.

We have very little information about what causes social phobia. There are many biological theories, but none of them are currently in a state that is particularly convincing. Cognitive and behavioral therapists cite maladaptive, anxiogenic thought patterns and traumatic exposures as the cause of social phobia. Psychoanalysts believe that the social anxiety and avoidance seen in social phobia stem from unconscious conflict, often centering around a fear that too much success and notoriety will have dangerous consequences. All these ideas are speculation. Very little scientific research exists to guide us to the cause of social phobia.

The treatment of social phobia has been much better studied than its causes. Both medication and cognitive/behavioral strategies have been fairly extensively studied and from this work we can piece together a series of recommendations for how to approach the problem of social phobia.

Cognitive/Behavioral Treatments

Let's start with cognitive and behavioral strategies. People with social phobia tend to entertain specific thoughts that increase their anxiety when in social and performance situations. They assume, for example, that their nervousness is easily detected by everyone they come in contact with and that they will be judged harshly for it. In reality, most people do not condemn nervous people. When we see a performer who looks nervous we usually feel sympathetic (unless, of course, we are paying a fortune to see that performance); but people with social phobia generally expect to be judged with derision.

They consistently overestimate how anxious they *appear*—as opposed to how anxious they *feel*—and the harshness of the audience's opinion. These thoughts fuel the social phobic's anxiety. The cognitive therapist attempts to retrain the social phobic to think more realistically. The therapist does not tell the patient, "There, there now, you don't have to feel so nervous." Merely patronizing a social phobic patient is ineffective; rather, the cognitive therapist attempts to teach the patient to consider the full range of possibilities before leaping to catastrophic conclusions. Here is an example of that kind of treatment:

A Case Demonstrating Cognitive Therapy. The patient is a 34-year-old woman with social phobia who has to make a presentation at a meeting for work tomorrow. She is terrified.

Therapist: What do you think will happen?

Patient: I'm already scared out of my mind. I start shaking just thinking about going in there. I know the minute I stand up I'm going to lose my voice and blush and perspire. I'll look like a complete idiot. They will think I'm a thorough fool.

Therapist: You feel pretty nervous right now just thinking about it?

Patient: You bet. I probably won't sleep a wink tonight.

Therapist: You know, even though you feel nervous now thinking about tomorrow's presentation, you haven't lost your voice. You're talking a little fast, but I can understand every word you are saying. Do you actually lose your voice completely when you speak in front of a group?

Patient: Well, my throat gets very dry and I feel like I'm going to choke.

Therapist: Have you ever choked?

Patient: No, but once I started coughing like crazy.

Therapist: What did you do?

Patient: Well, it was sort of funny because one of the men in the audience rushed to give me a glass of water and he spilled it on the floor. Everybody laughed at him and that sort of relaxed me.

Therapist: So in that case you were able to get your voice back and complete the presentation?

Patient: That time I did, but I can't be sure I'll be able to tomorrow and this is a very important meeting.

Therapist: But the first thing I want you to recognize is that sometimes your voice is okay in these situations and sometimes it isn't, so you can't be so certain you are going to lose it tomorrow. Part of what makes you so fearful is that you have assumed that it is 100 percent the case that tomorrow you are going to lose your voice, no matter what. Maybe someone will spill a glass of water on the floor tomorrow and you'll be okay.

In this vein, the therapist works with the patient to adopt a more realistic assessment of the likelihood she will not be able to speak. By showing the patient that there is even a chance, based on previous experience, that she may be able to talk, she will feel calmer. This kind of work requires great attention to detail and persistence on the part of the therapist, who must challenge every one of the patient's catastrophic beliefs. The idea is that in time the patient will learn to challenge them herself and reduce her overall level of anxiety.

Next the therapist works on the patient's insistence that if she doesn't give a good presentation, she will be judged a complete idiot.

> *Therapist:* Have you ever seen anyone be nervous during a presentation?
> *Patient:* Of course, but not like me.
> *Therapist:* You'd be surprised how nervous some people feel and not actually show it. But if you remember a particular instance in which someone was nervous giving a presentation, can you recall what you thought of them?
> *Patient:* Well, I thought they were pretty nervous and that the presentation would have been better if they weren't so nervous.
> *Therapist:* Do you remember if you thought the person should be fired or shot or anything like that for being nervous?
> *Patient:* Of course not.
> *Therapist:* The point I'm getting at is that even if you appear nervous— and remember that we don't really know yet exactly how nervous you really appear—you believe that everyone in the audience will hate you and think you are completely worthless. Now if I thought that was going to happen to me if I gave a talk, you better believe I'd be terrified myself and avoid giving that talk. But the fact is that it is unlikely anyone will really have that harsh a judgment. They might think, according to you, "Well she seems nervous," but not "What an idiot, where did they get this moron from?"

If the therapist can teach the patient to evaluate the risk of giving a presentation in a more realistic way—that is, to stop believing that she will be condemned—the patient will naturally feel less threatened. Once again, this is going to take a lot of hard work on both therapist's and patient's parts.

Behaviorally, exposure treatment is very useful and follows the same general guidelines as those explained above for the specific phobias. If you take someone who is afraid of heights and dangle them from a skyscraper by the heels, it is unlikely you will make much headway in curing their phobia. Similarly, if a social phobic has to give a talk in front of a thousand people on a difficult topic, she will probably be extremely anxious. But by starting with less stressful presentations and working her way up, the social phobic may learn to tolerate the anxiety that comes from public performance. Hence, the therapist may ask the patient to give her next presentation to two friends first, then to a group of less familiar coworkers who nevertheless are her peers, and then perhaps to one of her bosses. The therapist may even ask the patient to give her presentation in the office and videotape it; often the patient will see that she appears much calmer than she feels. The therapist may also teach the patient some standard tricks, like focusing on the face of a friendly-looking person during the presentation.

Another important behavioral approach to the treatment of social phobia is assertiveness training. A particularly meek and socially avoidant person may indeed be overlooked at parties and meetings. This serves to reinforce the social phobic's belief that he is ineffectual in social situations. In fact, the patient may lack the skills necessary to make an impact on other people in a gathering. Assertiveness training seeks to help such patients acquire these skills. Here is an example:

An Example of Assertiveness Training. Joe, an accountant, lived a lonely existence because of his social phobia. He worked alone in an office for a large company and feared talking to his boss, coworkers, or just about anyone besides his parents. He forced himself to go to a party several weeks before a therapy session and reported to the therapist what happened.

Joe: I sort of hung out in the corner the whole time. There was one woman there who looked like she might be friendly, but I couldn't bring myself to talk to her. My heart was pounding too much. I think she probably would have thought I was weird.

Therapist: Was there anyone at the party you knew?

Joe: Oh yeah, there were a few people.

Therapist: Did you think about talking to them?

Joe: Not really, I sort of got hung up on this one woman and just wound up feeling nervous and mad at myself for not being able to talk to her.

Therapist: So you didn't talk to anybody?

Joe: That's right.

Therapist: That was a bad strategy, Joe. Obviously, talking to a woman you don't know is going to produce more anxiety for you at this stage than talking to other people. So instead of trying to do something, you wound up doing nothing. Now, a better way to start this thing would be to pick out someone you know and try talking to them.

Joe: That's hard for me. I always feel like I'm interrupting what's going on or maybe they don't want to talk to me.

Therapist: Okay, well the first thing is to figure out when it's a good opportunity to say something. Then you have to be sure you have some sort of smile on your face. It's not fun at a party to be approached by someone who looks like he is about to die. You have to tell yourself that this is what people do at parties, they talk to each other. No one who is worth talking to is going to get mad at you at a party if you smile and say, "How are you, how have things been going?" Obviously, you don't just barge in and do that. If someone looks like they're in the middle of a heated discussion, then that's not a good time. But start by picking someone who you are familiar with and just say, "Hey, how's it going?"

This may seem trivial, but a patient like Joe needs exactly this kind of help figuring out how to maneuver in social situations. If he can be successful a few times his confidence will improve and he can move to the next level. With some work, he may even be able to talk to the friendly-looking woman some day.

Cognitive therapy, exposure, and assertiveness training are three effective methods of treating social phobia. Different combinations of these will be most appropriate for different patients. Exposure may be more important for some patients with discrete social phobia while assertiveness training may be more important for people with generalized social phobia.

Behavioral treatments for social phobia are sometimes conducted in a group format. For this particular problem group treatment makes sense. Members of the group practice presentations with each other and also conduct exposure exercises, such as eating in restaurants. Some studies have indicated that group therapy for social phobia is very effective, although these studies are not yet definitive.

Medication Treatments

Medications also work for social phobia. One medication strategy is to block the physical symptoms that patients with social phobia experience with drugs in a class called beta adrenergic blockers. The idea here is that patients with social phobia fear that the palpitations, shaking, blushing, and hyperventilating they experience during social and performance situations will be noticed by others, leading to embarrassment and humiliation. Beta adrenergic blocking drugs block adrenaline, a hormone produced by the adrenal gland, from stimulating organs in the body like the heart and sweat glands. They generally stop heart racing, drenching perspiration, and tremulousness. Then, with these physical manifestations of anxiety blocked, the patient may be able to face the phobic situation with less fear of being embarrassed or looking foolish.

Beta blockers are generally safe and are given to people with social phobia in two ways. For people who know exactly when they are going to be in a difficult situation—having to give a speech or teach a class, for example—a relatively short-acting beta blocker called propranolol (Inderal) can be given in a dose of 20 or 40 mg about one hour before the scheduled performance. Many musicians take propranolol before performances in this way to cut down on shaking caused by stage fright that might affect their performance.

For patients who get socially mediated anxiety at less predictable times—that is, those with more generalized social phobia—a longer acting beta blocker called atenolol (Tenormin) can be taken daily in a dose of 50 or 100 mg.

The advantages of beta blockers over other medications are that they work relatively quickly and have few side effects. These medications are commonly prescribed to people with heart problems like angina, with high blood pressure, and with migraine headaches. Patients with diabetes, asthma, low blood pressure, or certain types of heart disease may not be able to take them, but most people with social phobia tolerate beta blockers like propranolol and atenolol with very little in the way of side effects.

There are, however, clear doubts about how effective beta blockers are for social phobia. It is safe to say that many people with discrete-type social phobia who use propranolol on the intermittent basis described above find it helpful. This is a virtually risk-free intervention. On the other hand, atenolol for more generalized social phobia, while safe, is not always effective and may not be better than placebo.

The benzodiazepine-type antianxiety drugs also work for patients with social phobia. Once again these can be taken on an intermittent basis for people with discrete social phobia—often in combination with propranolol—or regularly for people with more generalized social phobia.

More recently, doctors have begun to prescribe antidepressants of the class called selective serotonin reuptake inhibitors (SSRIs) for social phobia—examples are Prozac (fluoxetine), Zoloft (sertraline), and Paxil (paroxetine). As the case with other anxiety disorders for which SSRIs are used, the patient need not be depressed for them to work in helping social phobics. Because patients with anxiety disorder are very sensitive to antidepressant medication and may initially get even more anxious when they are prescribed, SSRIs are typically started in very low doses for patients with social phobia and then the dose is gradually increased. SSRIs take four to six weeks to work.

As discussed in Chapter 4, SSRIs like Prozac and Zoloft are well tolerated by most people and are medically very safe. Some people, however, get jittery or experience some insomnia from them. Others may get an upset stomach or develop nausea. Sexual side effects of the SSRIs are most troublesome: some patients—both male and female—have difficulty achieving orgasm while taking SSRIs. Sometimes this adverse side effect mysteriously goes away, but it can be a reason to stop the drug if it continues. In my experience, few patients with social phobia find losing the ability to have an orgasm to be an acceptable trade-off for being able to give speeches or be the life of the party.

By far, the most effective drug for social phobia is the monoamine oxidase inhibitor (MAOI) called Nardil (phenelzine). If all else fails, Nardil usually works. Sometimes the response is dramatic and the patient who has been shy and socially avoidant for an entire lifetime becomes outgoing, comfortable with all kinds of social interactions, and at ease during performances.

Nardil is a tricky medication to use, however. Patients on Nardil must adhere to a special diet that excludes, among other things, cheese, red wine, beer, and many medications. Nardil also causes many side effects, including weight gain, low blood pressure, and sleep disturbance. Some patients become overstimulated from Nardil and may even become overconfident in social situations. For all of these reasons, many doctors prefer to try other solutions to social phobia before Nardil. If nothing else works, Nardil should be tried, but it is best to see an experienced psychopharmacologist who regularly prescribes Nardil and who is available to provide close supervision.

Psychodynamic Treatments

Once again we have the question of whether to recommend psychoanalytic psychotherapy for social phobia and once again the situation is complex. There are many theoretically plausible reasons to explain why early life experiences could make someone fearful to stand out socially. Some psychoanalysts believe that patients with social phobia are actually compensating for an unconscious wish to be exhibitionistic. Others feel that social phobia arises from an unconscious fear that being noticed by others will lead to drastic consequences. For example, a patient may have had a very competitive but unsuccessful parent who gave subtle messages that he would not tolerate being surpassed by the child. Such a person might come to believe, on an unconscious level, that being too successful would arouse the anger of the parent and lead to a loss of approval and affection. Young children equate such a parental dismissal as catastrophic, hence the adult with this background actually believes that he or she will face severe punishment if noticed too much by others. As protection, the patient avoids the public eye and becomes socially avoidant.

These are only examples of possible psychoanalytic explanations for the development of social phobia. Are they true? Obviously, we cannot prove them, but no theory has been proven for the cause of social phobia. More important, does psychoanalytic therapy, which seeks to make conscious these hidden wishes and fears, work to relieve social phobia? Here there is a difference between psychoanalytic therapy on the one hand and behavioral and medication treatments on the other. We now have reasonable scientific proof that the latter work, but for the former we must rely solely on the testimonials of psychoanalysts and their patients.

The New Psychiatry Approach to Social Phobia Treatment

A New Psychiatry approach attempts to integrate different types of therapy into an individualized—and effective—treatment. It is reasonable to start with behavioral therapy. Behavior therapies increasingly appear effective for social phobia and are relatively brief. Patients may be offered intermittent use of the beta blocker propranolol (Inderal) or a short half-life benzodiazepine such as Xanax even while beginning behavior therapy if immediate relief of symptoms is necessary.

If behavioral intervention is not successful, even with use as needed of beta blockers and benzodiazepines, a reasonable next step would be to try regular use of an SSRI (Prozac, Zoloft, and Paxil are currently available). If, after a six-week trial of one of these, there is no response, the next step should be Nardil (note that several weeks must elapse between stopping an SSRI and starting Nardil, an MAOI). Psychoanalytic therapy may be started at anytime for those patients who are interested in long-term treatment and for whom exploration of unconscious material appears to be of likely benefit.

It is very important, above all, not to make light of social phobia. It is not simply a case of "the jitters" and it can lead to severe impairment in occupational and social function and to drug and alcohol abuse. The steps for treatment recommended in Table 37 are a reasonable approach to tackling a serious emotional problem.

Obsessive Compulsive Disorder (OCD)

Whenever someone worries a bit too much about something, it is common for others to say, "You're so obsessive." Similarly, a person who pays a lot of attention to detail, checking her work several times, for example, might be called "compulsive." This is not what we mean by obsessive compulsive disorder.

Obsessive compulsive disorder can be one of the most severe psychiatric disorders and it is often difficult to treat. Patients with obsessive compulsive disorder (OCD) may have one or both of two key symptoms, obsessions and compulsions.

Obsessions are repetitive, senseless thoughts that the patient with OCD cannot stop thinking about. These are not merely everyday worries and they are never realistic.

Case Studies of Obsessions

Here are some examples of obsessions that meet the criteria for OCD.

The Case of John. John, a 30-year-old car mechanic, every day must sing to himself all the songs that are sung during church services on

TABLE 37

RECOMMENDED STEPS IN TREATING SOCIAL PHOBIA

1. Begin cognitive/behavioral therapy with an experienced therapist who has been specifically trained in this method and has treated patients with social phobia successfully. The treatment will include some combination of cognitive therapy to reduce anxiety-producing thinking, exposure to phobic situations, and assertiveness training. It may be conducted in a group format. Treatment should last between two and six months.

2. For patients with a discrete social phobia, like an inability to deliver a speech to an audience, intermittent use of the beta blocker propranolol can be started. Usually, 20 or 40 mg is given one hour before the phobic situation. If this is not sufficient, it can be combined with a low dose of a short half-life benzodiazepine, often 0.5 mg of Xanax or Ativan. This should not be taken on a regular basis, only before a situation known by prior experience to produce an anxiety attack.

3. If step 1, even combined with step 2, fails, begin one of the SSRI medications (Prozac, Zoloft, or Paxil). A very low dose is given at first (usually about 5 mg of Prozac, 25 mg of Zoloft, or 10 mg of Paxil) and then the dose is slowly raised over the first few weeks. The patient takes the medication every day for at least six weeks. If it works, medication is continued for six more months.

4. If step three does not work, stop the SSRI and wait six weeks after Prozac, or two weeks after Zoloft or Paxil, to start Nardil. Be sure you know the dietary restrictions in detail. Nardil comes in 15 mg pills; the usual effective dose is between 45 mg and 90 mg a day. If it works, the patient will stay on it for at least six months.

5. Consider starting psychoanalytic therapy if you are inclined toward long-term treatment and if you and the therapist have a reasonable belief that exploration of unconscious material may be helpful. Psychoanalytic treatment usually lasts at least one year and involves at least one session a week.

Sunday morning and he must do it five times. He is not allowed to make any errors. If he does, he must start over again. There are several rules for how fast he must "think" through these songs, how loud they should be in his head, and the correct order of songs. He generally takes about 30 minutes to complete this ritual, and since he has to do it five times daily he winds up spending at least two and half hours at it each day. He has had to rearrange his schedule to accommodate this obsession and sometimes, on ''bad days,'' he does not get to work at all because he has made too many errors during the first run-through and has to keep on trying. If you ask John why he does this, he can only tell you that he has tried to suppress the urge to mentally sing the songs but experiences overwhelming anxiety that can only be relieved when he gives in. John understands that these obsessions serve no purpose (he is not, actually, particularly religious) and would like nothing better than to stop.

The Case of Mary.   Mary, a physics professor, is burdened throughout the day by thoughts and images of death. She sees people she loves lying in coffins. She imagines in full detail car and train wrecks. When she drives by a hospital she cannot help ruminating about people dying. Often, she gets the idea in her head that she has been responsible for many deaths herself. Once, for example, she drove across a railroad track just a split second before the lights and sirens began to indicate an oncoming train. Mary started thinking that the train had stopped short to avoid hitting her car, resulting in many passengers being thrown to their deaths against the sides of the train. These thoughts obviously made no sense. Mary, nevertheless, searched the newspapers and listened to the news for evidence that there had been a fatal train wreck. Even though she found no such reports, she continued to obsess about the deaths of people on the train. Interestingly, Mary does not suffer from symptoms associated with clinical depression as described in Chapter 10. She has a good appetite, sleeps well at night, and enjoys her work.

Perhaps these stories seem so absurd that it is difficult to imagine people really do such things. But patients with OCD are in fact just like John and Mary. Their obsessions directly interfere with their ability to function, but no matter how hard they try to stop their obsessions they cannot be suppressed. Patients with obsessions develop terribly high levels of anxiety if they try to avoid their obsessions. At the same time, the obsessions themselves cause anxiety.

Case Studies of Compulsions
The second symptom, compulsions, involves repetitive actions or behaviors that a patient feels compelled to carry out, sometimes in response to obsessions. Here are some examples.

The Case of Alfred.   Alfred can almost never get the thought out of his head that he has touched something that has contaminated his hands. This recurrent thought is, of course, an obsession. But in addition, Alfred feels compelled to wash his hands about three times every hour. Each handwashing must be thorough and cover every inch of skin from fingertips to wrists. Nothing short of a fire in the building could stop him from washing. The skin on Alfred's hands is worn away from the constant washing and he is under the continuous care of a dermatologist. Alfred is not psychotic—that is, he does not really believe that he has been contaminated and he admits that nothing terrible, such as fatal disease, would actually happen to him if didn't wash his hands so often. But about every 20 minutes he gets the thought that he might have touched a contaminated object and that he must wash his hands. If he tries to resist washing, he gets unbearably anxious and can think of nothing except the dirt on his hands. Carrying out the ritual gives him momentary relief and allows him to continue with his regular routine.

The Case of Ronald. Ronald was hospitalized because of compulsions. He cannot sit down in a chair until he carries out a rigidly prescribed series of actions. He must first brush the seat of the chair, then the back, then the seat again. Each brushing must include 26 strokes to the left and 26 to the right. Then the chair must be turned to the right four times, then left four times, and turned completely around eight times. There is more, and the entire compulsion takes about 30 minutes. If a single mistake is made, Ronald must start all over again. He also has rituals for lying down on his bed to go to sleep. Some days he decides not to get out of bed in order to avoid having to go through the rituals. Other days he paces about his apartment for hours rather than starting the whole process necessary to sit down. Once again, Ronald cannot give a reason for all of this and will tell you he wishes he could stop. But he has given up trying to resist for many years.

Obsessive compulsive disorder was once thought to be a rare illness, but more recent data suggest it may occur in as many as three percent of the American population. Some people with OCD are able to function in various job and social roles, but it is critical to making the diagnosis that the symptoms clearly interrupt normal function and produce great distress. OCD is often a heart-rending condition to observe; the patient is fully aware of what he is doing and desperately wants to stop. Attempts to suppress the obsessions or stop the compulsions, however, only produce unbearable anxiety and the patient becomes a slave to his symptoms.

OCD is about equally common in men and women and may start in very early childhood. A fascinating book by Dr. Judith Rapaport of the National Institutes of Health called *The Boy Who Couldn't Stop Washing* details the cases of several children with OCD. Without treatment, OCD is likely to be a lifelong condition.

Conditions That Resemble OCD

There are three conditions that are closely linked to OCD that I will mention in this chapter. *Trichotillomania* is a compulsion to pull out one's hair. In severe cases patients pull clumps of hair out to the point that they need to wear a hat or wig all of the time. The patient is unable to give any reason for this behavior and often has no other obsessions or compulsions.

Body dysmorphic disorder is actually listed in the *DSM* system as a "somatization disorder," along with others like hypochondriasis. Patients with body dysmorphic disorder become obsessed with an imagined defect in their physical appearance. They think that the curve of the head is odd-looking or that there are bumps on the face that are ugly. No one can persuade these patients, who usually look just fine, that they are exaggerating their physical defects way beyond reality; the patient is unable to stop focusing on the perceived problem.

Giles de la Tourette's syndrome, often called simply *Tourette's disorder,* begins before age 18 and involves both motor tics (sudden, involuntary movements like lipsmacking or body jerks) and vocal tics (a sudden, involuntary noise; sometimes but not always an obscene word). It is now clear that patients with Tourette's disorder are more likely to have OCD than people without Tourette's disorder, but the reason for the association remains unknown.

A Biological Disorder

I believe that research will someday prove that OCD is largely a biologically mediated illness. I have to use the phrase "I believe" because scientists have not yet proven a biological basis for OCD. Still, the symptoms exhibited by patients with OCD do not seem linked to any kind of life stress or adverse childhood experiences. Rather, the patient seems locked into some involuntary neurological process that forces him to carry out certain thoughts or actions. OCD has been likened, not without reason in my opinion, to epilepsy, in which sudden involuntary bursts of activity in the brain lead to seizures. Our impression with OCD patients is that something in the brain isn't firing properly.

Evidence for a biological basis of OCD comes from several sources. First, it has been known for many years that obsessions and compulsions can develop for the first time in a previously healthy individual following traumatic brain injury or a brain infection such as encephalitis. Second, laboratory studies suggest that patients with OCD have a deficiency in activity of a particular brain chemical called serotonin. Drugs that increase serotonin activity appear to be effective treatments for OCD. Third, modern brain-imaging studies persistently show abnormalities in specific parts of the brain, including structures called the caudate, basal ganglia, and prefrontal cortex. With recent knowledge that OCD runs in families, it now appears a very good bet that some cases may be inherited.

This does not mean, of course, that medication is the only answer for OCD. In fact, nonmedication treatments of OCD have an important role.

Obsessive Compulsive Disorder: Treatment

Traditionally, OCD has been thought of as one of the most difficult psychiatric illnesses to treat. This remains the case, although modern drug and behavioral therapies have significantly improved the prognosis. Although Freud had a fascinating theory to explain the cause of OCD, it is now widely agreed by both psychoanalysts and others that psychoanalytic psychotherapy is not effective for OCD.

Most patients with OCD will need to be treated with a combination of medication and behavioral therapy. Medication is effective for both obsessions and compulsions; behavioral therapy is most effective for compulsions. The recommendations that follow apply to OCD, trichotillomania, and body dysmorphic disorder.

Medications for OCD

Most patients with OCD should be started on medication once the diagnosis is made. While future research may document that certain patients with OCD can be effectively treated with behavior therapy alone, most experts currently agree that medication is necessary for the majority of patients. Drugs that increase the amount of serotonin available to brain receptors seem to work best, and there are two kinds of these. The first kind is a drug that belongs to the tricyclic antidepressant class, called Anafranil (clomipramine). It was available throughout the world except the United States for many years, but was finally made available in this country only a few years ago. Anafranil has the most potent serotonin effects of the tricyclic drugs and has been shown to be clearly effective for OCD. Patients are usually started at about 50 mg daily and the dose is raised over several days to a maximum dose of 200 mg. It takes about four to six weeks to work.

While Anafranil is effective—perhaps the most effective drug for OCD— it does have side effects. It is one of the most sedating of the tricyclic drugs and has the typical tricyclic side effects, called anticholinergic side effects: dry mouth, constipation, sweating, blurry vision, and some difficulty initiating the urinary stream. It may be slightly more likely to produce a seizure than the other tricyclic drugs and therefore the current recommendation is to keep the dose to 200 mg or less, although in research trials many patients have taken much more without difficulty. Anafranil, like many antidepressants, may also delay the time it takes to have an orgasm. Patients with certain heart conditions, a type of glaucoma called narrow-angle glaucoma, and those with enlarged prostates may be advised by their doctors not to take Anafranil.

The second class of drugs effective in treating OCD are the antidepressants called selective serotonin reuptake inhibitors (SSRIs), which are mentioned frequently in this chapter. Included in this group are Prozac (fluoxetine), Zoloft (sertraline), Paxil (paroxetine), and Luvox (fluvoxamine). OCD patients typically need fairly high doses of SSRIs (that is, for example, 80 mg daily of Prozac or 200 mg daily of Zoloft). SSRIs also take four to six weeks before they work for OCD.

SSRIs typically have fewer side effects than Anafranil. Some patients may experience initial jitteriness, anxiety, nausea or stomach upset, and the drugs can cause insomnia. They are very safe from a medical standpoint and there are very few patients who will be advised not to take them. Sexual side effects are perhaps the most troublesome with SSRIs, with many patients complaining of difficulty achieving orgasm while taking them. Sometimes this can be handled by lowering the dose; in other instances, orgasmic difficulties simply disappear in time.

There are other drugs that have been said to be useful for OCD, including the antianxiety agent BuSpar (buspirone) and such monoamine oxidase inhibitors as Nardil (phenelzine), but the real choices are between SSRIs and Anafranil.

Because SSRIs are usually better tolerated than Anafranil, they are a very good place to start. The patient is usually begun on one of the four currently available, the dose is raised to the highest tolerated, and then a four-to-six-week wait is begun to see if it works. If it does not, many psychiatrists then switch to Anafranil and wait another four to six weeks.

For patients who fail to respond to an SSRI alone and then to Anafranil alone there are several other strategies available. One is to combine the two medications. Some patients have found that the combination of an SSRI and Anafranil can turn a previous nonresponder into a responder. Because of interactions between the two medications, however, the combination must be done very carefully by an experienced psychopharmacologist.

A second strategy is to try to augment the effectiveness of either the SSRI or Anafranil by adding something else. Fenfluramine (Pondomin) is a serotonin-stimulating drug usually prescribed to help people lose weight, which has been reported to augment the response to SSRIs and Anafranil in this way. There are also reports that BuSpar (buspirone) has this augmenting property.

Behavioral Therapy for OCD

Patients with OCD should almost always be in behavioral psychotherapy along with medication. The key components of this kind of therapy for OCD are exposure and response blocking. Many OCD patients, like Alfred in our example earlier, have a morbid fear of contamination. An exposure therapy involves actually having the patient put his hands in dirt and leaving them there for prolonged periods of time without washing. This is often first done in the therapist's office. The patient might, for example, bring in a pot full of mud and smear it on his hands, then leave it there for 30 minutes. This will produce tremendous levels of anxiety at first, but ultimately the anxiety level will go down as the patient recognizes that no untoward events occur from the mud exposure.

Response blocking is a difficult behavioral technique to carry out and requires a skilled therapist. It operates on the principle that carrying out a compulsive ritual is actually a positive reinforcement for the patient with OCD. This is because once the patient carries out the ritual, say hand washing, his anxiety level temporarily drops. Hence, hand washing reduces anxiety for the patient, conditioning him to do it every time he feels anxious. By stopping the patient from carrying out the ritual, he is prevented from getting this kind of reinforcement. Eventually, the high levels of anxiety experienced while contemplating the need to carry out the ritual will go down and the urge to hand wash will be reduced.

There is also a cognitive component to some treatments for OCD in which the therapist rehearses with the patient the obsessions and reviews all of the evidence for and against accepting the patient's worries. The therapist may instruct the patient to attempt to block the thoughts or to limit the time spent obsessing to a prescribed time of day. In general, however, behavioral interventions have been more successful for compulsions than for obsessions.

Psychosurgery

With the combined use of medication and behavioral therapy patients with OCD today often get substantial relief. Cures are less common, however, and patients may need to remain on medication for many years. Further, at least 30 percent of patients with OCD have a poor or inadequate response to even the best treatment attempts. One seemingly extreme strategy for patients who have failed to respond to every possible treatment attempt, including several different medications and years of good psychotherapy, is psychosurgery.

We do not take psychosurgery lightly. Like electroconvulsive therapy (ECT), the use of psychosurgery has lead to some mistrust of psychiatrists. There is a mistaken notion that psychiatrists use brain operations as a means of subduing political subversives or people who simply don't agree with the doctor's point of view. The implication in the movie *One Flew Over the Cuckoo's Nest* is that at the end the main character has been given a ''lobotomy'' against his will, which renders him a passive, childlike individual.

While I cannot answer for doctors who may have abused psychosurgery in the past, it is now a last-ditch but still acceptable choice for certain patients with OCD. These are patients whose lives are completely ruined by the illness and who respond to nothing. Recall the case of Ronald, presented earlier, who cannot sit in a chair until he has completed endless rituals. Ronald's OCD completely alters his life; he cannot work or socialize. He is compelled to spend his entire day moving a chair around. Hopefully, Ronald will respond to some medication and to therapy, but what if absolutely nothing works. It is reasonable for someone like Ronald to consider surgery.

Modern psychosurgery involves very small disruptions of specific brain pathways. Scientists are experimenting now with a method of using lasers to do this, which does not even require cutting into the skull. The amount of disruption of the brain is very small and in general there is very little change in the patient's personality or intelligence level after the operation. But some patients do experience a substantial reduction in their OCD symptoms to the point that they can lead more or less normal lives. When OCD is completely intractable, there should at least be a discussion about whether psychosurgery could be helpful.

Posttraumatic Stress Disorder (PTSD)

For the anxiety disorders discussed so far, we are never quite sure what role real-life events play in producing the symptoms. But for posttraumatic stress disorder, the illness, by definition, always begins with a terrible and tragic occurrence in the patient's life. This diagnosis has been terribly misused, especially by lawyers and their clients trying to win large cash settlements in disputes. Often, the event in these cases is something that a person might not like to go through or might make most people angry but is far from awful enough to meet our criteria for traumatic.

Posttraumatic stress disorder (PTSD) follows an event that would be expected to cause severe distress in anyone. Being a Holocaust survivor, a soldier who sees his best friend killed in battle, a participant in an automobile crash that leaves several people dead, or being a rape victim are examples of traumatic events capable of causing PTSD. Having a nasty boss, being shoved in a bar by a drunk patron, or getting bitten by a neighbor's dog, while all unfortunate, are not generally felt severe or unusual enough to cause PTSD.

Following the really traumatic event, sometimes immediately and sometimes not until several months later, patients with PTSD develop two characteristic symptoms: flashbacks to the event and emotional numbing. Flashbacks may occur while awake, in dreams, or both, but in either case the patient feels as if he or she is reliving the original traumatic event over and over again. The flashbacks are not simply bad memories; the patient actually feels as if the event is occurring. For example, a Holocaust survivor with PTSD may see a uniformed guard in front of a museum and suddenly feel as if he is once again in a concentration camp. A Vietnam War veteran who witnessed three of his closest buddies blown to bits by a land mine hears a car backfire and runs for cover, feeling suddenly that he is in the midst of gunfire.

Emotional numbing is a persistent inability to experience life with the full range of emotion that was possible before the traumatic event. Events both happy and sad seem to leave the PTSD patient relatively unmoved; the ability to participate in life is lost.

In addition to these major symptoms the patient with PTSD also experi-

TABLE 38

*Treatment Plan for Obsessive Compulsive Disorder**

Step 1:	Begin medication, usually one of the SSRI drugs (Prozac, Zoloft, Luvox, or Paxil), and get up to a relatively high dose in the first few weeks.
	AND
	Begin behavior therapy, with components such as exposure and response blocking.
Step 2:	Wait at least six weeks to see if the drug works. If it does, stay on it for at least one year. If you stop it and your symptoms come back, go back on the drug. Also, complete the behavior therapy program and if it works see your therapist again from time to time if any symptoms return.
Step 3:	If the first drug does not work, switch to Anafranil and get the dose up to 200 mg if you can tolerate it. Wait at least six weeks to see if it works. Continue behavior therapy.
Step 4:	If neither the SSRI or Anafranil work, try one of the augmentation or combination strategies mentioned in the text.
Step 5:	If absolutely nothing works and your symptoms are severe and incapacitating, ask your doctor to discuss surgery with you. Get several opinions from different doctors before going ahead with this to make sure you have exhausted every other possibility.

*These steps apply to patients with trichotillomania and body dysmorphic syndrome as well.

ences a variety of common anxiety and depressive symptoms, including loss of energy and the ability to concentrate, tension, jumpiness, insomnia, and appetite disturbance. Sometimes these symptoms evaporate on their own after several months, but for some patients PTSD can linger for years or even a lifetime. The more uncontrollable the trauma, it seems, the more severe are the symptoms. Some have observed that PTSD is worse when the trauma is man-made, such as war, torture, or rape, than when it is a natural disaster, such as an earthquake or flood.

The Controversy Over Repressed Memories

An emerging controversy in the PTSD field is the extent to which people can suffer from the symptoms of PTSD because of traumatic events for which they have absolutely no memory. Recently, some therapists have created what they call the "profile" of a patient who had been sexually abused as a child but has no recollection of these events. In the course of treatment, the therapist attempts to help the patient "remember" what happened. The argument here is that traumatic events, like sexual abuse, may be entirely repressed by the young child, obliterating all memory in adult life. The symptoms of PTSD are apparent in the adult, however.

This has been controversial because it is clearly open to misinterpretation and exploitation. Proponents of the idea that PTSD can follow unrecollected childhood sexual abuse often insist that critics are merely sexist. They cite recent surveys showing the high prevalence of childhood sexual abuse and note that this abuse is usually, but not always, perpetuated by adult men against young girls. Male scientists and therapists, they believe, attempt to deny that unrecollected childhood sexual abuse can cause later PTSD because they do not want to deal with the issue and because they do not take seriously the plight of women in male-dominated societies.

On the other hand, some therapists and scientists fear that impressionable patients with emotional problems may be talked into remembering childhood sexual abuse that never really occurred, so-called false memories. Unscrupulous therapists could use this as a means of hooking patients into years of psychotherapy to resolve feelings about an event that never took place. Some women who were indeed the victims of childhood sexual abuse and remember what happened with perfect clarity may feel that their awful experience is being trivialized if therapists attempt to talk large numbers of women into believing that they too were sexually abused even if they don't remember it.

My best advice here is to use caution in your own situation. I believe it is absolutely true that men would like the issue of childhood sexual abuse to go away, even men who would never entertain the idea of doing it themselves. Men are often unable to understand the horrible impact of sexual abuse on young children and tend to make light of it. Many women who have been the victims of childhood sexual abuse complain that male doctors and therapists—and sometimes female doctors and therapists as well—treat it as a minor event.

At the same time, patients should never let themselves be talked into anything. If you do not remember ever being sexually abused, don't assume you were just because a therapist thinks you fit the "profile" of someone who must have been abused. Remember that your own memories are to be taken seriously; don't ever let a therapist insist that something happened to you if you don't have the slightest inkling that it did happen. And also remember that there are different types of sexual abuse, not all of which are guaranteed to produce lifelong symptoms. Many brothers and sisters will expose their genitals to each other on a few occasions in early childhood before puberty; while I personally think this is to be strongly discouraged and forbidden by attentive parents, it is common and should not have devastating effects on a young woman's development. Rape and incest, on the other hand, will almost always produce substantial symptoms, but are so horrible that they will generally be recalled by the victim. I absolutely do not mean to imply in this discussion that childhood sexual abuse as a cause of PTSD should be taken lightly or that it is impossible for the abuse to have been forgotten; rather, I want patients to be cautious about accepting interpretations from therapists that are not synchronous with what the patient actually remembers.

PTSD May Have a Biology
It is interesting that despite the fact that PTSD is the one psychiatric syndrome that always involves a real-life event, it may still have a biology and may still be, in part, genetic. We often mistakenly think that everything in the human body is laid down in stone when we are born and cannot be changed by experience. Obviously, this is not true and there are many examples of how our behavior changes the physical aspects of our bodies. If you smoke cigarettes you will vastly increase your chances of developing lung cancer. If you exercise vigorously you will have stronger bones and muscles. Similarly, there is now evidence that if you are subject to severe traumatic stress you may alter some aspects of brain function. During times of stress and anxiety the hormone cortisol, which is heavily regulated by a hormone called CRH that the brain makes, is often secreted in greater than usual amounts. Some researchers have now shown that there are changes in cortisol physiology in patients with PTSD. Others have found that the brain neurotransmitter called noradrenaline may act differently in people with PTSD compared to people who have not undergone severe traumatic stress. There is a hint that the tendency to develop PTSD after traumatic life events may be partially under genetic control, although this is very tentative.

The Treatment of PTSD
In treating PTSD, there is some therapeutic benefit in the simple process of supportive listening. Some PTSD patients feel guilty about what happened to them, either because they have a secret belief that they could have done something to prevent it or because they have survived while others perished. Consider a patient with PTSD who was a passenger in a car that crashed, killing the driver and another passenger. She secretly harbors the belief that she had seen the car going through the red light that hit the car she was in moments before the crash. Why didn't she scream to the driver to stop? In most cases, it turns out the patient's belief that she could have changed the course of events is a fantasy and it is sometimes helpful to review these guilty ruminations and correct them. Survivor guilt is a common phenomenon

among PTSD patients. Many survivors of the Nazi Holocaust experience this, wondering why they were spared. Again, helping the patient understand that he or she is trying mentally to control irrational events is part of the therapeutic approach to PTSD.

Because PTSD can be devastating to the patient's ability to function or enjoy life, psychiatrists have tried a variety of medications to resolve the symptoms. In fact, it is hard to think of any drug that has not been tried for patients with PTSD. Unfortunately, very few scientific studies have been done of medication use for PTSD, so it is very difficult to say with certainty what works and what only seems to work because the doctor and patient want it to work.

So far, the antidepressant drugs mentioned several other times in this chapter called SSRIs (selective serotonin reuptake inhibitors) seem to hold the most promise for treating PTSD. In the United States this class includes Prozac (fluoxetine), Luvox (fluvoxamine), Zoloft (sertraline), and Paxil (paroxetine). Although few high-quality scientific studies have been published, there is some evidence from a few reports that these drugs can help decrease some of the symptoms experienced by PTSD patients, including intrusive memories of the traumatic event, emotional blunting, depression, and anxiety. If medication is going to be used, one of these drugs is a reasonable place to begin. They generally have few side effects and are quite safe from a medical standpoint. More can be read about them in the chapters on psychiatric drugs and depression in this book.

Another approach to the medication treatment of PTSD is to treat the most prominent symptoms with the appropriate drug. For example, if a patient is mainly bothered by flashbacks and memories of the traumatic event, drugs that are known to treat obsessive compulsive disorder, like the SSRIs or Anafranil (clomipramine), are a reasonable choice. If avoidance of events associated with the traumatic event is the principle symptom, antiphobic drugs like the tricyclics (imipramine, desipramine, or nortriptyline) or SSRIs are called for. Depression and emotional numbness can be treated with any of the antidepressants. Anxiety, tension, and hyperarousal might respond best to such antianxiety drugs as the benzodiazepines (Valium, Librium, Xanax, or Ativan) or BuSpar (buspirone). Some psychiatrists have found that the anticonvulsant drug Tegretol (carbamazepine), which is used to treat some patients with bipolar mood disorder (formerly known as manic depression), also seems to help patients with PTSD.

There is obviously a great need to do more research on the treatment of PTSD. It seems that today's world is replete with opportunities to expose people to extreme, cruel, and often humiliating traumatic experiences. We now suspect that such experiences alter both psychological and physical function and believe that attention to both aspects with psychotherapy and medication is probably the best approach to treatment of posttraumatic stress disorder.

12.
Schizophrenia

I HAVE TWO purposes in writing this chapter about schizophrenia. Like all other parts of this book, my first purpose is to explain what the illness is and what treatment options exist. But to a greater extent than with any other chapter I hope to appeal to the reader's conscience and make him or her more compassionate toward people suffering with schizophrenia. I believe that many psychiatrists have always believed in the importance of extending kindness and empathy to patients with schizophrenia and their families, but it is now a clear conviction of the New Psychiatry that we treat schizophrenia as a severe and often devastating brain disease.

Let me begin with the second purpose. Perhaps more than any other group of people with a severe medical illness, people with schizophrenia suffer from constant taunts, bigotry, ignorance, and hostility. Labels like "crazy," "mental case," "lunatic," and "fruitcake" are hurled at them, even by supposedly sensitive people and often in the most prestigious media. Calling a person with schizophrenia a "head case" or "nuts" is no less prejudicial and bigoted than using words like "nigger," "faggot," "bitch," or "kike," but people with schizophrenia have not had, until recently, powerful lobbying groups to protect their interests and fight against such prejudice. The fact is that the very nature of the illness makes it extremely difficult for people with schizophrenia to stand up for themselves and present their case to the world. As you will see, this problem has retarded progress both in the research to understand what causes schizophrenia and in the attempt to provide safe and humane treatment.

There is no question that schizophrenia is a severe brain disease caused by malfunction in one or more neurotransmitter systems in the central nervous system. No credible authority believes any longer that social circumstance, poverty, poor mothering, or willful behavior causes schizophrenia. Scientists are rapidly honing in on the exact nature of the brain disorder that causes schizophrenia. We are almost certain at this point that some cases are genetic while others are probably caused by environmental insults that disturb the developing brain during fetal life. Two parts of the brain, the temporal lobe and the prefrontal cortex, appear to be most involved and two brain chemicals—dopamine and serotonin—are prominently mentioned by scientists in their attempt to understand exactly what goes wrong in the schizophrenic brain.

What It Is Not

That is a capsule version of what schizophrenia is. Before going into greater detail, let's consider some of the things schizophrenia is not. First, it has nothing to do with "split personalities." The term *schizophrenic* is sometimes used in popular literature to mean someone who is torn between two competing personalities or who acts in two radically different ways at different times. This has nothing to do with the illness psychiatrists and psychologists recognize as schizophrenia. Second, a person with schizophrenia is no more likely to be a violent psychopath than anyone else in the world. Recently, the company that manufactures the G.I. Joe doll was criticized for calling a new doll billed as the violent enemy of G.I. Joe as "schizophrenic." In fact, patients with schizophrenia are more likely to be the *victims* of violence than the perpetrators. While it is true that some famous cases of violent acts have been committed by people who probably did have schizophrenia— like the Son of Sam—the illness itself is not defined by any propensity to harm others, and the vast number of violent crimes committed in the world are not carried out by people with schizophrenia. Adolph Hitler, for example, clearly did not have schizophrenia; there is no psychiatric "excuse" for his behavior. Third, patients with schizophrenia do not live in peaceful bliss. A popular movie in the 1960s called *The King of Hearts* portrayed the patients in an asylum as peaceful, "otherworldly" types surrounded by a supposedly "insane" world of war and violence. Although I personally like the movie for its antiwar message, the patients in it bear very little resemblance to people with schizophrenia. Schizophrenia produces terrible suffering, leading many of its victims to contemplate or even attempt suicide.

Emil Kraeplin

The only proper way to regard schizophrenia is as an illness. The great German psychiatrist Emil Kraeplin gave the world the first real description of schizophrenia, which he called "dementia praecox." Kraeplin noted that patients with schizophrenia tended to follow a downhill course, ultimately developing a disorder that involved marked loss of intellectual ability. He differentiated it from what he called manic depressive psychosis, a disorder he felt often involved the same symptoms as dementia praecox but lacked this deteriorating course. Manic depressive patients seemed to Kraeplin to recover from each psychotic episode and return to normal function until the next episode.

Kraeplin's description is still important to the modern psychiatrist, although today we know that not all patients with schizophrenia deteriorate and not all patients with manic depression (which we now call bipolar mood disorder) recover fully between episodes. In making the diagnosis of schizophrenia we look for both a characteristic set of symptoms and for some evidence that these symptoms last for several months.

The symptoms that patients with schizophrenia have are called psychotic symptoms. Loosely speaking, these are the symptoms that represent a "break with reality." There are three main types of psychotic symptoms: *hallucinations, delusions,* and *thought disorder.*

Hallucinations

Hallucinations occur when a person hears, sees, smells, or feels something that isn't really there. The most common form of hallucination in patients with schizophrenia is auditory hallucination—hearing voices. The patient with schizophrenia who hears voices does not think the voices are merely his own thoughts; the voices sound to him as if someone is really talking. Sometimes the patient is surprised or annoyed that other people cannot hear the voices. There may be one voice or several and they may be the voices of strangers or of people the patient knows. These voices usually do not say calming, soothing, or complimentary things to the patient. Sometimes they criticize him, or tell him to do things he wouldn't ordinarily do, or comment on whatever he is doing at the time. Some patients talk back to the voices, making it obvious that a patient is listening to them. Other patients remain secretive about the voices and sometimes deny hearing them.

Delusions

Delusions are false ideas that no amount of reality can change. These are not opinions, religious beliefs, preferences, or even eccentric ideas but clearly false notions that the patient holds on to no matter what. One common type of delusion in patients with schizophrenia is the paranoid delusion in which the patient is convinced that others are out to get him. ''Paranoid'' does not mean overly sensitive; people who often read criticism into other people's benign comments sometimes refer to themselves, incorrectly, as paranoid. Rather, a paranoid person believes that for no good reason there are people out there who want to do him harm. Some paranoid patients think that strangers are staring at them and talking about them; others think that the CIA or FBI are after them or even that Martians are watching them.

There are many other kinds of delusions that patients with schizophrenia may have. They may believe that there are strange things growing inside their bodies or that they really come from another planet. In each case the belief is patently incorrect but the patient cannot be persuaded.

Thought Disorders

Thought disorder involves a disruption of the normal thinking process to the point that the person cannot communicate coherently. When the patient with a thought disorder talks, the listener quickly realizes that much of what he says makes no sense. Sometimes, but not always, the patient can explain that this is because he is having trouble making sense of his own thoughts. Odd or socially unacceptable thoughts do not constitute a thought disorder.

Related to thought disorder is the behavioral disorganization seen in some patients with schizophrenia. The patient may do truly bizarre things, like collect garbage or wear heavy coats and sweaters on a hot day. Often, the patient is unable to give any coherent explanation for these behaviors.

Once again, it is important to make the distinction between odd or eccentric thoughts and actions and the symptoms of schizophrenia. Psychiatrists are not interested in labeling political subversives or counterculture types as "schizophrenic." Schizophrenia should be applied to people with symptoms that are clearly abnormal, not merely unusual or perhaps distasteful.

A Case Study of Schizophrenia

Here is an example of a patient brought to a hospital emergency room exhibiting several different symptoms of schizophrenia.

The Case of Jon.   Jon, a 36-year-old man, is brought to the emergency room by police after his neighbors in his apartment building complained that he had been yelling and screaming for three nights in a row well into the early morning hours. When the police arrive they hear shattering glass in the apartment. They need to get the superintendent to open the door because Jon doesn't respond to their beating on it. When the police get in they see a fearful sight. Jon has piled all the furniture in the whole apartment in one corner and is smashing some glasses. He is not wearing any clothes and looks as if he has not showered or shaved in a week. When the police come in the room, Jon looks terrified. He cowers behind the pile of furniture and refuses to move. The police cannot understand much of what he says, but they are able to convince him to go with them to the hospital.

In the hospital emergency room Jon appears to calm. He sits quietly except for occasional gesticulations. He also seems to be listening to an imaginary voice and he talks incoherently to it. A psychiatrist introduces himself to Jon and asks his name.

"Jon, name is Jon Frankenstein and the monster is after all of us— that's because of those guys in blue [he points to a security guard in the emergency room] who are the devil and they chase us and me too."

"Jon," says the psychiatrist, who cannot yet find out his last name, "the police officers who brought you here said you were shouting and breaking things. Why were you doing that?"

"Because of the monsters who were screaming at me. I thought I could crush them with the glasses. I almost had to light a match."

"Did you hear monsters yelling at you?"

"Yes, they have been yelling at me. They are sent there by the devils, ever since my brother moved out. He sent them to get all my money."

"What do the voices tell you?"

"They tell me to pile up the furniture and to light the matches and stuff like that."

Fortunately, it is possible for the psychiatrist to get some history from Jon. He is able to tell his age and relate that his brother and his brother's girlfriend had been living in the apartment with him until about two weeks earlier. They left, but Jon did not know where they went. Since they left he has been hearing voices and become convinced that there are monsters and devils in the apartment who are trying to control his mind. In order to keep them out of his brain, Jon related, he had stopped washing or shaving and only ate bread and candy bars.

This patient clearly has three psychotic symptoms. He is experiencing auditory hallucinations (hearing voices), he has delusions (he believes that monsters and devils are trying to control his mind), and he has a thought disorder (very little of what he says makes much sense, although the psychiatrist is able to piece together something of a story through a combination of patience and painstaking questioning).

At this point, however, we know that Jon is psychotic, but we do not know if he actually has schizophrenia. This is because there are several different ways a person can become psychotic. Drugs and alcohol can produce psychotic states; so can a variety of medical conditions, like brain tumors and systemic lupus. Finally, other psychiatric illnesses, like the manic phase of bipolar mood disorder, can also involve psychosis. Before making a diagnosis of schizophrenia, therefore, it is necessary to rule out drug and alcohol intoxication and a variety of medical problems.

Jon is admitted to the hospital and through some detective work his brother is located and asked to come to the hospital. The brother is able to give more pieces to the puzzle. Jon, it turns out, has had psychotic symptoms since he was 19 years old. He has been admitted to the hospital more than ten times since then. Although he was once a college student who received good grades, had friends, and wanted to become an engineer, he had never been able to hold a job and spent most of his time either attending various psychiatric clinics or sitting in front of the television set smoking cigarettes. He is generally withdrawn and isolated, especially when he is taking medication, but from time to time he becomes increasingly psychotic and begins to insist that all kinds of supernatural beings are talking to him and trying to harm him.

With this history the diagnosis of chronic schizophrenia seems secure. All medical tests are negative and, in any event, there are very few medical conditions that would cause psychosis but no other physical symptoms for 17 years. Jon denies using drugs, his blood and urine are negative for drugs and alcohol, and his brother confirms that he does not drink much alcohol or use street drugs. Finally, mania seems highly unlikely because when Jon is psychotic he does not have a euphoric mood and he has never had a clear-cut period of depression that would be necessary to make a diagnosis of bipolar mood disorder.

The diagnosis of schizophrenia, then, rests both on the presence of typical psychotic symptoms and on a course of illness that includes either prolonged psychosis or many episodes of psychosis. We do not make the diagnosis of schizophrenia in someone having their first episode of psychosis, although we worry a great deal that such "first break" patients may actually go on to develop schizophrenia. A small number of people with psychosis in early adult life recover and never have another episode; that is a fortunate outcome. About one-third of patients, however, develop a relentless course like Jon in which psychotic episodes follow each other, with less and less return to full functioning in between each episode.

Positive and Negative Symptoms

The psychotic symptoms of thought disorder, disorganized behavior, hallucinations, and delusions are often referred to as "positive" symptoms, not because they are good but because they represent the production of abnormal behavior. They are distinguished from a series of symptoms called "negative" symptoms, which represent the absence of normal behaviors. Negative symptoms include social withdrawal, lack of facial expression, inability to experience or express emotion, apathy, inability to derive pleasure, and sometimes intellectual decline, with actual loss of reasoning and cognitive abilities. Many patients with schizophrenia begin with mainly positive symptoms but, over the course of many years of illness, develop an increasing number of negative symptoms. These patients will often sit for hours on end, sometimes on park benches or street corners, staring into space, motionless. Negative symptoms can start early in the course of schizophrenia, however, or, in some instances, be the only symptoms. The latter is an especially difficult diagnostic problem because patients with only negative symptoms are hard to distinguish from patients with depression. The difference is that patients with negative symptoms do not really feel sad, guilty, and hopeless. They often feel very little emotion at all.

Subcategories of Schizophrenia

There are many different ways to subcategorize schizophrenia. Table 40 gives some subtypes commonly employed. *Paranoid*-type schizophrenia is diagnosed when paranoid delusions predominate the clinical picture. Such patients will often not hear voices or have thought disorder. The patient maintains a fixed, irrational belief that people are trying to harm him. *Disorganized* schizophrenia occurs when thought disorder and bizarre behavior are the predominant symptoms. When negative symptoms predominate the clinical picture, the diagnosis of *deficit* schizophrenia is made. *Undifferentiated* schizophrenia is diagnosed when no single symptom predominates but the patient has many different kinds of psychotic symptoms. Jon would probably be given the diagnosis of undifferentiated schizophrenia.

Catatonia is a somewhat controversial category. Catatonic patients are virtually motionless. They sit like statues, are mute, and have no facial expression. Sometimes, if you lift up one of their arms it stays in place rather than dropping down. This sometimes alternates with periods of extreme, purposeless agitation

TABLE 39
SOME OF THE SYMPTOMS OF SCHIZOPHRENIA

I. Positive symptoms
- Hallucinations (hearing, seeing, feeling, or smelling things that are not really there)
- Delusions (false ideas that the patient will not give up no matter how much evidence to the contrary is presented)
- Thought disorder (a disturbance in thinking that leads to an inability to communicate coherently)

II. Negative symptoms
- Social isolation and withdrawal
- Apathy
- Alogia (decreased speech)
- Anhedonia (inability to derive pleasure)
- Loss of affect (inability to experience or express emotion)
- Cognitive impairment (loss of memory, the ability to solve problems, and reasoning capacity)

or with periods when the patient exhibits random body movements and jerks. Catatonia is rare, and when it occurs, it often does so in a patient who actually has bipolar mood disorder (manic depressive illness) or a neurological disease, not schizophrenia. Another controversial subtype of schizophrenia is called *simple* schizophrenia. This refers to people who in early adult life show a marked change in personality over a several-year period, becoming aimless, withdrawn, and unmotivated. In time, such people become isolated, unfriendly, and aloof. They do not appear as ill as people with the deficit type of schizophrenia because their intellectual abilities remain intact and they are capable of carrying on conversations. This category is controversial because it was sometimes used to label people as severely ill who were merely shy, withdrawn, and socially uncomfortable. It is not used much today.

Another important but difficult to apply subtype is *schizoaffective disorder.* Some patients with schizophrenia show a picture that is mixed between schizophrenia and a mood disorder. That is, when they get psychotic they also have signs and symptoms of either mania or depression. The distinctions here are very complex because it is possible to have pure depression with psychotic symptoms or pure mania with psychotic symptoms and not be considered schizophrenic at all. In those cases the psychotic symptoms are what we call "mood congruent," that is, the hallucinations and delusions

TABLE 40
SOME SUBTYPES AND VARIANTS OF SCHIZOPHRENIA

• Paranoid	Delusions that others are trying to plot against or harm the patient dominate the clinical picture.
• Disorganized	Thought disorder and bizarre behavior dominate the clinical picture.
• Deficit	Negative symptoms dominate the clincial picture.
• Undifferentiated	Patient has a variety of psychotic symptoms, but none of them predominate.
• Catatonic	Patient is virtually immobile much of the time, with some episodes of extreme agitation and random physical movements; very rarely seen in patients with schizophrenia.
• Simple	A somewhat disfavored term for patients who have a marked deterioration over time in the ability to socialize with others, to the point of leading lonely, isolated, withdrawn lives.
• Schizopreniform	Patient has all the signs and symptoms of schizophrenia but the illness has lasted less than six months.
• Schizoid personality disorder	A person with a lifelong style of social isolation, aloofness, and little regard for human contact; may be genetically linked to schizophrenia.
• Schizotypal Personality Disorder	Similar to schizoid personality but patient also exhibits a pattern of peculiar and odd behavior; may be genetically linked to schizophrenia.

are depressing in the case of a depressed patient or euphoric and grandiose in the case of a manic patient. In schizoaffective disorder you might have a depressed patient who hears voices commenting on his actions like: "Now you are eating your lunch, now you are walking down the hall." These auditory hallucinations are typical of patients with schizophrenia but atypical for depression. Such a patient might be given the diagnosis of schizoaffective disorder, depressed.

The *DSM-IV* system requires that the patient have symptoms of schizophrenia for at least six months before the diagnosis is made. Patients with psychotic symptoms typical of schizophrenia for less than six months are given the provisional diagnosis of schizophreniform disorder. If the illness then lasts, this is changed to schizophrenia.

There are two personality disorders that are also discussed in Chapter 15 that may be variants of schizophrenia: schizoid personality disorder and schizotypal personality disorder. Personality disorders are enduring styles of feeling, acting, and responding to the world that are considered maladaptive because they cause the patient discomfort and harm. We used to call them ''neuroses,'' but this term has fallen into disfavor in some circles. There is a whole range of personality disorders and they are laid out in more detail in Chapter 15. The reason for considering them here is that a number of studies looking at the family patterns and genetics of schizophrenia have found a possible relationship between schizophrenia and both schizoid and schizotypal personality. It is possible that people with these personality disorders carry the gene or genes for schizophrenia without themselves getting the complete illness. Nevertheless, they may be capable of passing on the gene to their children who then do develop full-blown schizophrenia.

People with schizoid personality resemble in many ways what we called ''simple schizophrenia'' in an earlier part of this chapter—basically, they have virtually no need for human contact. They are not shy or socially phobic; they really don't care if they are with people or not. They tend to be cold, talk little, and do not care what other people say or think about them. People with schizotypal personality have these same traits plus what can only be described as ''peculiar'' or ''odd'' behavior. They may believe they can influence events in the world by their own thoughts, or think that television or radio programs are conveying special, personal messages to them. They may be very suspicious of others and often talk in a very vague and circuitous way.

It is important to understand that neither schizoid or schizotypal personality disorder involves psychotic symptoms. These people usually do not get hospitalized and psychiatrists are very wary of treating them with medication. Most of these patients are not interested in psychotherapy because they are fairly content with their lonely, isolated lives. They often evoke sympathy from others because of their seeming loneliness, but the patients themselves often are not all that interested in changing things.

How Schizophrenia Starts

Schizophrenia develops very differently in different people, although some general statements can be made. Men usually show signs of schizophrenia earlier than women. It is common for schizophrenia to begin around age 18 or 19 in men and unusual to see it for the first time after age 30. Women, on the other hand, often do not show signs until their twenties and can have their first psychotic break after age 30. It is very uncommon for anyone to first develop schizophrenia after age 40; psychotic symptoms in someone of that age who has never been psychotic before usually come from an illness besides schizophrenia, like alcoholism or bipolar mood disorder.

Poor people living in cities are more likely to develop schizophrenia than wealthy people living in the country. Scientists are now fairly certain that this is not because poverty and crowding cause schizophrenia. Rather, people become poor and gravitate toward cities because schizophrenia makes it very difficult for them to earn a living and they wind up on welfare or in large institutions. Although it is critical to provide better residential and community care for people with schizophrenia, better housing won't cure the illness.

In some cases there are incipient signs of schizophrenia in childhood. Such children who are destined to develop the illness are withdrawn, isolated kids who are made fun of by other children. They never seem to fit in and sometimes exhibit odd or eccentric behavior. In other instances childhood and adolescence are completely normal and psychotic symptoms come on rather suddenly and without warning in early adult life. Right now, we really have no reliable way of predicting who will get schizophrenia in later life.

Schizophrenia Presents in Different Ways: Some Case Examples

Here are some examples of patients with schizophrenia with different presentations.

The Case of Ronald.   Ronald, who is 36 years old, is an example of someone who shows signs of abnormal behavior even in childhood. Today, he is sitting in a chair in a hospital, rocking back and forth and muttering to himself. He has a vacant look on his face and when spoken to only reluctantly interrupts the conversation he appears to be having with unseen companions. His hair is not combed and he has a beard that has not been attended to for weeks. He has just been brought into the hospital by his mother, who says that Ronald started refusing to take his medication three weeks ago and now sits in a chair at home all day long, refusing to change his clothes, bathe, or speak to anyone. She is getting alarmed because he also has been eating less and less. He offered no resistance to coming to the hospital.

Ronald's mother tells the doctors that she thought there was something wrong with him when he was a very young boy. He seemed cranky and hard to relate to even as a five-year-old. In school he was always described by teachers as ''polite, but very quiet.'' He showed little interest in playing with other children and never seemed to care how he dressed for school. He spent most of his time reading books and listening to the radio. A test of his I.Q. indicated above-average intelligence at age 11, but Ronald did not do very well in school because he rarely participated in class and seemed completely disinterested. He was also very clumsy and poor at sports. Other children considered him weird and often treated him cruelly, but he appeared relatively indifferent to these insults and kept mainly to himself.

In high school Ronald started refusing to go to school from time to time, complaining that his head hurt and he couldn't concentrate. He became fixated on books about astronomy and relentlessly read one book after the other about stars, galaxies, and space travel. Teachers complained to Ronald's parents that every essay he wrote for school was always about the same topic. Ronald never had a girlfriend or even a date in high school and rarely went to the movies or out with friends. He graduated from high school and enrolled in community college. One day he started grimacing and laughing in the middle of a class and was asked to leave. He left school and refused to return.

After dropping out of college Ronald took a job as a clerk in a store, but was quickly fired for poor attendance at work. He preferred to sit at home and read his astronomy books. One day, his father discovered a diary Ronald had been keeping for months. In it, Ronald had detailed a complicated but difficult to follow system of interplanetary communication between himself and several people from outer space. His parents wondered, hopefully, if perhaps he was writing a science fiction novel, but Ronald became furious when he discovered that his parents had read the diary and left the house. His parents had to call the police and Ronald was found sitting in an abandoned car three days later, apparently having had nothing to eat in the interval. He was taken to the hospital where he was treated for frostbite. A psychiatrist was called.

The psychiatrist interviewed Ronald and found that he had a complicated delusional system involving outerspace creatures who sent him messages through astronomy textbooks. Ronald insisted that the words in the books were secret messages meant for him that he had translated into English in his diary. He was furious that his parents had read his secret decoding and believed that his space friends would soon beam him up to another planet from the abandoned car. Ronald acknowledged that he could often hear the space people talking to him. They would generally reassure him that they were soon coming to get him and that he should keep his communications with them a secret. Ronald was afraid to go home because he thought it would be disloyal to his space friends. The psychiatrist made the following suggestion: "It is very painful to go around feeling as frightened as you do. It is possible that some medication could make you feel less afraid and I would like you to try it." Ronald, unlike many patients with schizophrenia who refuse medication, agreed to take the pills.

The medication, an antipsychotic drug called Haldol (haloperidol), had a calming effect on Ronald and he went home. His parents continued to give him medication over the next few weeks and they noticed some change in his behavior. He stopped sitting in the chair all day and began to engage in conversations with his parents. He read the newspaper and watched television instead of restricting himself to books about stars and planets. He laughed at humorous programs on television and for the first time in several years went to the movies and also to a shopping mall with his parents. He asked if he could buy a new shirt and seemed interested in trying on sweaters.

The medication also had side effects, however. Ronald began complaining that he felt jumpy and agitated. He developed a tremor and some stiffness in his muscles. He found it hard to get up in the morning. After several months he stopped taking the medication and within weeks he was back in his chair reading books about stars. He became less and less communicative and finally stopped eating because, it later turned out, he got the idea that "earth food keeps me on earth and I can't stay on earth too much longer." He was hospitalized for a second time and again responded to medication.

This is a fairly typical story of chronic schizophrenia. By the time Ronald is 36 he has been hospitalized half a dozen times. When he takes his medication he becomes more outgoing and able to engage in several different kinds of activities. At one point he even enrolled in a job training program. But after a while he always stops the medication, mainly because of side effects but also because he never accepts that there is anything wrong with him, and he winds up back in the hospital. He never has to be forced to go into the hospital or to take medication once the doctors give it to him, and his hospital stays are relatively brief. There is no suggestion, however, that Ronald will break this pattern unless a better medication is found that has fewer side effects so that Ronald will stay on it.

Some might argue that Ronald should be permitted to live his life however he wants to. His parents, of course, disagree. They want their son at least to be able to eat, go the store, and talk. They contend that without medication Ronald would probably starve or freeze to death in an abandoned car someplace. No one ever has to tie him down or force drugs down his throat. He is never a threat to anyone besides himself. Ronald really has never voiced an opinion about what should happen to him one way or the other. Mostly, he thinks he is going to get to another planet someday and he does not seem to care all that much what people tell him to do until that day arrives. Hopefully, most people will recognize that Ronald is suffering from a serious brain disease that deserves treatment. He probably had signs of the illness from early childhood. There is a suggestion that medication can help him, but so far the drugs he has tried have not helped enough and he has not agreed to stay on them for very long. Unless we are prepared to let Ronald die, we will have to continue to hospitalize him at considerable expense to his family and to society.

The Case of Martin.   Martin, in his forties, had a different kind of presentation than Ronald. He showed absolutely no signs of any difficulty until things suddenly unraveled in early adulthood. He was a star student and athlete in high school and went off to a prestigious college with high hopes of becoming a doctor someday. No one in his family had ever seen a psychiatrist as far as Martin's parents knew, and they never had any inkling that there was anything wrong with Martin throughout his childhood. They were a little concerned, however, when Martin began calling home frequently during his second year of college complaining that the courses were too hard and that the teachers were all unfair. Then one day Martin got into a fight with one of his dorm mates whom he accused of stealing money from his room. The charge was clearly false and the other students in the dorm thought Martin was acting very strangely and started avoiding him. One day Martin made an appointment to see one of the assistant deans at the college and told the dean he wanted to make a formal charge of discrimination against one of the teaching assistants. In vague and rambling sentences Martin told the perplexed dean that the teacher had it out for him because Martin had different "political, social, and economical ideas than the professor." He accused the teacher of plotting to have him flunk out of school by telling all the other teachers that Martin was a "homosexual and child molester."

The dean doubted Martin's story but still decided to check. In fact, the teaching assistant barely knew Martin because Martin had not been coming to class or turning in any papers. From this developed a sad story. Martin had developed a number of clearly paranoid ideas about people talking behind his back and trying to harm him. He accused classmates of stealing his notes, dorm mates of stealing his property, and teachers of ganging up to get him thrown out of school. He stopped using the telephones on campus, believing they had all been tapped to pick up his conversations. He had written several fairly incoherent letters to the president of the college accusing various teachers of plotting against him.

The school officials asked Martin to see a doctor in the student health service. Their first concern was that Martin might be taking drugs. Certain drugs, like amphetamines, can produce paranoia, although Martin's pattern of sustained and complex delusional ideas are difficult to produce with drugs. Nevertheless, Martin adamantly denied using any street drugs and blood and urine screens were completely negative. His physical examination was also normal and the doctor could find no obvious reason for Martin's odd behavior. Because Martin complained that he could not sleep well and felt tense and uptight the doctor prescribed a sleeping pill.

A few days after the visit to the doctor, Martin was arrested by campus police after he stormed into a class that he wasn't enrolled in and began cursing at the teacher, insisting that she was part of the plot to get him thrown out of school. Martin did not attempt to assault the teacher, but his behavior was threatening and out of control. He was brought to the hospital emergency room where a psychiatrist evaluated him. In the emergency room Martin detailed his very paranoid and delusional ideas and threatened to have "all my lawyers expose you to the government and to society for the terrible injustices you are portraying [sic] against the people of this universality [sic]." Because of the relatively sudden onset (over a period of a few months) of Martin's psychotic behavior, the psychiatrist repeated some of the medical tests, including screens for drugs, but everything was normal. The psychiatrist also asked a neurologist to examine Martin to rule out the possibility that a brain tumor was causing his symptoms. The neurological examination, however, was entirely normal. The psychiatrist diagnosed Martin with an acute psychotic illness and prescribed antipsychotic medication. Martin was hospitalized and after one week of taking the medication most of his paranoid ideas were gone. Two weeks into the hospitalization a psychiatrist interviewed Martin and this is how the conversation went:

"Do you remember why you were admitted to the hospital?"

"Yeah, I was screaming at a teacher in a classroom."

"Why did you do that?"

"I thought she was part of a plot to get me thrown out of school. I thought if I exposed her in front of everyone then I might be saved."

"What do you think about all of that now?"

"It was a stupid thing to do, I really must have frightened the hell out of her."

"What do you think about the plot against you?"

"Well, I got carried away with that. I felt, you know, like people were looking at me funny and talking about me and then I got a lousy grade on a paper and I started thinking that the school was against me."

"Do you believe those things now?"

"No, not exactly."

"What do you mean by 'not exactly'?"

"Well, I do think some of the guys in my dorm think I am gay or something and have it in for me and make fun of me. But I don't think the teachers are involved. I got carried away on that one."

Martin now has some insight into his illness, although it is clear that he is still suspicious and worries that some people are saying things about him behind his back. At this point, the doctors felt that it was safe to release Martin from the hospital. They recommended that he continue to take the medication and see a psychiatrist regularly. His diagnosis at discharge was schizophreniform disorder because, although he clearly had psychotic symptoms, the duration of the illness was too short to make a diagnosis of schizophrenia. At this point it was entirely possible that Martin would make a full recovery.

Sadly, Martin did not and at the age of 43 he is a resident in a special home for patients with schizophrenia. After his first psychotic episode Martin had many more, always filled with paranoid delusions. When paranoid he became terrified that someone was about to kill him. He once threatened his mother with a kitchen knife after developing the idea that she was poisoning his food with arsenic. He never returned to college. Medication had less and less of an effect over time for him, and although it now reduces the intensity of his symptoms he maintains a fixed delusional system that includes the belief that people on the street know who he is and are monitoring him for the "authorities." Martin has made three serious suicide attempts, always at times when he felt most endangered, and in one of them nearly died. His diagnosis is clearly chronic paranoid schizophrenia.

The obvious difference between Ronald and Martin is the onset of schizophrenia. In Ronald's case there was evidence of an abnormality from childhood; in Martin's case childhood was actually well above average and the psychosis struck at age 19. I have painted two fairly bleak pictures; not all patients with schizophrenia wind up as chronically ill as Martin and Ronald. Many, especially those who consistently take medication and respond to it, do much better than these two and are able to live on their own in the community. But I must emphasize that Martin and Ronald are by no means unusual cases. Their situations are tragic. It is no wonder that many scientists working for the pharmaceutical industry, academic institutions, and the National Institute of Mental Health, have turned so much of their attention to trying to understand what causes schizophrenia and how to treat it.

Schizophrenia: What Are the Possible Causes?

For most illnesses described in this book, the section on possible causes is full of controversy and fighting among various schools of thought. Usually, we have psychoanalysts, psychobiologists, and behaviorists battling over each illness. This is not the case for schizophrenia. Almost no one believes any longer that schizophrenia is anything other than a biological illness. While there are many differences of opinion about what causes schizophrenia, these are confined mostly to the realm of the psychobiologists. Psychoanalysts and behaviorists have largely acknowledged that whatever causes schizophrenia must have something to do with abnormal brain function.

This was not always the case. For much of the early twentieth century schizophrenia was regarded as an attempt by the "ego" to break with reality. Patients with schizophrenia were believed to be suffering with such terrible unconscious conflict that there was no solution but to give up entirely on the real world and live in a fantasyland of hallucinations and delusions. Freud's notion of what caused paranoid delusions had to do with unconscious homosexual urges that he believed are so unacceptable to the patient that he begins to externalize the conflict and believe that everyone is out to get him. Most of these theories have been repudiated by modern psychoanalysts for two reasons. First, there is not a shred of evidence to support them. Second, psychoanalysis and psychoanalytic psychotherapy have proven almost entirely useless in the treatment of schizophrenia. Indeed, some patients with schizophrenia actually get worse during these therapies because of the intensity of the self-scrutiny, which makes them anxious.

There were other psychological theories. Family therapists talked about the "double bind" in which a patient's parents would supposedly give him such impossibly contradictory messages about everything that total emotional escape becomes the only answer. Some psychologists concocted the particularly ridiculous notion of the "schizophrenigenic mother": an angry, controlling, and demanding woman who literally drives her children to psychotic behavior. This idea was based almost totally on sexism; nobody ever talked about the schizophrenigenic father. Sadly, blaming parents for causing schizophrenia was once a common phenomenon, leading to depressed, guilt-ridden people who not only had to watch their children suffer from a mysterious and sometimes devastating illness but who were also encouraged to believe they caused it. Fortunately, outstanding groups like the National Alliance for the Mentally Ill (NAMI) have cropped up in the last decade to enable families of people with schizophrenia to band together for their own defense and to advocate for patients with the illness.

Schizophrenia Is a Genetic Illness

Perhaps the first thing to pierce the psychological theories of schizophrenia were studies begun in the 1940s demonstrating that schizophrenia is a familial illness that is passed on in some cases through a genetic mechanism. We still do not know if all cases of schizophrenia are genetic but we are almost certain that at least some cases are caused by the inheritance of abnormal genes. It is also clear that while bad parents can do a lot of harm to their children, they do not make them develop schizophrenia. Moreover, while stress and psychological trauma will make a patient with schizophrenia worse, these things are not the cause of the disorder.

How do we know that schizophrenia is at least in part genetic? The first clue came from ground-breaking studies that showed that people with schizophrenia are far more likely to have first-degree relatives with schizophrenia than are people without schizophrenia. Thus schizophrenia runs in families. In fact, while the prevalence of schizophrenia is about one percent of all people in the world, a person with one parent who has schizophrenia has more than a 10 percent chance of having it also, while a person with two parents with schizophrenia has a 40 to 50 percent chance.

This evidence still leaves open the question whether schizophrenia could be caused by growing up in an environment in which children are exposed to family members with the illness. Is it a case of genetics or copying abnormal behavior? Nowadays the question seems to have an obvious answer: No one who observes patients with schizophrenia could take seriously the idea that children learn to hear voices or believe the FBI is tapping their phone. If we found that diabetes runs in families (which it does), we would never leap to the absurd conclusion that children somehow learn to elevate their blood sugar levels to mimic their parents, but in the area of psychology and abnormal behavior these possibilities are given serious consideration.

How can we separate the effects of genes from those of the environment? The solution is to study twins. There are two kinds of twins, identical and fraternal. Identical twins (called monozygotic by scientists) develop when a single fertilized egg splits in half and forms two fetuses. All of the genes in one identical twin are exactly the same as in the other identical twin. Identical twins must always be the same sex, have the same hair and eye color, and grow to the same height (or nearly the same height, but that is a complication not worth getting into now). Fraternal twins (called dizygotic), on the other hand, develop when two eggs are fertilized at the same time. Fraternal twins are genetically like ordinary brothers and sisters; they share some genes but not others. If a disease is truly genetic and one identical twin has it, then the other will almost always have it also (notice I say ''almost always'': once again, this is a complicated point about genetics that I needn't go into at this point). On the other hand, if one fraternal twin has a genetic illness the other one doesn't necessarily have to get it because she may not have gotten the responsible gene. Scientists say that the ''concordance rate'' for a genetic disease must always be higher in identical twins than in fraternal twins. If a disease is not genetic, however, but is caused by something in the environment that occurs after birth, then both fraternal twins should get the disease because they grew up in the same environment and both identical twins should get it for the same reason. Thus, in the case of a nongenetic cause, the concordance rate will be the same for identical and fraternal twins.

We now know that the concordance rate for schizophrenia is much higher for identical twins than for fraternal twins, giving us as good proof as possible that the illness is at least partially under genetic control. If one identical twin has schizophrenia the other has about a 50 or 60 percent chance of having it also, but if one fraternal twin has it the other one has only about a 10 percent chance of having it also. Notice that this last number is still greater than the 1 percent chance an average person has of getting the illness because fraternal twins do share about 50 percent of their genes. But clearly the concordance rate for identical twins is highest.

Scientists all around the world are now trying to take the genetic work to the next level and find the actual gene or genes that cause schizophrenia. This is done by the very powerful techniques of molecular genetics. So far, no one has been successful, but most of us believe it is only a matter of time until the genes will be found.

There's More to Schizophrenia Than Genetics

But genetics is not the end of the story for the cause of schizophrenia. Notice that the concordance rate for schizophrenia between identical twins is high (about 50 percent) but not 100 percent. If a gene causes schizophrenia and identical twins get exactly the same genes, then how could one identical twin get it and not the other?

There are some very complicated genetic reasons why this might occur, but most scientists have now come to believe that having an abnormal gene may not be enough to give everyone schizophrenia. Something else must also be necessary. The something else is not bad parents or stress, but appears to be one of several biological phenomena.

One of the things that galvanized the field of schizophrenia research into taking that position was an elegant piece of work done by scientists Richard Suddath, Daniel Weinberger, and Fuller Torrey at the National Institute of Mental Health in Washington, D.C., in the early 1990s. Fuller Torrey is one of the most indefatigable champions of the biological theory of schizophrenia and he managed to locate a series of identical twinships in whom only one identical twin has schizophrenia. These are called "discordant" for schizophrenia. Suddath and Weinberger obtained pictures of the brains of these discordant twins using a technique now in widespread medical use called magnetic resonance imaging (MRI). This is a safe way to take pictures of the brain and other parts of the body without using X rays. What the scientists found is that the identical twins with schizophrenia had slightly smaller brains than the ones without schizophrenia. The abnormality was most apparent in a part of the brain called the temporal lobe, an area that controls emotions and memory. Their work, which was published in the *New England Journal of Medicine,* stands with a large body of research that has convinced us that patients with schizophrenia have an abnormality in the size of the temporal lobe, particularly on the left side of the brain. It seems clear in the case of the identical twins that something must have happened to the twin's brain who got schizophrenia and that something is probably not an abnormal gene. Otherwise, the other twin would have a small temporal lobe as well.

Many scientists have used brain-imaging techniques, while others have studied the brains of deceased patients with schizophrenia to convince us that the temporal lobe, plus one other part of the brain—the prefrontal cortex—are most affected in patients with schizophrenia. It is somewhat astounding how rapidly this information was gathered. We now tentatively believe that something goes awry in the development of the temporal lobe in some patients with schizophrenia while they are still fetuses in the mother's uterus and that this probably happens during the second trimester of pregnancy, the fourth through sixth months.

Genes and Environment Interact

What could cause this? It appears most likely to be an interaction between abnormalities in the genes that direct brain development during fetal life and some other insult. There are many candidates for this "other insult." One possibility is a viral infection during pregnancy. Another is that antibodies that normally protect the brain against bacteria or viruses get mixed up and start attacking the developing brain itself as if it was a foreign invader. Still another possibility, recently made believable by the work of Columbia University psychiatrist and epidemiologist Ezra Susser, is that a subtle nutritional deficiency may cause some developing temporal lobes to grow abnormally. All of these possibilities, and several others, are now under intense investigation by many scientists and we have every right to expect that the next ten years will bring important revelations about what causes schizophrenia.

One very difficult question to answer is, if the brain of a person with schizophrenia develops abnormally during fetal life, why aren't people born with the illness and why do many patients show no signs of it until they are 18 or older? We do not know the entire answer to this question, but two points are relevant. First, the human brain really doesn't stop developing until late adolescence. Perhaps it is only when every part of the brain is complete and "laid in stone" that an illness like schizophrenia develops. Second, many genetic diseases are silent through childhood years. A good example is Huntington's disease, a severe and fatal brain disease that is known to be caused by a single abnormal gene. Most people do not show signs of Huntington's disease until adulthood or even middle age. Hence, it is not so remarkable that a brain disease like schizophrenia with certain genetic underpinnings might not become obvious until a person has passed through childhood.

Brain Chemicals and Schizophrenia

There is still one more important piece of biology to explain. We might ask, How could an abnormality in the development of one or two parts of the brain lead to schizophrenia? As described in Chapter 20, it is mostly likely that an illness like schizophrenia operates through some disruption in the way brain cells communicate with each other. Chemicals called "neurotransmitters" carry signals from one brain cell (called the "neuron") to another, and scientists think that an abnormality in one neurotransmitter—dopamine—might have a lot to do with the symptoms of schizophrenia.

There are many reasons to think that the dopamine system is responsible for many of the symptoms of schizophrenia. Foremost among them is the simple fact that all the drugs that treat psychotic symptoms block the ability of dopamine to bind to its receptor, the dopamine receptor. When this was first discovered it lead to a flurry of research activity centered around the "dopamine hypothesis," which says that patients with schizophrenia have too much dopamine in their brains. We now know that this hypothesis is too simplistic, but an excess of dopamine activity, particularly in the temporal regions of the brain, may be involved in causing the "positive" psychotic symptoms of schizophrenia—such as hallucinations, delusions, and thought disorder. A deficiency in dopamine activity in the part of the brain called the prefrontal cortex may explain the "negative" symptoms of withdrawal, apathy, loss of pleasure, and decreased intellectual function.

More recently some scientists, like Herbert Meltzer in Cleveland, have suggested that another neurotransmitter, serotonin, may also be overactive in brains of people with schizophrenia. One reason for this idea is that the new antipsychotic drugs, like clozapine (Clozaril) and risperidone (Risperdal), block both dopamine and serotonin. Because clozapine seems to be superior to the older antipsychotic drugs that block dopamine but not serotonin, some scientists think that both neurotransmitters are involved in causing the illness.

The pace of this research is quickening dramatically. On the one hand, it remains very discouraging to patients with schizophrenia and their families to live without a definite answer about what causes schizophrenia, but on the other hand, most realize that at the current rate of progress true breakthroughs are near. Research has convinced almost everyone that schizophrenia is a brain disease that is partially genetic and that results in important disruptions in normal brain development and neurotransmitter function. Even without an exact reason why people get schizophrenia, scientists are already using some of this new information to guide their development of new treatments.

Schizophrenia: An Approach to Treatment

With the understanding that schizophrenia is a brain disease has come the recognition that successful treatment will have to involve the use of medication. As we will see, nonmedication interventions play an important role in helping people with schizophrenia, but almost all patients will have to take medication if their symptoms are going to be reduced or controlled. Unlike the situation with depression and anxiety disorders, there are no legitimate debates any longer about whether drugs or psychotherapy are better for treatment of schizophrenia. Medication is clearly the effective and appropriate choice for most patients; psychotherapies will also benefit many. Table 41 gives specific treatment approaches for five common situations involving patients with schizophrenia:

1. The patient has been brought to the emergency room, acutely psychotic.
2. The patient presents to the psychiatrist with psychotic symptoms, but it is not an emergency.

3. The patient persistently refuses treatment.
4. The patient does not respond to several different typical drugs.
5. The patient has mainly negative symptoms.

But this statement does not mean we have particularly good medication treatments for schizophrenia. In fact, the current treatments are a definite mixed blessing. Antipsychotic medication does diminish the "positive" symptoms of schizophrenia in a majority of patients. Patients with schizophrenia who take them will have fewer hallucinations and delusions and their thinking will normalize. Some will even experience the total elimination of psychotic symptoms and be able to function fairly well in school and at work. Occasionally, there are dramatic stories of patients with schizophrenia making a complete recovery and going on to very successful lives.

TABLE 41

AN APPROACH TO THE TREATMENT OF SCHIZOPHRENIA

A. *The Patient Has Been Brought to the Emergency Room, Acutely Psychotic:*
   1. Obtain medical and psychiatric history, physical exam, and blood tests.
   2. With patient's permission, give a dose of a high-potency antipsychotic drug either orally or by injection. Five milligrams of Haldol or Prolixin is a common choice.
   3. Wait awhile, making sure the patient is in a safe place. If agitation and the potential for violence continue, many psychiatrists now advocate giving repeated doses of a benzodiazepine drug, lorazepam (Ativan), either orally or by injection, until the patient is calm.
   4. When calm, the patient may need to be admitted to the hospital. The patient is then started on antipsychotic medication. Risperidone (Risperdal) is an increasingly common first choice for patients with schizophrenia. It is started in a dose of 1 mg twice a day, increased to 2 mg twice a day on the second day, and then 3 mg twice a day thereafter. Slower dose increase is often better tolerated.

B. *The Patient Presents to the Psychiatrist with Psychotic Symptoms, but It Is Not an Emergency:*
   1. Make sure there are no medical problems or drug use that may be causing the psychosis.
   2. Begin an antipsychotic medication, often risperidone as in section A.4. above.
   3. Attempt to involve the family in family therapy and the patient in social skills and other rehabilitative therapies.

C. *The Patient with Schizophrenia Persistently Refuses Treatment:*
   1. Determine if the reason is that the patient hates the side effects of the drug. This is often because the patient feels sedated or is experiencing the neurological side effect called akathisia caused by antipsychotic drugs. If this is the problem, switch drugs to one that is less likely to produce the side effect the patient complains about.
   2. If the patient still persistently forgets to take medication, consider putting the patient on one of the long-acting, depot formulations. The two available are called Haldol Decanoate and Prolixin Decanoate. They are given by injection once every two to four weeks.
D. *The Patient with Schizophrenia Does Not Respond to Several Different Typical Antipsychotic Drugs:*
   1. Try adding one of the mood-stabilizing drugs, such as lithium or Depakote.
   2. If this does not work, consider switching to the atypical antipsychotic drug clozapine (Clozaril).
   3. If the patient is still psychotic, consider electroconvulsive therapy (ECT), which is sometimes effective in stopping psychotic symptoms.
   4. Continue to try to employ family and rehabilitative psychotherapies.
E. *The Patient with Schizophrenia Has Mainly Negative Symptoms:*
   1. Determine if the problem is really post-psychotic depression. If it is, start an antidepressant drug like Tofranil (imipramine).
   2. Determine if the problem is a side effect of the antipsychotic medication called akinesia. If it is, administer one of the medications that reduces this side effect, like Cogentin (benztropine) or Artane (trihexyphenidyl).
   3. Consider adding one of the dopamine-enhancing drugs to the traditional antipsychotic drug. Mazindol is an example. This should be done carefully, under the supervision of an experienced psychopharmacologist.
   4. Consider switching to one of the atypical antipsychotics drugs because these may be better at reversing negative symptoms. The two currently available are risperidone (Risperdal) and clozapine (Clozaril).

The current drugs, however, have very substantial risks and side effects. Studies have clearly shown that patients have a good chance of relapsing and becoming psychotic again if they stop taking the drugs. Yet, patients with schizophrenia generally do not like taking antipsychotic medication because of the side effects, making compliance with treatment a major issue. One of the side effects of some antipsychotic drugs, tardive dyskinesia (TD), is an uncomfortable neurological problem that can become permanent even if the patient stops taking the medication. The drugs can also be very sedating and produce in some patients a zombielike appearance. Such patients may not be actively psychotic but they are not well either, often losing their motivation to do things and becoming comfortable sitting in one place for hours. The side effects of some of the antipsychotic drugs can mimic the "negative" symptoms of schizophrenia.

It is extremely encouraging that drug companies have recently picked up the pace of searching for better antipsychotic drugs. A very old drug called clozapine (Clozaril), which has many advantages over traditional antipsychotic medications, was recently introduced into the American market, with a big impact. Risperidone (Risperdal) was released in the early winter of 1994, promising several advantages over the older drugs. Experimental drugs like seroquil, sertindole (Serlect), and olanzapine (Zyprex) are being vigorously tested by drug companies and psychiatrists. We desperately need better drug therapies for schizophrenia.

Categories of Antipsychotic Drugs
We can divide antipsychotic drugs into two categories: *typical* and *atypical*. These are shown in Table 42. Someday, the atypical ones may become the only drugs doctors prescribe, so, it is hoped, the term *atypical* will become obsolete. For now, however, these are the terms that are generally used.

Typical Antipsychotics
The typical antipsychotic drugs were first introduced in the late 1950s and all have the property of strongly blocking the ability of the neurotransmitter dopamine to bind to its receptor in the brain. The typical antipsychotic drugs can further be subdivided into the high-potency and low-potency typical antipsychotic drugs. High-potency drugs—such as Haldol (haloperidol), Prolixin (fluphenazine), Stelazine (trifluoperazine), and Navane (thiothixene)—are generally not very sedating and do not have much effect on blood pressure, but they have a great ability to cause a series of neurological side effects called "extrapyramidal symptoms" or EPS. Low-potency drugs—such as Thorazine (chlorpromazine) and Mellaril (thioridazine)—are much more sedating and tend to lower blood pressure, but they are somewhat less likely to produce EPS. A drug called Trilafon (perphenazine) is midway between low- and high-potency drugs.

TABLE 42
THE ANTIPSYCHOTIC DRUGS

Category	Examples	Used For	Some Prominent Side Effects
Typical: High-potency	Haldol, Prolixin, Navane, Stelazine	Positive symptoms	EPS (dystonia, Parkinsonism, akathisia), tardive dyskinesia
Typical: Low-potency	Thorazine, Mellaril	Positive symptoms	Sedation, low blood pressure, tardive dyskinesia
Atypical	Clozapine	Patients who do not respond or cannot tolerate other antipsychotics, positive and negative symptoms	Agranulocytosis, seizures, weight gain
Atypical	Risperidone	Positive and negative symptoms	EPS at higher doses, low blood pressure

Sides Effects of Typical Antipsychotics

What are these neurological side effects that cause such concern for patients taking antipsychotic drugs? The ones called EPS occur in three main forms: Parkinsonian-like effects, dystonias, and akathisias.

Dystonias are fairly abrupt stiffening in muscles, sometimes resulting in sudden contraction of the arms, neck, or face. These can usually be quickly reversed with medication, including the antihistamine Benedryl (sometimes given intravenously for immediate relief), Cogentin (benztropine), and Artane (trihexyphenidyl).

Parkinsonian-like effects involve tremor, muscle rigidity, and slowing of movement. The patient often has a sad, masklike facial expression even if he doesn't feel sad. These symptoms resemble those seen in patients who actually have Parkinson's disease. They are probably caused by the blocking of dopamine in a particular part of the brain called the basal ganglia. Medications can be given to reverse the Parkinsonian-like symptoms, but some patients manifest them anyway. Examples of these medications are Cogentin, Artane, and Kemadrin (procyclidine).

Akathisia is a subjective feeling patients with schizophrenia often get when taking typical antipsychotic drugs. They feel as if they cannot sit still. This jumpiness may not be apparent to observers, but patients will say things like "my legs are restless" or "I feel like I'm jumping out of my skin." Akathisia is an important reason that patients often refuse to take antipsychotic drugs. Doctors often don't take it as seriously as other side effects because they don't see it, but for patients it may be the worst of the routine neurological side effects of antipsychotic drugs. It can be treated with a variety of drugs, including propranolol, clonidine, and such benzodiazepines as Valium, Ativan, or Xanax, although these "antidotes" for akathisia are often only partially useful.

The most dread side effect of typical antipsychotic drugs is, however, *tardive dyskinesia (TD)*. Patients usually don't show signs of this until they have taken the drugs for years, although elderly people and some younger patients may show signs after as little as a few months. TD involves involuntary movements of muscles. It may start with undulating movements of the tongue and move to include lip-smacking and grimacing. These are completely uncontrollable by the patient. Some patients may get TD involving large-muscle groups, with involuntary movements of the arms or rocking back and forth. If these signs of TD are noted immediately and the drug stopped they usually go away, but then the patient may become psychotic again. In a small number of patients, TD remains even after the antipsychotic drug is stopped. Patients should be tested by the doctor for the presence of early signs of TD at least annually, usually using a procedure called the Abnormal Involuntary Movements Scale (AIMS). There is some evidence that lower doses of antipsychotic medication reduce the risk of TD slightly.

The list of side effects to antipsychotic medications does not end here. Most of them produce substantial weight gain. Some increase the risk of having a seizure. Rarely, they cause a medical emergency called neuroleptic malignant syndrome in which the patient develops high fever and decreased consciousness. Clearly, typical antipsychotics are a trade-off. Without them the patient may never stop being psychotic and may even have to be hospitalized permanently. With them, better functioning is possible but serious side effects can occur.

The Atypical Antipsychotic Drugs

The atypical antipsychotics currently include just two drugs that can be prescribed in the United States, clozapine (Clozaril) and risperidone (Risperdal). Others, including olanzapine (Zyprex), seroquil, and sertindole (Serlect), will probably be released soon. These drugs are less effective in blocking dopamine binding than the typical antipsychotics but have the additional effect of strongly blocking the binding of another neurotransmitter, serotonin, to its receptor. They also have a number of other biological properties that are different from the typical antipsychotics, and scientists do not yet know which of them is responsible for the actual clinical differences between typical and atypical drugs.

Clozapine hit the American market with a splash, even though it had already been prescribed in many other countries—China and France, for instance—for years. The reason for the excitement was twofold: first, clozapine appears to relieve psychotic symptoms in about 30 percent of patients who do not respond to any of the typical antipsychotic drugs and, second, clozapine appears to have little potential to produce neurological side effects like EPS and TD that the typical drugs cause. Unfortunately, about 1 percent of patients who take clozapine develop a serious blood disorder called agranulocytosis in which the bone marrow stops making one type of white blood cell that is needed to fight infection. Unless the drug is stopped immediately, the patient with agranulocytosis usually succumbs to overwhelming infection and dies. The situation can be prevented by testing the blood every week for the number of white blood cells; if it drops below a certain critical level, the doctor orders the patient to stop the medication and the white blood cell count rises to normal in virtually all cases. Still, the need for and expense of weekly blood monitoring has limited the use of clozapine to patients who are very ill with schizophrenia and fail to respond to other medications.

Even without agranulocytosis, clozapine has some troublesome side effects. It produces weight gain in most patients, increases the risk of seizures, and can make the patient salivate uncontrollably. Overall, though, patients seem to mind taking clozapine less than they do the typical antipsychotic drugs.

Risperidone (Risperdal) appears to work as well as the typical drugs but seems to have less potential for causing the neurological side effects such as EPS. Unlike clozapine, it does not produce agranulocytosis and the seizure risk is not high. A note of caution here: although doctors have every right to believe that risperidone won't cause TD at anywhere near the rate as the typical drugs, TD is a side effect of medication that takes years of drug use to become apparent. Also, we cannot know with absolute certainty that risperidone has a low potential to cause EPS until it has been around for many more years. Right now, many doctors consider risperidone the "drug of first choice" for patients with schizophrenia. They prescribe it to the patient first, hoping it will work and not produce EPS. If it does work, patients seem relatively agreeable to taking it, making compliance less of a problem with risperidone than other antipsychotic drugs.

In Table 41 on pages 292-293 I present some specific treatment approaches to different situations involving patients with schizophrenia.

Psychotherapy for Schizophrenia

So far, I have discussed only medication treatments for schizophrenia. This is because they are the mainstay of therapy for the illness. Still, there is great value for some patients in adding particular types of psychotherapy to the medication. The two most extensively studied are *family therapy* and *rehabilitation therapy.*

When discussing family therapy for patients with schizophrenia it is critical to emphasize once again that families do not cause schizophrenia. Hence, family therapy is not intended (or at least, should not be intended) to cure schizophrenia by "straightening out" the family. Rather, family therapists recognize that many patients with schizophrenia are unable to live on their own and remain with their families throughout adulthood. A supportive, knowledgeable family can be a great help to a patient with schizophrenia. In addition, family therapy can help family members cope with the constant emotional pain and frustration of seeing someone they love struggle with a serious illness. There is evidence, primarily from the excellent work of social worker Gerard Hogarty, that family therapy combined with medication decreases the likelihood of psychotic relapse in patients with schizophrenia compared to medication alone. Remember, however, that even Hogarty, a great proponent of the use of family therapy for patients with schizophrenia, insists that the patients continue to take their medication.

Some patients with schizophrenia also benefit enormously from the kind of rehabilitation treatments that have been studied by California psychiatrist Robert Liberman. This is not psychotherapy aimed at helping the person understand his unconscious, but a serious attempt at teaching patients with schizophrenia how to establish relationships and learn social skills. Once again, this kind of therapy is done in conjunction with medication.

Schizophrenia: When the Patient Refuses Treatment

All of the treatment recommendations discussed so far are fine if the patient agrees to them. But patients with schizophrenia sometimes refuse treatment. Often this is because of paranoid delusions that convince the patient that doctors are trying to poison him. Sometimes voices tell the patient to refuse treatment. In many instances patients with schizophrenia refuse treatment because they cannot stand the side effects of the medication, especially the sedation and the akathisia sometimes caused by antipsychotic drugs.

Patients generally have a right to refuse treatment, but doctors have a responsibility to try to convince them to accept useful therapy. No one would fault a doctor for trying to convince a patient with diabetes to take insulin or a patient with a broken leg to have it set and placed in a cast. Similarly, doctors should try to convince patients with schizophrenia to take medication that will eliminate psychotic symptoms. The first step in dealing with a patient with schizophrenia who refuses treatment is to try to convince him that the treatment is not harmful and will help.

When that fails, the law and medical ethics require that doctors determine whether the refusal to take medication could lead to a tragedy. Rather than allow a psychotic patient to jump in front of a car or attack someone, it seems reasonable to administer an antipsychotic drug that may clear up the hallucinations and delusions responsible for the patient's violent potential. It does not seem right to permit someone in the clutches of psychosis to end his life; the patient has the right to make that decision with a clear mind, free of psychotic interference.

But do we have the right to force the patient to take medication? This has become one of the most controversial areas of psychiatry. In general, it is now necessary to get a judge's permission to give antipsychotic medication to a patient against his will.

In most states, a psychotic patient who poses a clear and immediate threat to either harm himself or someone else can be made to enter a hospital against his will. This is called civil, or involuntary, commitment. Usually, the patient has the right to request a court hearing to determine if the commitment is to continue; in most states the patient is given a lawyer who can present his case to the judge for release from the hospital.

But even if the judge orders the patient to remain in the hospital, doctors cannot administer drugs to the patient against his will without another court order. It is often the case that the judge decides it is too dangerous to grant the patient's wish to be released from the hospital but grants the patient's decision to refuse medication. This can obviously result in a very long hospitalization, because without medication there is little chance the patient will get much better.

Contrary to some popular belief, psychiatrists do not go around committing people to hospitals against their will. I have sometimes been called by a distraught parent of an adult with schizophrenia who pleads with me to "commit" the patient. Usually, the son or daughter with schizophrenia has been threatening to harm family members but refuses to see a doctor. The family has the idea that a psychiatrist has the legal power to order the patient into the hospital. This is not the case. The only solution for the family is to call the police and convince them to take the patient to an emergency room. Police are often reluctant to get involved with these requests; they are also limited in their legal authority to force someone to go to the emergency room. An involuntary commitment can usually only proceed if a patient is brought to the emergency room and if it is absolutely clear that the patient is dangerous.

The bottom line here is that today psychiatrists have relatively little power to administer treatment against the will of a patient. They must generally rely on persuasion to get the patient to take treatment. Often, families are better able to convince a patient with schizophrenia to accept antipsychotic medication.

Schizophrenia: Concluding Remarks

Readers may think that the only impediment to successful treatment of schizophrenia is getting the patient to accept the treatment. This may make it sound as easy as convincing a five-year-old child with strep throat to agree to swallow her antibiotic tablets. Perhaps I have painted too rosy a picture of the treatment of schizophrenia. This reflects our current optimism that breakthroughs and new medications are emerging at a very fast rate right now. But it is important to balance the picture. A walk down a main street in any big American city will immediately reveal homeless people with schizophrenia who obviously are acutely psychotic. Twenty-five percent of America's psychiatric beds are still filled by patients with schizophrenia and 10 percent of patients with schizophrenia will commit suicide rather than continue living with their hallucinations and delusions.

We do a terrible job in the United States and in many Western countries at providing proper housing, food, and medical care for people with schizo-phrenia. There is evidence that patients with psychotic illnesses are more readily accepted in third-world countries and have a milder course of illness. Here, we continue to stigmatize and ostracize patients with schizophrenia and often make it nearly impossible for them to take advantage of new treatments as they come along.

Some have argued that it is "cost effective" to provide good treatment for patients with schizophrenia because this decreases the need for expensive hospitalizations. That may be the case, but it should be beside the point. Schizophrenia is a terrible illness and we need to spend considerable money in two areas to take care of it: on research into its causes and on better treatment facilities, housing, and medical care. Given current scientific prog-ress, our lack of compassion and our failure to provide adequate services for patients with schizophrenia is a national shame.

13.
Eating Disorders

THERE ARE TWO kinds of eating disorders: *anorexia nervosa* and *bulimia nervosa*. Both of them are serious, even at times life-threatening. But in the popular mind and press they have taken two very different courses. Anorexia is seen by everybody as a fairly easy condition to diagnose that is almost always extremely serious and requires vigorous, often emergency treatment. It is not the kind of illness that people casually say they have or that gets written about in magazines.

Bulimia, on the other hand, virtually has become a fad. Princess Diana, probably the most famous bulimic of all times, catapulted the illness into international headlines. There are reports in popular magazines and articles in journals that vast numbers of teenage and college-age women have bulimia. There are bulimia programs and clinics and it sometimes seems that anyone who overeats a bit and then feels guilty decides she has bulimia.

Almost everyone in the United States, and in much of the entire Western world, eats too much. That is why obesity looms as one of the major public health problems we now confront. But is any substantial portion of this overeating the result of a psychiatric disorder? I am going to take the very conservative and probably controversial stance that while bulimia nervosa is a genuine and serious psychiatric illness, most people who eat too much do not have it. In my view, we need to see eating disorders as fairly well defined disturbances that do not affect large numbers of people. It is, I feel, a dangerous trend to use a psychiatric label, in this case bulimia, to explain away a common problem that affects many people worldwide—lack of will-power when confronting a delicious and fattening meal. What this has done is to line the pockets of unscrupulous purveyors of "mental health" approaches to eating and also trivialized some very severe psychiatric illnesses.

Anorexia Nervosa

Let's begin by discussing the more readily defined eating disorder, anorexia nervosa. By all accounts, this is the disorder that killed the popular rock-and-roll star Karen Carpenter, whose painful decline brought widespread national attention to the illness. Carpenter's was by no means an isolated case. Unless treated aggressively, anorexia nervosa is eminently capable of killing its victims.

Anorexia is a disorder almost entirely confined to females. Somewhere between 90 and 95 percent of people with anorexia are women. The illness usually begins in adolescence, but can start earlier or later, and it is characterized by the patient starving herself.

What Are the Signs of Anorexia?

Patients with anorexia believe they are too fat. Sometimes they begin a diet and exercise regimen that seems quite reasonable and even wins the praise of friends and family. They cut back on junk food and reduce their fat intake, something doctors and parents are always urging teenagers to do. They increase their exercise, starting to jog and swim. Again, everybody thinks this is a very good idea. But then troublesome signs emerge. The family notices that the patient is pushing her food around on the plate every night at dinner but not eating anything. If anyone makes a comment, the patient says she is not feeling well, or lies and says that she had a big lunch earlier in the day. Maybe she will eat a few pieces of lettuce. If pushed too hard to finish dinner, some young women with anorexia get angry and storm away from the table. Then the parents feel guilty and leave her alone.

TABLE 43

Signs of Anorexia Nervosa

- Constant preoccupation with weight and "feeling fat"
- Excessive weighing, looking in the mirror, measuring the body for fat
- Increased exercise
- Strange diets, refusing to eat, playing with food at mealtime
- Use of laxatives and diuretics
- Self-induced vomiting (purging)
- Loss of menstrual period (amenorrhea)

People also start to notice that the patient is exercising with increasing degrees of fanaticism. It isn't merely a good two-or three-mile jog several times a week but hours of intense working out every day. The patient seems to put a higher priority on the workout than anything else and becomes nearly frantic if she can't complete a very detailed and particular exercise regimen daily.

Now people begin to notice that the patient is getting very thin. Her face seems drawn and pale. In the locker room before gym class, friends see that her ribs are protruding; they begin to worry about her. Someone asks her why she is getting so thin. The patient seems defensive and denies that she is thin.

In fact, patients with anorexia never think they are thin enough. Even when they become entirely emaciated to the point at which their lives are in danger, they insist they are too fat. A hallmark of anorexia nervosa is this complete distortion of body image. It is not a put-on. Hard as it may be to believe when confronting a person who looks like they have been living in a concentration camp, the patient with anorexia truly believes that she is too fat and becomes obsessed with the mission to continue to lose weight.

In order to speed the weight-reduction process, patients with anorexia often begin to abuse laxatives, diuretics, and appetite suppressants, including amphetamines and over-the-counter preparations. Some, but not all, will occasionally eat and then induce vomiting. The patients ultimately appear to be very depressed and completely obsessed with their weight, but most of these mood and anxiety symptoms are entirely secondary to the near-starvation status with which they live.

Medical Implications

This kind of starvation has many serious medical implications. Most women with anorexia eventually stop having their menstrual periods. This can lead, among other things, to demineralization (softening) of the bones. Almost no organ of the body likes to be deprived of nutrients, and severe drops in blood pressure and heart rhythm disturbances can occur. The production of many hormones is altered. Overall, anorexia is a dangerous psychological and medical condition. Patients usually require hospitalization for refeeding to prevent them from starving to death.

What Causes Anorexia Nervosa?

Perhaps the leading psychoanalytic theory is that anorexia represents an unconscious need to control at least one aspect of the person's life. Remember that the patient with anorexia, almost always a young woman, loses her period and distorts her body. Psychoanalysts have speculated that these women are unconsciously resisting sexual impulses; because they feel that they cannot control any aspect of their lives, these young women hit upon one thing they can take charge of: how much they weigh. Anorectic girls stop being sexual or reproductive beings. I think, to be honest, that there is some truth to this theory, but it is very difficult to prove. Psychoanalytic treatment of patients with anorexia nervosa is not notably effective, perhaps mainly because as with any psychoanalytic therapy it takes a long time and in most cases treatment of anorexia has to be fast or the patient will die.

The issue of control is also at the root of many behavioral- and family-therapy-oriented theories. Although it sometimes seems as if the family dinner hour is fading from the American scene, it can be a ritual in many households. In some, according to theorists, it becomes symbolic of a stifling atmosphere that occurs in some families. The parents are rigid disciplinarians who demand too much excellence and perfection from their children. Indeed, it has been observed that young women with anorexia nervosa are often excellent but compulsive students. Refusing to eat is seen as the anorectic patient's method of seizing control of her life and refusing to be compliant in all areas. The fanatic exercise and laxative abuse become secret rebellions against parents who demand too much and give too little love and affection. I do think there is merit to these ideas and some of them have been translated into therapeutic success.

Biological theories of anorexia nervosa are hardly worth going into, in my opinion, because they are not very convincing. A women with anorexia has dozens of biological abnormalities: almost any test you do will be abnormal; but most of these abnormal results are because the patient is starved. After refeeding, most of the test results become normal. It is hard to make a convincing case at this point that any particular biological abnormality is really the *cause* of anorexia nervosa.

Political and sociological theories have some appeal, but I tend to think they are overstated. They often begin with the correct observation that anorexia is almost exclusively a disorder that affects women. In our society, there is tremendous pressure for women to maintain an appearance that is sexually appealing to men. That generally means thin. Add to that the current emphasis on healthier diets and exercise and we have even added pressure on women to be thin and work out. Feminists note that these pressures are applied much more to women than to men in Western society. Again, there is much truth to these statements, but they still don't help us understand why some women develop anorexia nervosa. There must be something that affects these individual women beyond cultural demands that makes them willing to starve themselves nearly to death.

Treatment of Anorexia Nervosa

The first task in treating someone with anorexia nervosa is to restore weight to a safe level. Often this needs to be done in the hospital. By the time patients with anorexia nervosa come to clinical attention, they have often lost so much weight that their health is in jeopardy. It is actually dangerous under these conditions to refeed someone too rapidly. Weight restoration must be done carefully under medical supervision.

In most cases, the doctor makes a "behavioral contract" with the patient regarding eating. The patient is placed at bed rest in the hospital and can only earn privileges like watching television or going for walks if she eats her meals. Trips to the bathroom are made only with supervision so that self-induced vomiting is not possible. Usually, as the patient gains weight her mood improves, most of the abnormal medical and laboratory findings normalize.

Less often, the patient adamantly refuses to eat and must be force-fed. This is usually done by placing a tube through the nose into the stomach (a nasogastric tube) or by intravenous feeding. This is obviously an extreme solution and some may say an unfair one. Essentially, it is a way of preventing the patient from committing suicide. Let me state my unequivocal belief that all measures should always be taken to prevent a person from committing suicide because of psychiatric disease. Hence, if a patient with anorexia refuses to eat and is going to die I insist that the patient be force-fed.

TABLE 44

A Treatment Approach for Anorexia Nervosa

1. Hospitalization is often necessary. It is essential if weight loss is so severe that the patient's life is in danger.
2. Begin a weight restoration program immediately, usually by granting the patient privileges only when she eats a previously agreed upon amount.
3. Use force-feeding only in the most dire, emergency conditions when death would otherwise occur.
4. Begin an intense cognitive/behavioral psychotherapy program.
5. Involve the patient's family in family therapy, particularly if she is still living at home.
6. Consider psychoanalytic psychotherapy.
7. Maintain contact with therapists for a sustained period of time after hospital discharge.

The need for force-feeding is, fortunately, unusual. Most women with anorexia do eat according to the contract. This does not address the issue, however, of the patient's belief that she is fat or her desire to continue to lose weight. The only effective treatments for this so far discovered are psychotherapies. Although almost every drug in the world has been tried, at the present time there is absolutely no convincing evidence that medication plays a role in successfully treating anorexia nervosa. Obviously, if the patient has another psychiatric problem, say depression, it may be necessary to use a psychiatric drug. But usually patients with anorexia will not benefit from drugs.

Most experts on anorexia nervosa now recommend combining individual and family therapy, the latter only when the patient is an adolescent or young adult who is living with or is at least heavily involved with her family. The individual therapy usually includes cognitive and behavioral elements. The cognitive portion is aimed at confronting the patient's distorted body image and providing information about nutrition. The behavioral part gives the patient assignments to eat a certain amount in return for specific rewards.

Throughout the treatment attempts are made to improve the patient's self-image and help her find effective ways of expressing her feelings to her family.

Psychoanalytic psychotherapy is often also employed with patients with anorexia nervosa. Often, this centers on unconscious fears the patient may have about sexuality and assertiveness. Patients with anorexia nervosa sometimes live with such inner rage that they unconsciously fear if they express their anger they will go completely out of control and become nearly murderous. They are often also frightened or repulsed by sex. If such issues seem important to an individual patient, then psychoanalytic therapy may play a role in treating this patient with anorexia nervosa.

Family therapy is usually recommended as well. Usually, by the time a patient with anorexia is first seen by a clinician, family life has become a battlefield. The patient's entire relationship with her mother and father often degenerates to battles over eating. The more the parents yell at the patient to eat, the more she refuses and also takes laxatives. The first job of the family therapist is to insist that the parents stop ordering their daughter to eat and try to reestablish communication on other topics. At the same time, it is wrong to blame parents for anorexia nervosa. As I have stated repeatedly in this book, we have no right to blame anyone for causing psychiatric disorders for which we do not really know the cause. Obviously, by the time we first see a girl with anorexia nervosa and her family, they are often in pretty sorry shape, suffering from endless arguments, tension, and recriminations. But is this situation the cause or the result of the serious illness that threatens to kill the child? The key is not to blame anyone in the family but to try to get them to talk to each other in meaningful ways. Other children in the family beside the patient should usually also be included.

Short- and Long-Term Prognoses for Anorexia

The short-term prognosis for anorexia patients is fairly good. Most will gain enough weight to be medically safe and make some gains in therapy. They are often discharged with high hopes that things will go well.

Unfortunately, the long-term prognosis for anorexia is not so optimistic. Many patients relapse and resume their self-starvation and exercise obsession. The only way to prevent this is continued, long-term psychotherapy. Although I rarely advocate this, for anorexia nervosa I believe that psychotherapy should generally be a long-term proposition.

Bulimia Nervosa

What Are the Signs of Bulimia Nervosa?

The hallmark of bulimia nervosa is the binge. But what is a binge? The *DSM* system says it is an amount of food ''larger than most people would eat during a similar period of time and under similar circumstances.'' Does that mean a second helping of cake? Three hamburgers instead of two? Five cookies instead of three? The definition is so loose that almost anyone who thinks they eat too much could qualify. And bulimia seems to be a disorder people like to have. Instead of saying, ''I have a weight problem because I eat too much,'' many people say, ''I cannot control my eating because of the disease I have called bulimia.''

T A B L E 45
SIGNS OF BULIMIA NERVOSA

- Binges, at least twice a week for three months
- Self-induced vomiting (purging)
- Preoccupation with weight and body appearance

In classic bulimia the patient consumes truly enormous amounts of food in rapid sequence and then forces herself to vomit it up. Within the span of a few minutes, the patient consumes a loaf of bread, peanut butter eaten directly out of the jar with a spoon, and drinks a jar of honey. Then she sticks her fingers down her throat and purges. There is little difficulty labeling this as abnormal behavior. It is also driven behavior; the patient feels truly out of control and often repulsed by what she has done.

Without trying myself to draw a boundary around what should and should not be called bulimia, I would like to urge a person who thinks she has it to read the description of a binge I have just given. You should have a problem that at least approximates what I have described, because then there is a chance that psychiatric treatment will help you. If your problem is more like compulsive overeating and weighing more than you should, then the psychiatrist or psychologist you see is probably going to have the same problem that you do and not be particularly helpful.

What Causes Bulimia?

As with anorexia, we really do not know what causes bulimia. This is again an illness that almost exclusively affects women. Patients with bulimia often do have other psychiatric conditions, including depression, obsessive compulsive disorder, and substance abuse. There is evidence that they are more likely to have been sexually abused as children than women who do not have bulimia. Once again, there are all kinds of hypotheses, many of them similar to those for anorexia, but none of them are particularly convincing.

Treatment of Bulimia

Unlike anorexia nervosa, bulimia usually does not become life-threatening and most bulimic patients can therefore be treated without admission to the hospital. The first thing to assess in treating bulimia is whether there are other psychiatric disorders also present. Patients with bulimia frequently also suffer from depression, alcohol and other substance use problems, and anxiety disorders such as obsessive compulsive disorder. Proper treatment approaches to these conditions can be found in other parts of this book.

TABLE 46

A TREATMENT APPROACH FOR BULIMIA

1. Determine if the patient is also suffering from other psychiatric disorders, particularly depression, substance abuse, and anxiety.
2. Begin a cognitive/behavioral psychotherapy program.
3. For more serious cases or if psychotherapy is not working, begin an antidepressant medication, usually Prozac, Zoloft, or Paxil.
4. Consider psychoanalytic psychotherapy.

Two kinds of treatment have been found useful for bulimia, cognitive/behavioral therapy and medication. Combining these two will probably offer patients with severe forms of bulimia the best chance of recovery, while patients with milder forms may benefit from cognitive/behavioral therapy alone. Hence, the basic treatment for bulimia at this point should include cognitive/behavioral therapy with medication added in more severe cases.

The cognitive/behavioral therapy used for bulimia involves several components. On the cognitive level, the first step is to carefully examine and list all of the thoughts that go through the patient's mind before a binge. Often, a patient with bulimia feels depressed and anxious prior to a binge and says to herself, ''I am fat and ugly anyway, why not just eat whatever I want.'' At other times, the patient bargains with herself, thinking, ''I will eat one doughnut and have a Coke and that will be it for the rest of the day.'' Then, after eating the doughnut and Coke, she feels horrible and thinks, ''I am disgusting. I have no control. I ate the doughnut and now I might as well eat the whole box.'' And so she does. One slip leads to such massive self-hatred that the patient indulges in even greater self-destructive binge eating.

All of these thoughts can be corrected through cognitive therapy. The thought, ''I am fat and ugly anyway, why not just eat,'' is challenged by the therapist who insists that the patient review the evidence she is fat and ugly and admit that binge eating is responsible for her being fat. The thought that one can eat a restricted food once and not eat the rest of the day is similarly challenged. Is this ever really successful? Isn't it the case that after a while the patient usually feels hungry and eats despite any deals she made with herself earlier in the day? Finally, the patient needs to understand that one slip does not have to create an avalanche. The patient is taught to understand that controlling bulimic eating is an extremely difficult task and that mistakes are going to happen. Rather than condemn herself if she slips, the patient is taught to forgive herself. She is trying very hard and deserves credit for what she has already accomplished. This new way of thinking reduces the chance that a mistake will lead to a binge.

The behavioral part of the therapy for bulimia is equally important. Patients are generally given diets that are low in fat and calories and taught to take a "time-out" of at least several minutes between feeling the urge to binge and actually going to the refrigerator. By the breaking the cycle of responding immediately to the urge to binge, patients are sometimes able to avert some of the binges. Patients also construct plans with the therapist to engage in alternative activities during the time of peak binge urges.

Recent studies have shown that these cognitive/behavioral therapies can be very successful. Patients may meet with the therapist once a week for between three and six months to complete the program.

Medication, particularly antidepressants, also has a role in the treatment of bulimia. Many patients are prescribed the selective serotonin reuptake inhibitor (SSRI) drugs Prozac (fluoxetine), Zoloft (sertraline), or Paxil (paroxetine). Since patients with bulimia are also often depressed or have obsessive compulsive disorder, these drugs may be particularly useful for bulimic patients because they will treat the other problems effectively as well. Nevertheless, a patient with bulimia does not have to be depressed in order to benefit from one of the SSRI-type antidepressants.

The older antidepressants, called tricyclics (see Chapter 4), are also effective for treating bulimia but are not used first because most of them tend to make the patient gain weight. Monoamine oxidase inhibitor (MAOI) antidepressants such as Nardil (phenelzine) and Parnate (tranylcypromine) are similarly effective but not used because the dietary restrictions placed on patients who take them are sometimes difficult for bulimic patients.

One effective antidepressant, called Wellbutrin (buproprion), is specifically not used for the treatment of bulimia. For entirely unclear reasons, Wellbutrin may cause seizures in patients with bulimia.

Because patients with bulimia often feel highly anxious just before a binge, some take antianxiety medications such Valium (diazepam) or Xanax (alprazolam). These belong to a class of drug called the benzodiazepines that are described in Chapter 11 and are very effective in controlling anxiety. There is little reason to think they actually help patients with bulimia, however, and should probably be avoided whenever possible.

The issue of longer-term, psychodynamic therapy often comes up for patients with bulimia. Patients with bulimia frequently suffer from poor self-image and low self-esteem. They often have difficulty maintaining relationships and complain of sexual difficulties. Some of these problems are directly related to the bulimic symptoms and improve considerably when cognitive/behavioral therapy and medication reduce the frequency of the binges. In patients who still have residual problems with self-esteem after these treatments are applied, and for whom unconscious conflict and childhood difficulties seem to be the cause of some of their problems, it is reasonable to consider psychoanalytic psychotherapy. It must be borne in mind, however, that the primary aim in the beginning of treatment for patients with bulimia is the practical one of eliminating the binges. This is best done with cognitive/behavioral therapy and possibly antidepressant medication.

Prognosis for Bulimia

The prognosis for bulimia is generally superior than that for anorexia, but vigilance is still warranted because relapses are common. Patients should be alerted to return to the therapist and possibly restart medication as well if they resume bingeing.

The treatment approach I have outlined here will not help people who think they weigh too much or think they eat too much and need to lose weight. Doctors really don't have a reliable cure for that. It will help people who suffer from the illness bulimia. Once again, being clear about the diagnosis and the limitations of psychiatric therapy will vastly decrease disappointment.

14.
Drug and Alcohol Abuse

THE USE OF intoxicating substances is probably the world's oldest public health problem. While most people focus on the abuse of illegal drugs such as heroin and cocaine, it has always been the case—and probably always will be—that the most abused substance throughout the world is alcohol. Alcohol abuse is the most common psychiatric disturbance among men in the United States. It is a significant problem for women too.

Substance abuse is not always considered a psychiatric illness. Many abused drugs, other than alcohol, are illegal and therefore drug abuse is partially an issue for the criminal justice system. Some forms of drug abuse, like heroin abuse, raise significant social issues. Psychiatrists often like to pontificate about the political, criminal, and social aspects of drug abuse, but in truth we have no particular expertise on these matters, only our own personal opinions. Some psychiatrists think drugs should be legalized, others do not. Some think drug abusers should be put in jail, others insist they need help finding jobs and a way out of poverty. Everyone is entitled to his or her opinion, but the New Psychiatry is medicine, not politics. Our interest is in evaluating whether the mental-health field has anything to offer a patient with a substance abuse problem. Can we reliably help him break his addiction?

The issue for psychiatrists, then, is whether there are treatments that effectively stop people from abusing drugs. The answer, of course, is that some types of therapy and medication can reduce drug abuse. Sadly, this is an area where psychiatrists have probably had their least success. It is extremely hard to stop someone from drinking too much alcohol or snorting cocaine or injecting heroin. Still, I will review a number of treatments that are sometimes effective. It is also interesting to note that for some forms of drug abuse we think there may be a medical component to the cause. If these things can ever be proven, we might do a better job with treatment.

Alcohol Abuse

A recent study indicates that nearly 25 percent of the American population abuses alcohol at some time in their lives. Men are more than twice as likely as women to have a serious alcohol use problem.

How to Know If It Is Abuse
By abuse I do not simply mean getting drunk occasionally or having one or two drinks at night. Alcohol abuse refers to a consistent pattern of drinking

when it is clearly harmful. The patient persistently misses work or school, gets into fights, drives while intoxicated, or gets arrested for disorderly conduct while drunk. A person is said to be dependent on alcohol when in addition to abuse there is evidence that the body has made a physiological adjustment to alcohol. Signs of dependence include having a withdrawal syndrome when alcohol consumption is stopped. The withdrawal syndrome may be limited to shakes, rapid heart beat, and physical restlessness, but at its most serious it can include seizures, hallucinations, and a potentially life-threatening condition called delirium tremens (DTs). Other signs of physical dependence are a need to drink more and more to avoid withdrawal, spending increasing amounts of time trying to get alcohol, and continuing to drink even in the face of obvious physical damage from alcohol, such as hepatitis or bleeding from the gastrointestinal tract.

Interestingly, a small amount of daily alcohol intake may be good for health, at least for men. There is accumulating scientific evidence that one or two drinks a day protects men from heart disease; it is not clear if this is true for women, and there is some reason to fear that alcohol use may promote breast cancer.

My own feeling, however, is that there are better ways to cut down on the heart attack risk, such as exercise, losing weight, stopping smoking, and treating high blood pressure. Maybe small amounts of aspirin and vitamin E taken daily will also help. Excessive use of alcohol causes disease to almost every organ of the body and causes untold numbers of fatal accidents every year. We learned earlier in this century that it is pointless to try to make alcohol illegal, but we should never forget that alcohol abuse is a major-league killer.

People who abuse alcohol usually deny it. For that reason, in the discussion of the medical approach to treating alcohol abuse, we need to start by defining who has a problem. In the paragraphs above I list some of the official psychiatric criteria for alcohol abuse and dependence and these are repeated in Table 47. But there are two better ways to identify a person with alcohol use.

The criteria for alcohol abuse and dependence listed in Table 47 come from the *DSM-IV* manual of the American Psychiatric Association and represent the standard way that doctors make the diagnosis of alcohol abuse or dependence. If you substituted the word *cocaine* or *heroin* for *alcohol* anywhere in the table, you would get the same result: official criteria for abuse and dependence for those substances. Obviously dependence on a substance like alcohol is considered more serious than abuse. Dependence essentially means addiction: the person cannot stop drinking, and if they try they get a serious, sometimes life-threatening, physical withdrawal reaction.

The two easier ways to identify a person with a drinking problem are to apply the CAGE criteria and to do the two-week abstinence test that I described in *The Essential Guide to Psychiatric Drugs.*

TABLE 47
THE SIGNS OF ALCOHOL ABUSE AND DEPENDENCE
(Adapted from the *DSM-IV*, American Psychiatric Association, 1994)

Abuse

You often miss work or just don't do your job properly because you drink

You drive or operate dangerous machinery after drinking

Drinking gets you into legal problems like arrests for disorderly conduct or fighting

You get into fights because you have been drinking

Dependence

It takes more and more alcohol to get the same effect (this is called tolerance)

When you stop drinking you get a set of physical symptoms that include shaking, feeling dizzy, heart pounding, nervousness, and sometimes seizures and hallucinations (this is called alcohol withdrawal)

Even if you try, you can't stop drinking

You spend a lot of time doing things necessary to get alcohol

You stop doing the things you want to do because of drinking

You continue to drink even though you know it is causing you serious health problems

The CAGE questions were developed by researchers from the University of North Carolina. If you think that you or anyone you know may be drinking too much, ask the following four questions:

1. Have you ever felt you ought to *C*ut down on drinking?
2. Have people *A*nnoyed you by criticizing your drinking?
3. Have you ever felt bad or *G*uilty about your drinking?
4. Have you ever had a drink first thing in the morning to steady your nerves or get rid of a hangover (*E*ye opener)?

From Ewing, J.A.: "Detecting alcoholism." The CAGE questionnaire. *JAMA* 12: 1905–1907, 1984.

The two-week abstinence test goes like this: decide right this moment that no matter what you will not have a drop of alcohol to drink for the next 14 days. There are three essential parts to this: (1) You have to make the decision right now; if you say I'll start tomorrow or next week but you can't do it this minute, then there is a reason you need to have a drink today and you should take very seriously the probability that reason is you have a problem with alcohol. (2) The "no matter what" part means that if in the middle of the two weeks you have an important business meeting at which it might look odd if you don't have a drink or you have to go to a wedding or even if there is a religious ceremony at which alcohol is usually used you still can't have a drink. There are no excuses. (3) The "not a drop" part means absolutely zero alcohol. You can't cook with it or put a little in your coffee or take a sip from your wife's glass of wine. None.

The two-week abstinence test is hardly foolproof. If you can't do it, you probably have a drinking problem. If you can do it, you may still have one because some alcohol abusers can, with great force of will, get through two weeks and then go right back to drinking too much. A person who is truly alcohol-dependent will not get much passed the first day; in fact, for a very seriously alcohol-dependent person, the two-week abstinence test is medically dangerous. If you have gotten the shakes before when you tried to stop drinking, then you have a serious drinking problem and should go to a rehab program rather than trying to stop drinking on your own. Despite these warnings, the two-week abstinence test, like the CAGE questions, can be used by individuals to find out whether they have drinking problems.

There are other warning signs that people, incredibly, ignore. Blackouts are one of them. People with serious drinking problems sometimes "blackout." They don't necessarily loose consciousness, but they loose all recollection of a period of time while they were intoxicated. This is not simply falling asleep while drunk, but probably represents a severe neurological reaction to drinking in which brain cells responsible for memory are affected. Some scientists believe that permanent brain damage occurs after too many blackouts. Another warning sign is doing things you wouldn't ordinarily do after drinking. Here is an example of that.

A Case Study of Alcoholism. Bernard is a 33-year-old construction worker who saw a psychiatrist because of mild depression. In the course of one visit to the doctor, he revealed that he was frequently unfaithful to his wife. He had never had an extensive affair; one-night stands were his habit. He wanted to discuss this in terms of his relationship with his wife and dissatisfaction with the relationship, but the psychiatrist noticed that the one-night stands always occurred with women he met in restaurants or bars or at parties. It turned out that Bernard usually was drunk when he got involved with these women. The next day, sober, he usually regretted having been unfaithful. While there may have been problems with his marriage, it turned out that Bernard was in the habit of spending more money than he should, making crass comments and insulting people, and having sex with women besides his wife after drinking a lot of alcohol. The first thing to do to help him (and probably deal with his depression as well) was to get him to stop drinking. Work on his marriage could come later.

The biggest problem when trying to help a drinker is to get him to recognize that there is a problem. My best advice is that if it ever crossed your mind for the merest of moments that you might drink too much, or if you have ever had that thought about someone close to you, assume there is a drinking problem until proven otherwise. Alcohol abuse and dependence are devastating and deadly and it is best to be overcautious and maintain a very high index of suspicion.

Are There Biological Causes of Alcoholism?

There is some evidence that alcohol abuse may be a genetic problem. Dr. Mark Schuckit of the University of California in San Diego studied the nonalcoholic sons of alcoholic fathers and compared their responses to alcohol to nonalcoholic sons of nonalcoholic fathers. The subjects with alcoholic fathers had a number of abnormal biological responses to a dose of alcohol. This suggests that there may be something passed on genetically that predisposes people to become alcoholic. Recently, studies using powerful molecular biological techniques have indicated that there may in fact be an abnormal gene on a specific chromosome in alcoholics. Although definitive evidence is still lacking, many scientists now think it is likely that at least some forms of alcoholism represent an inherited illness.

Other evidence suggests that some drinking problems may arise from an attempt to "treat" an anxiety or mood disorder. One study showed that as many as 30 percent of patients admitted to an inpatient hospital unit to be detoxed from alcohol had begun drinking after developing panic attacks. The scientists suggest that alcohol was originally used by these people to relieve the anxiety disorder, but that the patients went on to become alcoholic. While I doubt that anywhere near 30 percent of alcoholics actually started drinking to relieve anxiety or depression, it is highly likely that some alcoholism does begin in this way. In evaluating any alcoholic patient, therefore, it is always critical to obtain a complete psychiatric history.

Treatment of Alcohol Abuse

Regardless of the cause of alcoholism, the treatment always begins with the same first step—detoxification and abstinence. For alcohol-dependent people detoxification is a medical procedure. In such cases the body has become addicted to alcohol and stopping drinking immediately can cause serious physical problems, sometimes even resulting in death. A patient in acute alcohol withdrawal is usually admitted to the detox unit of a hospital and may be treated with medication to block the withdrawal symptoms.

Once the detoxification procedure is complete, the next step is to enforce complete alcohol abstinence. There are tidbits of evidence that some alcoholics can drink small amounts on occasion without relapsing, but to me this is playing Russian roulette. To really treat alcohol abuse, absolutely no alcohol is the best advice. And at present the best way to achieve that goal is to join Alcoholics Anonymous (AA).

Psychiatrists have tried to find ways of treating alcohol abuse themselves, and some of these efforts are described below. But in fact doctors have relatively little to offer an alcoholic patient who wants to stop drinking. AA is clearly the most successful route. It was the first of the so-called Twelve-Step programs that are currently also applied to addiction to other drugs and even now to other types of compulsive behavior, such as gambling, overeating, and sexual obsession. Whether it works for these nondrug compulsions is questionable, but Twelve-Step programs clearly are effective for drug abuse. They start with the acknowledgment that one does indeed have a drug abuse problem and progress through stages of conquering the addiction. It is critical to attend meetings regularly and to be honest about each and every "slip."

Members of AA chapters benefit from the help they get from other members, including the simple knowledge that there are many people just like them who are also alcoholic. In most chapters a new member is assigned a "buddy" or "partner," usually a veteran of AA. The new member is encouraged to call the buddy at any hour of the day or night if he feels he is about to slip and have a drink. AA discourages members from criticizing each other if slips occur; a guilty alcoholic who feels ostracized from the group is someone who is a set-up to get drunk. When slips occur, the member is encouraged to talk about what happened and try to figure out how to avoid the errant alcohol intake in the future. On the other hand, AA does not permit members to harbor rationalizations or excuses about drinking. It is blunt in insisting that a drunk is a drunk. There is no such thing as being "a little alcoholic" or of special circumstances in which a drink is needed or allowed. To be successful in AA a member must strip himself bare of any illusion that his drinking is any different from a drunk lying in the street. Even the fanciest corporate businessman must admit that he is a drunk to make it in AA.

In the past, AA discouraged alcoholic patients with other psychiatric illnesses from taking psychiatric drugs, a clear mistake. Patients with bipolar mood disorder (formerly called manic-depressive illness) often abuse alcohol, for example, particularly when manic. These people will benefit from AA and must stop drinking, but they also have to take a mood-stabilizing drug like lithium. Most chapters have changed their minds about this and now accept the use of psychiatric medications. AA is correct, however, that antianxiety medications of the benzodiazepine class, like Valium and Xanax, should be avoided by most people with a history of alcohol abuse because they are highly prone to abuse these drugs also.

Alcoholics Anonymous and psychiatric treatment of concomitant psychiatric illnesses, then, are the best approaches to alcohol abuse. Other forms of psychotherapy are not the appropriate treatment for alcoholism. No form of psychotherapy has ever been shown effective in stopping people from drinking, but it can be helpful later as an addition to AA in helping people cope with the stresses of their lives.

There are two drugs that are also used in the treatment of alcoholism that should be mentioned. Antabuse (disulfiram) is a drug that interferes with the body's ability to break down some of the components of alcohol. If a person who takes Antabuse has a drink, he will become violently ill, usually developing severe headache, difficulty breathing, retching, vomiting, and dizziness. Going through this once is more than enough to convince most alcoholics not to drink again. The problem is that the patient has to take the Antabuse pill every day and many patients, even ones who think they are motivated to stop drinking, "forget" to take the pills. Also, many doctors are frightened about prescribing it because the Antabuse-alcohol reaction is so severe it sometimes amounts to a medical emergency.

Recently, there has been a flurry of reports that a drug called naltrexone (Revia) may block the craving for alcohol and the high that people get after they drink. This is a surprise because naltrexone is an old drug that blocks the ability of opiates like heroin to bind to the opiate receptor in the brain. No one ever thought that it would have any effect on alcohol. At this point, the use of naltrexone to treat alcoholism is still experimental but promising, and it will probably be increasingly used in conjunction with AA in the future.

Of all the addictions, alcohol is by far the most devastating to the public health. It is also the only addiction that society tolerates and, to some extent, even encourages. People who don't drink are often looked at as boring. I am not about to start a campaign against drinking; most people are able to consume alcohol in safe and reasonable amounts. But there are thousands (actually millions) of people in this country who cannot. These people make their families miserable, eat up a disproportionate amount of health care, and kill on the highways. It would be hard to think of an illness that deserves more research attention than alcohol abuse. For now, we have to make due with some fairly good treatments and do what we can to stop ignoring the enormity of the problem.

Cocaine Abuse

About 15 years ago I had a conversation with a leading figure in psychiatric research. He told me he had been reading about a group of South American Indians who supposedly ate coca leaves on a regular basis and had chronically high blood cocaine levels. These Indians allegedly lived long, normal, and happy lives. Because cocaine has actions in the brain that are remotely similar to what some antidepressant medications do, this psychiatrist asked me if it wouldn't be a good idea to study cocaine as a possible antidepressant drug.

Only a few years after this occasion, the neighborhood in which I work in New York City because ravaged by the spread of cocaine. We now know that cocaine is the most powerfully addicting of all abused substances. From a pharmacological point of view, cocaine is the world's most dangerous drug.

If you put a male rat in a cage with a dish of alcohol, some food, and a female rat, he will drink a little alcohol, eat some food, and have sex with the female. You can substitute heroin, Valium, or barbiturates for the alcohol and get pretty much the same result. But if you put cocaine in the dish, the male rat will keep eating it until it dies. He won't eat or even look at the female. All he wants to do is keeping taking the cocaine until he starves.

A New Plague

Humans take cocaine by a number of routes. It can be injected or "snorted" (sniffed into the nose). It can be taken in the highly purified form called *crack.* However it is ingested, it is powerfully reinforcing, which means that it makes people want to take it over and over again. A person addicted to cocaine will do almost anything to get more, including kill people. Cocaine and crack cocaine have stimulated an unprecedented wave of violence in cities all over the United States. From once casually considering it as a possibly interesting substance to study in our laboratory, we now spend research time trying to figure out how to stop people from using cocaine. Psychiatrists did not face the prevalence of such addictions 20 or more years ago. Today, they are widespread and require new treatments.

The Biology of Cocaine

Cocaine affects neurotransmitter or brain chemicals. Essentially, once someone takes cocaine there is a sudden burst of brain chemical activity that stimulates many parts of the brain. Some people say they get an intense feeling of confidence and well-being after taking cocaine. There are people who can take it once in a while without getting addicted, but no one should ever count on this because it seems that almost anyone is capable of getting hooked even after casual use. I have sometimes read about politicians who think it might be a good idea to legalize cocaine. They think this would cut down on the crime associated with the sale of cocaine. I think these politicians might just as well attack the population with mustard gas or germ warfare; it would have nearly the same effect.

I make this point so strongly because it is important to convey the fact that there are vast differences among drugs that people abuse. Sometimes, people believe that heroin, alcohol, and cocaine are all the same thing— substances some people take too much of. But there are incredibly important differences. Cocaine is purely evil, has absolutely no redeeming value of any kind, and should never be made legally available to anyone.

Scientists are now trying to figure out just what it is about cocaine that makes it so powerfully addicting. Some people report a "rush" when they take cocaine, especially after sniffing or snorting it because this leads to tremendously high blood levels and rapid transport to the brain. Then, the effect wears off and a craving for cocaine develops and that appears to be the real culprit. This craving demands satisfaction. Among other effects, cocaine increases the amount of a neurotransmitter called dopamine that is available to stimulate brain cells. The craving for cocaine is probably caused by a physiological adjustment in the brain; the brain starts to demand excessive levels of dopamine and other neurotransmitters. Without cocaine, addicts experience a horrible depressed-like feeling that is intolerable. Unfortunately, there is just so much dopamine the brain can produce, and after a while the cocaine addict needs to take more and more cocaine to squeeze out every last drop of neurotransmitter from every brain cell that makes it. After a while the cocaine "high" lasts for a very short period of time and the addict may need to snort cocaine every hour to ward off the intense craving. In some addicts no amount of cocaine is enough and they live chronically depressed lives, always searching for more cocaine but never getting enough to satisfy the brain's demand. The brain has become exhausted.

There are other physical consequences of cocaine use. Snorting the drug leads to irritation of the mucous membrane of the nose, and eventually holes in the nasal septum occur. The drug also overstimulates the heart, leading to well-publicized cases of sudden death after cocaine use. I believe I have made it clear that cocaine is a physiological disaster.

Treatment for Cocaine Abuse

The only approach to treatment is to get the patient to stop taking the drug, something that is extremely difficult. If you can get the cocaine addict into a rehab program early enough, you may have a chance to induce him to stop. He will need intense counseling and supervision. The patient will have to be cajoled and supported through the withdrawal phase when the desire to get cocaine is intense. Some people will need to be hospitalized. Tranquilizers are sometimes given to ease some of the withdrawal pain. Cocaine abusers are encouraged to join Twelve-Step programs like Narcotics Anonymous.

Still, the relapse rate is high. Because of this we are especially interested in trying to find drugs that will intervene at two points in the cocaine abuse cycle: to block the high and to block the craving. We think that if we can find such a drug we can stop addicts from getting either the rush that hooks them on the drug or from experiencing the horrible withdrawal reaction that literally forces them to keep getting more. So far, no such agent has been identified. At first, it was thought that one of the tricyclic antidepressant drugs, desipramine (Norpramin, Pertofrane), had the ability to block the high, but more recent research has cast doubt on its usefulness. A drug called buprenorphine, which can be used to treat heroin addiction, looks as if it may block cocaine craving, but once again further research is crucial to establish this. Because psychological treatments for cocaine addiction have not worked well enough and many cocaine abusers relapse even after intense treatment, it is well worth the effort to try to find some pharmacological agent that can replace cocaine without itself causing a high or a craving.

Heroin Addiction

When I started to write this section, someone said to me not to bother. "Heroin addicts don't read books like this," he said. Not true. We think of heroin addicts as shady characters living in tenement basements and doing nothing but sticking needles in their arms. In fact, heroin addicts come from all walks of life and all socioeconomic strata. Because heroin addiction has been around for so long, we know a fair amount about how to treat it. Our biggest problem in treating heroin addiction in the United States is a lack of enough treatment programs to accommodate all of the people who need and want to stop abusing heroin.

Heroin is a member of a class of drugs called opiates. They derive from the poppy plant. Opium, once itself an abused drug, was probably the first of the opiates. Another opiate is morphine, which is actually one of the most effective drugs for treating severe pain in medically ill patients. There are also "synthetic" opiates, drugs that have been manufactured as painkillers. These include Talwin, Dilaudid, and Levodromoran. All of these can be abused.

The Biology of Heroin

The brain has a specific receptor for opiate drugs, called the opiate receptor. It turns out that our bodies actually make several substances that naturally bind to opiate receptors. These are called endorphins and enkephalins. It is believed that these naturally occurring opiate substances are produced at times of physical and possibly emotional stress and act as natural painkillers. There is good evidence, for example, that long-distance runners become relatively insensitive to physical pain because of high endorphin levels. Some believe that acupuncture works to suppress pain by stimulating the release of endorphins. It was once thought that psychiatric illnesses, like depression, might result from an endorphin deficiency, but this has not turned out to be the case. At this point, scientists are not sure they understand exactly why we have opiate receptors or make endorphins.

Heroin also binds to the opiate receptor, producing a calm and relatively pain-free state. It can be injected, snorted, or smoked. Injection produces high blood levels. The risk of contracting AIDS among heroin users comes from the sharing of needles used to inject heroin, not from the heroin itself. When heroin addicts inject themselves, they insert the needle into a vein, draw some of their blood into it, and then push the plunger to inject the drug. Some of their blood remains on the needle and in the syringe. If they then pass the needle to someone else, he or she will inject the first person's blood into his or her own vein. If that blood contains the virus that causes AIDS (called HIV), the second injector can become infected. Some have advocated providing heroin users with free, sterilized needles to prevent the needle-sharing practice and help stop the spread of AIDS, but this has been a very controversial suggestion (I cannot resist inserting that it is a suggestion I absolutely endorse, although sadly it may be too late given the large numbers of heroin addicts already infected with HIV).

Once a person becomes addicted to (or *dependent on,* to use the technical term) heroin, there is a craving for the drug shortly after the effect wears off. This craving is intense and will lead the heroin addict to go to great lengths to get more heroin, including committing crimes. The craving for heroin is generally not felt to be as intense as that for cocaine, however. In part, this is because heroin purchased on the street is very impure and most addicts actually inject very small doses. There is, however, a very characteristic physical withdrawal syndrome that occurs when heroin addicts stop their heroin. This includes profuse perspiration, racing heart, shaking and tremulousness, runny nose, tearing, and extreme agitation. A person in the midst of heroin withdrawal will find it almost impossible to sleep and may go for days in an intense, agitated state until the withdrawal state subsides. The withdrawal is so painful that the heroin addict will usually try to get more drug.

Treatment of Heroin Addiction

There are two approaches to treating heroin addiction. One is to try for an immediate drug-free status. The other is to substitute a similar but less dangerous drug for heroin, called methadone.

There are many drug-free rehabilitation programs in the United States for heroin addicts. Often, the patient must first be medically detoxified. A drug called clonidine (Catapres) can be given to people who are withdrawing from heroin to block many of the distressing physical symptoms that occur when heroin is stopped abruptly. Some heroin users are then placed on a drug that prevents heroin from binding to the opiate receptor in the brain. This drug, called naltrexone (Revia), can be taken once a week and effectively blocks the effects of heroin. A person who then takes heroin gets absolutely no effect from it. Naltrexone is fairly safe, but can cause problems in patients with liver disease. After a time on naltrexone, many former heroin users stop taking it but remain in the drug rehabilitation program.

Drug-free programs can be residential or outpatient, but typically begin with very intense counseling and group therapy sessions. Later, patients may attend sessions on a weekly basis. Most of them require that the patient give periodic urine samples, which are tested for drugs, including heroin. Patients who persistently have "positive" urines, indicating ongoing drug use, are often asked to leave the program. Success rates vary from program to program. Many heroin users are able to turn their lives around and remain permanently drug-free, but relapse rates are nevertheless high.

The use of methadone to prevent heroin use is by now a standard and widely used treatment. Methadone is given out mainly by government-approved methadone clinics. Patients also attend counseling sessions and must submit urine samples to prove they are not taking heroin or other illegal drugs.

Methadone is an opiate that is taken orally. It produces much less of a "high" than heroin, but satisfies the heroin users' craving for heroin. Because it is given out by clinics, patients do not need to engage in illegal activities to get methadone. They also do not need to use needles, thus eliminating the risk of getting infected with the AIDS virus. There is no question that methadone maintenance, which can last for years for some patients, is an effective treatment for heroin addiction. The major problem is the serious shortage of methadone clinics. Heroin users must sometimes wait for months on waiting lists to get into a methadone clinic. An expansion of the number of methadone clinics is clearly needed.

After taking methadone daily for months or years, some former heroin users then move to drug-free programs. They can make this transition by first using clonidine to block withdrawal symptoms when they stop methadone and then taking naltrexone as described above. Although purists object to the substitution of one addicting drug for another (that is, methadone for heroin), there is no question that methadone maintenance is one of the most successful methods of ending a person's addiction. Most of us wish we had a methadone-like drug to help people addicted to alcohol or cocaine.

Marijuana

We have finally come to our senses about marijuana, recognizing in most states that it is a minor problem compared to alcohol or cocaine. Marijuana is not particularly addicting; there is little craving for marijuana even among habitual users and little physiological withdrawal when a habitual user stops taking marijuana. Most people who smoke or eat marijuana get a mild "high," but it is probably less intense than that obtained from alcohol and certainly nothing like cocaine. Occasionally, a person will report feeling suspicious and paranoid while under the influence of marijuana; such people usually do not take it again. Interestingly, patients with panic disorder (described in Chapter II) frequently report getting intense panic attacks after smoking marijuana. They invariably leave the stuff alone.

I do not mean, however, to endorse marijuana as a great substance. It is doubtful that marijuana smoke is particularly good for the lungs, and we quite frankly do not know what other physically harmful effects it might have. Hence, habitual smoking is probably not a terrific idea. Also, marijuana is intoxicating and can lead to automobile and other accidents.

But perhaps the biggest problem with marijuana is not that it causes psychological problems but that it is used to excess by some people with other psychological problems. Psychiatrists frequently see patients who suffer from a variety of emotional problems that cause them to lead relatively isolated and unproductive lives. Such patients may suffer from chronic depression or an anxiety disorder or they may have one of the personality disorders described in Chapter 15. Characteristically, these people are unmotivated and have trouble supporting themselves. They waste time and have few friends. Marijuana seems to be a preferred drug for them, perhaps because it eases the pain of their lonely lives. But marijuana also seems to further dull their motivation and drive, making them even more listless. I believe that in these cases marijuana is more of a symptom than a cause of the psychiatric problem, but I nevertheless always try to encourage the patient to stop smoking it on the grounds that it probably makes the situation worse.

It is not physically difficult to stop smoking marijuana because there is no withdrawal syndrome to speak of following cessation. Hence, the patient is simply urged and cajoled to give it up.

Stimulant Abuse

It is my impression that the abuse of stimulants like amphetamines, Ritalin (methylphenidate), and diet pills is less of a problem now than it was in the 1950s and 1960s. Perhaps this is because people who are prone to abuse stimulants have all found cocaine. Also, I think doctors have drastically curtailed prescribing stimulants to patients for the purpose of weight loss and this has cut down on some of the abuse.

Most stimulants act on the brain by increasing the release of chemical neurotransmitters. The person who takes a stimulant often gets a "high" characterized by a feeling of emotional giddiness and stimulation. They may also feel anxious and agitated. Stimulants like the amphetamine Dexedrine (dextroamphetamine) speed up all biological processes so that metabolic rate is also increased and some weight loss can occur. We now know that stimulants are a poor way to lose weight because the body eventually stops responding to the stimulant; unless ever increasing doses are taken, the drugs lose their effect and all the weight is gained back.

There are many stories of actors and dancers getting hooked on stimulants, often supposedly because directors insist that they lose weight and send them to unscrupulous diet doctors who prescribe them. Judy Garland was supposedly an example of this. Some people then get addicted to them, finding that if they stop the stimulant they immediately experience crushing depression, often to the point of feeling suicidal. There is no actual physical withdrawal when stimulants are stopped, but the psychological withdrawal effect is profound and can motivate some people to start taking them again. Stimulants can produce insomnia and high blood pressure and in some individuals may produce paranoia and hallucinations. In fact, scientists used to give amphetamines to normal volunteers in order to induce a temporary psychotic state that they thought resembled schizophrenia. This enabled them to conduct scientific studies of psychosis.

There is a place for stimulants in psychiatric practice. Dexedrine is occasionally useful for some patients with severe depression who fail to respond to any other forms of antidepressant treatment. Ritalin (methylphenidate) is a useful drug for treating both children and adults with the condition known as attention deficit disorder. Neurologists use stimulants to treat patients with narcolepsy, a condition in which the patient suddenly falls asleep without warning many times a day. Under close medical supervision, which includes watching for any signs of psychosis and monitoring blood pressure, stimulant drugs still have their place. They should not be used for weight loss, however, and never taken without careful supervision from a physician who is experienced in prescribing them. And that does not mean a diet doctor. If you have a feeling that the doctor is pulling out his prescription pad casually and writing a prescription for Dexedrine, don't take it. Dexedrine should only given to patients for psychiatric reasons after very careful consideration and an attempt to use all other possible treatments has failed.

Caffeine

One other stimulant needs to be mentioned: caffeine. It is said that the only addictions doctors don't consider addictions are the ones that they themselves suffer from, and caffeine fits that description for me. But caffeine is a stimulant that people (like me) get hooked on. It doesn't cause psychosis and there is no evidence at this point that it is harmful to physical health, but caffeine is definitely addicting. People who drink a lot of coffee and then stop suffer a bona fide withdrawal reaction that usually includes headache, sluggishness, and constipation. Caffeine is especially bad for people with such anxiety disorders as panic disorder because it clearly makes them more anxious. I usually recommend that someone who wants to reduce their caffeine intake should cut down slowly, perhaps by eliminating one cup of coffee every three or four days. This reduces the withdrawal problem. Americans seem to think that having a cup of coffee is a good way to relax: actually, it makes most people more anxious.

Nicotine

Smoking is in every sense an addiction, perhaps the most deadly of all addictions. There is little question that if cigarettes were invented today the government would immediately ban them. It is hard to believe that a substance that absolutely and without any doubt kills people is allowed to be manufactured and sold. But it is and I doubt that my ranting and raving about cigarettes is going to be particularly helpful, so now on to what psychiatrists have to say about nicotine.

We know that nicotine is addicting. We also know that cigarette smoking causes almost every disease known, including most forms of cancer, lung disease, heart disease, and stroke. We know that it is very difficult to stop smoking and that most smokers try and fail many times before they are ever successful. As an ex-smoker myself, I think that there should be a Hall of Fame for all the people who have quit; it is difficult to do and requires a lot of fortitude.

Treatment of Nicotine Addiction

If will power alone is not enough, there are several things to try. A number of behavioral therapy programs now exist that are successful in helping people to stop smoking. These programs identify all the cues and motivations that cause people to light up. For example, most smokers crave a cigarette after eating, so the behavioral therapy for smokers encourages them to get up from the table and go do something right after eating, thus cutting down on the chances of smoking. I used to need a cigarette right after talking to my boss, so I arranged not to talk to him for two weeks while I was trying to quit. That helped (and perhaps not so surprisingly, my boss didn't seem to miss me that much). Definitely enroll in one of these programs.

Some people have found that hypnosis helps. I am all for trying it, although I caution people that there is very little systematic evidence that hypnosis is really an effective way to stop smoking.

There are two pharmacological aids for quitting smoking: Nicorette gum and nicotine patches. Both of these are helpful, although they work best when combined with a behavioral program. Nicorette gum contains nicotine and is chewed whenever the smoker has the urge to have a cigarette. It satisfies the craving for nicotine but, because no smoke is inhaled, poses much less of a health risk than smoking. It is used as a transition to complete abstinence; after using the gum for a few weeks, the ex-smoker is often able to stop chewing it without resuming smoking. Nicotine patches slowly release nicotine into the bloodstream, again satisfying the craving for nicotine and serving as a transition to complete nicotine abstinence. The gum is now available OTC, but the patches are only available by prescription.

Depression and Cigarette Addiction

Dr. Alexander Glassman and others have shown that people who cannot stop smoking despite an earnest effort (or many efforts) often have a history of depression. It is thought that some element of cigarette smoking may actually be acting as a mild antidepressant in such people. Consequently, researchers are now trying to learn if antidepressant medication might be useful in helping people stop. So far, the scientific jury is out on this issue.

Drug and Alcohol Abuse: Concluding Remarks

Is the New Psychiatry trying to let people ''off the hook'' for their addictions by blaming them on biological causes beyond our control? That is a recent and fairly absurd charge. The truth is that the New Psychiatry is asking the question, Why is it so hard for people to stop taking substances they know are harming them? To be sure, many of the reasons for drug and alcohol abuse are social rather than medical. People living under conditions of poverty and adversity may find solace in substances that offer instantaneous relief from depression and anxiety. But the great majority of poor people do not drink to excess, shoot heroin, or sniff cocaine. There is a growing possibility that some component of addictive behavior is indeed biologically driven and therefore may be researched and treated. One problem with this research is that it always seems behind the times. We are now vigorously studying cocaine, but who knows what the next drug of abuse will be. Perhaps drugs already used on the street, like ''Ecstasy,'' ''Crystal Meth,'' or ''Special K,'' all powerful inducers of brain neurotransmitter function, will form the basis of the next drug abuse epidemic.

Whether it is under someone's control or not, the main mission is to find the quickest, most efficient way of stopping people from abusing drugs and committing crimes to get them. Of course it would be best if all alcoholics joined AA tomorrow and never had another drink, but that is never going to happen. Some of them may take naltrexone, however, and the ones who do just may never drive their cars into yours or develop liver cancer and need a transplant. Yes, we wish all heroin addicts would just stop, but until that happens we accept methadone maintenance as a second-best because you don't have to shoot anyone to get money for methadone and you won't get AIDS taking it. The New Psychiatry is clear on the issue of addictions: a little less political posturing and a lot more research and treatment is needed.

15.
Neuroses, Personality Disorders, and the Problems of Living

THERE ARE FEW areas in which the New Psychiatry struggles as much as the so-called neuroses or personality disorders. Time and again we have stressed in this book that the New Psychiatry attempts to rise above parochial turf wars, trying instead to integrate the best aspects of psychoanalysis, cognitive and behavioral theory, and biological psychiatry. The aim is to find treatments that are safe and can be shown to work scientifically. Diagnosis is key; treatments are specifically linked to the exact disorder the patient suffers from, just as we do in all the rest of medicine.

But we have a terrible time defining what *neurotic* actually is. As will become clear, the *DSM* system has attempted to supply us with categories of neurotic illnesses, called *personality disorders,* under its Axis Two. But many people feel these categories do not sufficiently capture all the nuances of human character and therefore do not help us when we think there is something abnormal about someone's personality.

The *DSM-IV*'s definition of personality disorder, the modern equivalent for neurosis, is not bad: "A Personality Disorder is an enduring pattern of inner experience and behavior that deviates markedly from the expectations of the individual's culture, is pervasive and inflexible, has an onset in adolescence or early adulthood, is stable over time, and leads to distress or impairment." It then lists ten specific personality disorders, some of which are discussed in more detail later in this chapter.

Already, however, you have probably noticed where the difficulties begin. How do we *define* "enduring pattern of inner experience"? That's not so easy as asking a depressed person if she has lost her appetite or even a psychotic person what the voices are saying to him. If we could really capture "inner experience," we would still have the problem with "enduring." Does it mean someone has to act the same way all the time to qualify for a personality disorder? In this chapter we distinguish personality disorders from "problems of living." The latter refer to transient situations that distress us, like having difficulty finding a job or a marital problem, but do not represent ongoing disorders of character and personality. Even here distinctions often get blurred. What may seem like a problem of living may actually be the maladaptive response to a situation characteristic of someone with a personality disorder.

And what constitutes markedly deviant experience and behavior? That surely must be in the eye of the beholder, even if we are able to establish cultural norms (which is not easy). And what do we do if someone's personality is perfectly acceptable to him but irritates everyone else? Is the angry, belligerent, obnoxious person we all know off the hook, personality disorderwise, because his inner experience and behavior don't lead to "distress or impairment"?

The New Psychiatry, frankly, does not yet have an answer for all of these questions. There is research going on to find out whether different personality styles are biologically determined, by genes for example. There is some research trying to figure out if any of the psychotherapies used for personality disorders actually work. All we can do at this point is apply some of the principles of the New Psychiatry to try to guide us in recommending therapy. The overriding principles are: (1) Can we identify something that both patient and doctor think needs to be fixed? and (2) Can we design a treatment for the individual patient that both doctor and patient can evaluate?

Let's begin with a case study to illustrate some of the problems in defining personality disorders and neuroses.

A Case Study: Is This Neurotic? I recently passed by the office of a colleague at the hospital late one evening as I was leaving work for the day. His door was open and I saw he was furiously banging away at his computer. "You're working pretty late," I said to him, "what are you doing?"

"I'm reworking the numbers from the study we published last month," he replied, not looking away from the computer screen, which was occupied with a vast array of statistics.

"Why would you do that?" I asked. "That paper is already published."

"I know, but I keep having the feeling something is wrong in the data. I've been checking it for three hours so far and I can't find anything wrong. I guess I'm just neurotic about these things."

The word *neurotic* crops up again, I thought to myself. What does my colleague mean by it? He is himself a psychologist who knows the technical meaning of these terms. Did he really mean to imply that there was something "abnormal" about his behavior? Is there something wrong with a scientist who thinks his interpretation of data might have been incorrect and spends time checking it?

To some people he is merely careful and scrupulous. There are almost infinite possibilities for mistakes to creep into scientific studies, many of which are unavoidable and often undetectable. Scientists worry about this a great deal. Some scientists are more relaxed than others, just like any other group of people. More relaxed scientists worry less than less relaxed scientists. My colleague is not a particularly relaxed person. I can imagine that the very hint of any error in his work would bother him a great deal, causing more than a few sleepless nights. So there I found him late one evening trying to find if, in fact, there was an error.

Some might say, however, that his behavior was abnormal. There was minimal basis for him to think he had made a mistake. The article about his research had been reviewed by experts, accepted by a scientific journal, and published. He had been looking for errors and not found a single problem; why not give it up, go home, and watch television? By this view, my friend's activity was obsessive and excessive, definitely neurotic.

You can see that the problem here is all a matter of interpretation and degree. When do the ordinary features of human personality become distorted to the point that psychiatrists should consider them abnormal and the subject of treatment? Is everyone who ever worries, brags, or acts in a way that is not clearly in his best interest a candidate for psychotherapy for a neurotic problem? Couldn't the argument be made that everybody is neurotic and needs to see a shrink? But if we are all neurotic, doesn't that mean being neurotic is normal?

Freud's View

The idea that everyone is neurotic actually derives from an interpretation of the work of Sigmund Freud. In Freud's great book *Civilization and Its Discontents,* he makes a reasonable case that Western civilization by its very design produces neurotic people. After all, we are born with a variety of urges and impulses, mainly sexual and aggressive, that society does not tolerate. So we are forced to repress and deny these impulses in order to fit in with the rest of civilization. We all have natural sexual impulses, for example, but we are not allowed to have sex whenever, wherever, and with whomever we choose. We get angry, but must constantly suppress our desire to maim or kill even the most irritating offenders. The price of civilization, Freud argued, is neuroses.

How might Freud view my scientist colleague? His need to check his work represents a symptom. He is denying himself pleasure by sitting for hours at his computer terminal checking his work. He should be home, enjoying himself, even basking in the glory of getting his paper published. Instead, he is inflicting needless pain on himself. An analysis of his behavior might reveal that he is secretly, and probably unconsciously, guilty about being successful. He is afraid of the envy of his colleagues and unconsciously believes that by being successful he has simply made himself a target for the wrath of other scientists who will want to destroy him rather than let him get ahead. Now we are arriving at a fairly primitive level, the level of the unconscious mind. What the scientist thinks he is doing is sitting at a computer poring over complex scientific data to see if his hypotheses are correct. What he is really doing, according to the Freudian interpretation, is struggling to defend himself against the murderous rage of envious rivals.

The process of getting to all of this unconscious material is, of course, the process of psychoanalysis, described in more detail in Chapter 2. Obviously, it would take more than a glib comment from me to show the scientist the roots of his behavior and help him overcome his need to check his data endless times. I am not sure, to be frank, I believe the Freudian interpretation myself. But the issue at hand is whether his behavior is a disorder.

I think everyone would agree that if my colleague spent hours a day for weeks and months checking his data, finding everything in perfect order, but still not feeling reassured that nothing was wrong, that he has a problem. And if he has a lifelong pattern of worry, self-doubt, perfectionism, and an inability to enjoy himself, we would probably all agree that he suffers from some kind of disorder. On the other hand, if this is an isolated incident of doubt, if by and large the scientist is overly careful and scrupulous but able to enjoy life, we might be reluctant to say he is suffering from an actual psychiatric disturbance.

When Is Protest Neurotic?

Let's give another example. While waiting outside on line to get into a movie on a very cold winter night recently, I heard yelling and screaming coming from the front of the line. A woman was berating the theater manager for not letting the people go into the theater so they could keep warm while waiting for the movie to begin. "It is freezing cold out here and the lobby of your theater is large enough to hold all these people. Why don't you set the line up inside?"

The manager tried to brush her off. "That's how we do things," he said, rather rudely.

She was not consoled and got angrier. "Well, it's a terrible way to do things. You are making all these people freeze for no reason. I think we should all just rip up our tickets and leave."

This went on for quite a while. The woman got angrier and angrier; the manager gave her little consideration and treated her like a lunatic. Eventually, I started fearing the woman was going to do something violent. She seemed so angry and the manager was really provoking her by refusing to offer even the rudiments of a excuse for keeping the line outside. I was personally freezing and believed the woman was absolutely correct; the manager was being intransigent. Yet neither I nor anyone else on the line said a word. No one came to the woman's defense or supported her position. Her anger was overwhelming and it seemed to frighten the crowd more than the freezing cold made us want to get inside. Everyone watched the scene, which ended eventually without violence and without us getting inside one second earlier, more discomfited by the woman's anger than our freezing noses.

Obviously, there was something different about this woman than most of the other people on the line. To be sure, she was absolutely correct in what she said. Yet she alone was capable of getting incensed to the point of provoking an argument. Most of the people on the line, myself included, wondered if there was something wrong with her.

Now, if we didn't have a small group of angry people willing to challenge the establishment when it is wrong, we would never make social progress. This woman was really fighting for the "people" against a "business." Is that a psychiatric problem? How do we reconcile the fact that she is absolutely correct and possibly a crusader with the equally undeniable fact that her level of anger was far greater than most people are capable of generating over waiting in a line. Most of us suffered in silent annoyance; she could not bear the injustice of being made to freeze so that the theater manager could maintain his line where he wanted it to be.

There are tremendous variations in the amount of anger people are able to experience and generate. We all know people who seem deficient in their ability to get angry. A waiter brings them a cold steak and they eat it rather than complain. A driver cuts them off and they do not even think about honking. On the other hand, there are people who seem unable to stop being angry. They walk into a restaurant and automatically, it seems, complain that they have been given a bad table and that the rolls aren't brought fast enough. No one can change lanes in front of them on a highway without getting barraged by honking and flashing lights. The first person gets taken advantage of all the time; the second one is so chronically angry that no one wants to be around him. Clearly, these do not seem to be particularly adaptive ways to behave.

Let us return to the women on the line. Maybe she has just had it that day and is finally letting off steam. She calms down, enjoys the movie, and later writes a letter to the president of the corporation that owns the movie theater suggesting a change in the way they maintain their lines. This seems fine and we are less likely to think she has an emotional problem. But supposing this kind of unrelenting rage is a lifelong pattern. She is constantly indignant and fighting the system. She gets a parking ticket and becomes incensed, even though she was parked at an expired meter. A friend shows up unavoidably late for a lunch date and she cannot help making angry comments at several points during the meal. She is angered by nine out of ten social contacts she makes. Now we wonder if this woman doesn't have a problem.

Personality Disorder Replaces Neurosis

Through the years, psychiatrists and psychologists have noticed that there are certain patterns and clusters of behavior that can be labeled and that seem to get some people into trouble in their lives. Because the word *neuroses* was so overused, when the *DSM-III* system was created it was proposed that the term be dropped entirely, something that shook up the mental-health world because we were so used to using it. A new category of Axis Two disorders was created and called *personality disorders.* The *DSM-III* people were trying to get rid of the term *neurosis* because they felt it was a psychoanalytic term and implied agreement with the psychoanalytic view that these conditions are the result of early childhood experience and unconscious conflict. They thought they could describe these disorders in a purely descriptive way, without making any theoretical statements, and thus sought to rename them as personality disorders. Thus for example, our scientist who checked his data all the time might be said, according to *DSM-III* (or *DSM-III-R* or *DSM-IV*), to have obsessive compulsive personality disorder. *DSM-IV* does not even have the word *neurosis* in the index or glossary.

What are these "personality disorders"? Here is what the *DSM-IV* definition is supposed to mean. They are conceived of as enduring patterns of behaving, thinking, and feeling that interfere with someone's ability to enjoy her life, feel fulfilled and successful, and maintain meaningful relationships. There are two elements to this definition. First, the condition is enduring. People do not develop a personality disorder for a few months and then get rid of it. These patterns of behavior often take shape in adolescence and are relatively fixed throughout life. Treatment may alter them, but to some degree most therapists agree that it is generally not possible to completely change someone's personality with psychotherapy. Second, the condition has to have a negative impact on the person's life. Psychiatrists are not in the business of altering people's personalities for the fun of it. The point of working on a personality disorder is to improve the patient's quality of life. This can be tricky at times because people with some of the most severe personality disorders sometimes think the rest of the world, not them, is screwed up. Our woman who started the fight on the movie line is an example; she probably thinks her anger is entirely justified and that there is nothing wrong with her. But in time people with uncontrollable anger usually recognize there is some kind of a problem because they have no friends. While it may not be obvious to them that their rage is responsible for this, they do recognize that something about them drives people away. Hence, the negative-impact-on-life criteria is met.

Value Judgments Abound

I want to acknowledge one final time that there are definitely "value judgments" involved in this personality disorder business. Here psychiatrists are open to the claim that psychiatric treatment may be misused to impose the doctor's point of view on the patient. For example, I once took care of a 35-year-old woman who came to see me because she felt chronically bored and depressed. Although she was a college graduate, she had stopped working ten years earlier when she had her first child. Her youngest was now six and attending school. I reached the conclusion that she felt unfulfilled because she was staying home all day to take care of the children and maintain her home. I decided to try to understand what was inhibiting her from resuming her professional career.

One day, however, my patient made a calm but firm admonishment: "Dr. Gorman, you obviously believe that women should work and that college-educated women should be professionals. I think that is just your point of view. I and lots of women I know are perfectly happy being housewives and I would feel guilty if I went back to work instead of being home for my children."

My patient was correct: I do have a definite opinion that women should do the same things that men do, including having careers. But clearly this is my political point of view. It is not a psychiatric disturbance, neither neurotic nor a personality disorder, to believe otherwise. In this instance, I was clearly misusing psychotherapy to impose my beliefs on my patient.

Personality Disorders: The Categories

I will turn now to describing the main personality disorders. I deliberately do not describe all of the *DSM-IV* categories because I do not believe that all of them are useful or common. I have almost never seen or heard of a patient who legitimately deserves diagnoses like "avoidant personality disorder" or "dependent personality disorder," for example. Some of the personality disorders are probably related to schizophrenia, like "schizoid personality disorder," "schizotypal personality disorder," and, probably, "paranoid personality disorder." These are therefore dealt with in Chapter 12 on schizophrenia. Here I will discuss five types of personality disorder that will fit most of the people seeking treatment for neurosis: *obsessive compulsive, histrionic, narcissistic, antisocial,* and *borderline.*

Obsessive Compulsive Personality Disorder
A little compulsiveness is probably a good thing. It is what makes us value order, rules, and reason. People wear watches because they want to keep track of time and avoid being late; they check their work to avoid mistakes; and they accept responsibility for what they do because that is the best way to be sure things get done correctly. We look for these traits when we choose an accountant, doctor, or plumber.

But it is not difficult to imagine these traits being carried to an extreme that produces unhappiness and inefficiency. Here is an example.

The Case of Roger. Roger is an account executive at a small brokerage firm. He is 37, married with two children, and moderately successful. But he has watched many of his peers, who are no more intelligent than he, advance much further in his company. Roger is perennially dissatisfied with his life, but he has difficulty figuring out what the problem is. He does not meet our diagnostic criteria for depression or any of the anxiety disorders, but he is not a very happy person either.

It is interesting to hear how Roger's wife describes him. Although she loves him very much, there are many aspects of his personality that irritate her. He is virtually preoccupied with rules and order. Every morning he makes a list of things he should do that day and no deviations from completing the list are permissible, no matter what. He gives his wife a list of things also, like people to call and appointments to make. If everything isn't done according to plan, he gets nervous and upset. Roger's wife is also upset that he refuses to spend money on enjoyable things and gives little to charity. He insists on maintaining a frugal family budget. Finally, Roger seems to care more about work than anything else. He works longer hours than he has to and even on weekends his conversations are dominated by work-related topics.

With all this emphasis on perfectionism and hard work, why isn't Roger more successful? Because an excessive devotion to regulations and order inhibits people from using creativity, insight, and hunches that separate an efficient worker from a star. Roger spends too much time at work keeping his desk neat; he goes through his tasks in rigid order, often missing the opportunity to grab on to something really important because it does not come up in the predetermined order he set for himself. He is viewed by coworkers as rather humorless and grim; his attention to detail makes them feel guilty because no one else seems capable of following all the rules the way Roger does.

These are classic features of obsessive compulsive personality disorder. Note that it has nothing to do with the anxiety disorder discussed in Chapter 11 called obsessive compulsive disorder. The latter involves obsessive and meaningless ruminations and compulsive rituals, which people with the personality disorder do not have.

What is missing from Roger's life is fun. He is locked in by reason and logic. It makes him nervous and uncomfortable to let himself go, but he recognizes that he is missing out on a lot of things. Sometimes he fantasizes about escaping it all and moving to Vermont to live in the woods and make pottery; these escapist fantasies are common among people with obsessive compulsive disorder because they forever want to get away from all the rules and details.

There are conflicting points of view about what causes this and most personality disorders. Psychoanalytic thinkers believe that obsessive and compulsive personality traits essentially protect people from unconscious anger. Indeed, obsessive compulsive types are prone to anger and irritation whenever their lists cannot be completed or a job is not done to their satisfaction. Behaviorists think that people acquire personality traits by mirroring the behavior of their parents who reinforce them as children for following rules and obeying authority. Psychobiologists have shown that many aspects of personality are actually inherited characteristics.

It is often said that men are more prone than women to have obsessive compulsive disorder, but I think the evidence for this is rather thin. It is probably true that society tolerates obsessive compulsive behavior in men better than it does in women. A man who is rigid, stubborn, orderly, and overly conscientious might be considered to be serious and trustworthy by many people and a good bet as an employee; women are expected to be warm, charming, and flexible, so these same traits in a woman are more likely to be criticized. We see many women with obsessive compulsive personalities and many men who do not have them.

Psychotherapy can help people with obsessive compulsive personality disorder. The first task is to demonstrate for the patient that his attitudes and behavior are responsible for his unhappiness. Often, people with obsessive compulsive disorder think they are victims of other people's carelessness and irresponsibility. Obsessive compulsives often harbor a barely conscious idea that because they are so "good" and law-abiding, they should receive rewards and consideration from other people. Roger is often upset that he and his wife do not have sex often enough, for example. A therapist was able to show him that merely because he is a "good" husband who works hard for his family, never has affairs, and always buys his wife a birthday present does not mean that he will be seen by a woman as romantic or sexually attractive. Roger thinks that he and his wife have signed a contract: if he acts in a responsible and loyal way, his wife should want to have sex with him at least twice a week. But Roger's wife never signed that contract. She wants Roger to be warm and loving, to act in a more spontaneous way. Similarly at work Roger thinks he does not get ahead because the other workers cut corners and use political manipulations. He believes that a dutiful, loyal, and conscientious employee should be the first promoted. In fact, conscientiousness is only one criteria for career success; people get promoted for creativity and ingenuity as well.

Because personality disorders are ingrained and longstanding, they do not disappear with brief treatment. Psychodynamic-type psychotherapies are usually required for improvement to occur, but they do not always work. It is very important for people considering psychotherapy for obsessive compulsive disorder to understand that there is absolutely no guarantee that they will get better.

On the other hand, there are several reasons that people with obsessive compulsive personality disorder, by virtue of the very nature of their neurotic problems, may be too hard on psychotherapy and fail to see its benefits. Psychotherapy is an emotional process and change occurs slowly and subtly. Obsessive compulsives have difficulty waiting for anything and insist on concrete evidence for everything. Roger, for example, may think that unless he and his wife are having sex twice a week after two months of psychotherapy that the therapy isn't working. In fact, it would take longer for him to change than two months and there is also his wife's feelings to consider. Also, people with obsessive compulsive personality disorder are almost always tight with money and they are very prone to complain constantly about the cost of therapy, rather than getting down to work. Finally, it is often very hard for obsessive compulsive types to recognize and then talk about their feelings; they usually like to talk about facts and evidence. This is a problem for psychotherapy, which almost always needs to deal with feelings and emotions. Hence, people with obsessive compulsive disorder must understand that the very nature of their problems often makes therapy a slow-going process.

Histrionic Personality Disorder

In many ways, histrionic personality disorder is the opposite of obsessive compulsive personality disorder. People with histrionic personality disorder are, if anything, excessively emotional and flamboyant. They seem prone to throw caution to the wind, to be very extroverted, and to be dramatic. They hate details, order, and rules.

Once again, a lot of the description of histrionic personality sounds absolutely charming. Who wouldn't want to be a free spirit, unhindered by excessive attention to details and worry? Actors and actresses, whom we often admire and envy, are sometimes perfect role models of successful people with histrionic features. But let us look at an example in which having a histrionic personality disorder is not a particularly good thing.

The Case of Susan. Susan, aged 26, started crying after about ten minutes of her first visit with a psychiatrist. Her "boyfriend" had just told her he was seeing several other women and was not prepared to make a commitment to her. Susan felt hurt and enraged; she thought the relationship, which had lasted about three months, was progressing toward marriage. Although Susan told the psychiatrist that she felt so horrible she wanted to die or "just disappear," she spoke in a very animated voice, describing her situation and feelings in dramatic terms. While listening to her, the psychiatrist thought to himself that very depressed people usually talk slowly and haltingly and need prodding to fill in details. Susan, on the other hand, sounded like she was in front of a television camera. Also, unlike most very depressed people who think life is not worth it, Susan was beautifully dressed. She wore a very short skirt, a fairly low cut blouse, and plenty of makeup. Depressed people usually have difficulty paying attention to their appearance, but Susan must have spent a lot of time putting her makeup on that morning.

As Susan continued her story, the psychiatrist started wondering what the basis was for Susan's belief that her "boyfriend" was going to marry her. In three months they had had many telephone conversations, about half a dozen dates, and slept together three times. It seemed like fairly minimal contact to substantiate a belief that an intense, committed relationship was developing. Also, Susan seemed to grasp at every comment the man had made to convince herself he was truly interested in her; she ignored many signs that he was involved with other women. Their relationship began after a chance meeting at a business function. Susan invited the man to her apartment, had sex with him, and accepted his excuse that he had to get up early for a business meeting the next morning for not staying with her all night.

As the psychiatrist listened to Susan (who did a lot of talking), he learned that she had a series of "relationships" in which she had a very different understanding about what was going on than did the man involved. The psychiatrist noted that Susan had a tendency to sleep with men after one or two dates, then believe she was involved in a serious romantic relationship. It was striking to the psychiatrist that so intelligent a person as Susan—she was a very successful advertising executive— could so misread other people's intentions. Susan also had a great deal of difficulty in managing her personal affairs: she was constantly bouncing checks, forgetting appointments because she did not keep an appointment book, and jumping from one task to another. She also seemed to need to be the center of attention in almost every setting and often felt ignored when in fact she was merely being treated like everybody else.

Put in this way, the features of histrionic personality disorder don't sound all that attractive. Susan can come across as charming, engaging, and sometimes seductive, but her personality traits also lead her to be chronically disorganized, self-involved, and unproductive.

The theoretical reasons advanced for the cause of histrionic personality disorder have always seemed particularly unsatisfying to me. One idea is that the histrionic personality is compensating for all kinds of repressed sexual urges. These individuals actually feel very insecure and doubt that anyone will love them. Their seeming seductiveness and sexual flamboyance is really only a desperate attempt to get love and attention. In reality, they are unconsciously frightened by their sexual desires and overwhelmed by the fear of abandonment. Everything they do is an attempt to get attention in order to be sure they will never be alone.

Therapists generally love to treat patients with histrionic personalities because they talk a lot in therapy sessions and seem to have their feelings on the tips of their tongues. The job with a histrionic patient is sometimes the opposite of what needs to be done with obsessive compulsive patients: the latter must struggle to get to their emotions and feelings, but histrionic patients often must be taught to *think* about what they do and to avoid reacting immediately to every emotion. Histrionic patients frequently do not like being told to give up their provocative behavior and sometimes quit therapy in a huff. Other times they successfully seduce the therapist and convince her that they are merely victims of all the mean, uncaring people in the world. In such cases, therapy sometimes lasts forever, with the therapist merely empathizing with the patient rather than actively identifying for her the things she is doing that get her into trouble.

Once again, patients with histrionic personality disorder must carefully reevaluate with the therapist at periodic intervals whether progress is being made. It is very easy for histrionic patients to get comfortable with long therapies when nothing much more than handholding is going on. On the other hand, psychodynamic-type therapies can be very helpful for histrionic patients.

Narcissistic Personality Disorder

The vast majority of people who see psychiatrists suffer from some degree of low self-esteem. This is so common that low self-esteem is rarely given as the criteria for any of the psychiatric illnesses, either in Axis One or Axis Two. But one personality disorder is distinguished by the opposite pattern, excessive self-esteem. What is wrong with that? Almost everything, because people with narcissistic personality are, by and large, the most difficult people to like that anyone can imagine. Sooner or later, the ability of narcissistic people to offend everyone catches up with them and they wind up lonely, depressed, and hopeless.

Here is an example of a person with narcissistic personality who has not yet reached the burnout stage.

The Case of Jim. Jim, an attorney, felt a little anxious one day while arguing a case in front of a jury. He noticed his hand was shaking and thought his voice quivered a bit. He went on to lose the case, which enraged him because he was certain that he had done a terrific job and could not fathom how a jury could decide against him. The only thing he could imagine was that his anxiety might have been obvious to the jury and worked against him; perhaps they thought he was not convinced himself that his case was better. Jim remembered reading an article in a business magazine about successful performers taking medication to stop them from shaking while onstage and decided to see a psychiatrist who specialized in performance anxiety and to get the medication.

When the psychiatrist asked Jim to explain his problem, he launched into a diatribe as follows: "I am, I must tell you, a very successful attorney. Some of the most famous people you could know are my clients [he then proceeded to rattle off a list of people who the psychiatrist had actually never heard of]. I never saw a psychiatrist before, but I think I may be experiencing some anxiety, which is ridiculous because you have to believe me, I am really one of the best trial attorneys in California."

This went on for nearly fifteen minutes. The psychiatrist merely listened;

Jim never indicated that he had any interest in a reaction from the doctor. Jim seemed mostly interested in getting "whatever drug that is that all those movie stars and symphony conductors take," as if taking that drug would put him in the same club as them. The only time he seemed to acknowledge that there was another person in the room was when he said, "I found you by looking in that directory of the best doctors in Los Angeles. I know you are the top in this field, which is why I am coming to you." The point here was not that Jim was trying to pay a compliment to the psychiatrist but rather that he wanted him to know that only the best doctors were good enough for him.

Although the consultation was scheduled for an hour and a half, Jim seemed to assume that he could stay all day. When asked about his personal life, he proudly listed the three "gorgeous young models" he was involved with and told a somewhat irrelevant story about having had sex with two woman at the same time several years before. He had never been married: "So far, I don't need to get married, I can get it without being married, and I need to find a woman who is beautiful and bright enough for me." He bragged about the expensive gifts he bought his girlfriends and explained that he was furious at one of them because he recently found out she was simultaneously having a relationship with another man, one who was several years younger than Jim. The fact that Jim never had any intention of maintaining a monogamous relationship with her seemed beside the point to him.

Psychiatrists are supposed to remain neutral and nonjudgmental, but it should be obvious that doing so in the presence of a narcissistic character like Jim is nearly impossible. Jim is grandiose, entitled, and arrogant. But the real problem is that he is almost entirely lacking in empathy. He seems to have no ability to see or feel things from anyone else's point of view than his own.

Sometimes, people with narcissistic character can be very successful. Because they crave and thrive on attention and admiration they will often go to great lengths to please people, although this is never done out of a sense of altruism. But people can be fooled by narcissists and believe they are acting kindly. Some politicians fit the bill perfectly for this kind of behavior. Narcissists are easily enraged, however, because they truly believe they are special and deserve unqualified admiration and special privileges.

Eventually, as I said earlier, all of this catches up with most narcissists. They age, lose their physical attractiveness, and suffer from competition with younger people. They have done nothing to develop relationships and more and more they become ignored and isolated. Only then does it sometimes become possible to feel empathy for them; an aging narcissist is a pathetic thing.

Psychoanalysts have struggled to understand how someone becomes pathologically narcissistic. To my mind, the best theories suggest that in childhood people destined to become narcissistic are treated with neglect and emotional deprivation, perhaps by narcissistic parents. Unable to get the kind of admiration and love children need from their parents, the future narcissist learns to get it from himself. He builds a fantasy world in which he is the center of attention and everyone must love him. This is perhaps an appropriate adaptation to the situation, but it is easy to see how it goes awry in adult life. In my chapters on the Axis One conditions like depression and schizophrenia, I stress over and over again that bad parents do not cause these illnesses; I do believe, however, that neglectful and inconsistent parents are fully capable of producing narcissistic personality disorder.

It is very hard to treat people with narcissistic personality disorder. The patient does not really want to change; he thinks he is better than fine as he is. The therapist invariably does not like the patient. It is not a good setting for treatment. If treatment for narcissistic personality disorder is going to work it usually needs to be a very long treatment. What takes place is that the patient learns to have a relationship with the therapist. The therapist constantly points out the ways in which the patient ignores other people and inflates his own worth. Over time, the patient becomes more interested in how other people feel and more aware of his own bad behavior. It is hard to imagine how a short-term behavioral or cognitive therapy would have any meaningful impact on a narcissist.

Antisocial Personality Disorder

These are the career criminals, the people who have committed crimes since childhood. There is a great deal of debate about whether antisocial personality disorder should even be considered a psychiatric problem. Maybe these are just criminals who should be dealt with in the criminal justice system and not by mental health care providers.

To meet the *DSM-IV* criteria for antisocial personality disorder, a person must be at least 18 but must have shown a pattern of breaking the rules from before age 15. Antisocial personality types are typically impulsive, hostile, and aggressive people who lie, cheat, steal, and endanger the lives of others without feeling guilty or remorseful. The striking thing about them is that they seem to lack a conscience—or superego, as the psychoanalysts call it.

There is evidence that antisocial personality disorder runs in families and may be partially genetic. It is also linked to alcohol and drug abuse, so that first-degree relatives of people with antisocial personality disorder have a higher rate than normal of being substance abusers. Because of this, there is a suspicion that antisocial personality disorder may in part be a biological disorder, involving some inherited abnormality in brain function. Perhaps the inability to feel guilt when committing a criminal act or harming someone stems from a neurological defect. Although the evidence linking antisocial behavior to genetic factors is fairly strong, there is a great deal of controversy surrounding the notion that antisocial personality is a biological disorder. To some, this will be used merely as an excuse by criminals to justify breaking the law. Already, as described in Chapter 19, the insanity defense has been stretched to some very incredible limits and there does appear to be a substantial risk that criminals will get off simply by saying, "It wasn't my fault that I murdered him, it was my brain disease that I inherited from my father that made me do it." Still, there is compelling reason to continue to do research looking at the possibility that at least some forms of antisocial behavior do represent abnormal brain function.

Is there any psychiatric treatment for antisocial people? By and large the answer is no. Scientists have looked for medications that might change antisocial behavior, but so far none have emerged. A wide variety of behavioral and psychoanalytic therapies have been advocated, but there is no convincing evidence that any are particularly effective. Sadly, antisocial personality remains a fairly malignant disorder that, because we have no medical treatment, generally winds up the responsibility of courts and prisons.

Borderline Personality Disorder

For years I have responded to the question, "Am I a borderline?" with the answer, "I really don't understand what that term means." Originally, the term *borderline* was developed to identify people who seemed somewhere between psychotic and neurotic. A disorder called "pseudoneurotic schizophrenia" was the forerunner of borderline personality disorder, again intended to identify a situation in which a person was not quite psychotic but seemed much more impaired than a neurotic.

If this definition seems vague, it is. Nowadays, we try to define psychotic illnesses with a fair amount of precision, intending them as specific disorders that include hallucinations, delusions, or thought disorder (see Chapter 12 for a fuller explanation of psychosis). It is hard to see how someone could be "almost" psychotic. Similarly, what does it mean to be more ill than neurotic? Does it mean one has a particularly bad case of obsessive compulsive or narcissistic or histrionic personality disorder?

Adding to the confusion is the fact that psychiatrists and other mental-health professionals often use the word *borderline* as an epithet. If a patient does something particularly annoying or disagreeable the therapist is apt to call the patient borderline mainly to denote the fact that the patient is giving him a hard time. Borderline patients are notorious among psychiatrists for "acting out," that is, for threatening suicide all the time, calling the therapist at all hours of the day or night, missing appointments, and not paying the bill.

Does borderline really describe a distinct type of personality disorder? Let me try to give an example of a patient I believe most clinicians would call borderline.

The Case of Allison.   Allison is a 29-year-old laboratory technician who made a suicide attempt one night after having a fight with a boyfriend. She went into the bedroom of his apartment shortly before he was due home from work, using a key she had pressured him to give her, made four superficial cuts in her wrist with a razor blade, and swallowed ten 5-mg Valium tablets. When her boyfriend came home, he found her fast asleep on the bed, the sheets covered in blood. He called the police, who brought Allison to the emergency room. In the emergency room she was barely arousable, but her vital signs were stable [it is virtually impossible to commit suicide with Valium]. The doctors sutured one of the cuts in her wrist; the others were too superficial to require stitches. They determined that Allison was not in medical danger and waited for her to wake up from the overdose.

After she woke up, Allison was seen by a psychiatrist in the emergency room. She was extremely hostile, demanding to be released. The psychiatrist explained that he could not let her leave the emergency room because she had just apparently tried to kill herself. Allison angrily insisted that she had a perfect right to kill herself and that she was going to sue the doctor and the hospital if they did not let her go.

The psychiatrist tried to find out why Allison had made the suicide attempt. It turned out that her boyfriend was an alcoholic and cocaine abuser who had told her the day before that he was going to return to his wife. Enraged, Allison decided to kill herself. She had not felt particularly depressed and had not been considering suicide until the moment the boyfriend gave her the bad news. It was clear that Allison wanted to punish her boyfriend by forcing him to confront the spectacle of her bleeding body draped across the bed. It also became apparent that Allison understood that neither the superficial cuts she put in her arm nor the ten Valium tablets were truly capable of killing her. This was an angry and dramatic gesture rather than the desperate behavior of a despondent person.

The psychiatrist could feel himself becoming somewhat irritated with Allison. She refused to cooperate with most of his attempts to understand what was bothering her, forcing him to drag it out of her. She insisted she would sue the hospital if not released, yet refused to discuss whether she wanted to make another suicide attempt. After several hours of this, the patient agreed to call her mother, who came to the emergency room. Allison's mother appeared more annoyed at her daughter than concerned, but nevertheless agreed to take her to her home and watch over her until the next day, when she would be brought to see a psychiatrist for a follow-up appointment.

The next day, Allison came to the psychiatrist's office in a much calmer state. She had had a long talk with her boyfriend and he had decided not to go back to his wife after all. They had had ''fantastic sex'' the entire night and now Allison seemed almost giddy with hope that everything would work out. She also had decided that she should see a therapist for a while to work out "my issues." These included the fact that she had been fired four times in the last two years, usually after getting into fights with bosses, that she had gotten pregnant three times in the last four years, each time having an abortion, and that she felt that none of her friends really liked her.

It turned out that Allison had been scratching her wrist with razor blades repeatedly for several years. She described a chronic feeling of inner "emptiness." This was clearly not depression. Allison constantly referred to an inability to understand who she really was and a feeling that "I am like an onion, if you peel away the layers you eventually have nothing. No core. Nothing." At times she would drink or eat excessively in an attempt to fill the void; at other times she would meet men in local bars, take them home, and have sex with them.

Allison also suffered from severe interpersonal difficulties. She would establish very intense relationships with people very quickly, then virtually suffocate them with her neediness and demands. Eventually, friends and lovers would pull back, always putting Allison in an indignant rage. Her version was always that she had been victimized by someone else's neglect; in fact, her constant demands and anger chased most people away.

Thus, Allison's life is marked by intense, often inappropriate anger, emptiness, self-destructive and impulsive behavior, and markedly unstable relationships. Most of this came to be reflected in her relationship with her new therapist. She began therapy by idealizing her therapist and deciding that he was going to be her salvation. She demanded to have an unlimited number of sessions and the right to call the therapist at least once a day at his home if she felt the need. She insisted that she should be his most important patient. In time, as the therapist tried to limit her demands and failed to be her salvation, Allison began to devalue the therapist and see him as neglectful and incompetent. She constantly disrupted the therapist's schedule by canceling sessions at the last minute, then demanding make-up sessions. She never paid the bill on time. The therapy, like Allison's life, was chaotic.

In the *DSM-IV* there is a list of characteristic traits for making the diagnosis of borderline personality disorder. These include "frantic efforts to avoid real or imagined abandonment," unstable relationships, self-destructive and impulsive behavior, highly reactive mood, empty feelings, and intense anger that is usually inappropriate to any given situation. Patients with borderline personality sometimes develop full-blown major depression (as described in Chapter 10), drug and alcohol abuse, eating disorders (like bulimia or anorexia, see Chapter 13), and any of the anxiety disorders. They can also suffer from brief, transient psychotic episodes in which they may have paranoid delusions or even auditory hallucinations (hearing voices). When depressed or suffering from an anxiety disorder, patients with borderline personality disorder usually have a difficult time responding to the usual therapies for these Axis One disorders. Hence, the presence of a severe personality disorder like borderline makes recovery from such conditions as depression and panic disorder more problematic.

There are a million theories about what causes borderline personality disorder. Recent evidence appears to corroborate what many theorists have long believed, that inconsistent and inadequate parents can produce borderline children. Parents of future borderline patients seem themselves to be emotionally unstable and immature; they often move quickly from being overprotective and intrusive with their children to acting in a cold, distant, and punitive manner. This obviously disrupts the emotional development of the child. Borderline patients seem never to develop a consistent idea of who they are and where they fit into the world. To make matters worse, they often make it impossible for people to be kind or empathetic to them because of their easily triggered rage.

There are also biological theories for borderline personality disorder and some evidence that people with this condition suffer from abnormalities in brain chemical function. Particular emphasis is placed recently on the possibility that there is a deficiency in the function of the neurotransmitter serotonin.

The treatment usually recommended for borderline personality disorder is psychodynamic psychotherapy. Dr. Otto Kernberg has written extensively about the special approach necessary for patients with borderline personality and his method is probably the most popular among therapists today. It is based on a very complex understanding of unconscious mental processes in borderline patients. The treatment recommended usually involves a minimum of two sessions per week for many years. Patients do not undergo actual psychoanalysis; there is no couch and no "free-association." In fact, although the therapists must have detailed information about the patient's childhood history, the therapy is largely based in the "here and now." This means that the therapist attempts to direct the patient's attention mainly to how she acts in the present, particularly in her relationship with the therapist. As the relationship between doctor and patient grows, the patient invariably "acts out" most of her conflicts in the relationship with the therapist. This gives the therapist the opportunity to confront the patient with her inappropriate anger and her propensity to go through cycles of first idealizing the therapist and then devaluing the therapist.

Cognitive and behavioral therapists have also recently begun describing and studying treatment for borderline personality disorder. These emphasize social-skills training and behavioral change rather than attempting to repair basic personality structures. Interestingly, all theories aside, therapists wind up spending a lot of time dealing with very practical issues when treating borderline patients. Hence, my guess is the cognitive/behavioral and psycho-dynamic approaches to treating borderline personality disorder will wind up in practice being fairly similar.

It is difficult to know to what degree long-term therapy actually helps patients with borderline personality disorder because there are very few published outcome studies. It is clear that many patients are able to gain stability in their lives and form relationships. Hence, the success of the therapy needs to be judged on a case-by-case basis. Often borderline patients require very long therapies, sometimes lasting for ten or more years. There is obviously a great deal of reluctance on the part of health insurance companies to cover this expense, and it is getting increasingly difficult to provide patients with borderline personality disorder with the kind of treatment that they need. My own feeling is that for patients who truly have borderline personality disorder, very long term therapy is usually the only hope for improvement and should be offered.

Medications are sometimes useful. There is mounting evidence that antidepressants, particularly the serotonin reuptake inhibitors (SSRIs) like Prozac (fluoxetine), Zoloft (sertraline), and Paxil (paroxetine), can sometimes relieve depression and irritability in borderline personality disorder patients. If a borderline patient develops a brief psychotic episode with paranoid delusions or hallucinations, this is usually treated with antipsychotic medications described in Chapter 4.

Problems of Living

There are a whole range of difficulties that people can encounter in their lives that may benefit from seeing a psychiatrist. Difficulty coping with a child, a severe business reversal, the death of a spouse, or the ending of a relationship may cause substantial distress. In these cases, the person may not have any psychiatric disorder, including any of the personality disorders. In *DSM,* distressed reactions to common events are called "adjustment disorders," but many clinicians see these as "problems of living." Unlike the events that cause posttraumatic stress disorder (see Chapter 11), the kinds of things that produce "problems of living" are not life-threatening or "out of the range of normal human experience." Rather, they are untoward events that can happen to anyone, but are still unpleasant and difficult to handle.

Most people in such situations never consult psychiatrists or therapists. But it can be helpful to talk to someone who will be caring and objective and who will not expect reciprocal emotional help. It is sometimes useful to have a person to dump all of one's fears, sorrows, and anguish on without having to consider that person's feelings or reactions. This is the "one-way" emotional street that a therapist can provide. Here is an example.

The Case of Melissa. Melissa, a 19-year-old college student, was doing well until her boyfriend decided to leave college and move to another state. The breakup was sudden. Naturally, Melissa felt sad and angry. She spent time talking to her friends about her feelings, but most of them were having their own problems with relationships and did not seem able to understand the depths of Melissa's despair. Her parents were sympathetic, but treated the situation as "just a stage everyone goes through." Melissa started having trouble concentrating on her studies and shunned opportunities to socialize. A friend suggested she find someone "professional" to talk to, and so Melissa asked to see a counselor at the student health service of her college. Melissa cried in the counselor's office when talking about the breakup with her ex-boyfriend and also said, "Sometimes I just don't know what to do next." This concerned the counselor, who wondered if Melissa was suffering from depression, and referred her to a psychiatrist. The psychiatrist quickly ascertained that Melissa was not clinically depressed but was understandably heartbroken. Melissa also felt "weird" because no one seemed to understand what she was going through. The psychiatrist explained to Melissa that she was suffering from a normal and understandable reaction to an adverse life event. He told her not to be hard on herself; that anyone would feel awful in her situation. He promised her that in time she would feel better and encouraged her to try, difficult as it might be, to resume her usual activities.

Melissa came to see the psychiatrist a few more times but, as expected, she felt much better within a week. Both she and the psychiatrist decided she did not need extended treatment.

In this case, Melissa did not have any serious psychiatric illness but seeing a psychiatrist for a few visits clearly helped her. It is probably true that she would have eventually pulled out of her upset state without any help, but seeing the psychiatrist eased her burden and made her life a little easier.

I don't think there is anything wrong with this; psychiatrists and other mental health professionals are good at helping people get through rough spots in life. It would have been wrong, as some unscrupulous therapists sometimes do, to have tried and convinced Melissa that she was seriously disturbed or needed medication or long-term therapy. But a few visits to the psychiatrist were helpful and appropriate. I hope that whatever form of health-care reform we get does not exclude people, especially poor people who are dependent on third-party payers for their health care, from getting this kind of brief treatment.

PART IV **Special**
TOPICS

16.
How Much Should It Cost and Who Should Pay?

As THIS CHAPTER is written there is great uncertainty about how health care will be financed in the future. Every day we read about new proposals to extend health insurance to all Americans, and every day we see these proposals shot down by Congress or the President. The plans not only vary on how health care will be paid for, they vary about how much health-care Americans should receive and how much choice they can have in selecting their own doctors.

Psychiatric care has always had a unique position in health-care economics and that position has usually been a simple one: it is generally not included. Most current health insurance policies either place limitations on reimbursement for psychiatric treatment or refuse to cover it at all. A typical policy will pay 80 to 100 percent for medical care, except when a psychiatrist is involved; then it might pay 50 percent or less. Health insurers say this is necessary because otherwise everyone would enter long-term psychotherapy and see psychiatrists or other therapists several times a week for years. No health insurance plan could afford that, they claim, so they put limitations on how much is reimbursed and how often a patient can see a therapist.

Even Medicare, the government's health insurance plan for people over 65, severely limits psychiatric care. In fact, Medicare pays so little for psychiatrists that it is virtually impossible for someone over 65 to see one privately; only clinics can afford to take care of senior citizens who need to see psychiatrists.

Some have argued that the severe psychiatric disorders should be covered at the same rate as all other medical problems, leaving the restrictions only on the treatment of neurotic illnesses and "problems of living" that generally require extensive psychotherapy. This would mean coverage for people with illnesses like schizophrenia, depression, bipolar mood disorder (manic depression), panic disorder, and obsessive compulsive disorder at the better rate. Medication and cognitive/behavioral treatments are usually sufficient to treat these illnesses; psychodynamic psychotherapies lasting many years are not generally required. But many disagree with this proposal for several reasons. First, there are those who believe that all psychiatric illnesses should be treated equally and that psychotherapy should be reimbursed at the same rate as medication treatment. Second, it would be difficult to police psychiatrists to know for sure that everyone they said had schizophrenia or depression really had these conditions rather than neurotic illnesses. Third, even a cognitive/behavioral therapy can take up to 20 sessions and be expensive for an insurance company to cover. With this kind of debate going on even among psychiatrists themselves it is no wonder that insurance companies and the government have been able to elude coverage for psychiatric illness.

The current champion of psychiatric patients and their families is Tipper Gore, wife of Vice President Al Gore, who is a strong proponent of equal coverage for psychiatric care under health-care reform. At present, one prominent plan for health-care reimbursement would cover about 20 sessions a year and would also extend coverage for psychiatric hospitalization beyond the two or three weeks that most policies now cover. Although this kind of coverage does not achieve actual parity with other medical conditions—no limitations are placed on how often a person can see a doctor if she has cancer or heart disease as long as the visits are necessary—it would clearly be better than what most people currently have available.

Until some form of health-care reform that includes psychiatric illnesses is established, however, it will remain very hard for people to afford to see psychiatrists. Most will have to foot the bill largely out of their own pockets and rely on very paltry reimbursements from insurance companies. Some will only be able to get care in low-cost clinics, which vary widely in quality from outstanding to barely acceptable.

The fact that psychiatric care usually has to be paid directly by the individual angers many patients and creates the impression that mental illness is not real and that psychiatrists are gouging them with very high prices. The fact is that psychiatrists are usually the lowest or next-to-lowest paid medical specialists. Neurologists, internists, gynecologists, dermatologists, and surgeons all earn more than psychiatrists. People do not realize how much dermatologists and surgeons charge because their fees are usually largely picked up by insurance companies. Psychiatrists are also at a disadvantage compared to other specialists because they cannot pack in high volumes of patients in a day's work. A psychotherapy session must last 45 minutes to an hour; even medication sessions can take 20 to 30 minutes. Also, psychiatrists do not perform procedures or minor surgery, which are very lucrative; all they have to sell is their time, and there are limited numbers of hours in a week when patients can come to see the psychiatrist.

Fees vary enormously from psychiatrist to psychiatrist depending on experience, reputation, and sheer ability to collect what they want to charge. In the chapters about the different types of psychiatric treatment, I have provided information about picking the right doctor and therapist for your individual situation. Part of making that choice will inevitably include the cost. The first rule is to be sure that you ask before the first visit with any psychiatrist what the fees will be for different services. The first visit may be longer than other visits and therefore the cost of that may be greater. Be sure you find out. There may be different fees depending on whether you are going to see the psychiatrist for psychotherapy or just for medication management.

If a therapist refuses to discuss fees with you, it is probably best to find someone else.

The most expensive psychiatrist or psychologist is not necessarily the best. Some very senior and famous individuals command very high fees, but they are not always the most accessible or personable individuals.

Once a fee is set, you should consider it your responsibility to pay it promptly. Remember that the psychiatrist you are seeing is deriving his or her income from fees charged patients; it pays the rent on the office, the telephone bill, and the malpractice insurance. Nothing will bog down a therapy faster than making your therapist resent you because you are not paying the bill. If you are having trouble paying, make sure you alert the therapist quickly.

Your psychiatrist should be willing to fill out insurance claim forms for you promptly, but don't expect her to be an expert about what your policy will or won't cover. There are many different policies and each has different requirements for reimbursement. You should contact your insurance carrier and find out what psychiatric care is covered and at what rate.

Sometimes a patient who had been in treatment with a psychiatrist will, for unforeseen reasons, run into financial trouble and be unable to pay. Psychiatrists, like all physicians, have a responsibility—both ethically and in most states legally—to continue to care for patients even if they develop serious financial problems. Your doctor should *not* abandon you under these conditions. You and the therapist should try to work out some arrangement until your financial condition improves. If the change in your financial situation seems irreversible, the therapist is responsible to continue to treat you through any current crisis period and to help you find more affordable treatment when your condition permits.

In most situations, therapists should not charge patients for phone calls. The only exceptions are: (1) when the therapist and patient agree that a full session is to take place by phone because one of them cannot make it to the office, or (2) a patient needs to call the therapist very frequently (at least several times a day or week) and talk for extended periods of time. Otherwise, psychiatrists, unlike taxi drivers and corporate lawyers, should not have their ''meters'' running every time a patient calls for brief advice or to report a problem with medication.

The fact is that reimbursement for psychiatric illness is biased and unfair. Insurance companies, Medicare, and Medicaid all add to the horrible stigma levied against people with emotional problems by treating their claims for reimbursement as if the patient is begging for a handout. Citizens groups and mental-health professional organizations should continue to lobby hard to change this situation. Until it is changed, however, it is important for patients not to treat their therapists as the enemy. If you think you have a psychiatrist who is charging you too much, complain or change psychiatrists. But do not expect psychiatrists to assist you in deceiving health insurance companies or to subsidize the treatment.

17.
What Does
"Confidentiality" Mean?

THERE ARE VERY few rules in medicine that are absolutes, but the requirement that psychiatrists strictly maintain their patients' right to confidentiality
comes close. With the very few exceptions listed below, you should expect
that your doctor will not reveal anything about you to anyone without your
express permission.

In some ways, this is an unfortunate situation because it is partially
motivated by the stigma attached to seeing a psychiatrist. In a perfect world
the fact that someone suffered from depression or panic attacks would be
nothing to be ashamed of and we would be no more reluctant to say we
saw a psychiatrist than we are to tell our friends that we went to the dentist
or dermatologist. We are rightfully pleased when famous individuals like
Betty Ford, Governor Chiles of Florida, and Mike Wallace acknowledge
that they have psychiatric problems and have sought treatment.

Nevertheless, it can be harmful to some people's standing in the community
if it is known that they are seeing a psychiatrist. Furthermore, psychiatrists
encourage patients to reveal the most intimate details of their lives, including
all of their secret wishes and desires. We promise our patients that we will
keep all of these secrets. We are absolutely obligated to keep those promises.

Some patients have asked me to identify myself as Jack Gorman if I call
them at work. I always agree. They have asked me to fill out their bills
myself rather than have my secretary do it so that no one but me knows
they are seeing me. I agree to this as well. To the extent possible, I feel I
owe it to my patients to protect their privacy.

This does not mean that a psychiatrist or other therapist is barred from
listening to what other people have to say about a patient. For example, if
the husband or wife of a patient believes there is something important that
the psychiatrist must know—like suicidal wishes or excessive drinking—it
is appropriate for the doctor to listen. He must not, however, report any
information to the spouse unless the patient gives consent.

There are a few exceptions to this general principle of strict confidentiality.
According to the so-called Tarasoff rule, a psychiatrist is expected to violate
his patient's confidentiality and warn a third party if he has heard the patient
threaten to harm that person. The Tarasoff rule originated from a case in
California in which a psychiatrist's patient told the doctor he intended to
murder a former girlfriend, and then carried out the threat. The doctor was

successfully sued by the victim's family for not warning her and the police about the threat. Patients should know, then, that a psychiatrist will not keep secret any threat to harm another person.

When a patient threatens to kill himself, the situation is trickier. Should the doctor warn a spouse or other family members so that they can watch the patient who is suicidal but refuses hospitalization? Many patients would regard this as a serious breach of their right to confidentiality, yet a psychiatrist would probably rather violate the privacy rule than risk have a dead patient.

A court can also order a psychiatrist to produce records or testify about a patient. If a patient is arrested for a crime or sues someone for damages, the psychiatric record can be subpoenaed and the doctor be forced to reveal everything that is in it. Most psychiatrists do not keep records with the idea that someday they may have to be produced in court. Records are kept of what the patient says, how the treatment goes, and what the diagnoses are. You may not want the psychiatrist to write some things down; for the most part, that wish can be accommodated. For example, a patient revealed to me that she was having an affair but feared that this might come out in a custody action her husband was bringing against her as part of the couple's divorce. I did not feel that I needed to write this down (I was sure I would remember what she had told me) and agreed to keep it out of my record. Unless ordered to reveal it by a judge, I felt this patient's decision whether to reveal her affair to her husband was entirely her own and need not come out through my chart notes.

There are times when embarrassing revelations cannot be prevented, however. Once I received a request from a patient's attorney to produce my office notes about her. She was apparently suing a driver following an automobile accident in which she claimed had injured her back. The problem was that when I first saw the patient she had told me that she had suffered from back trouble for many years preceding the car accident. I had written that down. My records would obviously reveal that the patient was lying about the car accident; in fact, it hadn't hurt her back at all. When I told her what was in my records she was forced to amend her lawsuit.

Let me reiterate, however, that these exceptions notwithstanding, the rule of confidentiality should be honored by psychiatrists as a major ethical principle. If you have any reason to suspect that your therapist is talking about even the most trivial aspect of your life or treatment to anyone without your express, clear, and unambiguous permission, you should challenge the therapist, order him to stop, and consider filing a complaint with the responsible regulating authorities.

18.
Is Sex With A Therapist
Ever Okay?

THERE ARE A few exceptions to the rule of confidentiality that therapists must maintain. There are *no* exceptions to the rule forbidding physical contact between therapists and their patients. Under no circumstances should a therapist ever touch a patient except to shake hands or to perform a medical procedure like drawing blood or taking blood pressure. No kissing, no fondling, no holding hands, and absolutely no sex. Never.

Recently, an article appeared in a major psychiatric journal in which the authors asserted that it could be permissible for a psychiatrist to have sex with a consenting patient after one year had elapsed following the complete termination of therapy. I adamantly disagree. One hundred years could elapse as far as I am concerned; it is still not appropriate.

The reason for this is that psychiatrists have an unfair advantage over patients. They encourage patients to tell them all of their secrets, to trust them, to look to them as authority figures who can help them. Patients sometimes develop sexual feelings toward their therapists; this is called *transference* in psychoanalytic circles, but whatever the technical term it is always the manifestation of an artificial relationship between patient and doctor. The two do not meet as equals; the patient expects the doctor to be influential and in control. Under these circumstances there is always the possibility that sex between therapist and patient represents the therapist exploiting his advantage and coercing the patient, even if the patient agrees to have sex or actually encourages it.

Psychiatrists who find themselves physically attracted to patients need to think carefully about what is going on in the therapy. Even if the patient is acting in a seductive manner, this must be considered part of the condition that must be dealt with therapeutically, not acted on. If the therapist cannot get sexual thoughts about a patient out of his mind, he should tell the patient that he does not feel qualified to help the patient and recommend treatment elsewhere. We often encourage psychiatrists who are burdened by sexual thoughts about their patients to get supervision or treatment themselves. We never tell the psychiatrist he should ask the patient for a date or go to bed with her.

Even innocent contact should be avoided. Although it may seem cold, I do not put my arms around patients to comfort them or hug them or hold their hands. It is impossible to know for sure if this will be seen by the patient as a partially seductive move.

When a patient expresses sexual interest in the therapist she should not be insulted or criticized. Rather, the therapist should explain that this is a common occurrence during therapy and that it is important to understand why the patient has these feelings. Such an exploration can reveal a great deal about the patient's way of thinking about the world. Here is an example.

A Case of a Patient Expressing Sexual Interest in Her Therapist. A 23-year-old graduate student told her 50-year-old therapist that she found him attractive and wished she could have sex with him. The patient was a very attractive young woman and the therapist could not avoid admitting to himself that he felt flattered that she felt that way about him. Still, the therapist was realistic enough to recognize that he was not a movie star or heartthrob and that the contact he had with his patient was entirely limited to one weekly session for the previous year. During those sessions the young woman discussed problems about her family and job. She knew that her therapist had a Ph.D. in psychology and the name of the university that gave him the degree, some details about his professional credentials, and had figured out that he was married because he wore a wedding band.

How on that basis could she possibly make a decision that she would like to have sex with him? The patient was not suffering from a psychiatric illness such as acute mania that makes people hypersexual and indiscriminate about their sexual encounters. She knew very little of a personal nature about this man who was her therapist, but still began fantasizing regularly about going to bed with him. She began wearing sexy outfits to her sessions and expressed a wish to discuss details of her sex life. At several intervals she openly expressed the wish that the therapist could just "loosen up and be more real with me." One time she even said, "It is sort of elitist of you not to even consider having an affair with me. You are just acting like the powerful therapist who is too superior to get involved with me. It's actually very insulting and rejecting. It would at least make me feel better if you admitted you were turned on by me and sometimes think about having sex."

This actually gave the therapist a clue about what was going on. The patient was essentially complaining that she felt ignored and rejected by the therapist. She wanted him to be more personal. The therapist understood that his patient had a very distant father who rarely complimented or encouraged her. She remembered one time when she was about ten years putting on a pretty dress and hoping her father would tell her she looked pretty [something fathers *and* mothers for that matter, should always do, by the way], but he never said a word. Over time, the patient became angry at the lack of personal warmth from her father. Now, she was experiencing what psychoanalytically trained therapists call *transference:* she was transferring onto her therapist emotions she had developed about her father. As an adult, the patient had an unconscious belief that seducing her therapist would reassert her power over him and force him to become a warmer and more personal figure to her. Sex was actually irrelevant; the patient was merely trying to use it as a means of correcting very old feelings of rejection.

Now this is a very tricky area, because had the therapist merely said to his patient something stupid like "You really don't want to have sex with me, you want to have sex with your father," the patient would have been well within her rights to either laugh at him or feel terribly hurt and rejected. The patient had a conscious wish to sleep with the therapist; the therapist's job was to carefully and sensitively show her the meaning for that wish. Over the course of several sessions the therapist was in fact able to help her recognize the reason behind her sexual fantasies and to get closer to her childhood feelings of paternal neglect. In this case, a careful handling of a patient's wish to have sex with her therapist was used to help the patient learn more about herself.

This is going to be a short chapter for a good reason: there is nothing more to say on the issue. Sex between therapists and patients is always wrong. Next case.

19.
What Are the Legal Aspects of Psychiatry?

IT SEEMS THAT psychiatrists often like to play lawyer and lawyers often like to play psychiatrist. Perhaps that is why psychiatrists, more than any other medical specialists, seem to wind up in courtrooms so often. In a previous chapter about schizophrenia I have already discussed one scenario in which psychiatrists get involved with the legal system: the occasional need to commit a dangerous person to a hospital against his will (see pages 147–148). In this chapter, I will discuss two other instances of psychiatrists getting involved with the legal system—the insanity defense, and the decision to declare an individual incompetent to handle his affairs.

The insanity defense originates from 19th-century British law and began with a perfectly reasonable premise. Clearly, there are psychological states that render a person unable to be responsible for his actions. In such situations, reasonable people agree that special consideration should be made and that the usual criminal punishments may be unfair. Let's start with an obvious example. Tumors in certain parts of the brain can have severe effects on behavior, rarely even making a person violent. If a person with such a tumor hits somebody, almost no one would think it fair to put him in jail; the solution would be to first get a doctor to testify that the patient has a brain tumor, then to treat the tumor.

Things get a little more difficult with psychiatric illness because it is more difficult to "prove" in the legal sense. Still, we might all agree that a patient with bipolar illness who, in the middle of a psychotic manic episode, developed the delusion that he was the smartest businessman in the world and wrote a check to his stockbroker for $100,000 one day should not be put in jail for trying to pass bad checks. Rather, he should be put on antipsychotic medication and lithium, which will almost always cure the delusion and return him to a normal state of functioning. Similarly, a patient with schizophrenia who hears voices (auditory hallucinations) telling him that men with blond hair are devils and should be killed to protect the world needs to be in the hospital, not in prison. In most of these cases, psychiatrists should have no trouble demonstrating the nature of the illness and convincing district attorneys that medical treatment, not prosecution, is the proper course.

Thus, there clearly is a need for an "insanity" defense to protect patients with serious psychiatric illness when they are obviously unable to be responsible for their actions. With modern diagnostic criteria, these fairly straightforward cases are generally not difficult to diagnose and psychiatrists usually sound sensible and credible when explaining what has happened.

But of course the American legal system never keeps things simple or obvious. Psychiatrists are now being called upon to declare people innocent of crimes because of abnormalities that hardly seem straightforward. We have murderers who say they have multiple personalities, rapists who insist they should not be held responsible because they themselves were abused as children, and people who seem perfectly normal claiming they committed crimes while "temporarily insane."

These scenarios have made psychiatrists seem at times like circus performers. Lawyers clap and psychiatrists jump through whatever hoop that will support the side they have been hired to help. In some very famous murder trials, juries of people with no medical or mental health training are asked to figure out which shrink is correct, the one who says the criminal is perfectly sane and just a bad guy, or the one who says the criminal only commits crimes when he is under the temporary influence of psychotic symptoms. Juries are asked to differentiate between true psychotic illness, such as schizophrenia, and such a personality disorder as borderline when even experts don't agree about what a "borderline" really is.

Does multiple personality disorder actually exist? Probably, but it is almost certainly extremely rare and hard to prove. Almost anyone can say they have it as a defense for committing a crime. Then lawyers can hire teams of psychiatrists and psychologists who will testify on both sides of the issue, leaving juries, judges, and the general public scratching their heads.

Does a history of abuse as a child render an adult "insane" and therefore not responsible for crimes? This seems more of a philosophical question than a medical one. Yet increasingly defense attorneys are arguing that adults who admit to serious crimes should not be put in jail because childhood abuse—ranging from parental to societal—somehow altered their mental functioning and made them prone to violence.

The fact is that psychiatrists and psychologists are probably no better qualified than anyone else to testify in these cases. We really don't know the answers the lawyers and judges are asking us. We are reasonably certain that in some cases psychotic illnesses do make people violent and that in those cases imprisonment is wrong. If the question is whether someone accused of a crime has schizophrenia or another psychotic illness, then psychiatrists should be able to help. But we cannot honestly say that we know very much that is scientifically credible about multiple personality disorder and hence should not be telling juries that it is perfectly understandable that a person might murder when one personality is in control and then be perfectly polite and sweet while in the clutches of another. We also do not know at this point whether getting abused as a child produces changes in brain or emotional function that really do render a person unable to resist committing a crime as an adult years later.

None of what I have to say on this issue will make much difference because there is big money to be made in the psychiatric defense business. Psychiatrists are often staggered at the amount of money attorneys earn and cannot resist getting involved in legal cases so that they can charge the same hourly fees. Quite honestly, I have done some of this myself and it is very easy to convince oneself that the motivation for getting involved in a legal case is to help the person on your side rather than to earn a big fee. But I do wish that psychiatrists and psychologists would ask themselves two questions before testifying in a courtroom: (1) Do we really have sufficient medical knowledge at this point to answer the questions being asked? and (2) Will the testimony psychiatrists give on both sides of a case be so confusing and contradictory that it will merely make psychiatry in general look ridiculous and purely subjective?

None of us wants to see a sick person go to jail for something he could not help doing. Nor do we want to see a dangerous criminal get off because a lawyer convinced a jury he had a mental disorder. Still, there are limitations on what psychiatrists really know, and testimony in legal cases should never go beyond those boundaries.

A similar caution is in order for situations in which psychiatrists are asked to help decide the legal competence of an individual. Here again, there are conditions that affect emotional and brain function to a point that the ability to make reasonable choices and decisions is compromised. Such people may then be taken advantage of, giving away money because they did not comprehend the contract they were being asked to sign, or signing up to participate in research studies without the ability to understand what the consent form was informing them about the experiment.

The law in most states provides a mechanism whereby an *incompetent* person—that is, someone whose mental state is such that decision-making capacity is seriously eroded—may actually lose some of his rights to sign contracts or manage affairs. Here, the legal system usually places a surrogate or guardian in the position of ''protecting'' the patient's interests. In most cases this is a useful way of protecting an ill person from making self-destructive decisions. A patient with Alzheimer's dementia will eventually lose most memory for recent events. Such an unfortunate person often becomes entirely unable to understand what is written in a contract and could easily be mislead into giving away a life's hard-earned fortune. Similarly, we can imagine a situation in which scientists believe they have a wonderful new drug that might cure schizophrenia, but a particular patient with schizophrenia may be so under the influence of psychotic symptoms such as delusions and hallucinations that although he agrees to take the drug he really does not understand the potential risks. To protect such individuals, psychiatrists are often asked to decide the nature and extent of the disability and, if it is extensive, recommend the appointment of a surrogate to help make decisions.

Psychiatrists can then get themselves into some very tricky situations. It is not always completely clear whether a person who may even be suffering from a serious brain disease can or cannot understand things. Many conditions, like schizophrenia, have highly variable courses so that a patient may have better cognitive function at one time than at others. Families often put great pressure on lawyers and psychiatrists to have someone declared incompetent so that they, and not the patient, can manage the money and make the decisions.

It is important again to recognize the limitations psychiatrists work under. Psychiatrists do not "declare a person incompetent"; that is something judges do. Rather, psychiatrists can make a diagnosis and explain a patient's symptoms and how those symptoms may affect the ability to make reasoned, informed choices. We can say that someone has Alzheimer's disease with a reasonable amount of certainty, even though at present we do not have blood tests or X rays that help much with the diagnosis. We can also do neuropsychological tests that give us some idea about the amount of memory loss and the ability to comprehend spoken and written instructions. We can then give an opinion about how likely it is at a given time that a patient can make choices and decisions.

In the case of a patient with a psychotic illness like schizophrenia, the psychiatrist should usually be able to make a diagnosis and characterize the symptoms. The degree to which hallucinations or delusions are influencing the patient's judgment can be assessed.

But in all of these proceedings, psychiatrists, contrary to some people's beliefs, cannot read minds and do not know exactly what someone does or doesn't understand. Sometimes we are surprised when a very psychotic patient asks a question that reveals he knows exactly what is being asked of him. At other times we see people with what we think are relatively mild degrees of dementia making very careless errors and poor decisions.

Anytime there is a question of limiting a person's rights to make a decision, there should be more opinions that just one. At least two psychiatrists should independently examine the patient, and it is preferable that each see the patient on more than one occasion in case the situation is fluctuating. The psychiatrists should carefully acknowledge any lack of certainty they have in making diagnoses; if they are not entirely sure the patient has schizophrenia, they should say so. The doctors should also interview any "interested" parties and find out who is going to benefit if the patient's decision-making rights are abridged. And the psychiatrists should encourage the lawyers and judges involved to put the fewest possible restrictions in place and to review the case at regular intervals. Protecting the patient should always be the first concern.

20.
What Will More Research in Psychiatry Teach Us?

I HAVE SAVED the best part for last: research about the causes and treatments of psychiatric illness is going to make dramatic progress in the next decade.

Sound like a very bold statement? Indeed, it is, but not an incorrect one. Never before have scientists been so interested in how the brain works or in what controls behavior and emotion. At last, sophisticated biomedical technology is being applied to the nervous system and to an understanding of illnesses such as schizophrenia, depression, and panic disorder. There are all kinds of new insights, some of which have already led to important improvements in treatment.

The brain is surely the most complex and difficult to study organ of the body. It is a concentrated mass of cells called neurons that each send out long fibers called axons, branching hundreds and thousands of times. Each time the axons of one neuron meet another neuron there is a connection called a synapse (actually, an empty space between the two cells that are linked by chemical neurotransmitters). There are millions, probably billions, of synaptic connections in a single brain. Although the human brain does not process information as fast as modern computers, it is vastly more complex and mysterious, able to do things that computers (despite their most enthusiastic supporters) will never be able to do. This mass of cells, axons, synapses, and chemical messengers is encased inside a hard bony structure, the skull. Between the skull and the brain itself are a number of membranes and also something called the *blood-brain barrier,* a complicated system that prevents most things carried in the bloodstream from getting into the brain, and most things in the brain from getting into the blood. The brain controls every function in the body, and perhaps because of this the body protects the brain at all costs.

This makes the brain inaccessible. An X ray of a lung tells us if there is pneumonia; an ordinary X ray of the head does not show the brain at all. A simple blood test reveals anemia or diabetes; blood tests tell us virtually nothing about what is going on in the brain. A cardiologist can put a tube directly into the heart and see what is going on; try doing that to a brain and you'll quickly have absolutely nothing going on. A kidney specialist can biopsy a piece of the kidney and look at it under a microscope; psychiatrists and neurologists are not apt to ask for brain biopsies too readily.

The inability to directly study the organ of interest, the brain, has made it difficult to do research in psychiatry. But recently, powerful new brain-imaging techniques enable us to get very detailed pictures of the brain and to actually measure the activity of its different parts during various activities. These brain-imaging techniques have names like magnetic resonance imaging (MRI), single photon emission tomography, and positron emission tomography. All are safe, using little or no radiation, and all provide us with the ability for the first time to take a direct look at what the brain does in health and disease. Using these techniques, scientists have been able to show that certain parts of the brain of patients with schizophrenia are smaller than is seen in people without schizophrenia. They have found exactly where in the brain cocaine acts. They have been able to trace different chemical neurotransmitters and have found out a lot more about what they do during different emotional states. The work is just beginning and is as yet incomplete, but medicine usually advances quickly when technological breakthroughs are made. Psychiatry is now exactly at that point.

And brain imaging is only one example of an exciting new development. Neuroscientists have now been able to grow brain cells in tissue culture so that they can be studied directly. From this, very exact knowledge about molecular events that occur during the transmission of brain signals has been obtained. Some of the recent molecular work has revolutionized our understanding of human memory, showing us for example that gases like nitric oxide and carbon monoxide may be normal parts of the brain chemical messenger system.

Understanding the brain better will lead to the development of more specific treatments. The important new class of antidepressant medications called selective serotonin reuptake inhibitors (SSRIs) are safer than previous drugs for depression because scientists learned how to make drugs that affect only one chemical neurotransmitter, serotonin, instead of several, as do older drugs. In the treatment of schizophrenia, scientists are now involved in making "designer" antipsychotic drugs that target only selected chemical systems in selected regions in the brain. In all of this, the goal is to affect an illness without disturbing other parts of normal brain function.

The advances are hardly limited to biotechnology and medications. Scientists, using sophisticated knowledge about study design and statistical analysis, have now conducted the first reasonable experiments to test the effectiveness of psychotherapy. In many instances they have shown that psychotherapy is in fact beneficial for selected groups of patients with specific illnesses. We hope in the not too distant future we will know what, if any, kind of psychotherapy is exactly right for an individual patient with a specific psychiatric illness.

But for every advance there are many false starts. That is the nature of science. Often I pick up a newspaper or magazine and read a story about a supposedly miraculous new cure for a psychiatric illness. People who have experienced horrible traumatic events are supposed to recover from the psychiatric sequelae simply by watching a therapist move his fingers back and forth; a vitamin is heralded as the cure for memory loss and depression; a fancy new gadget is claimed to relieve anxiety forever. The people who present these "therapies" are sometimes dedicated believers and sometimes charlatans, but they all lack one essential thing: scientific evidence that the treatment works.

Because humans are suggestible creatures and because, to paraphrase Yogi Berra, we want to see what we believe, it is often easy to convince ourselves that a new treatment is effective. Sadly, the vast majority of new treatments are really no better than placebo. The only way to find out is to conduct rigorous scientific research using our old standby, the scientific method. What makes us so excited about psychiatry as the twentieth century comes to an end is that for the first time the same scientific method that brought us penicillin, insulin, and aspirin is being applied to psychiatric illness.

That method involves many things, but the most essential is the experiment. The scientific method says that we should not believe anything until properly conducted, unbiased experiments prove it is true. To do that in psychiatry we will need three things: dedicated scientists, funds from the government and private foundations, and, perhaps most important of all, courageous patients who are willing to take some risks in return for the hope that someday their illness will be treatable. There are those who still believe that psychiatric illness is not important and not worth spending time or money on. Such people sometimes join antiscience movements that pretend to be protecting the "rights" of psychiatric patients. In fact, what they are doing is continuing the horrible neglect by the scientific community of psychiatric illness that only now is being corrected.

This is truly a crossroads period for psychiatry and for patients with psychiatric illness. In this book I have tried to tell you many of the things that psychiatrists now know and can do something about. Hopefully, it is apparent to all readers that psychiatrists can be very successful in treating many different kinds of illnesses. In fact, our track record for relieving the suffering of illness is as good as most other medical and surgical specialties. So there is ample reason to see a psychiatrist and try to get help if you have even the slightest inkling you may have a psychiatric illness. The New Psychiatry absolutely offers help that is safe and effective as long as the consumer is well educated.

But there is a tremendous amount we just don't understand yet and a lot of suffering we cannot reverse. With the proper support from the public, scientists can now begin to make progress. Everytime I have to tell a mother or father that their child might have schizophrenia or hear about a depressed person who has committed suicide I know that it is worth a lot of effort and money to keep looking for better treatments. Psychiatric illnesses are painful and serious. People who have them should not ignore them; people who have the ability to help find solutions for them should advocate for more research and better delivery of psychiatric care. That way, the New Psychiatry will continually be made new, and hope for all people suffering with psychiatric illness will never diminish.

Where to Call or Write for More Help

For general information:

National Alliance for the Mentally Ill
  200 North Glebe Road
  Suite 1015
  Arlington, VA 22203
  (800) 950-NAMI

National Mental Health Association
  1021 Prince Street
  Alexandria, VA 22314
  (800) 969-NMHA

National Institute of Mental Health
  Public Inquiries,
  5600 Fishers Lane
  Room 7C-02
  Rockville, MD 20857

For information about depression and other mood disorders:

National Depressive and Manic Depressive Association
  730 North Franklin Street
  Suite 501
  Chicago, IL 60610
  (312) 642-0049
  (800) 826-3632

National Foundation for Depressive Illness
  P.O. Box 2257
  New York, NY 10116
  (212) 268-4260
  (800) 248-4344

National Institute of Mental Health
DEPRESSION Awareness, Recognition, and Treatment
(DART)
5600 Fishers Lane, Room 10-85
Rockville, MD 20857
(301) 443-4140
(800) 421-4211

For information about panic disorder and other anxiety disorders:

Anxiety Disorders Association of America
600 Executive Boulevard
Suite 513
Rockville, MD 20852
(301) 231-9350

Mental Health Clinical Research Center at
The New York State Psychiatric Institute
722 West 168th Street
New York, NY 10032
(212) 960-2442

Obsessive Compulsive Foundation
P.O. Box 70
Milford, CT 06460
(203) 878-5669

For information on eating disorders:

National Association of Anorexia Nervosa
and Associated Disorders (ANAD)
P.O. Box 7
Highland Park, IL 60035
(708) 831-3438

Anorexia Nervosa and Related Eating Disorders, Inc.
P.O. Box 5102
Eugene, OR 97405
(503) 344-1144

American Anorexia/Bulimia Association, Inc. (AABA)
425 East 61st Street
New York, NY 10021
(212) 891-8686

National Eating Disorder Organization
445 East Grandille Road
Worthington, OH 43085
(614) 436-1112

Suggestions for Further Reading

Amada, Gerald. *A Guide to Psychotherapy.* New York: Ballantine Books, 1983.

Andreasen, Nancy C. *The Broken Brain.* New York: Harper & Row, 1984. This is a classic, explaining brain function in psychiatric illness. It is written by a psychiatrist who also has a Ph.D. in English Literature and is the editor of the *American Journal of Psychiatry.*

Barlow, David. *Anxiety and Its Disorders.* New York: The Guilford Press, 1988. Dr. Barlow pioneered the cognitive and behavioral approach to anxiety disorders and this is one of his main texts.

Barondes, Samuel H. *Molecules and Mental Illness.* New York: Scientific American Library, 1993. Dr. Barondes is a leader in research on the biology of brain and behavior.

Beck, Aaron T. *Depression: Causes and Treatment.* Philadelphia: University of Pennsylvania Press, 1973. Dr. Beck is one of the founders of cognitive therapy and this is the classic in the field.

Berger, Diane, and Lisa Berger. *We Heard the Angels of Madness: A Family Guide to Coping with Manic Depression.* New York: Quill/William Morrow, 1991.

Burns, David D. *Feeling Good: The New Mood Therapy.* New York: New American Library, 1981. The cognitive approach to treating depression, turned into a very approachable and reader-friendly version for the general audience.

Diagnostic and Statistical Manual of Mental Disorders, Fourth Edition. Washington, D.C.: American Psychiatric Association, 1994. This is the *DSM-IV,* the official listing of all psychiatric illnesses. Also gives descriptions of the illnesses and other information.

Falloon, Ian R. H., Jeffrey L. Boyd, and Christine W. McGill. *Family Care of Schizophrenia.* New York: The Guilford Press, 1984.

Fieve, Ronald R. *Prozac: Questions and Answers for Patients, Family, and Physicians.* New York: Avon Books, 1994.

Foa, Edna B., and Reid Wilson. *Stop Obsessing.* New York: Bantam Books, 1991. Drs. Foa and Wilson represent the cognitive and behavioral approach to treating obsessive compulsive disorder.

Engler, Jack, and Daniel Goleman. *Consumer's Guide to Psychotherapy.* New York: Simon & Schuster/Fireside, 1992.

Gorman, Jack M. *The Essential Guide to Psychiatric Drugs.* New York: St. Martin's Press, 1995. The revised edition.

Greist, John H., and James W. Jefferson. *Depression and Its Treatment.* Washington, D.C.: American Psychiatric Press, 1984.

Greist, John H., James W. Jefferson, and Isaac Marks. *Anxiety and Its Treatment.* Washington, D.C.: American Psychiatric Press, 1986.

Heimberg, Richard G., Michael R. Liebowitz, Debra A. Hope, and Franklin R. Schneier (editors). *Social Phobia.* New York: The Guilford Press, 1995.

Jamison, Kay Redfield. *An Unquiet Mind.* New York: Alfred A. Knopf, 1995. One of the leading researchers of bipolar mood disorder tells her own story about overcoming manic and depressive episodes.

Kass, Frederic I., John M. Oldham, and Herbert Pardes (editors). *The Columbia University College of Physicians and Surgeons Complete Guide to Mental Health.* New York: Henry Holt, 1992.

Keefe, Richard S. E., and Phillip D. Harvey. *Understanding Schizophrenia.* New York: The Free Press, 1994.

Kernodle, William O. *Panic Disorder* (second edition). Richmond, VA: William Byrd Press, 1993. This is a very readable and informative account of current theories and treatments.

Klein, Donald F., and Paul H. Wender. *Mind, Mood, and Medicine.* New York: New American Library, 1982. Still an important book to read for anyone considering taking psychiatric medication.

Klein, Donald F., and Paul H. Wender. *Understanding Depression.* New York: Oxford University Press, 1993. Drs. Klein and Wender have written a number of books that make complicated concepts very accessible to the general reader.

Kocsis, James H., and Daniel N. Klein (editors). *Diagnosis and Treatment of Chronic Depression.* New York: The Guilford Press, 1995.

Kramer, Peter D. *Listening to Prozac.* New York: Penguin Books, 1993. This is the book that started the media interest in Prozac. It is well written and informative.

McNally, Richard J. *Panic Disorder: A Critical Analysis.* New York: The Guilford Press, 1994. Although Dr. McNally is primarily known for his work in the cognitive and behavioral aspects of anxiety disorder, this book gives a very fair and scholarly overview of the panic disorder field.

Minuchin, Salvador. *Family Kaleidoscope.* Cambridge, MA: Harvard University Press, 1984. Dr. Minuchin is one of the leading names in family therapy.

Oldham, John M., and Lois B. Morris. *The New Personaility Self-Portrait— Why You Think, Work, Love, and Act the Way You Do.* New York: Bantam Books, 1995.

Person, Ethel S. *By Force of Fantasy: How We Make Our Lives.* New York: Basic Books, 1995. The former director of the Columbia University Psychoanalytic Center is one of the most engaging writers and deep thinkers in the field.

Papolos, Demitri F., and Janice Papolos. *Overcoming Depression.* New York: Harper Perennial, 1992.

Rapoport, Judith L. *The Boy Who Couldn't Stop Washing.* New York: E.P. Dutton, 1989. The best-seller that describes obsessive compulsive disorder by one of the country's leading mental-health scientists.

Rosenthal, Norman E. *Winter Blues.* New York: The Guilford Press, 1993. Dr. Rosenthal is one of the leaders in the study of seasonal affective disorder, and this book is an accessible description of the problem and its solution.

Ross, Jerilyn. *Triumph Over Fear.* New York: Bantam Books, 1994. The president of the Anxiety Disorders Association of America gives her own story of overcoming anxiety as well as important information for all people with anxiety disorders.

Schuyler, Dean A. *A Practical Guide to Cognitive Therapy.* New York: W. W. Norton, 1991.

Sheehan, David V. *The Anxiety Disease.* New York: Bantam Books, 1983. This is one of the classics in the field of anxiety disorders.

Torrey, E. Fuller, Ann E. Bowler, Edward H. Taylor, and Irving I. Gottesman. *Schizophrenia and Manic-Depressive Disorder.* New York: Basic Books, 1994. Dr. Torrey has been one of the most effective and outspoken spokesmen for research about serious mental illness; Dr. Gottesman is one of the leading genetic researchers in the field.

Woolis, Rebecca. *When Someone You Love Has a Mental Illness.* New York: Jeremy P. Tarcher/Perigee Books, 1992.

List of Tables

Drug Directory

Note: Brand names are in caps, generic names in lower-case letters.

Drug Name	Page Described
alprazolam (XANAX)	222
amitriptyline (ELAVIL, ENDEP)	202
ANAFRANIL (clomipramine)	264
ANTABUSE (disulfiram)	317
ARTANE (trihexyphenidyl)	295
atenolol (TENORMIN)	257
ATIVAN (lorazepam)	222
AVENTYL (nortriptyline)	243
AURORIX (moclobemide)	203
benztropine (COGENTIN)	295
buproprion (WELLBUTRIN)	203
BUSPAR (buspirone)	220–221
carbamazepine (Tegretol)	210
CATAPRES (clonidine)	296
chlordiazepoxide (LIBRIUM)	222
chlorpromazine (THORAZINE)	294
clomipramine (ANAFRANIL)	264
clonazepam (KLONOPIN)	245
clonidine (CATAPRES)	296
clorazepate (TRANXENE)	222
clozapine (CLOZARIL)	297
CLOZARIL (clozapine)	297
COGENTIN (benztropine)	295
DEPAKOTE (divalproex sodium)	204
desipramine (NORPRAMIN, PERTOFRANE)	202
DESYREL (trazodone)	202
DEXEDRINE (dextroamphetamine)	324
dextroamphetamine (DEXEDRINE)	324
diazepam (VALIUM)	222
disulfiram (ANTABUSE)	317
divalproex sodium (DEPAKOTE)	204
DOLOPHINE (methadone)	322
doxepin (ADAPAN, SINEQUAN)	202
EFFEXOR (venlafaxine)	203
ELAVIL (amitriptyline)	202
ELDEPRYL (selegiline)	203
fenfluramine (PONDOMIN)	265
fluphenazine (PROLIXIN)	294
fluvoxamine (LUVOX)	203
fluoxetine (PROZAC)	203

Drug Name	*Page Described*
HALCION (triazolam)	77–78
HALDOL (haloperidol)	294
haloperidol (HALDOL)	294
imipramine (TOFRANIL)	202
INDERAL (propranolol)	256–257
KEMADRIN (procyclidine)	296
KLONOPIN (clonazepam)	245
LIBRIUM (chlordiazepoxide)	222
lithium (ESKALITH, LITHOBID, and others)	209
lorazepam (ATIVAN)	222
LUDIOMIL (maprotiline)	202
LUVOX (fluvoxamine)	203
maprotiline (LUDIOMIL)	202
MELLARIL (thioridazine)	294
methadone (DOLOPHINE)	322
methylphenidate (RITALIN)	324
moclobemide (AURORIX)	203
naltrexone (REVIA)	317
NARDIL (phenelzine)	202–203
NAVANE (thiothixene)	294
nefazodone (SERZONE)	203
NORPRAMIN (desipramine)	202
nortriptyline (AVENTYL, PAMELOR)	202
olanzapine (ZYPREX)	296–297
oxazepam (SERAX)	222
PAMELOR (nortriptyline)	202
PARNATE (tranylcypromine)	202–203
paroxetine (PAXIL)	203
PAXIL (paroxetine)	203
perphenazine (TRILAFON)	294
PERTOFRANE (desipramine)	243
phenelzine (NARDIL)	202–203
PONDOMIN (fenfluramine)	265
PROLIXIN (fluphenazine)	294
procyclidine (KEMADRIN)	296
propanolol (INDERAL)	256–257
protriptyline (VIVACTIL)	202
PROZAC (fluoxetine)	203
REVIA (naltrexone)	317
RISPERDAL (risperidone)	297
risperidone (RISPERDAL)	297
RITALIN (methylphenidate)	324
selegiline (ELDEPRYL)	203
SERAX (oxazepam)	222
SERLECT (sertindole)	296–297
sertindole (SERLECT)	296–297

Drug Name	*Page Described*
sertraline (ZOLOFT)	203
SERZONE (nefazodone)	203
SINEQUAN (doxepin)	202
STELAZINE (trifluoperazine)	294
TEGRETOL (carbamazepine)	204
TENORMIN (atenolol)	257
thioridazine (MELLARIL)	294
thiothixene (NAVANE)	294
THORAZINE (chlorpromazine)	294
TOFRANIL (imipramine)	202
TRANXENE (clorazepate)	222
trancylcypromine (PARNATE)	202–203
trazodone (DESYREL)	202
triazolam (HALCION)	77–78
trifluoperazine (STELAZINE)	294
trihexyphenidyl (ARTANE)	295
TRILAFON (perphenazine)	294
VALIUM (diazepam)	222
venlafaxine (EFFEXOR)	203
VIVACTIL (protriptyline)	202
WELLBUTRIN (buproprion)	203
XANAX (alprazolam)	222
YOCON (yohimbine)	86
yohimbine (YOCON)	86
ZOLOFT (sertraline)	203
ZYPREX (olanzapine)	296–297

Index

About the Author

Jack M. Gorman, M.D., received his B.A. *summa cum laude* from the University of Pennsylvania and then his M.D. from the College of Physicians and Surgeons of Columbia University. After an internship in pediatrics at the Babies Hospital in New York City, he received residency training in psychiatry at the Columbia University/New York State Psychiatric Institute program, where he was also chief resident. Dr. Gorman has remained on the faculty of the Department of Psychiatry of Columbia University and its affiliated New York State Psychiatric Institute since finishing his residency. He is presently Professor of Psychiatry and Chief of the Division of Clinical Psychobiology. Dr. Gorman is the author or coauthor of more than 200 professional articles and is an active research scientist in a number of mental-health areas, including anxiety disorders, depression, schizophrenia, and the neuropsychiatric aspects of AIDS. He is also the deputy editor of the *American Journal of Psychiatry* and a member of the American College of Neuropsychopharmacology. His first book for the general audience, *The Essential Guide to Psychiatric Drugs,* has been read by thousands of people with psychiatric illnesses and their family members. Dr. Gorman lives in New York City with his wife, Dr. Lauren Kantor Gorman, also a psychiatrist, and his two daughters, Rachel and Sara.